T0328114

Systems Thinker's Toolbox
Tools for Managing Complexity

Systems Thinker's Toolbox
Tools for Managing Complexity

Joseph Eli Kasser

CRC Press
Taylor & Francis Group
Boca Raton London New York

CRC Press is an imprint of the
Taylor & Francis Group, an **informa** business

CRC Press
Taylor & Francis Group
6000 Broken Sound Parkway NW, Suite 300
Boca Raton, FL 33487-2742

First issued in paperback 2020

ISBN-13: 978-1-138-60676-0 (hbk)
ISBN-13: 978-0-367-78088-3 (pbk)

Library of Congress Cataloging-in-Publication Data

Names: Kasser, Joseph Eli, author.
Title: Systems thinker's toolbox : tools for managing complexity / Joseph Eli Kasser.
Description: First edition. | Boca Raton, FL : CRC Press/Taylor & Francis Group, 2018.|
Includes bibliographical references and index.
Identifiers: LCCN 2018026594| ISBN 9781138606760 (hardback : acid-free paper) |
ISBN 9780429466786 (ebook)
Subjects: LCSH: Project management--Technique. | Systems engineering.
Classification: LCC T56.8 .K36 2018 | DDC 658.4/04--dc23
LC record available at https://lccn.loc.gov/2018026594

Visit the Taylor & Francis Web site at
http://www.taylorandfrancis.com

and the CRC Press Web site at
http://www.crcpress.com

To my wife Lily, always caring, loving and supportive.

To Hsiao-Szu, Janie, Jos, Joyce, Lai Poh, Queenie, and Stephanie, the proactive administrative staff in TDSI at NUS with whom it was both an honour and pleasure to work.

To Prof T.S. Yeo, the director at TDSI who provided an outstanding role model of a manager.

Contents

List of Figures

List of Tables

Preface

This is not another book about systems thinking; this is a book on how to actually do it. This book provides you with the tools for systems thinking and solving problems, and if you use them, you will have an advantage over those who are not using systems thinking.

This book is written for a wide audience. It's written for people like you who are struggling to deal with the day-to-day problems they face in life. If you're a student, a project manager, a systems engineer, or just somebody who needs to tackle problems, this book provides a desk reference of more than 100 tools and examples of how to use them.

Some of the tools are widely known, others have been around for a while but are not so widely known, several of the tools are not even associated with systems thinking, and some of the tools are original coming out of the research that I've been doing for the last 30 years.

The story begins in 1981 when I talked myself into my first job as a project manager. The project succeeded but according to all traditional approaches and measurements the project should have failed. It took me years to realise that the project succeeded because I was using the systems approach without realizing it.

All the tools, original and otherwise, have been used successfully in the real world as well as in the classroom. For example, after I introduced CRIP Charts in my postgraduate class on software engineering at University of Maryland University College, towards the end of the semester one of the students told me that she was using the charts in her work and her management was absolutely delighted with them. The tools and their predecessors helped me to achieve success in my project management and systems engineering endeavours. So in this book I show you how to use the tools and how they are linked to other tools.

What is the systems approach? It's basically a problem-solving approach that looks at the problematic or undesirable situation in its context from a number of different viewpoints and then works out the root cause of the symptoms causing the undesirable situation. It then goes on to conceptualize at least two different solutions that will remove the undesirability, selects the best one and then turns it into reality. Of course, all this is supposed to be done within schedule and budget. This book will give you the tools to do the job.

Acknowledgments

This book would not have been possible without the co-authors of the papers upon which some of these chapters are based, and colleagues and friends who helped review the manuscript:

Prof Derek K. Hitchins
Edouard Kujawski
Angus Massie
Dr Xuan-Linh Tran
Victoria R Williams
Associate Prof Yang Yang Zhao

Author

Joseph Eli Kasser has been a practicing systems engineer for almost 50 years and an academic for 20 years. He is a Fellow of the Institution of Engineering and Technology (IET), a Fellow of the Institution of Engineers (Singapore), and the author of *Perceptions of Systems Engineering* (CreateSpace, 2015), *Holistic Thinking: Creating Innovative Solutions to Complex Problems* (CreateSpace, 2013), *A Framework for Understanding Systems Engineering* (CreateSpace, 2nd Edition 2013), *Applying Total Quality Management to Systems Engineering* (Artech House, 1995), and many INCOSE symposia and other conference and journal papers. He is a recipient of NASA's Manned Space Flight Awareness Award (Silver Snoopy) for quality and technical excellence for performing and directing systems engineering. He holds a Doctor of Science in Engineering Management from the George Washington University. He is a Certified Manager, a Chartered Engineer in both the UK and Singapore, and holds a Certified Membership of the Association for Learning Technology. He has performed and directed systems engineering in the US, Israel, and Australia. He gave up his positions as a Deputy Director and DSTO Associate Research Professor at the Systems Engineering and Evaluation Centre at the University of South Australia in early 2007 to move to the UK to develop the world's first immersion course in systems engineering as a Leverhulme Visiting Professor at Cranfield

University. He spent 2008–2016 as a Visiting Associate Professor at the National University of Singapore where he taught and researched the nature of systems engineering, systems thinking and how to improve the effectiveness of teaching and learning in postgraduate and continuing education. He is currently based in Adelaide, Australia. His many awards include:

- National University of Singapore, 2008–2009 Division of Engineering and Technology Management, Faculty of Engineering Innovative Teaching Award for use of magic in class to enrich the student experience.
- Best Paper, Systems Engineering Technical Processes track, at the 16th Annual Symposium of the INCOSE, 2006, and the 17th Annual Symposium of the INCOSE, 2007.
- United States Air Force (USAF) Office of Scientific Research Window on Science program visitor, 2004.
- Inaugural SEEC "Bust a Gut" Award, SEEC, 2004.
- Employee of the Year, SEEC, 2000.
- Distance Education Fellow, University System of Maryland, 1998–2000.
- Outstanding Paper Presentation, Systems Engineering Management track, at the 6th Annual Symposium of the INCOSE, 1996.
- Distinguished Service Award, Institute of Certified Professional Managers (ICPM), 1993.
- Manned Space Flight Awareness Award (Silver Snoopy) for quality and technical excellence, for performing and directing systems engineering, NASA, 1991.
- NASA Goddard Space Flight Center Community Service Award, 1990.
- The E3 award for Excellence, Endurance and Effort, Radio Amateur Satellite Corporation (AMSAT), 1981, and three subsequent awards for outstanding performance.
- Letters of commendation and certificates of appreciation from employers and satisfied customers, including the:
  - American Radio Relay League (ARRL).
  - American Society for Quality (ASQ).
  - Association for Quality and Participation (AQP).

- Communications Satellite Corporation (Comsat).
- Computer Sciences Corporation (CSC).
- Defence Materiel Organisation (Australia).
- Institution of Engineers (Singapore).
- IET Singapore Nework.
- Loral Corporation.
- Luz Industries.
- Systems Engineering Society of Australia (SESA).
- University of South Australia.
- United States Office of Personnel Management (OPM).
- University System of Maryland.
- Wireless Institute of Australia.

Other Books by This Author

- *Perceptions of Systems Engineering*, Createspace, 2015.
- *Conceptual Laws and Customs of Christmas*, Createspace, 2015.
- *The 87th Company, The Pioneer Corps: A Mobile Military Jewish Community*, Createspace, 2013 (Editor).
- *Holistic Thinking: Creating Innovative Solutions to Complex Problems*, Createspace, 2013.
- *A Framework for Understanding Systems Engineering*, Createspace, 2nd Edition 2013.
- *Applying Total Quality Management to Systems Engineering*, Artech House, 1995.
- *Basic Packet Radio, Software for Amateur Radio*, First and Second Editions, 1993, 1994.
- *Software for Amateur Radio*, TAB Books, December 1984.
- *Microcomputers in Amateur Radio*, TAB Books, November 1981.

1
INTRODUCTION

The best way of solving simple and complex problems is to use the systems approach based on systems thinking. However both the systems approach and systems thinking are not taught very well. In fact, there are many things that are not taught very well in the 20th-century problem-solving paradigm. While there are indeed many tools that are taught for problem-solving, project management, and systems engineering, they are all taught as separate tools. They are not taught as interdependent tools. For example, in project management, risk management is taught as a separate process from general management or project management. Similarly, in systems engineering, risk management is taught as a separate process from mainstream systems engineering. In the real systems approach, everything is related as part of a system. While these words are often used, they not really implemented.

The literature focuses on the "what" of the systems approach, namely what it is and the benefits it bestows. This book focuses on the "how": how to use the systems approach and how to apply systems thinking by providing a set of tools. The tools in this book consist of products such as Lists (Section 9.4), processes such as the Process for Tackling a Problem (Section 11.5), and templates such as the Problem Formulation Template (Section 14.3). Because the tools are grouped in the different chapters, Section 1.6 provides an alphabetical list to facilitate locating a specific tool quickly. This book:

- Contains more than 100 different conceptual tools for solving problems.
- Is different. Not only does it teach the tools for solving problems, it relates them together; you will notice many cross references in this book.
- Provides examples of how to use many of the tools.

1

- Provides a number of original tools that were developed as part of the research into systems engineering and systems thinking that led to a practical approach to teaching and applying systems thinking to solve problems. I could probably write a whole book on each of those tools, but I hope I've given enough information on how to use them in the appropriate sections of this book.
- Contains a number of items included because in the course of my teaching the systems approach paradigm I often heard myself saying, "And you won't find that in the textbooks." Well, now you can find it in at least one book.
- Is written for a project managers, systems engineers, and other problem solvers as a desk reference to provide a reminder of the tools that are available for solving different types of problems so they won't rely on their usual problem-solving tool that may not be suitable for a specific problem.
- Is written for students because I've noticed that few postgraduate students have been taught how to deal with class exercises, and many do not have any idea of how to manage the time they have available in which to do exercises (which will reflect in the real world as managing the time they have available to do projects and other tasks) using Prioritization (Section 4.6.6) and other time management tools.
- Shows how many of the tools in use today are related, and you will recognize them. However, these tools are not thought of as being part of systems thinking because they were not taught as such.
- Mentions the current non-systems approach as well as the system approach in many sections since the systems approach is different to what is currently being taught.
- Can be used by the beginner as a cookbook of tools, but the advanced systems thinker can also use the individual tools to build custom complex tools.

1.1 How to Read and Use This Book

The first section to read is the section on Systems Thinking (Section 1.4) followed by the Holistic Thinking Perspectives (HTP) (Section 10.1) and the Problem Formulation Template (Section 14.3). This order is suggested because Section 1.3 discusses systems thinking and systematic and systemic thinking, and Section 10.1 discusses the HTPs which are used throughout this book. As explained later in this book, we often make sure that everybody is viewing something from the same perspective by saying something like, "Let's make sure everybody is on the same page" (Chapter 10). Well, the set of viewpoint pages in this book, in most instances, are the different HTPs. The Problem Formulation Template (Section 14.3) helps you think through the problem before beginning to tackle it, and you will find many examples of the Problem Formulation Template in different situations throughout this book.

Each section that describes an existing tool is a descriptive summary which should provide enough information on how to use the tool and is not intended to be comprehensive. For the more complex tools, many books and Internet pages have been written about them. The original tools developed in this research however are described in more detail. If you know the name of the tool, look it up and read about it. To learn about the other tools, remember that this is a reference book, so don't read this book sequentially in a linear manner, but prepare for several passes through it. This book is non-fiction. Non-fiction books are different to fiction; stories, novels, and thrillers that are designed to be read in a linear manner from start to finish. This book is designed to help you learn and use the content in the following manner:

1. **Skim this book.** Flip through the pages. If anything catches your eye and interests you, stop, glance at it, and then continue flipping through the pages. Notice how the pages have been formatted with dot points (bulleted lists) rather than in paragraphs to make skimming and reading easier.
2. For each chapter:
   1. Read the introduction.
   2. Skim the contents.
   3. Look at the drawings and photographs.
   4. Read the summary of the chapter.
   5. Go on to the next chapter.
3. **If you don't understand something, skip it on the first and second readings.** This book uses examples from many

different disciplines and domains; don't get bogged down in the details.

4. Work though this book slowly so that you understand the message in each section of each chapter. If you don't understand the details of the example, don't worry about it as long as you understand the point that the example is demonstrating.

5. Refer to the list of acronyms in Table 1.1 as necessary.

6. Visualize (Section 7.11) and create innovative solutions to complex problems using the material you have gained from this book, your reading and experience.

Step 1 should give you something you can use immediately. Steps 2 and 3 should give you something you can use in the coming months. Step 4 should give you something you can use for the rest of your life. Step 6 is the rest of your life.

1.2 Thinking

Thinking is the action that underlies problem-solving and decision-making. Thinking can be divided into three parts:

1. Non-systems thinking.
2. Systems thinking.
3. Critical Thinking.

Auguste Rodin's bronze casting *The Thinker*, first presented to the public in 1904, shows a seated man in a thinking pose. What is he thinking about? Nobody knows. How does he think? Nobody knows. Where do ideas come from? Nobody knows. What we do know is that thinking is a cognitive act performed by the brain. Cognitive activities include accessing, processing, and storing information. The most widely used cognitive psychology information processing model of the brain based on the work of Atkinson and Shiffrin (Atkinson and Shiffrin 1968) cited by Lutz and Huitt (Lutz and Huitt 2003) likens the human mind to an information processing computer. Both the human mind and the computer ingest information, process it to change its form, store it, retrieve it, and generate responses to inputs (Woolfolk 1998). These days we can extend our internal memory using paper notes, books and electronic storage as shown in Figure 1.1. We use our mental capacity to think about something

Table 1.1 Acronyms Used in this Book

AC	Actual Cost (ACWP)
ACWP	Actual Cost of Work Performed (AC)
AHP	Analytical Hierarchy Process
ATM	Automatic Teller Machine
BAC	Budget at Completion
BCWP	Budgeted Cost of Work Performed (EV)
BCWS	Budgeted Cost of Work Scheduled
BPR	Business Process Reengineering
C3	Command, Control, Communications
C3I	Command, Control, Communications, and Intelligence
C4ISR	Command, Control, Communications, Computers, Intelligence, Surveillance and Reconnaissance
CASE	Computer Assisted Software Engineering
CDR	Critical Design Review
CM	Configuration Management
CONOPS	Concept of Operations
CONOPS	Concept of Operations Document
COTS	Commercial-Off-The-Shelf
CPI	Cost Performance Index
CPM	Critical Path Method
CQ	Looking for a contact (seek you)
CRIP	Categorized Requirements in Process
CSV	comma-separated values
CV	Cost Variance
DMSMS	Diminishing Manufacturing Sources and Material Shortages
DOD	Department of Defense
DRR	Delivery Readiness Review
DSM	Design Structure Matrix
DSTD	Defence Systems and Technology Department
dTRL	dynamic TRL
EAC	Estimate at Completion
EDF	Engaporean Defence Forces
EV	Earned Value (BCWP)
EVA	Earned Value Analysis
ETC	Estimate to Completion
ETL	Enhanced Traffic Light
EVA	Earned Value Analysis
FCFDS	Feasible Conceptual Future Desirable Situation
FDD	Feature Driven Development
FP	Function Point
FRAT	Functions Requirements Answers and Test

(*Continued*)

Table 1.1 (Continued)   Acronyms Used in this Book

HKMF	Hitchins-Kasser-Massie Framework
HTP	Holistic Thinking Perspective
ICD	Interface Specification Document
INCOSE	International Council on Systems Engineering
IRR	Integration Readiness Review
ISM	Interpretive Structural Modelling
IST	Ideas Storage Template
IV&V	Independent Validation and Verification
JIT	Just in time
KISS	Keep it Simple Stupid
MBE	Management by Exception
MBO	Management by Objectives
MBUM	Micromanagement by Upper Management
MVA	Multi-attribute Variable Analysis
NGT	Nominal Group Technique
NUS	National University of Singapore
OARP	Observations, Assumptions Risks and Problems
OODA	Observe-Orient-Decide-Act
OT&E	Operational Test and Evaluation
PAM	Product Activity Milestone
PBS	Product Breakdown Structure
PDCA	Plan Do Check Act
PDR	Preliminary Design Review
PERT	Program Evaluation Review Technique
PP	Project Plan
PV	Planned Value
PWC	Pair-wise Comparison
RFP	Request for Proposal
RTM	Requirements Traceability Matrix
QSO	Contact (communications "Q" code) exchange of messages
SEAS	Systems Engineering and Services
SEBOK	Systems Engineering Body of Knowledge
SEEC	Systems Engineering and Evaluation Centre
SDP	System Development Process
SLC	System Lifecycle
SPARK	Schedules, Products, Activities, Resources and risKs
SPI	Schedule Performance Index
SRD	System Requirements Document
SRR	System Requirement Review
SSM	Soft Systems Methodology
SV	Schedule Variance

(*Continued*)

Table 1.1 (Continued) Acronyms Used in this Book

STALL	Stay calm, Think, Analyse and ask questions, Listen and Listen
SWOT	Strengths, Weaknesses, Opportunities, and Threats
TAWOO	Technology Availability Window of Opportunity
TBD	To Be Determined
TLC	Traffic Light Chart
TPM	Technical Performance Measure
TQM	Total Quality Management
TRIZ	Theory of Inventive Problem-Solving
TRL	Technology Readiness Level
TRR	Test Readiness Review
UDP	User Datagram Protocol
UniSA	University of South Australia
US	United States
VAC	Variance at Completion
WBS	Work Breakdown Structure
WP	Work Package

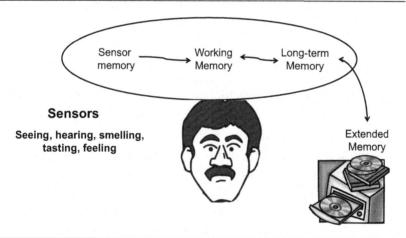

Figure 1.1 The extended human information system.

received from a sense (hearing, sight, smell, taste and touch). From a functional standpoint our mental capacities might be oversimplified as follows (Osborn 1963: p. 1):

- *Absorptive* – the ability to observe, and to apply attention.
- *Retentive* – the ability to memorize and recall.
- *Reasoning* – the ability to analyse and to judge.
- *Creative* – the ability to visualize, to foresee, and to generate ideas.

When we view the world, our brain uses a filter to separate the pertinent sensory input from the non-pertinent. This filter is known as a "cognitive filter" in the behavioural science literature (Wu and Yoshikawa 1998), and as a "decision frame" in the management literature (Russo and Schoemaker 1989). Cognitive filters and decision frames:

- Are filters through which we view the world.
- Include the political, organizational, cultural, and meta-phorical, and they highlight relevant parts of the system and hide (abstract out) the non-relevant parts.
- Can also add material that hinders solving the problem.* Failure to abstract out the non-relevant issues can make things appear to be more complex and complicated than they are and gives rise to artificial complexity (Section 13.3.1.1).
- The brain connects concepts using a process called reasoning or thinking.

1.3 The Systems Approach

"The systems approach is a technique for the application of a scientific approach to complex problems. It concentrates on the analysis and design of the whole, as distinct from the components or the parts. It insists upon looking at a problem in its entirety, taking into account all the facets and all the variables, and relating the social to the technological aspects" (Ramo 1973), namely, the systems approach is the application of Systems Thinking (Section 1.4) and Critical Thinking (Chapter 3). Moreover, the advantages of the systems approach to problem-solving have been known for centuries. The literature contains many examples including:

- "When people know a number of things, and one of them understands how the things are systematically categorized and related, that person has an advantage over the others who don't have the same understanding." (Luzatto circa 1735)

---

* For example, the differences between the Catholics and Protestants in Northern Ireland are major to many of the inhabitants of that country, but are hardly noticeable to most of the rest of the world.

- "People who learn to read situations from different (theoretical) points of view have an advantage over those committed to a fixed position. For they are better able to recognize the limitations of a given perspective. They can see how situations and problems can be framed and reframed in different ways, allowing new kinds of solutions to emerge." (Morgan 1997)

Yet the systems approach is rarely used when dealing with problems and issues. It seems that systems thinking which leads to the systems approach must be a learned skill because many people would say that human nature has a non-systems approach to thinking about issues. The non-system thinker views issues from a single viewpoint/perspective or when multiple viewpoints are used, they are individual non-standardized viewpoints in random order depending on the person. I often heard people saying, "Let's make sure we are on the same page," or engineers* saying "Let's make sure we are on the same wavelength" to try to ensure meeting participants were viewing something from the same perspective or viewpoint.

C. West Churchman introduced three standardized views in order to first think about the *purpose* and *function* of a system and then later think about *physical* structure in *The Systems Approach* (Churchman 1968). These views provided three anchor points or viewpoints for viewing and thinking about a system. Twenty-five years later, *The Seven Streams of Systems Thinking* (Richmond 1993) introduced seven standardized viewpoints. Richmond's seven streams were modified and adapted into nine Systems Thinking Perspectives (Kasser and Mackley 2008). The nine perspectives introduced nine standardized viewpoints which can be used in sequence or in a random order. The nine Systems Thinking Perspectives cover purpose, function, structure, and more and were later renamed as the Holistic Thinking Perspectives (HTP) (Section 10.1). The number of perspectives was limited to nine in accordance with Miller's Rule (Section 3.2.5). The nine perspectives and the Active Brainstorming tool (Section 7.1) improved the way students applied systems thinking in the classroom and seem to provide a good way of teaching applied systems thinking.

---

* This sentence is not meant to imply that engineers are not people.

1.4 Systems Thinking

Books on systems thinking don't teach it very well. There are books such as *The Fifth Discipline* (Senge 1990) which focuses on Causal Loops (Section 6.1.1) and seems to imply that systems thinking is the use of Causal Loops. There are books on the history and the philosophy and on what constitutes systems thinking, but there really aren't any practical handbooks on applying systems thinking to deal with problems and issues. Similarly the books on problem-solving tend to describe the process. They don't describe how to do the process. And the few articles that do, describe how to use a specific tool published in domain literature and do not get a wide distribution, so few people hear about it and even fewer people actually use it.

I found that out the hard way when I started to teach systems thinking at the University of South Australia (UniSA). I could describe the benefits and history of systems thinking, but no one at the Systems Engineering and Evaluation Centre (SEEC) could teach how to use systems thinking very well. We could teach Causal Loops (Section 6.1.1) in the manner of *The Fifth Discipline* (Senge 1990), but that was all. There weren't any good textbooks that approached systems thinking in a practical manner. So I ended up moving halfway around the world to Cranfield University in the UK to develop the first version of a practical and pragmatic approach to teaching and applying systems thinking to systems engineering under a grant from the Leverhulme Foundation.

1.4.1 The Two Distinct Types of Systems Thinking

Subsequent research identified that one reason for the lack of good ways of teaching systems thinking might be because if you ask different people to define systems thinking, you will get different and sometimes conflicting definitions. However, these definitions can be sorted into two types, namely:

1. *Systemic thinking*: thinking about a system as a whole.
2. *Systematic thinking*: employing a methodical step-by-step manner to think about something.

Many proponents of systems thinking consider either systemic or systematic thinking to be systems thinking not realising that each type of thinking seems to be a partial view of a whole, in the manner of the fable of the blind men perceiving the elephant (Yen 2008). For example, Senge wrote, "Systems thinking is a discipline for seeing wholes" (Senge 1990); accordingly, his book only covers systemic thinking. However, both types of systems thinking are needed (Gharajedaghi 1999). Consider each of them:

- Systemic thinking has three steps (Ackoff 1991):
  1. A thing to be understood is conceptualized as a part of one or more larger wholes, not as a whole to be taken apart.
  2. An understanding of the larger system is sought.
  3. The system to be understood is explained in terms of its role or function in the containing system.
- Systemic thinking has two facets:
  1. *Analysis*: breaking a complicated topic into several smaller topics and thinking about each of the smaller topics. Analysis can be considered as a top-down approach to thinking about something and is associated with René Descartes (Descartes 1637, 1965). It has been termed reductionism because it is often used to reduce a complex topic to a number of smaller and simpler topics.
  2. *Synthesis*: combining two or more entities to form a more complex entity. Synthesis can be considered as a bottom-up approach to thinking about something.

- Proponents of systemic thinking tend to:
  - Equate Causal Loops (Section 6.1.1) or feedback loops with systems thinking because they are thinking about relationships within a system (e.g. Senge 1990, Sherwood 2002).
  - Define systems thinking as looking at relationships (rather than unrelated objects), connectedness, process (rather than structure), the whole (rather than its parts), the patterns (rather than the contents) of a system and context (Ackoff, Addison, and Andrew 2010: p. 6).
  - Systematic thinking is mostly discussed in the literature on problem-solving, systems thinking, Critical Thinking, and systems engineering. It is often taught as the "problem solving process."

1.4.2 Systems Thinking and Beyond

Systematic thinking provides the process for systemic thinking which helps you understand the problematic situation. The
"beyond" part is where the problem definitions and solutions come
from. This is what I call holistic thinking. It emerged from the
research in 2008 and has been refined since then. It goes beyond
the two traditional components of systems thinking and includes
Critical Thinking as well as the internal, external, progressive, and
other HTPs (Section 10.1).

1.5 Problem-Solving

The systems approach to problem-solving is based on:

1. Visualizing (Section 7.11) the problem-solving process as
   a Causal Loop (Section 6.1.1), as shown in Figure 11.1, in
   which solutions evolve instead of the non-systems approach
   of visualizing the problem-solving process as a linear process
   from problem to solution.
2. Examining the problematic situation from a Perspectives
   Perimeter (Chapter 10), usually the HTPs (Section 10.1) to
   gain an understanding of the problem.
3. Going beyond systems thinking (Section 1.4.2) to determine
   the root cause or causes of the undesirability and Visualizing
   (Section 7.11) the solution.
4. Using the *Continuum* HTP to differentiate between subjective complexity and objective complexity and then abstracting
   objective complexity out of the problem. Objective complexity is being managed in many domains (Section 13.3).
   Distinguishing between objective complexity and subjective
   complexity in English is difficult because there isn't a single
   word that uniquely defines either concept (Section 13.3.1).
   The words "complicated" and "complex" have been used in
   the literature as synonyms to describe both types complexity. This book uses the words according to the following
   definitions:
   - *Complex*: objective complexity – made up of lots of things.
   - *Complicated*: subjective complexity – difficult to understand.

1.6 Alphabetical List of Tools

The tools presented in this book are grouped in various ways. Accordingly, Table 1.2 contains an alphabetical list of the tools to assist in speedily locating the different tools.

Table 1.2 Alphabetical List of Tools

TOOL	SECTION
2x2 format generic framework	5.1
Active Brainstorming	7.1
Annotated Outlines	14.1
Attribute Profiles	9.1
Association of Ideas	7.2
Bar Charts	2.1
Brainstorming	7.3
Budgets	9.2
Categorized Requirements in Process (CRIP) Charts	8.1
Cataract methodology for systems and software acquisition	11.2
Causal Loops	6.1.1
Cause and Effect Charts	2.2
Checkland's Soft Systems Methodology (SSM)	13.1
Comparison Tables	9.5.1
Compliance Matrix	9.5.2
Compound Bar Charts	2.3
Compound Line and Bar Charts	2.4
Concept Maps	6.1.2
Concept of Operations Document (CONOPS)	13.2
Constraint Mapping	7.4
Control Charts	2.5
Critical Thinking	3
Data or information tables	9.5.3
Decision Trees	4.6.1
Do Statement	3.2.1
Don't Care situation	3.2.2
Earned Value Analysis (EVA)	8.2
Enhanced Traffic Light Charts	8.16.2
Financial Budgets	8.3
Financial Charts	2.6
Five Whys	7.5
Flowcharts	2.7
Framework for tackling complexity	13.3
Functions Requirements Answers and Test (FRAT)	14.2.3

(Continued)

Table 1.2 (Continued)   Alphabetical List of Tools

TOOL	SECTION
Gantt Charts	8.4
Generic problem-solving process	11.1
Golden Rules	8.5
Graphics	6
Graphs	6.1.3
Hierarchical Charts	2.8
Histograms	2.9
Hitchins-Kasser-Massie Framework (HKMF)	5.2
Holistic Thinking Perspectives (HTP)	10.1
Idea Storage Templates (IST)	14.2
Just-in-time (JIT) decision-making	8.6
Keep It Simple Stupid (KISS)	3.2.3
Kipling Questions	7.6
Ladder of Inference	3.2.4
Lateral Thinking	7.7
Lessons Learned	9.3
Letter and word manipulation	7.8
Lists	9.4
Management by Exception (MBE)	8.7
Management by Objectives (MBO)	8.8
Mathematical tools	13.4
Miller's Rule	3.2.5
Mind Maps	6.1.4
Mission Statements	8.9
Multi-attribute Variable Analysis (MVA)	4.6.2
N^2 Charts	2.10
Nominal Group Technique (NGT)	7.9
Observations, Assumptions Risks and Problems (OARP)	14.2.2
Occam's Razor	3.2.6
Ordering and Ranking	4.6.3
Pair-wise Comparison	4.6.4
Pareto Charts	2.11
Perfect Score Approach	4.6.5
Perspectives Perimeter	10
Pie Charts	2.12
Plan Do Check Act (PDCA)	11.3
Polar Charts	2.14
Principle of Hierarchies	3.2.7
Prioritization	4.6.6
Problem Classification Framework	5.3

(Continued)

Table 1.2 (Continued) Alphabetical List of Tools

TOOL	SECTION
Problem Formulation Template	14.3
Process for creating technical and other project documents	11.4
Process for finding out-of-the-box solutions	11.6
Process for Tackling a Problem	11.5
Product-Activity-Milestone (PAM) chart	2.14
Program Evaluation Review Technique (PERT) Charts	8.10
Project Plans	8.11
Rich Pictures	6.1.5
Relationship Charts	6.1.2
Risk Management	12.2
Risk Rectangle	5.4
Schedules, Products, Activities, Resources and risKs (SPARK) Template	14.2.4
Slip Writing	7.10
STALL	3.2.9
Standard functional template for a system	14.4
SWOT	14.2.1
Systems thinking	1.3
Systematic thinking	1.4.1
Systemic thinking	1.4.1
Technology Availability Window of Opportunity (TAWOO)	8.12
Template for a management review presentation	14.8
Template for a document	14.5
Template for a presentation	14.6
Template for a student exercise presentation	14.7
Templates	14
Thank You	8.13
Theory of Inventive Problem-Solving (TRIZ)	11.7
Three Streams of Activities	8.14
Timelines	8.15
Traffic Light Charts	8.16.1
Trend Charts	2.15
Visualization	7.11
Waterfall Chart	14.9
Work Breakdown Structures (WBS)	8.18
Work Package (WP)	8.19
Working Backwards from the Solution	11.8
XY Charts	2.16
Zone of Ambiguity	13.5

1.7 Summary

Chapter 1 began with an overview of benefits provided by this book followed by a section on how to read and use this book. This chapter continued with a discussion on thinking and the systems approach, introducing systems thinking and the two distinct types of systems thinking: systemic thinking and systematic thinking, as well as the benefits of going beyond systems thinking into holistic thinking. This also contains a list of acronyms used in this book and a table listing the tools used in the book in alphabetical order to facilitate quickly locating each of the tools.

References

Ackoff, R. L. 1991. "The Future of Operational Research is Past." In *Critical Systems Thinking Directed Readings*, edited by Robert L. Flood and Michael C. Jackson. Original edition, *Journal of the Operational Research Society*, no. 30, 1979.

Ackoff, R. L., H. J. Addison, and C. Andrew. 2010. *Systems Thinking for Curious Manaers*. Axminster, Devon, UK: Triachy Press Ltd.

Atkinson, R., and R. Shiffrin. 1968. "Human Memory: A Proposed System and Its Control Processes." In *The Psychology of Learning and Motivation: Advances in Research and Theory (Vol. 2)*, edited by K. Spence and J. Spence. New York: Academic Press.

Churchman, C. W. 1968. *The Systems Approach*: New York: Dell Publishing Co.

Descartes, R. 1637, 1965. *A Discourse on Method*, trans. E. S. Haldane and G. R. T. Ross, Part V. New York: Washington Square Press.

Gharajedaghi, J. 1999. *System Thinking: Managing Chaos and Complexity*. Boston: Butterworth-Heinemann.

Kasser, J. E., and T. Mackley. 2008. "Applying Systems Thinking and Aligning It to Systems Engineering." In the 18th INCOSE International Symposium, at Utrecht, Holland.

Lutz, S., and W. Huitt. 2003. "Information Processing and Memory: Theory and Applications." Valdosta State University. Accessed 24 February 2010. http://www.edpsycinteractive.org/papers/infoproc.pdf.

Luzatto, M. C. circa 1735. *The Way of God*. Translated by Aryeh Kaplan. New York and Jerusalem, Israel: Feldheim Publishers, 1999.

Morgan, G. 1997. *Images of Organisation*. Thousand Oaks, CA: SAGE Publications.

Osborn, A. F. 1963. *Applied Imagination Principles and Procedures of Creative Problem Solving*. (3rd Rev. Ed.). New York: Charles Scribner's Sons.

Ramo, S. 1973. "The Systems Approach." In *Systems Concepts*, edited by R. F. Miles Jr, p. 13–32. New York: John Wiley & Son, Inc.

Richmond, B. 1993. "Systems Thinking: Critical Thinking Skills for the 1990s and Beyond." *System Dynamics Review*, no. 9 (2):113–133.

Russo, J. E., and P. H. Schoemaker. 1989. *Decision Traps*. New York: Simon and Schuster.

Senge, P. M. 1990. *The Fifth Discipline: The Art & Practice of the Learning Organization*. New York: Doubleday.

Sherwood, D. 2002. *Seeing the Forest for the Trees: A Manager's Guide to Applying Systems Thinking*. London: Nicholas Brealey Publishing.

Woolfolk, A. E. 1998. "Chapter 7: Cognitive Views of Learning." In *Educational Psychology*, pp. 244–283. Boston: Allyn and Bacon.

Wu, W., and H. Yoshikawa. 1998. "Study on Developing a Computerized Model of Human Cognitive Behaviors in Monitoring and Diagnosing Plant Transients." In IEEE International Conference on Systems, Man, and Cybernetics.

Yen, D. H. 2008. *The Blind Men and the Elephant*. Accessed 26 October 2010. http://www.noogenesis.com/pineapple/blind_men_elephant.html.

2
CHARTS

Charts are tools that we use all the time when thinking and communicating. They range from simple sketches on the back of an envelope or napkin to complex graphics produced by computers. This chapter discusses the following charts in alphabetical order:

1. Bar Charts in Section 2.1.
2. Cause and Effect Charts in Section 2.2.
3. Compound Bar Charts in Section 2.3.
4. Compound Line and Bar Charts in Section 2.4.
5. Control Charts in Section 2.5.
6. Financial Charts in Section 2.6.
7. Flowcharts in Section 2.7.
8. Hierarchical Charts in Section 2.8.
9. Histograms in Section 2.9.
10. N^2 Charts in Section 2.10.
11. Pareto Charts in Section 2.11.
12. Pie Charts in Section 2.12.
13. Polar Charts in Section 2.13.
14. Product-Activity-Milestone (PAM) Charts in Section 2.14.
15. Trend Charts in Section 2.15.
16. XY Charts in Section 2.16.

This book also discusses:

- Categorized Requirements in Process (CRIP) Charts in Section 8.1.
- Causal Loops in Section 6.1.1.

- Gantt Charts in Section 8.4.
- Program Evaluation Review Technique (PERT) Charts in Section 8.10.
- Traffic Light and Enhanced Traffic Light (ETL) Charts in Section 8.16.
- Waterfall Charts in Section 14.9.

Each type of chart shows information in a different way. Select the chart that helps you think about the information or presents the information you want the viewer to see in a way that is familiar to the viewer.

2.1 Bar Charts

Bar Charts are tools for comparing the values of independent variables on a single chart. The length of the bar represents the size of the variable. Bar Charts come in various forms and may show a vertical bar per grouping or several bars as needed to present the appropriate information. Sometimes the bars are shown horizontally. Depending on the chart, the bars may represent different variables at the same point of time, or the same variable at different points of time. One example is shown in Figure 2.1. Fred has been to a shooting range and fired six shots at a target. He plotted the distance from the centre of the target for each shot in the form of the Bar Chart shown in Figure 2.1.

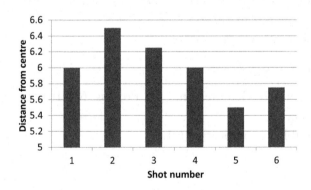

Figure 2.1   Bar Chart representation of the results of Fred's session.

2.2 Cause and Effect Charts

Cause and Effect Charts:

- Are specialized flow-charting tools used primarily in:
  - Tracking down the root cause (problem) of a specific symptom.
  - Identifying failure modes in failure analysis and risk management.
- Take the form shown in Figure 2.2.
- Are also known as:
  - *Ishikawa diagrams*: because of (the association with) Kaoru Ishikawa, the person who developed them.
  - *Fishbone Charts*: because of (the association with) the similarity in the shapes between the chart and the skeleton of a fish when there are a large number of items on the chart.
- Are often used in ideation sessions to examine factors that may influence a given situation.
- Facilitate:
  - Distinguishing between causes and effects or symptoms.
  - Determining the relationships between causes and effects.
  - Determining the parameters associated with causes.

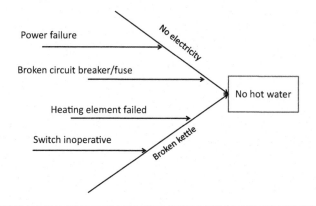

Figure 2.2 A Cause and Effect Chart.

- Consist of three parts:
  1. *The effect*: a situation, condition or event produced by a cause. The effect:
     a. Is shown as a box with a horizontal arrow in the centre of the chart, pointing to, and joined to the box.
     b. May be desirable or undesirable.
  2. *The primary causes*: drawn as sloping lines leading towards the effect box. The lines are labelled with "the cause".
  3. *The secondary parameters of the cause*: drawn as horizontal lines leading to the cause lines.

2.2.1 Using a Cause and Effect Chart

The Cause and Effect Chart is:

- Generally used in a manner that thinks backwards from the effect to the cause; an instance of the generic working backwards from the solution process (Section 11.8).
- Very useful when using the Five Whys (Section 7.5) to determine the cause of a failure in a complex situation where there may be more than one potential cause.

When using the systems approach to thinking about a process, you should generally also think about things that might go wrong with the process (risk management), and the appropriate Concept Map to link these thoughts is a Cause and Effect Chart.* For example, when thinking about making a cup of instant coffee, one of the things that might go wrong is that the water does not get hot. Figure 2.2 shows a typical Cause and Effect Chart drawn when trying to determine the type of failure that could cause the water not to get hot when using an electric kettle. The symptom is shown in the box on the right side, and in this case, the symptom is "no hot water". After some thought, two possible causes are identified: "no electricity" and a "broken kettle". Further thought postulates that "no electricity" might be due to a power failure or a tripped circuit breaker or blown fuse, and the "broken kettle" might be due to a failed heating element or switch. These ideas are connected as shown in Figure 2.2.

---

* Thinking about the different types of things that can go wrong is known by buzzwords such as contingency planning, risk management, and failure analysis.

2.2.2 Creating a Cause and Effect Chart

Create a Cause and Effect Chart by:

1. Creating the box containing the effect or symptom as shown in Figure 2.2. Label the box with the effect. In Figure 2.2, it is "no hot water".
2. Think about what could cause the effect and draw slanting lines into the box as shown in Figure 2.2. Label each of the lines with their cause.
3. Think about secondary causes for each slanted line and draw them as horizontal lines, as shown in Figure 2.2. Label each line with the cause.

2.3 Compound Bar Charts

A Compound Bar Chart is a tool that can be used to compare two sets of information about some attributes of something where the information is shown in the form of a Bar Chart (Section 2.1). In this example, the performance, speed, weight, length, width, height, payload, and flight duration of two different model airplanes (Series 1 and 2) have been evaluated. Each parameter has been evaluated on a scale of 0 to 5, and the resulting scores are shown in Figure 2.3. The chart shows that Series 1 is better in some respects, Series 2 is better in others, and the two model aircrafts received identical scores for speed. The same information is shown in Figure 2.4 but in the form

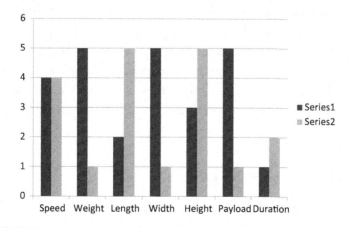

Figure 2.3 Compound Bar Chart for comparisons.

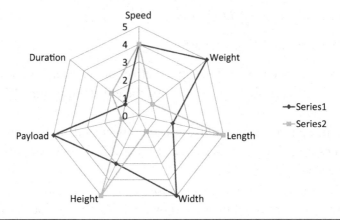

Figure 2.4   Kiviat Chart polar plot of model aircraft evaluations.

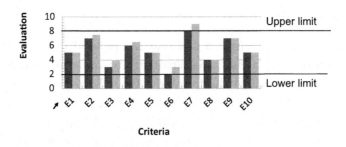

Figure 2.5   Performance evaluations over two periods.

of a Polar Chart (Section 2.14). When comparing a small number of parameters, either type of chart may be used, but when there are a large number of parameters to be compared, the Polar Chart is a better way of presenting the comparison results. Another example of a Compound Bar Chart is the performance evaluation Control Chart in Figure 2.5 which shows the performance evaluation for a candidate against the criteria E1 to E10 for two successive time periods. The figure is a Control Chart (Section 2.5) drawn as a Compound Bar Chart.

2.4 Compound Line and Bar Charts

There are times when a chart containing a mixture of lines and bars is useful, such as when thinking about cumulative values and values

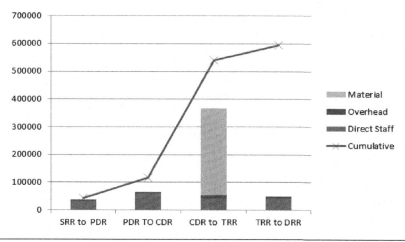

Figure 2.6   Compound Line and Bar Chart, NUS SDM5002, Session 7, 2014, Team Integral.

in specific time periods. Each type of chart shows information in a different way. Select the chart that helps you think about the information or presents the information you want the viewer to see in a way that is familiar to the viewer. For example, Figure 2.6 is a Compound Line and Bar Chart (Section 2.4).

2.5 Control Charts

Control Charts are:

- Tools by used by management to monitor and control a process.
- Trend Charts (Section 2.15) with upper and lower limit levels as shown on the line graph in Figure 2.7.
- Used to identify when pre-determined upper and lower limits have been exceeded.
- Useable in other situations as well (*Generic* HTP). For example, one use is in personal performance evaluations. Figure 2.8 shows a Control Chart used in performance evaluation. The person has been evaluated on nine (E1–E9) criteria, and when the information is plotted in the chart, is seen to exceed the upper limit on one of them, superior performance which might be recognized. In this figure the evaluation is plotted as a Bar Chart, not as a line chart. When the subsequent

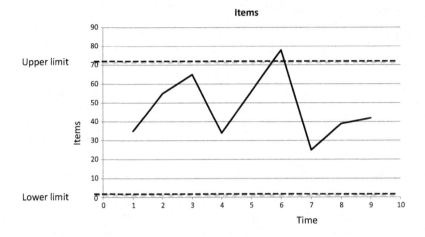

Figure 2.7   A typical Control Chart.

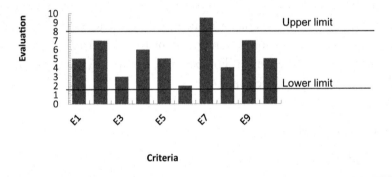

Figure 2.8   Control Chart for performance evaluation.

evaluation is added to the chart (for a different person), as shown in Figure 2.5, improvements can be seen. On the other hand, should the performance have dropped, someone should determine the reason.

While Control Charts are usually shown as Trend Charts using lines, in the performance evaluation scenario, the information is more easily extracted from the Bar Chart view (Section 2.1).

2.6 Financial Charts

Financial Charts are tools for thinking about and communicating financial information. They include Graphs (Section 6.1.3), Bar Charts

(Section 2.1) and Compound Line and Bar Charts (Section 2.4). When planning a Financial Budget (Section 8.3), a typical chart summarizing the information might be the one shown in Figure 2.9. It is a Trend Chart (Section 2.15) with two trend lines. The funds committed to the project trend line at $50,000 are not expected to change over the life of the project, so the line is drawn as a flat horizontal line. The budgeted line shows total planned budgeted expenditure over the 12 months of the project increasing each month by a planned value until it gets to about $45,000. Since the figure shows the planned budget before the project begins, nothing has been spent so the actual costs are zero.

Figure 2.10 is another type of Trend Chart showing the project financial status after nine months. The actual amount of funds

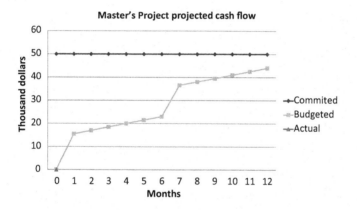

Figure 2.9 Project projected cash flows.

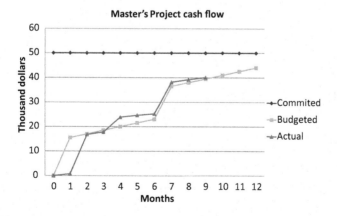

Figure 2.10 Project financial status after nine months.

spent has varied slightly from the planned amount but the project is currently expected to finish within budget. This type of chart is used in Earned Value Analysis (EVA) (Section 8.2). Figure 2.6 is a Compound Line and Bar Chart (Section 2.4) containing both a Line Chart and a vertical Bar Chart. The figure is a Financial Chart for a different project. The Trend Chart shows the cumulative expenditure over the project by for the time between the major milestones (Section 14.9). The vertical Bar Chart shows the expenditure for each milestone period as a stacked bar broken out by a number of categories of costs.

2.7 Flowcharts

A Flowchart is:

- A tool for describing a conceptual or real process.
- A tool for describing a sequence of activities/events.
- A graphic representation of the procedural association between items. It is often used when thinking about or discussing:
  - The relationship among parts of a process.
  - A signal (data) flow through a data processing system.

Depending on the content in which it is used, the Flowchart maybe used to think about something that exists or to conceptualize about something that is desired.

2.7.1 Types of Flowcharts

Perceptions from the *Continuum* HTP indicate that there are two types of Flowcharts, namely:

1. A process Flowchart.
2. A functional Flowchart.

Where:

- *A process* Flowchart shows the elements of the process in a time-ordered manner sequentially from start to finish. Since time does not go backwards, a process Flowchart must not contain any backward arrows. If a block of activities is going to be repeated, it has to be shown as a second block, identical to the first, but taking place later in time.

- *A functional* Flowchart is a Relationship Chart (Section 6.1.2). Since it's not time-dependent, arrows can loop back when functions are repeated; the most common example is a Causal Loop (Section 6.1.2).

2.7.2 Flowchart Symbols

The symbols for the four most common elements in a Flowchart are shown in Figure 2.11 in the context of describing adding water to something until there is enough water. The elements are:

- *Begin* and *end*, shown as ovals. These symbols show the entry point and the exit point of the Flowchart. They may be labelled "begin", "end", "start", or "stop" as appropriate.
- *Process, task, action, or operation*, shown as a rectangle. The label inside the rectangle shall contain a verb.
- *Decision*, shown as a diamond. A decision poses a question. The answer to the question determines the exit path out of the decision shape. So in Figure 2.11, the "no" response path flows back to the "add water" process symbol, while the "yes" path flows forward to the "end" symbol.
- *Connections*, shown as lines ending with an arrow in the direction of the flow.

Flowcharts may be drawn in various ways such as by hand freestyle, by hand using templates, or using computer software. When using

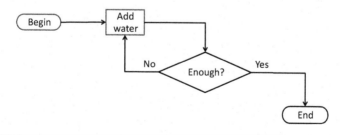

Figure 2.11 Flowchart for adding water showing the four most common flowchart symbols in use.

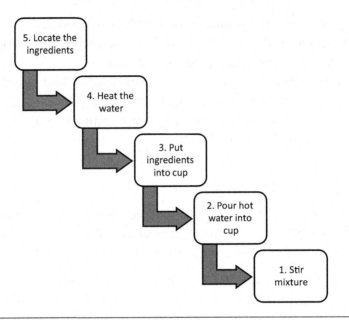

Figure 2.12   Process for making a cup of instant coffee.

software, the connections can sometimes be shown as thick arrows as in a process for making a cup of instant coffee shown in Figure 2.12.

2.7.3 Rules for Drawing a Flowchart

The rules for drawing a Flowchart are:

1. All information shall flow into process inputs.
2. All information shall flow out of process outputs.
3. The Flowchart shall show the sequential and concurrent nature of the activities.
4. The Flowchart shall show all the potential paths an activity can take. If those paths are not pertinent, they shall be deemphasized accordingly. One way of doing so is to colour the paths grey.
5. All of the decision points shall be shown accurately.
6. The Flowchart shall be drawn from top (start) to bottom (finish) or left (start) to right (finish).
7. There shall be no more than nine shapes in a Flowchart in accordance to Miller's Rule (Section 3.2.5).

2.7.4 Creating a Flowchart to Represent a Process

Creating a Flowchart requires thinking about the sequence of activities. For example, think about the process for making a cup of instant coffee. There are three ways to do this:

1. Starting from the ending and working backwards to the beginning, discussed in Section 2.7.4.1.
2. Starting from the beginning and working forwards to the ending, discussed in Section 2.7.4.2.
3. Starting in the middle and working backwards and forwards, discussed in Section 2.7.4.3.

2.7.4.1 Starting from the Ending Here you start with a completed product, namely the cup of instant coffee, and think about what you did to create it (Section 11.8). Working backwards from the completed stirred cup of instant coffee ready for drinking, you first thought of the last step you performed to realize the product and wrote it down. After writing down the step, you thought of the items you used when you performed the step. You then conceptually moved back to the previous set of activities that you used to make sure the items were ready when you needed them. So, you would end up with a list such as, you:

1. Stirred the mixture.
2. Added the ingredients to the hot water in the cup.
3. Poured the hot water into the cup.
4. Waited for the water to boil.
5. Started to heat the water.
6. Put the water into the kettle
7. Located the ingredients (coffee powder, creamer and sugar) and kitchen items (cup, spoon and kettle).

Or you could have written that you:

1. Stirred the mixture.
2. Poured the hot water into the cup.
3. Put the ingredients into the cup.
4. Waited for the water to boil.
5. Started to heat the water.

6. Put the water into the kettle
7. Located the ingredients (coffee powder, creamer, and sugar) and kitchen items (cup, spoon, and kettle).

Or you could have written that you:

1. Stirred the mixture.
2. Poured the hot water into the cup.
3. Put the ingredients into the cup.
4. Heated the water.
5. Located the ingredients (coffee powder, creamer, and sugar) and kitchen items (cup, spoon, and kettle).

Or you could have written a similar list of sequential ideas using slightly different wording. The first process was completely sequential; the second process contained two parallel activities in that you put the ingredients into the cup while the water was heating which shortened the time to create the product. The third version of the process was also sequential. In all three versions of the process, the "1. Stirred the mixture" step contained three sub-steps, namely:

1.1. Picked up the spoon.
1.2. Stirred the mixture in the cup.
1.3. Put the spoon down.

Similarly, in the third example the "4. Heated the water" step contained three sub-steps, namely:

4.1. Waited for the water to boil.
4.2. Started to heat the water.
4.3. Put the water into the kettle.

All three versions are acceptable at this time because they are just the initial ideas for the process. Note that each step is numbered and when a step is broken out into sub-steps the numbering is adjusted accordingly. In these examples, Step 1 is broken out into sub-Steps 1.1, 1.2 and 1.3, while Step 4 is broken out into sub-Steps 4.1, 4.2, and 4.3. This numbering style makes it easy to locate a sub-step in the process.

When working backwards, you can have a vision of the product in your mind and working out how you got there minimizes the probability of forgetting an ingredient (part) or a step in the process. However, when you draw the process as a Flowchart, irrespective if drawn forwards from the start or backwards from the finish, the Flowchart always appears as if it had been drawn from start to finish, as shown in Figure 2.12. From the *Generic* HTP, Figure 2.12 may also be considered as a simple Design Structure Matrix (DSM) (Eppinger and Browning 2012).

2.7.4.2 Starting from the Beginning Starting from the beginning means that you have to think forwards and ask questions. Here you might have thought about:

1. Locating the ingredients.
2. Heating the water.
3. Putting the ingredients into the cup.
4. Adding the hot water into the cup.
5. Stirring the mixture.

When you thought about locating the ingredients, you had to ask, "What are the ingredients?" You thought for a while and came up with the hot water, coffee, sugar, and creamer. Then you thought about heating the water and associated putting water into a kettle. The sequential process slowly took shape in your mind and is the same sequence of ideas as you developed starting from the ending.

2.7.4.3 Starting in the Middle Here the ideas come in no particular sequence and you write them down as they come. You then arrange them in Lists (Section 9.4) and Relationship Diagrams (Section 6.1.2), then in hierarchies showing how the parts come together to make up the product.

2.7.5 The Most Common Mistakes Made When Drawing Flowcharts

The most common mistakes made when drawing Flowcharts are:

1. ***Too many objects in the Flowchart***: a violation of Rule 7 in Section 2.7.3.
2. ***Inconsistent flow direction***: a Flowchart should have a consistent flow direction. It should be top-to-bottom or left-to-right.

Note, loops may violate this rule when the Flowchart contains a small number of elements.

3. *Inconsistent hierarchical arrangement* in which the elements are at different levels in the process hierarchy.

For example, Figure 2.13 describes the flow for a CQ function in an amateur radio contest which contains the following subfunctions:

1. *Call CQ*: the radio amateur operator calls "CQ" on an unused frequency indicating that she is looking for someone to respond.
2. *Reply?*: tests for a reply. If a reply is not received, the process advances to Step 3. If a reply is received, the process advances to Step 4.
3. *Enough?*: tests to see if the operator has been calling for a predefined time period without a response. If the time period has not been exceeded, the process flows back to Step 1 for another CQ call.
4. *Duplicate?*: tests to see if the station that responded to the CQ has already been contacted. If it has, the process flows to Step 5; if it has not, the process flows to Step 6.
5. *Send worked B4*: transmits a message to the other station that contact has already been made; the station has been worked

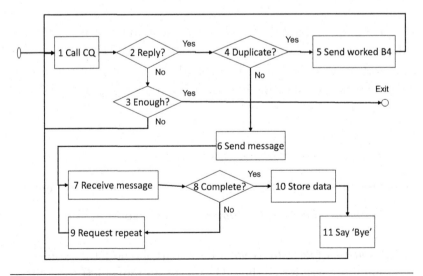

Figure 2.13   Initial call CQ function.

before (B4). The inference is that the other station will depart the frequency. The process then flows back to Step 1 and the first CQ call of the next sequence is transmitted.

6. **Send message**: transmits the contest exchange information and the process advances to Step 7.

7. **Receive message**: the operator receives a contest message exchange from the other station, and the process advances to Step 8.

8. **Complete?**: tests to determine if the received message is complete. If the message is not complete, the process advances to Step 9; if complete, the process advances to Step 10.

9. **Request repeat**: asks for a repeat of the message and returns to Step 7.

10. **Store the data**: stores the received message and corresponding transmitted data and advances to Step 11.

11. **Say "Bye"**: terminates the contact and the process flows back to Step 1.

Note that the blocks in Figure 2.13 have been numbered to facilitate discussing their content. Figure 2.13 contains a number of errors including:

- **Too many objects**: there are eleven which is a violation of Rule 7 in Section 2.7.3.
- **Elements from two levels in the hierarchy**, and should accordingly corrected to Figure 2.14. This type of mistake tends to arise because Figure 2.13 is generated while thinking about the process and is not converted into Figure 2.14 by grouping Steps 6, 7, 8, and 9 into a new higher level Step 6. One might also, as an alternative, have included Steps 10 and 11 into Step 6 and renamed the Step as a QSO function.
- **A potential indefinite loop** in Steps 7, 8, and 9 because unlike in Steps 1, 2, and 3, there is no timeout specified.
- **Inconsistent branch directions out of decision points** which make it harder to follow the logic. This means that one decision point may have a "yes" branch out of the right side and another decision point may have a "no" branch out of the same side. One way of avoiding this mistake is to flow "yes" out of the bottom of the decision and "no" out of the side. Another

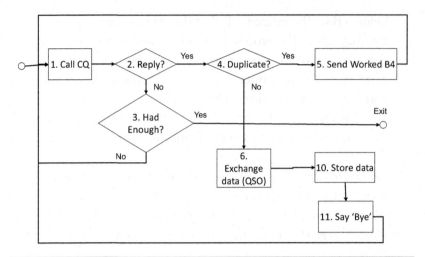

Figure 2.14   Adjusted call CQ function.

way is to flow out of the left and right sides as shown in Figure 2.11. You should use either way and not mix them.

- *Not showing directions (arrow heads) on the connections* which makes it difficult for other people to figure out the flow sequence.
- *Ambiguous branches* such as the one shown in Figure 2.15 which represents an approach to dealing with situations. Consider what happens after the "understand the situation block" in Figure 2.15. The flow can go back to "observe",

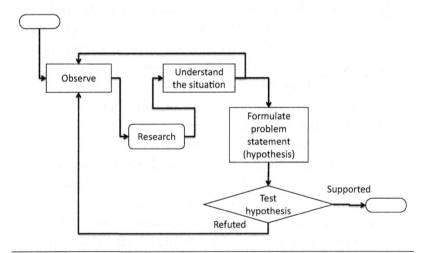

Figure 2.15   The scientific method (poor).

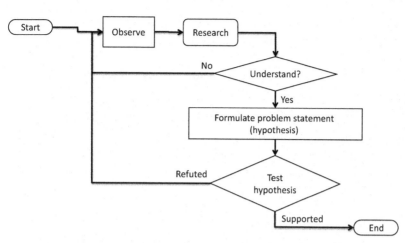

Figure 2.16 The scientific method.

down to "formulate problem statement", or in both directions. The implied decision is to return to "observe" until an understanding is achieved and then advance to "formulate the problem". Figure 2.15 should be redrawn as Figure 2.16 to remove the ambiguity by adding the decision point showing when each path is taken.

- **Failure to the use standard symbols** shown in Figure 2.11. Figure 2.15 also uses circles for the entry and exit points. The entry and exit points should be ovals as shown as in Figure 2.16.
- **Looping back in process Flowcharts.** Time does not flow backwards, so when process Flowcharts take the form of Causal Loops (Section 6.1.1), people tend to forget that time passes during the subsequent iterations and the need for baselining each iteration.

These mistakes generally arise because the person drawing the chart is familiar with the context, does a brain dump, and does not take the time to fix the chart before distributing it.

2.7.5.1 Creating Flowcharts When Designing Software Flowcharts are often drawn when designing the logic in computer software. This section now provides an example of creating a number of Flowcharts in the context of designing the software for a game which simulates an amateur radio contest and shows how some of the most common mistakes in creating Flowcharts appear and how they can be corrected.

2.7.5.2 Perceptions of an Amateur Radio Contest   From the *Big Picture* HTP, the purpose of an amateur radio contest is to simulate an emergency situation in which amateur radio operators are sending and receiving messages into and out of a disaster area and as such provide training in this type of operation.

From the *Operational* HTP, amateur radio operators perform a number of scenarios including:

- Searching for other amateur radio stations to contact.
- Calling CQ, a signal that the amateur radio station is waiting on a frequency for other amateur radio stations to contact them as shown in Figure 2.13.
- Exchanging messages with other amateur radio stations.

From the *Functional* HTP, functions can be thought of in a sequential manner, as shown in the top-level contest Flowchart in Figure 2.17 in which each item element is numbered to facilitate the discussion.

2.7.5.3 Creating the Flowcharts   Consider each element in Figure 2.17:

1. **Contacting someone** which can be done in several ways including:
   a. Calling CQ.
   b. Tuning the radio to find someone calling CQ and then calling them.
   c. Tuning the radio to find someone else in a contact to QSO (exchanging messages), waiting for the QSO to end, and then calling them.

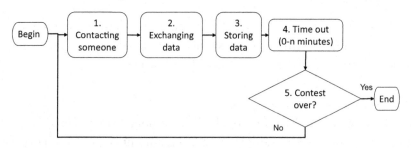

Figure 2.17   An amateur radio contest.

2. *Exchanging data* or messages, a function which can be done sequentially either by sending data first and then receiving data from the other station or vice versa.

3. *Storing the data* in the computer.

4. *Taking a timeout* for various reasons such as refreshment, comfort, equipment malfunctions and interference from members of the family.

5. *An "is the contest over" check* to terminate the software.

The Flowchart for the contacting someone or CQ scenario as developed by the software designer is shown in Figure 2.13. While it documents the functions, it contains several of the most common mistakes made when creating Flowcharts including:

- Non-standard entry and exit symbols (circles instead of ovals).
- The flow from item 6 to items 7 and 9 is backwards (saves space to draw it this way and the chart is still understandable, so this may be a valid exception).
- Items 6, 7, 8, and 9 are at a lower level in the system hierarchy than the remaining items.
- Too many items in the Flowchart.
- The "no" exits from the decision points are not labelled.

Figure 2.17 shows a partially adjusted Flowchart. Items 6, 7, 8, and 9 have been aggregated into a new higher-level exchange data function, item 6, and some of the other mistakes have been corrected. Two different versions of the exchange data function (item 6 in Figure 2.14) are shown in Figures 2.18 and 2.19 since participation in real

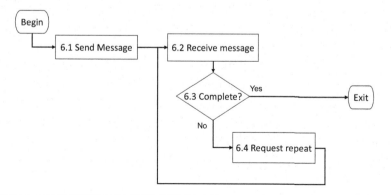

Figure 2.18 The exchange data function -1.

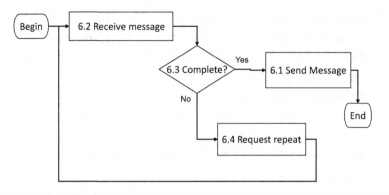

Figure 2.19   The exchange data function -2.

contests* have shown that both ways of exchanging messages are used and so need to be implemented in the simulation. The items have been labelled a 6.1, 6.2, 6.3, etc. to show that they are subfunctions of item 6.

In addition, each of the functions in Figures 2.18 and 2.19 must be shown in lower-level functional Flowcharts of their own.

2.8 Hierarchical Charts

Hierarchical Charts are:

- Tools showing relationships from the *Structural* HTP.
- Often used to describe reporting relationships in organizations, hence they are often known as organization charts.

For examples of the use of Hierarchical Charts, consider the problem of making a cup of instant coffee with creamer and sugar. When faced with a complex problem, we break it up into smaller, less complex problems (analysis), then solve each of the smaller problems and hope that the combination of solutions to the smaller problems (synthesis) will provide a solution to the large complex problem. When faced with the problem of making a cup of instant coffee, we use analysis to identify and create a List (Section 9.4) of the components that make up the complete cup of instant coffee. So the coffee powder, cup, hot water, cream, and sugar spring to mind. We then use synthesis to create the

---

* Application domain knowledge.

cup of instant coffee from the ingredients. We use Concept Maps to think of the relationships between the ingredients. When we think of the process, we think of mixing the ingredients, and in drawing the process flow chart (Section 2.7) we think of a spoon; when we think of heating the water, we think of a kettle and gas or electricity as the fuel.

A typical initial set of the items or parts used in making a cup of instant coffee is shown in Figure 2.20. The spoon is drawn as an assistant to the cup of coffee because it is used during the process of creating the cup of instant coffee and then discarded. The kettle and gas/electricity are associated with heating the water and so are shown in a similar manner as assistants to the hot water. However, this arrangement mixes concepts at different levels of the hierarchy and a better arrangement of the ideas is shown in Figure 2.21. The insertion of an abstract or virtual "ingredients" concept into the chart clarifies the arrangement of ideas, showing which ideas constitute the ingredients and which ideas are associated with other aspects of the cup of instant coffee.

However, Figure 2.21 should only be considered as an interim or working drawing. A better (simpler) final drawing is shown in Figure 2.22 which clearly distinguishes between the items associated with the cup of instant coffee and the aggregation of the spoon and kettle into an abstract concept called "kitchen items", the constituents of which are used in the process of creating the cup of instant coffee.

A common mistake in drawing Hierarchical Charts is the general mistake made in drawing Concepts Maps (Section 6.1.2.2) in which

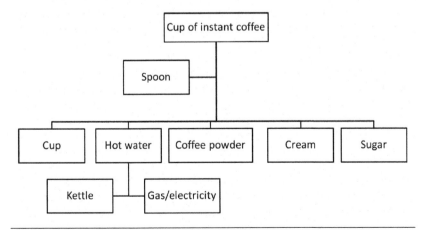

Figure 2.20 Initial set of ideas pertaining to a cup of instant coffee.

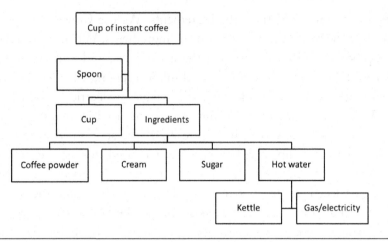

Figure 2.21   Hierarchical arrangement of items pertaining to a cup of instant coffee.

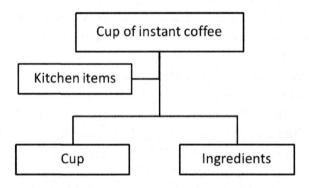

Figure 2.22   Top-level hierarchical chart for a cup of instant coffee.

a high-level chart such as Figure 2.22 is often extended to include the lower-level items such as in Figure 2.21 and Figure 2.23. The ideas or objects should have been sorted and aggregated prior to presentation and shown in the appropriate drawings. In this case, Figure 2.22 would show the entire system, Figure 2.24 would show the ingredients, and a third figure would show the kitchen items. Namely, the mistake is made up of the following two components:

1. We use a single chart for all the items instead of a set of charts, hence creating artificial complexity (Section 13.3.1.1).
2. We do not remove the clutter by grouping the items into a mixed hierarchy of less than nine items in accordance to Miller's Rule (Section 3.2.5).

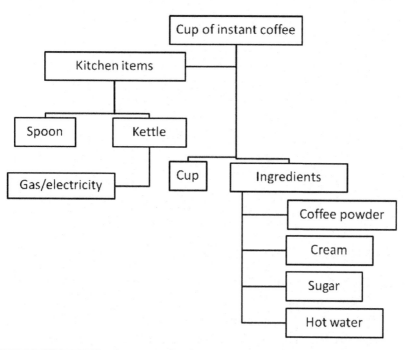

Figure 2.23 Sorted hierarchical arrangement of ideas pertaining to a cup of instant coffee.

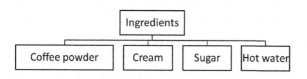

Figure 2.24 The ingredients.

2.9 Histograms

A Histogram:

- Is a specialized type of Bar Chart (Section 2.1) used in statistics to display a graphical summary of the distribution of data rather than the data (Pearson 1895). For example, Fred's hobby is shooting. After a session at the target range, Figure 2.36 shows the distance of Fred's shots from the centre of the target, as well as the angle. If Fred is interested in the number of shots hitting the target at specific range zones from the centre rather than the actual distances or angles, he could plot a Histogram to provide that information. Fred would create "buckets" for ranges of data, such as from 5.4 to 5.6 centimeters, 5.6 to

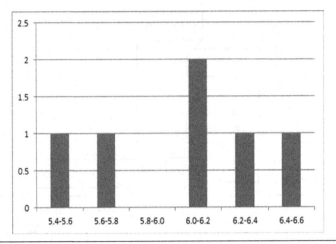

Figure 2.25   Histogram of Fred's shots grouping distance from target.

5.8 centimetres, etc., from the centre of the target at 0.2 centimetre intervals. He would then go through the data and increase the bucket count each time the value of a shot was inserted into a bucket. When he finishes the operation and displays the results, the Histogram would show up as depicted in Figure 2.25. As you can see, most of the shots were in the range 6.0–6.2 while none of the shots were in the range 5.8–6.0.

- Shows the relative distributions of items in a group. When the individual number of items is large, software can be used to calculate the data to be shown in the Histogram such as a chart summarizing the distribution of the final grades of students in a class at the end of a semester shown in Figure 2.26. The figure

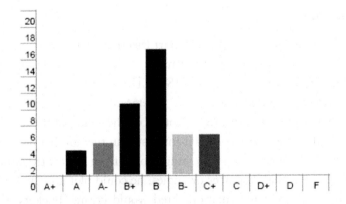

Figure 2.26   Histogram of student grades.

Table 2.1 N² Charts and DSM Inputs and Outputs

FUNCTION	N² CHART	DSM
Input	Column	Row
Output	Row	Column

shows that five students achieved a grade of A; six achieved a grade of A-, and so on. If the instructor wanted to grade on a curve, he or she could reduce the limit for a B grade to increase the number of B- grades.

2.10 N² Charts

The N² chart (Table 2.1):

- Was invented by R.J. Lano (Lano 1977).
- Is a table tool that shows relationships between entities, functions, people, organizations, equipment, etc.
- Appears in many different guises, including the Waterfall Chart (Section 14.9) of the System Development Process (SDP).
- Performs the same function as the Design Structure Matrix (DSM) (Eppinger and Browning 2012) but which reverses the flows in the rows and columns as summarized in Table 2.1.

2.10.1 The Basic N² Chart

The basic N² chart is based on a table in which the entities are listed across the columns and down the rows as shown in Figure 2.27. Since

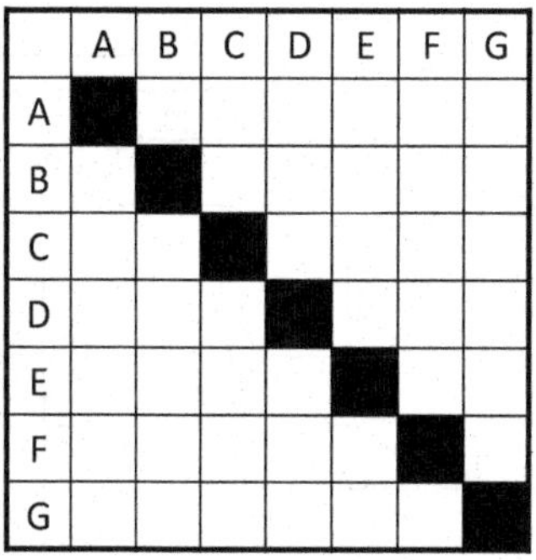

Figure 2.27 The table underlying an N² Chart.

an entity does not connect to itself, the common cell in the table is blocked out. The N² chart is a modified version of Figure 2.27 in which the heading rows and columns have been removed and the common cell contains the row and column designator. Inputs between entities are shown as a connection in a column, outputs as a connection in a row. The output from an early column flows out and down; a typical example is a Waterfall Chart (Section 14.9). So, for example, if there was a connection between the output of entity A and the input of entity C in Figure 2.27, an indication of the connection would be inserted in the cell in row A column C. As well as containing a simple indicator that a connection exists, cells can be populated with information such as priorities in the event of conflict or concurrency, data pertaining to interface such as type of connectors, data types and rates, etc. From the *Generic* HTP, Figure 2.12 may be considered as a DSM with the rows and columns abstracted out since the outputs are in columns and the inputs are in rows.

2.10.2 *The Aggregation Example*

Consider the following example of using N² Charts for aggregating entities. The set of functions shown in Concept Map format in Figure 2.28 needs to be aggregated or combined into a smaller but more complex set of functions. The Concept Map view of the functions in Figure 2.28 is not very useful for this purpose since it is difficult to see any useful pattern in the interconnections between the entities. However, when the functions are drawn in the form of the N² Chart as shown in Figure 2.29, you can see patterns in the interfaces.

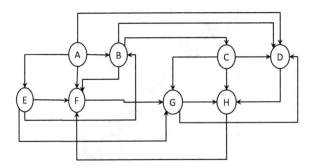

Figure 2.28 Complex Concept Map of relationships between functions.

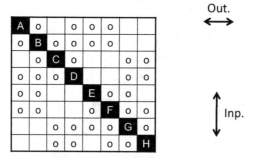

Figure 2.29 N² Chart of the relationships in Figure 2.28.

For example, entities B, C, and D all have inputs and outputs from each other, so they could be combined into one higher-level BCD entity. Entities E, F, and G show a similar pattern of interconnections and could likewise be combined into a higher-level EFG entity. The resulting higher-level representation of Figure 2.28 and Figure 2.29 is shown in N² and Concept Map formats in Figure 2.30. The Concept Map in Figure 2.30 is simpler than Figure 2.28 and Figure 2.29, but BCD and EFG have become more complex due to their each containing three elements.

Note that while the N² chart shows patterns suitable for aggregation, it does not show you which pattern to choose. In this instance, there are a number of alternate groupings including:

- ABEF, CD, and GH as shown in Figure 2.31.
- ABD, CGH, and EF shown in Figure 2.32.
- ABEF and CDGH.

The ease or difficulty of seeing the different arrangements depend on the initial sorting of the entities prior to drawing the chart in Step 3 of the process in Section 2.10.3.

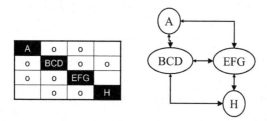

Figure 2.30 Higher level (more complex, less complicated) representations.

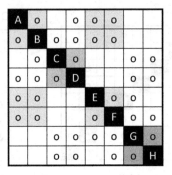

Figure 2.31   Alternate grouping -1.

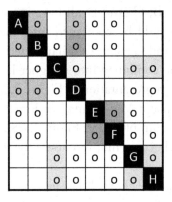

Figure 2.32   Alternate grouping -2.

2.10.3 Creating an N² Chart

Creating an N² Chart is a relatively simple process as follows:

1. Identify the entities in the area of interest often known as the system.
2. Make a List of the entities (Section 9.4).
3. Sort the entities into groups that seem connected without actually drawing any connections. This step facilitates seeing patterns in the chart once drawn.
4. Count the entities.
5. Create a table for the set of entities. Label the common cell in a meaningful manner.
6. Fill in the cells that contain the connections. Use an "x" or an "o" as in Figure 2.29 and Table 2.2 or provide the information as appropriate to the situation as in Table 2.3.

Table 2.2 Connections between Vivo City and Kent Vale

VIVO CITY												
0	Taxi											
0	10				0						0	
0	0	30			0	0			0	0	0	
0	0	0	143		0	0			0	0		
0	0	0	0	51	0	0				0		
0	0	0	0	0	188	0	Haw Par villa		0		0	
0	0	0	0	0	0	Clementi Rd			0			
							Back gate					0
0	0	0	0	0			Kent Ridge Terminal		0	0		0
0	0							33	0	33	0	0
0	0	0	0	0				183		183	0	
0	0	0	0						189		Front Gate	0
0					0			0		0	0	Kent Vale

Table 2.3   N² Chart Linking Locations by Transportation Option

VIVO CITY	SUBWAY, 10, 30, 143, 188	10, 30, 143, 188	10	TAXI, 30, 143	TAXI, 188	
10, 30, 143, 188	Haw Pah Villa	10, 30, 51, 143, 188	10	30, 51, 143	188	
10, 30, 143, 188	10, 30, 51, 143, 188	Clementi Rd.	10	30, 51, 143	183, 188	
10	10	10	Kent Ridge Terminal	189	33	
Taxi, 30, 143	30, 51, 143	30, 51, 143	189	Back gate		0
Taxi, 188	188	183, 188	33		Front gate	0
				0	0	Kent Vale

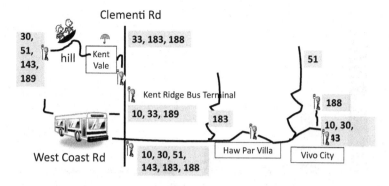

Figure 2.33 Rich Picture showing options for Vivo City to Kent Vale travel.

2.10.4 Inserting Data in the N² Chart

The examples shown in this section so far only show that a link exists between the inputs and outputs of the system elements. There is no reason why the linking cells should not contain information about the way the connection is made such as in the following example. In solving the problem of determining the fastest route for travelling from Vivo City and Kent Vale, based on the information in the Rich Picture shown in Figure 2.33, the initial N² chart showing the travel connections between Vivo City and Kent Vale is shown in Table 2.2. The chart starts at Vivo City and ends at Kent Vale and shows the interconnections between the transport routes and locations.

Now change the perspective and put the locations in the cells in the chart and link the locations by transportation option, namely using the *Continuum* HTP to perceive the bus, subway and taxis as signals travelling along the interfaces between the locations. This redesign shown in Table 2.3 shows clearly that the option to take the 10 and transfer at Kent Ridge Terminal provides fewer bus choices than all the others and reduces the number of options. Note how the N² chart in Table 2.3 provides information about the nature of the interface as well as the existence of an interface.

2.11 Pareto Charts

Pareto Charts:

- Were invented by Vilfredo Pareto (1848–1923).
- Are Histograms (Section 2.9) drawn with vertical bars showing the variables in order of increasing or decreasing length

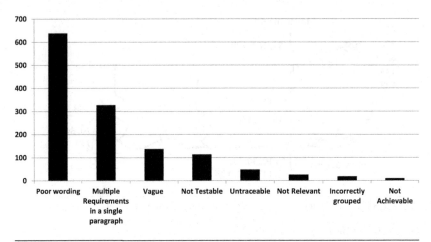

Figure 2.34   Number of defects in a requirements document shown as a Pareto Chart.

as shown in Figure 2.34. The figure shows the number and type of defects found when testing a requirement document in which the bars corresponding to the type of defect have been ranked according to the number of defects associated with the type. Consider the data shown in Table 2.4. Figure 2.34 graphically presents the information that poor wording and multiple requirements in a paragraph are the most common defects in the document. It is easier to see from the figure than the table that fixing those two types of defects alone will remove most of the defects in the requirement document.

- Are often used to display the degree that variables or parameters contribute to problems.

Table 2.4   Summary of the Defects Found in a Requirements Document

CATEGORY OF DEFECT	NUMBER OF DEFECTS
Poor wording	638
Multiple requirements in a single paragraph	327
Vague	137
Not testable	114
Untraceable	48
Not relevant	26
Incorrectly grouped	18
Not achievable	10
Total defects	1318
Total requirements	613

- Help to identify the few significant factors that contribute to a problem and separate them from the insignificant ones. The approach used to deal with the problem is to concentrate on the largest value first, then on the next largest and so on, such as repairing the requirements with poor words.

2.12 Pie Charts

A Pie Chart:

- Is shaped like a round pie, hence its name.
- Shows the relative values of each data item in a set as a percentage of the whole in the form of a circle or round pie. The value of each variable is represented by the size of the slice of the pie.
- Is best used to compare the size of a particular data item or slice with the whole rather than to make comparisons between different slices.
- Is often used instead of a Histogram (Section 2.9) to provide representations of summaries of data.

The same data as in the Pareto chart (Section 2.9) of Figure 2.34 is shown in Figure 2.35. The Pie Chart makes it very clear that the "poor wording" category of defects constitutes about 50% of the defects.

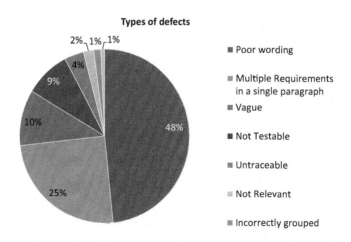

Figure 2.35   Number of defects in a requirements document shown as a Pie Chart.

2.13 Polar Charts

Polar Charts, sometimes called Kiviat Charts, Radar Charts, or Spider Charts, are used to show comparisons of a number of variables on a single chart where:

- Each spoke or axis on the chart represents a metric.
- The distance from the centre of the chart represents the metric's value plotted on that spoke.

For example, Fred's hobby is shooting. After a shooting session, he draws a Polar Chart shown in Figure 2.36 of the grouping of his shots in the target. The six-centimetre line is highlighted in the figure. Note the information shown in the figure; the distance and direction. Figure 2.36 shows the grouping of the shots, which suggests that Fred's shooting is pretty good, but he needs to adjust the sights on the weapon to move the centre of the grouping to the centre of the Polar Chart (target).

Polar Charts can be also used to compare two sets of information about some attributes of something, such as the performance the

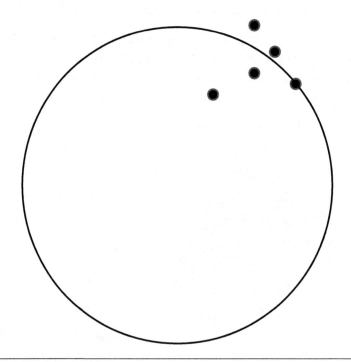

Figure 2.36   Polar plot of Fred's shots.

speed, weight, length, width, height, payload, and flight duration of two different model airplanes (Series 1 and 2). Each parameter has been evaluated on a scale of 0 to 5, and the resulting scores are shown in Figure 2.3. The chart shows that Series 1 is better in some respects, Series 2 is better in others, and the two model aircrafts received identical scores for speed.

2.14 Product-Activity-Milestone (PAM) Charts

The Product-Activity-Milestone (PAM) Chart (Kasser 1995):

- Is a tool to facilitate project planning by:
  - Defining a point in time (milestone).
  - Defining the product(s) or goals to be achieved by the milestone.
  - Determining the activities to produce the product(s).
  - Defining the resources needed to produce the product(s).
- Is designed to facilitate thinking backwards from the answer/ solution to the problem (Section 11.8).
- Is shown in Figure 2.37.
- Has been found to be a very useful project-planning tool for thinking about the relationships between the product, the activities that realize the product, and the milestone by which the product is to be completed.
- Is a Concept Map (Section 6.1.2) linking products, activities, and milestones.

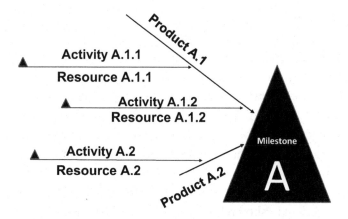

Figure 2.37 Product-Activity-Milestone (PAM) Chart.

- Can be used to think about the inputs to PERT Charts (Section 8.10). Note that the PAM Chart milestones are in triangles to relate them to Gantt Chart milestones (Section 8.4), while the PERT Chart milestones are in circles.
- Consists of four parts:
  1. *The milestone*: shown as a triangle.
  2. *The product(s) produced by or delivered at the milestone*: drawn as a sloping line(s) leading towards the milestone. Two products (A.1 and A.2) are shown in the Figure.
  3. *The activities that produce the products*: drawn as horizontal lines leading to the product line. They are listed above the line. Labelling reflects the activities associated with the product, so activities A.1.1 and A.1.2 are associated with producing product A.1, and activity A.2 is associated with producing product A.2. All activities shall start and end at milestones.
  4. *The resources associated with each activity*: shown as labels below the activity lines. They are listed below the line. Labelling reflects the resource associated with the activities, so resources for A.1.1 are listed below A.1.1, resources for A.2 are listed below A.2, etc.

2.14.1 Creating a PAM Chart

Use the following process to create a PAM Chart:

1. Start with a blank page.
2. Position a milestone at the right side of the paper.
3. Draw diagonal arrows for each product to be delivered at the milestone.
4. Draw horizontal activity lines that end at the product lines for each activity that creates the product. The starting point of each activity will be a previous (in time) milestone when the PAM Network Chart (Section 2.14.2) is completed.
5. Number the milestones, products, and activities where each milestone, product, and activity has an identical numeral component as shown Figure 2.37. The PAM triptych numbers

at each milestone must match, which facilitates identifying missing products and activities. The letter "A" identifies activities, "P" identifies products, and "R" identifies resources. Thus product P1 is produced by activity A1 using resource R1, which may consist of R1-1, R1-2, R1-3, etc.

The PAM Chart is a node in a project network because there is more than one milestone within a project. For example, consider the partial PAM Network Chart linking the products, activities, resources, and milestones in making a cup of instant coffee, shown in Figure 2.38. Working back from the last milestone (4), the product is a stirred cup of instant coffee ready to drink. The activity between milestones 3 and 4 is "stir the mixture", and the necessary resources are a spoon, the mixture, and a person to do the stirring. At milestone 3 the product is the "mixed ingredients", and there are two activities, adding hot water (between milestones 1-3) and adding the ingredients (between milestones 2-3). The product produced at milestone 1 is the hot water, and the resources needed consist of water, the kettle, electricity, and a person to do the job. The product produced at milestone 2 is the set of ingredients (instant coffee, creamer, and sugar) purchased separately or as a 3-in-1 packet. Look at the figure; can you see what is missing? No? Then what are you thinking

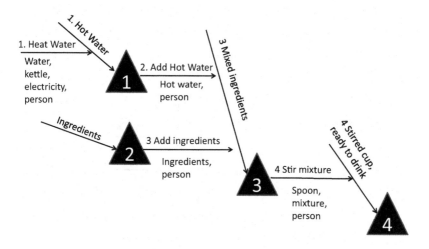

Figure 2.38 Partial PAM Network Chart for making a cup of instant coffee.

of putting the water and ingredients in before stirring the mixture? The answer is, of course, the cup.

2.14.2 The PAM Network Chart

The PAM Chart can be considered as a node in a network of PAM Charts. A typical partial PAM Network Chart is shown in Figure 2.39. Information in the figure includes:

- The ending milestone is 8.
- Two products are produced at milestone 8, products P8-1 and P8-2.
- Activity 8-1 produced product P8-1, activity A8-2 produced product P8-2.
- Activity A8-1 begins at milestone 2.
- Activity A8-2 uses resource R-2.
- There are no resources allocated to activity A8-1.
- Activities A6-1 and A8-2 do not follow from a prior milestone.
- There are no activities subsequent to milestones 6 and 7.

Accordingly, PAM Network Charts are not really useful as outputs from a project database because the PAM Network Chart can become complex and complicated very quickly when the number of milestones and products is more than nine, namely they are non-compliant with Miller's Rule (Section 3.2.5). The time taken by the activity and the milestone information should be presented in the corresponding

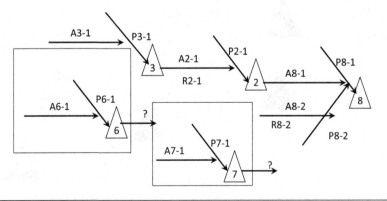

Figure 2.39   A Partial PAM Network Chart.

PERT Chart (Section 8.10). The resources and other information should be stored in the Work Package (Section 8.19) and presented in the appropriate manner. For example, timelines and schedules would be presented in Gantt Charts (Section 8.4).

Partial PAM Network Charts are useful as input tools for checking that the PAM triptych numbers are complete at each milestone, all activities begin and end at milestones and all the appropriate information has been identified and either inserted into the Work Package (WP) (Section 8.19) or a "TBD" (To Be Determined) has been inserted into the WP for the corresponding activity as a placeholder.

2.15 Trend Charts

Trend Charts:

- Are sometimes called Run Charts and show how the value of something changes over time.
- Plot time along the X-axis, with the parameter being depicted along the Y-axis. The example in Figure 2.40 plots (shows) the increase in items from 0 to 4.5 over three time periods. The figure shows that there was a change in the rate of increase in the first time period which might need to be investigated.
- Are used to compare changes in a number of variables over time.
- Are widely used in finance to show how the value of a stock or commodity changes over time.

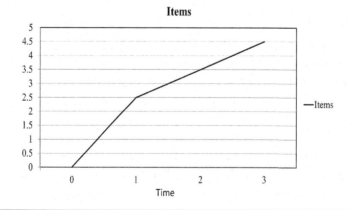

Figure 2.40 A Trend Chart.

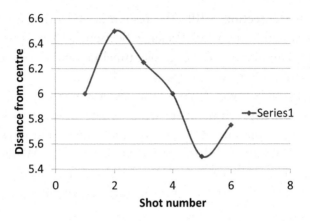

Figure 2.41   An XY Chart.

2.16 XY Charts

XY Charts, sometimes known as Scatter Diagrams, are tools (graphs) plotted to examine the relationship (correlation) between two variables (X and Y). One variable is plotted on the X-axis, the second on the Y-axis. The difference between a Trend Chart and a XY Chart is that a Trend Chart is always a plot of one or more parameters (Y-axis) as a function of time (X-axis). Lines between the points on the graph are optional in XY Charts. For example, Fred's hobby is shooting. After a shooting session, he draws the graph shown in Figure 2.41 that shows the distance from the centre of the target for each of the six shots he fired. The chart plots the distance from the centre in centimetres on the Y-axis for each shot and the shot number on the X-axis. While Figure 2.41 shows the distance from the centre, Figure 2.36 shows the grouping, distance, and direction. The difference in the information provided by the two figures illustrates the need to use the appropriate chart for the situation.

2.17 Summary

Chapter 2 discussed the following 16 charts commonly used by project managers and systems engineers for thinking about and performing problem-solving: Bar Charts, Compound Bar Charts, Financial Charts, Cause and Effect Charts, Compound Line and Bar Charts, Control Charts, Flowcharts, Hierarchical Charts, Histograms, N^2

Charts, Pareto Charts, PAM Charts, Pie Charts, Polar Charts, Trend Charts, and XY Charts. This chapter went into some detail for some of the more complicated charts. For example, it provided the rules for drawing a Flowchart and discussed the most common mistakes made when drawing Flowcharts. This chapter also discussed in detail N^2 Charts and the PAM Chart, a useful tool for project planning.

References

Eppinger, S. D., and T. R. Browning. 2012. *Design Structure Matrix Methods and Applications.* Cambridge, MA: The MIT Press.

Kasser, J. E. 1995. *Applying Total Quality Management to Systems Engineering.* Boston: Artech House.

Lano, R. 1977. "The N^2 Chart." In *TRW Software Series.* Redondo Beach, CA.

Pearson, K. 1895. "Contributions to the Mathematical Theory of Evolution. II. Skew Variation in Homogeneous Material." *Philosophical Transactions of the Royal Society A: Mathematical, Physical and Engineering Sciences,* no. 186:343–414.

3

CRITICAL THINKING

Critical Thinking is a ubiquitous tool that should be, but often isn't, used in project management, systems engineering, and most facets of our daily life. The literature on Critical Thinking contains lots of definitions of the term Critical Thinking and, of course, each one is different. From a practical perspective, the two aspects of Critical Thinking are that it:

1. Provides the rules for:
   - Thinking about ideas.
   - Communicating the ideas.
   - Evaluating the ideas.
2. Indicates the need for viewing an issue/situation/problem from multiple perspectives.

The literature on creativity and idea generation generally separates thinking up the ideas and evaluating the ideas. The literature on Critical Thinking, however, tends to combine the logic of thinking with evaluating the ideas using the terms "smart thinking" and "critical thinking". The term "critical thinking", by the way, comes from the word "criteria", not from "criticism". This chapter:

1. Views Critical Thinking from a Perspectives Perimeter (Chapter 10) in Section 3.1.
2. Discusses applications of Critical Thinking in Section 3.2.
3. Discusses six ways of evaluating Critical Thinking in Section 3.3.
4. Discusses the issues involved in creating student assignments to encourage Critical Thinking in Section 3.4.

3.1 Viewing Critical Thinking from a Perspectives Perimeter

There is a fairly large body of knowledge contained within the boundary of Critical Thinking. Much of this knowledge can be found by using Active Brainstorming (Section 7.1) to come up with questions that can be then answered by doing some research. The answers can be sorted and stored in the HTPs (Section 10.1); an example of using the HTPs as an Idea Storage Template (IST) is shown in Section 14.2. So, now view Critical Thinking from a Perspectives Perimeter (Section 10) made up of each of the HTPs.

3.1.1 *The* Big Picture *Perspective*

Perceptions from the *Big Picture* perspective include:

- *Purpose*: why the reasoning is taking place.
- *Assumptions* which underpin the reasoning; consequently, the assumptions must be reasonable, justifiable and clearly articulated.
- *Beliefs* which limit or guide the argument of the person doing the reasoning. These may be considered as cognitive filters.
- *Contextual concepts*: the theories, principles, axioms and rules implicit in the reasoning.
- *Point of view* or perspective from which the reasoning, based on the assumptions, using the information, takes place.

3.1.2 *The* Operational *Perspective*

Perceptions from the *Operational* perspective provide a black box view of Critical Thinking and include the:

- *Input to the reasoning process*: the information may come from any number of sources (senses [sight, sound, smell taste and touch] as shown in Figure 1.1, experience, the results of a literature search, etc.) from any point on the Perspectives Perimeter (Chapter 10).
- *Output, outcome, or conclusion from the reasoning process*: this could be a problem statement, a solution, or greater understanding of a situation (*Scientific* HTP). If done properly, it is the output of the Critical Thinking process.

- *Various scenarios in which critical thinking is used*: the literature contains a number of such scenarios including the following (Paul 1991: p. 78) cited by (Tittle 2011: p. 4):
  - Analysing or evaluating arguments, interpretations, beliefs, or theories.
  - Analysing or evaluating actions or policies.
  - Assessing and evaluating solutions.
  - Avoiding oversimplifications (*Quantitative* HTP).
  - Clarifying issues, conclusions, and beliefs.
  - Comparing analogous situations: transferring insights to new contexts (*Scientific* HTP).
  - Comparing and contrasting ideal with actual practice (*Generic* HTP).
  - Creating arguments.
  - Developing criteria for evaluation: clarifying values and standards (*Quantitative* HTP).
  - Developing one's perspective: creating or exploring beliefs, arguments, or theories.
  - Distinguishing relevant from irrelevant facts (application of domain knowledge).
  - Evaluating evidence and alleged facts.
  - Evaluating the credibility of sources of information.
  - Examining or evaluating assumptions.
  - Exploring consequences (*Temporal* HTP).
  - Exploring implications.
  - Generating solutions (*Scientific* HTP).
  - Giving reasons for something.
  - Listening critically: the art of silent dialogue.
  - Making interdisciplinary connections (*Generic* and *Continuum* HTPs).
  - Making plausible inferences, predictions, or interpretations (*Scientific* HTP).
  - Noting significant similarity and differences (*Generic* and *Continuum* HTPs).
  - Practicing Socratic discussion: clarifying and questioning beliefs, theories, or perspectives.
  - Questioning deeply: raising and pursuing root or significant questions.

- Reading critically: clarifying or critiquing texts.
- Reasoning dialogically: comparing perspectives, interpretations, or theories.
- Reasoning dialectically: evaluating perspectives, interpretations, or theories.
- Recognizing contradictions (Section 11.7).
- Refining generalizations.
- Thinking precisely about thinking: using critical vocabulary.
- *Self-analysis and evaluation of your own thinking*: In general the initial reaction to criticism is defensive rather than reflective. People tend to defend their thinking rather than reflect and accept comments. This, in turn, can lead to undesired consequences when people are not willing to admit mistakes and so continue in the wrong direction (one of the decision traps; see Section 4.2). Self-analysis and evaluation:
  - Need to be done to help you determine and overcome your own cognitive filters.
  - When not done, is one of the decision traps (Section 4.2).

3.1.3 *The* Functional *Perspective*

Perceptions from the *Functional* perspective provide an internal perspective. One of the ways the functions performed in the process of thinking can be aggregated into four states is shown in Figure 3.1.* While it is convenient to elaborate the process into sequential tasks for discussion purposes, it is not really a sequential process because ideas can be triggered in any state of the process, and depending on the idea generating technique employed, some states can be combined or bypassed. The tasks performed while thinking in this aggregation are:

- *Generating the raw ideas*: using idea generation tools such as the ones described in Chapter 7. Ideas relate to facts, myths, and values.
- *Storing the ideas*: using Idea Storage Templates (IST) (Section 14.2) or equivalents.

---

* The *Continuum* HTP points out that there might be others.

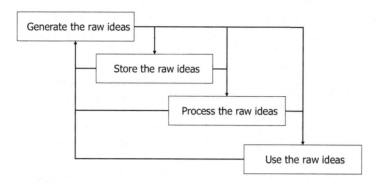

Figure 3.1 Functions of thinking.

- *Processing the ideas*: commonly called "reasoning". The process which builds an argument to support or refute a conclusion according to a specified set of rules.
- *Using the ideas*: to perform an activity such as providing a hypothesis or taking some action.

Ideas range in quality from profound to ridiculous, helpful to harmful, ennobling to degrading. It is therefore appropriate to pass judgment on them. However, fairness demands that you base your judgement on thoughtful consideration of the overall strengths and weaknesses of the ideas, not on your initial impressions or feelings. Be especially careful with ideas that are unfamiliar or different from your own because those are the ones you will be most inclined to deny a fair hearing. (Ruggiero 2012)

This statement leads to the second aspect of Critical Thinking; the judgement or evaluation of ideas discussed in Section 3.1.3.2.

3.1.3.1 Reasoning Reasoning, often used to associate effects with causes, may be deductive or inductive, as discussed below.

3.1.3.1.1 Deductive Reasoning The deductive reasoning process always provides a conclusion that is either true or false. It begins with statements called "premises" that are assumed to be true. The process then deduces what else is true if all the premises are true. The general principle is if *all* the premises are true, then the conclusion is true.

However, if any one of the premises is false, the conclusion is false. Consider the following three examples:

- 1: The fishy story
  - *Premises*: (1) All cats like fish; (2) Tabby is a cat.
  - *Conclusion*: Tabby likes fish.
    If the premise is true, the conclusion is true since Tabby is an instance of a class of animals called cats.
- 2: Where am I-1
  - *Premises*: (1) Singapore is in Asia; (2) I live in Singapore.
  - *Conclusion*: I live in Asia.
    The conclusion is true since Singapore is within Asia.
- 3: Where am I-2
  - *Premises*: (1) I live in Asia; (2) Singapore is in Asia.
  - *Conclusion*: I live in Singapore.

From the perspective of deductive logic, the conclusion is false since Asia is not within Singapore. However, since Singapore is within Asia, you can infer that there is a probability that the statement might be true.[*]

3.1.3.1.2 Inductive Reasoning The inductive reasoning process infers the probability of conclusions from observations in various non-deductive ways. It is the reasoning generally used in the Scientific Method (Section 11.1.10.5.1) to determine the hypothesis, by detectives solving crimes and physicians diagnosing causes of illnesses. Examples of inductive reasoning include:

- *Patterns of behaviour*: reasoning based on observing what seems to be a pattern of behaviour by something and creating a hypothesis for the pattern. You then make a prediction pertaining to the probability of future appearances of the something based on the hypothesis. For example, you notice that there has been a rain shower at about 4 p.m. local time every day from Monday to Thursday. On Friday morning, you use those observations to infer a hypothesis that there is a high probability of a similar shower on Friday afternoon at about

---

[*] But not how much of a probability without additional information.

the same time and decide to carry an umbrella. This is the type of reasoning used to predict the future price of shares on the stock market by projecting the trend forwards into the future.

- *Similarity*: generic reasoning which infers general principles or rules from specific facts. This type of generic reasoning is used with two items that are similar (having one or more common properties) to infer that properties pertaining to one item, also apply to, or can be inherited from, a similar item (*Generic* HTP).

- *Analogies*: generic reasoning which infers a property pertaining to one item also applies to a similar item. It is used to infer a property that has yet to be observed in one item based on observations of that property in a similar item. Unlike similarities which are used to infer generic properties, analogies are used to infer a specific property. This is the reasoning discussed in Section 10.1.5.9.3 used to infer which container holds the coffee.

- *Best explanation*: this reasoning process starts with a fact and concludes with the best explanation for this fact (Juthe 2005). Thus, having observed a situation, you infer the best explanation of that situation and state it in the form of a guess or hypothesis. For example, you have spent the afternoon in a windowless office. When you leave the building you notice that the street is wet. You infer that the best explanation of the cause of the situation is a rain shower. Occam's Razor (Section 3.2.6) is an example of the best explanation.

Inferences can become assumptions. Consider the following extract from the Babylonian Talmud in Tractate Sabbath.

R. Zadok said: 'It was the custom at the house of Rabban Gamaliel to give white clothes to the washer three days before the Sabbath, but colored clothes even on a Friday.' From this we have learned that it is harder to wash white clothes than colored ones. Abayi gave colored clothes to the washer and asked: How much wilt thou take for washing them? 'As much as for white clothes,' answered the washer. Said Abayi: 'The rabbis have preceded thee with their declaration' (that white clothes are harder to wash) (Rodkinson 1903).

Perceptions from the *Continuum* HTP indicate that there may be other reasons for not washing white clothes on a Friday. The washer may be set up to wash white clothes and coloured clothes on different days, and Friday is the day for washing coloured clothes. That may have nothing to do with the time it takes to wash clothes. It may have something to do with the quantity of each type of clothes that the washer receives from the public or the availability of staff on certain days. This is why it is important to document inferences as assumptions. In many situations, we do the equivalent of knowing the washer's schedule and can provide clothes according to the schedule so the reason for the schedule is a "Don't Care" situation (Section 3.2.2). However, in that rare instance where we do care about the reason, we need to know whether something is an inference/assumption or if it is really a fact.

3.1.3.2 Evaluating Ideas The second function of Critical Thinking is the judgement of the correctness or truthfulness of the both the reasoning (process) and the outcomes or conclusions from the reasoning (products). You do this in various ways, including by examining the:

- *Relevance of the information used in the premises*: for example, consider the following example of poor deductive logic.
  - *Premises*: (1) All cats like fish; (2) Brock is a dog.
  - *Conclusion*: Brock does not like fish.

  The validity of the conclusion cannot be determined because there is nothing in the argument that is relevant to dogs liking fish.
- *Nature of the links between two sequential events*: determining if the first event is indeed the cause of the second event. Correlation between events does not necessarily prove causation or contribute to the validity of the argument.
- Validity of the argument: particularly in inductive reasoning. For example, I tell students in class the following anecdote. I was visiting a fruit farm in Malaysia and saw a tree with purple plastic bags hanging from the branches. Being from Europe, tropical trees were strange and so I told the students that I thought I saw a plastic bag tree for the first time. The

students smiled. Why did they smile? They smiled because they knew that plastic bags don't grow on trees. But how did they know? They had enough prior domain knowledge about what plastic is made from to know that it does not grow on trees. The thinking sequence was:

1. *Observation*: plastic bags hanging on the branches.
2. *Reasoning*: since fruit hangs on branches and grows on trees, plastic bags are growing on the trees just like fruit.
3. *Conclusion/hypothesis*: I am looking at a plastic bag tree.

I illustrate the same point in an alternative way with the following question. I ask the students, "Do you know that electrical and electronic devices such as fans, air conditioners, television sets, and personal computers work because they are full of smoke?" The thinking sequence was:

1. *Observation*: electrical and electronic devices stop functioning after the smoke comes out of them.
2. *Reasoning*: electrical and electronic devices function until smoke comes out of them and then the devices cease to function.
3. *Conclusion/hypothesis*: electrical and electronic devices only function when they are full of smoke.

The conclusions are wrong in both examples, but you will need different domain knowledge in each example to know that the conclusions are false and why they are false. You will need to know about plastics in the first example and about electronics in the second example.

- *Relationships between the premises looking for missing premises.* Consider the following argument as an example:
    1. *Premises*: (1) Susie is a child. (2) Electrical tools are dangerous.
    2. *Conclusion*: Susie needs to be kept away from hammer-drills.
    3. *The missing premises* are (3) children need to be kept away from electrical tools and (4) hammer-drills are electrical tools. The validity of the missing premises in an argument also needs to be checked.

3.1.3.2.1 The Problem, Solution, and Implementation Domains When evaluating ideas, there needs to be a reference or some prior or researchable knowledge against which to evaluate the idea such as in knowing that the plastic bag tree conclusion is false because plastic bags don't grow on trees. This knowledge comes from a domain. There are three relevant domains relevant to Critical Thinking, namely:

1. The problem domain.
2. The solution domain.
3. The implementation domain.

It is tempting to assume that the problem domain and the solution domain are the same, but they are not necessarily so. For example, the problem domain may be urban traffic congestion, while the solution domain may be a form of underground transportation system to relieve that congestion. Lack of problem domain competency may lead to the identification of the wrong problem and lack of solution and implementation domain competencies may lead to selection of a less than optimal, or even an unachievable, solution system.

3.1.3.3 Process Used in Critical Thinking Arons provided the following illustrative list of thinking and reasoning processes used in Critical Thinking that underlie analysis and inquiry (Arons 1990: pp. 314–319):*

1. Consciously raising the following questions when studying some body of material or approaching a problem:
   • "What do we know …?"
   • "How do we know …?"
   • "Why do we accept or believe …?"
   • "What is the evidence for …?"
2. Being clearly and explicitly aware of gaps in available information. Recognizing when a conclusion is reached or a decision made in absence of complete information and being able to tolerate ambiguity and uncertainty. Recognizing when one is taking something on faith without having examined the "How do we know …?" and "Why do we believe …?" questions.

---

* Arons stated that the list is meant to be illustrative; it is neither exhaustive nor prescriptive.

3. Discriminating between observation and interference, between established fact and subjective conjecture.

4. Recognizing that words are symbols for ideas and not the ideas themselves. Recognizing the necessity of using only words of prior definition, rooted in shared experience, in forming a new definition and in avoiding being misled by technical jargon.

5. Probing for assumptions (particularly the implicit, unarticulated assumptions) behind a line of reasoning.*

6. Drawing inferences from data, observations, or other evidence and recognizing when firm inferences cannot be drawn. This subsumes a number of processes such as elementary syllogistic reasoning (e.g., dealing with basic prepositional, "if ... then" statements), correlational reasoning, recognizing when relevant variables have or have not been controlled.

7. Performing hypothetico-deductive reasoning;† that is, given a particular situation, applying relevant knowledge of principles and constraints and visualizing, in the abstract, the plausible outcomes that might result from various changes one can imagine to be imposed on the system.

8. Discriminating between inductive and deductive reasoning; that is, being aware when an argument is being made from the particular to the general or from the general to the particular.

9. Testing one's own line of reasoning and conclusions for internal consistency and thus developing intellectual self-reliance.

10. Developing self-consciousness concerning one's own thinking and reasoning processes.

---

* And missing premises (Section 3.1.3.1.2).

† The hypothetico-deductive method is an approach to research that begins with a theory about how things work and derives testable hypotheses from it. It is a form of deductive reasoning in that it begins with general principles, assumptions, and ideas, and works from them to more particular statements about what world actually looks like and how it works. The hypotheses are then tested by gathering and analyzing data and the theory is then either supported or refuted by the results (Crossman 2017).

3.1.4 The Continuum *Perspective*

Perceptions from the *Continuum* perspective provide the following concepts:

- *Multiple outcomes*: the *Continuum* HTP provides for inductive reasoning to produce multiple outcomes of the thinking process, each with different probabilities of occurrence. These are useful when thinking about different acceptable solutions, risks and opportunities.
- *Potential for errors or defects*: every part of the reasoning process is open to error such as incorrect theories, myths and assumptions, faulty input data, poor logic, etc., all of which lead to false or incorrect outcomes and the need to detect, prevent and compensate for these defects.
- *Breadth:* the degree to which the reasoning recognizes or employs arguments from several different HTPs.

3.1.5 The Temporal *Perspective*

Perceptions from the *Temporal* perspective indicate the need to consider not only the present but also:

- *The past*: the issues that have created the situation may still be present and need to be considered in the reasoning.[*]
- *The future*: there will always be further implications and consequences from any act of reasoning. These desirable and undesirable outcomes need some consideration.

3.1.6 The Structural *Perspective*

Perceptions from the *Structural* perspective indicate the need for:

- *Clarity* of the purpose, information, arguments and outcomes.

The *Structural* perspective is also used to identify the premises and conclusions in an argument by the words used in the statement. For example, words relating to:
  - *Premises* include "according to", "after all", "as", "assume", "because", "by", "considering", "for", "given", "hearing",

---

[*] Without assigning blame.

"if", "implied", "in fact", "reason", "seeing", "since", "smelling ", "suppose", and "whereas".

- *Conclusions* include "accordingly", "as a result", "conclude", "conclusion", "consequently", "deduce", "follows", "for that reason", "hence", "implied", "indicates", "infer", "means", "probably", "proven", "result", "seem", "shown", "so", "supports", "therefore", "then", and "thus".

You should always check the context in which the identification words are used to determine whether or not they are used in premises or conclusions because words have multiple meanings and some words such as "evidence" can be used to identify both premises and conclusions. Sometime the identification words are implied and not articulated. For example, a statement such as, "X's book on systems thinking is a load of rubbish, don't buy it" should be written with identification words such as "**Since** X's book on systems thinking is a load of rubbish, **the recommendation is** don't buy it".

3.1.7 *The* Quantitative *Perspective*

Perceptions from the *Quantitative* perspective indicate the need for:

- *Accuracy*: for example, consider statements such as, "four out of five people surveyed" and, "most people like ..." used in inductive reasoning. Taken on their own out of context, there is no way to determine the accuracy of the statements. Citing the source of such information may be one way to indicate the accuracy of the information.
- *Precision*: the need to use:
  - *Numbers instead of adjectives*: for example, use the appropriate number instead of the non-precise word "large".
  - *The appropriate degree of precision*: sometimes the number 3.14 is all that is required when the calculator displays 3.1415926535. Sometimes "approximately 3" will be enough.
  - *Tolerances on values*: Instead of describing the voltage needed to recharge your personal computer as 18 volts, you should use 18±v volts or whatever the actual range of the tolerance (v) is.
- *Depth*: the degree to which the argument reflects the degree of complexity of the issue (Section 13.3).

- **Sufficiency**: the number of premises and amount of information in the argument to support the conclusion.

When evaluating Critical Thinking, the *Quantitative* HTP provides the metrics used to evaluate a person's ability as discussed in Section 3.3.

3.1.8 *The* Scientific *Perspective*

The *Scientific* perspective is the idea contained in the conclusion, statement of the hypothesis, or guess that is stated after having thought about the situation and applying Critical Thinking.

3.2 Applications of Critical Thinking

There are many applications of Critical Thinking (cognitive tools) that are used all the time; most of them are just not generally recognized as being a part of Critical Thinking. The applications discussed in this section are:

1. The "Do Statement" in Section 3.2.1.
2. The "Don't Care" situation in Section 3.2.2.
3. The KISS principle in Section 3.2.3.
4. The Ladder of Inference in Section 3.2.4.
5. Miller's Rule in Section 3.2.5.
6. Occam's Razor in Section 3.2.6.
7. The Principle of Hierarchies in Section 3.2.7.
8. A process for critical analysis of arguments in Section 3.2.8.
9. The STALL technique in Section 3.2.9.

3.2.1 *The "Do Statement"*

The "Do Statement" (Chacko 1989) is a Critical Thinking tool which can be used in:

- Partitioning activities into lower level tasks.
- Refining lower-level requirements from high-level requirements.
- Determining sub-objectives for objectives in Management by Objectives (MBO) (Section 8.8).
- Tracing requirements and other objectives vertically in a hierarchy.

The "Do Statement":

- Is a forward looking approach to planning what to do to reach an objective and how the results of the activity will be measured.
- Links the low-level objects to the high-level objects according to the following statement:
  1. *Do* [the concrete activity]
  2. *In order to* [accomplish the organismic objective]
  3. *As measured by* [the operational measure of the concrete activity] or acceptance criteria.

Where:

- Organismic is derived from organism.
- The objectives hierarchy is based on a three-level linked hierarchy of objectives where:
  - Level 1 (highest) is the Organismic level
  - Level 2 is the Strategic level
  - Level 3 (lowest) is the Tactical level
- The concrete activity can be a new activity or a modification of an existing activity
    Use of the "Do Statement" in Project Planning (Section 8.1) contributes to the information in the following Work Package (WP) (Section 8.19) elements:
  - The activity (the concrete activity).
  - The reason for, or the objective of, the activity (to meet a directive from the next higher level in the hierarchy).
  - The product produced by the activity.
  - The acceptance criteria for the product (the operational measure of the concrete activity).
  - The links between the tasks.

When perceived from the *Generic* and *Structural* HTPs, the "Do Statement" contains:

1. A requirement.
2. A reason or rationale for the requirement traced to the next higher level in the hierarchy of the system.
3. The acceptance criteria for the requirement.

3.2.1.1 Using the "Do Statement"   The "Do Statement" can be used in most any situation to think through what needs to be done to meet a goal or fulfil a requirement/need and how the results will be measured. For example, let the organismic objective of Task 700 be to make a cup of instant coffee in a specific situation, namely:

> **700 Do** make a cup of instant coffee.
> **700 In order to** refresh the boss.
> **700 As measured by** the boss not complaining about his or her coffee.

A set of derived or lower level "Do Statement"s could then be created as follows:

> **701 Do** heat the water.
> **701 In order to** make a cup of instant coffee.
> **701 As measured by** the temperature of the water reaching 100 degrees Celsius.*
> **702 Do** pour boiling water into coffee cup
> **702 In order to** make a cup of instant coffee.
> **702 As measured by** the required amount of water in the cup.
> **703 Do** add instant coffee powder.
> **703 In order to** make a cup of instant coffee.
> **703 As measured by** a standard teaspoon.
> **704 Do** add sugar or sweetener.
> **704 In order to** make a cup of instant coffee.
> **704 As measured by** the required number of standard teaspoons or number of packets.
> **705 Do** add creamer or milk.
> **705 In order to** make a cup of instant coffee.
> **705 As measured by** the amount of creamer or fluid ounces of milk.
> **706 Do** stir the mixture
> **706 In order to** make a cup of instant coffee.
> **706 As measured by** five seconds of stirring at four revolutions per minute plus or minus two revolutions.

---

* The water should be 100 degrees for tea, not quite boiling for brewed coffee, and the temperature of instant coffee is a 'Don't Care' situation.

A better arrangement of the statement is to rearrange them as follows:

700 ***In order to*** [accomplish the organismic objective]
700 ***Do*** [the concrete activity]
700 ***As measured by*** the [operational measure of the concrete activity] acceptance criteria.

This rearrangement makes the ideas flow in a unidirectional manner by first describing the objective, then what has to be done to meet the objective, and lastly, how the results will be measured. Consider the following examples:

900 ***In order to*** use the river for recreation
900 ***Do*** reduce the pollution in the water
900 ***As measured by*** (i) a well-known political leader swimming in the river, (ii) the water meets a chemical analysis for non-polluted water. One measurement is emotional and the other is scientific. Both should be used.
1000 ***In order to staff*** the Widget project,
1000 ***Do*** hire the required number of personnel at each competency level.*
1000 ***As measured by*** filling the number positions at each competency level with competent personnel.†

Statement 1000 can then be broken out to lower level statements including:

1010 ***In order to*** hire the required number of personnel at each competency level
1010 ***Do hire*** three senior systems engineers
1010 *As measured by* three new senior systems engineers reporting for work.

---

* This requirement indicates a lack of systems thinking. The requirement is on the input, "'hire'". It does not consider that the staff need to be retained for the duration of the contract.
† This is a poor metric because it does not include retention of staff. The new employees could leave after the first day of work for some reason and the requirement would still have been met.

1020 In order to hire the required number of personnel at each competency level

1020 Do hire three junior systems engineers

1020 As measured by five new junior systems engineers reporting for work.

3.2.1.2 Creating the "Do Statement"   Consider making a cup of instant coffee. The top level function (organismic objective) is to make a cup of instant coffee. A set of "Do Statements" to provide a list of the functions, requirements and acceptance criteria to accompany Figure 2.22 can be used to identify lower level or sub-functions working backwards (Section 11.8) from the cup of coffee in the following manner.

2000 In order to make a cup of instant coffee.

2010 Do heat the water.

2010 As measured by the temperature of the water reaching 100 degrees Celsius.

2020 Do pour boiling water into coffee cup.

2020 As measured by the amount of water in the cup.

2030 Do add instant coffee powder.

2030 As measured by a standard teaspoon.

2040 Do add sugar or sweetener.

2040 As measured by the required number of standard teaspoons or number of packets.

2050 Do add creamer or milk.

2050 As measured by a packet of creamer or required fluid ounces of milk.

2060 Do stir the mixture using a spoon inserted at least 4 inches into the cup.

2060 As measured by five seconds of stirring at four revolutions per minute, plus or minus two revolutions.

3.2.2 The "Don't Care" Situation

The "Don't Care" situation is a Critical Thinking tool that simplifies dealing with complexity. It allows you to ignore things that are not pertinent or not relevant. For example, consider how the "Don't Care" situation is applied in:

1. Buying a new car discussed in Section 3.2.2.1.
2. Putting a tolerance on a requirement discussed in Section 3.2.2.2.
3. Simplifying software interfaces discussed in Section 3.2.2.3.

3.2.2.1 Buying a New Car If you're going to buy a new car, there are a large number of options open for you to select. How many of them do you really care about? Most people don't care about all of them. So there is no reason to consider all of them. That's one of the reasons Ordering and Ranking (Section 4.6.3) works. It picks out the most important aspects or items and abstracts out the remaining ones that we don't care about.

When writing requirements there is no reason to specify anything about which the customer doesn't care. This gives the designer a lot of freedom. We actually use this technique without naming it when we teach or tell engineers not to write requirements that tell people how to design the system. Rather write the requirements that describe what the system is supposed to do and how well it is supposed to do it; the functional and performance aspects. In this case we don't care how the system is designed, as long as it meets all the requirements and constraints and can be built within the cost and schedule budgets.

3.2.2.2 Putting a Tolerance on a Requirement The "Don't Care" situation is used when putting a tolerance on a requirement. For example, the need can be defined as, "The classroom shall accommodate more students than have signed up for the course". In this situation, the issues to consider include:

- The meaning of "accommodate". In this case it means provide a desk and a chair. It does not mean provide sandwiches, tea, and coffee.*

---

* Sometimes it is necessary to define what a word does not mean as well as what it does mean.

- The number of students that have signed up for the course. In this case, 27.
- Why is there a need for more? The answer is the need to accommodate last minute additions after the classroom is allocated.
- The history of last minute additions (*Temporal* HTP). Past experience sets the maximum class size at 35.

Do we care about the size of the classroom as long as it accommodates 35 people? If we don't care, that means we could be assigned a lecture theatre that would accommodate 500 or more students. Since classrooms usually are a limited resource, if we don't mind teaching in a lecture theatre even if the class sizes small, it gives the administrative staff assigning classrooms to classes a greater degree of freedom in making their decisions.

When writing a requirement for the size of the classroom to accommodate 35 people, they may or may not be a need to put an upper bound on the number of people the classroom shall accommodate. The requirement might be written in any one of the following ways:

1. The classroom shall accommodate between 25 and 35 students: setting both the upper and lower limits for the classroom size.
2. The classroom shall accommodate a minimum of 27 students: setting the lower limit for the classroom size.
3. The classroom shall accommodate more than 27 students: setting the lower limit for the classroom size.
4. The classroom shall accommodate no less than 27 students: setting the lower limit for the classroom size.
5. The classroom shall accommodate up to 27 students: setting the upper limit for the classroom size. This requirement is wrong; namely an error of commission (Section 4.4).
6. The classroom shall accommodate up to 35 students: setting the upper limit for the classroom size.

The best way to write the requirement is to use almost the same wording as in the need statement.

3.2.2.3 Simplifying Software Interfaces   The "Don't Care" situation makes interfacing computer programs very simple. For example,

I'm trying to interface to an amateur radio computer program (host program). I am writing an application program, and I want to know some of the information in the host program so my application can act on that information. The host program sends out User Datagram Protocol (UDP) messages announcing different types of information. This is the standard protocol for broadcasting messages, because UDP does not require the receiving station to confirm reception of the broadcast messages. So I need to know the format of the messages. I look up the Interface Specification Document (ICD) and start to read it. I can immediately detect that the "Don't Care" situation was not applied because the ICD tells me the following:

1. The host address and port number.
2. All messages are written or read using Qdatastream derivatives according to the version defined in this document.
3. Dates are in Unix time format.
4. The message is in "big endian" format.
5. The header format which is:
   a. A 32-bit unsigned integer magic number specified as eight bytes.
   b. A 32-bit unsigned integer schema number.
6. A list of the contents of each message schema which consists of various data elements which may be text, numbers or status where:
   a. Numbers can be formatted as a 64-bit unsigned integer, a 32-bit unsigned integer, Qwords, and as a floating point number.
   b. Text is formatted as UTF-8 bytes in a Qbytearray.
   c. Status information is in logic formatted as Boolean.

The programmers who wrote the host program were kind; the host program was written in C, and they supplied a copy of the software they used to encode, decode, send, and receive the UDP messages. The lack of systems thinking assumes everybody writing software to interface with the host program is also writing in C. I'm not; I'm writing in Delphi. So I have to know or look up how the various formats are defined in C. For example, how many bytes there are in 64-bit unsigned integers, in 32-bit unsigned integers, and in floating point numbers and in which order the bytes are written (first to last or last to first), in the interface message.

When I looked at the messages at the interface addressed to the host and port number, a typical short message converted to text looked like,

"DCBAABCD0000000200000060000000647736A562D59".
I can see:

- "DCBAABCD", the 32-bit unsigned integer magic number which identifies the host program at the start of the message; I don't need to decode it into a number to use it, I can use it as is.
- Some ASCII character bytes at the end of the message and decode them with an ASCII table. At first glance, they appear to identify the host software, so either these characters or the 32-bit unsigned integer magic number which identifies the host program at the start of the message is redundant. Actually I located another host program which performed the same functionality and generated the same messages. I then found that it could be distinguished from the first by the characters at the end of the message.

But what lies in between is a mystery because the programmers did not use the "Don't Care" situation. To completely decode the messages, I have to know:

1. The message type or schema (which is in the specification).
2. The specification of each message for each message type.
3. What a magic number is.
4. What Qdatastream derivatives are and which version is used.
5. How to deal with the Unix time format.
6. What UTF-8 bytes are.
7. The format of each message element.
8. The number of bytes used for each element.
9. What "big endian" means and how to deal with it.

Had they used the "Don't Care" situation, they would have formatted all the messages as text messages using comma-separated values

(CSV),* the same format used by spreadsheets. For example, a typical UDP message from "LAN-LINK", an amateur radio digital communications software application could look like, "LAN-LINK 4.5, 1, 2017/12/25, 12:00, G3ZCZ, 14277.8, SSB, 59, 59, 100, VK5WU, PK95ic, Joseph, S, R, QRP and whip ant" which is simple to read and someone who understands the application domain can easily figure out what the message means.

In the "Don't Care" situation life at the receiving end of the interface is so much simpler. You can pull out all the text characters between each of the commas and convert them to whatever format you need them in your software. This is an example of using the KISS principle (Section 3.2.3). In this situation, all you would have to know to decode the message is:

1. The message type.
2. A list of the data elements in each message type.†

You don't care:

1. What "big endian" is.
2. What a Qdatastream is.
3. What a magic number is.
4. What the Unix time format is.
5. What a Qbytearray is.
6. How many bytes C uses for each number.
7. About the format of those bytes in the message.

There might have been a time when an argument for transferring data in its C format when communicating between two programs written in C was valid because time would not be wasted in converting the numbers and the text in the interface message to and from their individual formats. That argument might have been valid back in the 1980s but today's computers are so fast that the time used is

---

* Except of course in situations where the contents of the messages are deliberately encrypted for security reasons.

† You would not even need that information if you could exercise LANLINK and look at the messages it generates.

negligible. In fact, I was faced with this same problem in 1981, when I had to design the interface communications protocol between the Luz system central computer and the local controllers for each of the mirrors (Kasser 2008). I chose to use the "Don't Care" situation and passed ASCII text messages across the interface. This allowed the additional benefit that I could test the serial input to any local controller with a handheld ASCII terminal just by typing in the ASCII command message and looking at the response. The people writing the software for the central station and the people writing the software for the local controllers didn't care about any of the internal ways in which the information was stored at each end of the interface. All they had to do was produce or decode the ASCII text message.

3.2.3 The KISS Principle

The "Keep It Simple Stupid" (KISS) principle:

- *Is a fundamental thinking and communicating tool* used or incorporated in all the remaining tools.
- *Should be used as a guide* when thinking about issues, situations, and problems to organize the concepts as a hierarchy.
- *Is mostly ignored* as seen by the profusion of complicated and complex drawings used in business, project management, systems and software engineering, etc. When ignored in the:
  - *Work or professional practice environment,* people tend not to question things they don't understand. Consequently, erroneous concepts perpetuate. They are not understood; they just passed on without question.
  - *Academic environment,* the students fail to learn much from the drawing since not much got into their short-term memory to be transferred to long-term memory (Figure 1.1). This practice leads to poor student understanding of the topics in the figure. The consequences are:
    a. Students who go out into the workforce and don't understand what they are doing so they follow the process.
    b. Students who become instructors who teach the book without understanding what they are teaching, which leads to more poor student understanding of the topics, which leads back to a) ... a positive feedback loop.

3.2.3.1 How to Keep Things Simple Things can be kept simple simply by doing some things and not doing other things. For example, in creating graphics (Chapter 6), the KISS principle can be stated in the form of the following requirements:

1. The number of elements of information in a graphic* shall be less than nine (complying with Miller's Rule [Section 3.2.5]).
2. All elements of information in a graphic shall be at the same level in the hierarchy (complying with the Principle of Hierarchies ([Section 3.2.7]).
3. When using logic to infer a conclusion from observations and other information, Occam's Razor (Section 3.2.6) shall apply.
4. Abstract out all the "Don't Care" (Section 3.2.2) elements of the situation.

The use of the single complex drawing creates artificial complexity (Section 13.3.1.1) which makes things complicated. Complying with these requirements:

- Forces you to actually think about the thing and sort out which parts of it are pertinent, and which parts are not,[†] instead of blindly presenting all the parts and hoping that the observers will be able to determine the appropriate degree of pertinence of each part.
- Reduces the artificial complexity (Section 13.3.1.1).
- Generally identifies missing concepts or ones that need to be adjusted when things that seemed to be clear to the originator in the original figure do not break out easily into the set.

Note, the original figure:

- Should not be discarded; it is a useful source for reference.
- May infrequently be used in a presentation as an introduction to give an impression of the issue or situation.
- Should not be used to try to explain the situation or issue.
- Should be replaced by the hierarchy of the high-level drawing and each of the lower level drawings in turn.

---

* A drawing, PowerPoint slide or any other kind.
† It also shows your level of competence.

3.2.4 Ladder of Inference

The Ladder of Inference (Argyris 1990):

- Is a Critical Thinking tool to:
  - Help to draw better conclusions or challenge other people's conclusions based on facts and reality.
  - Analyse hard data or to test assertions.
- Is a model of the way we think represented in a form of a ladder.
- Is a sequential seven-step process that climbs the ladder starting from the bottom.

The seven steps are:

1. We observe data generally by experiencing, seeing, and hearing.
2. We select data by viewing it through what is known as a cognitive filter based on our beliefs about the world and our existing knowledge.
3. We add meaning to the data based on experience, belief, and knowledge.
4. Since the data is a partial view of the situation, we fill the gap with assumptions based on inferences. In most instances we assume that other people have the same objectives and values that we do.
5. We then draw conclusions based on the assumptions. Once we've drawn conclusions, we begin to have feelings about those conclusions.
6. We adopt new beliefs or modify existing beliefs about the world.
7. We then take actions based on the conclusions.

We often perform the seven steps almost instantaneously without thinking about them. Sometimes we even say the conclusions are obvious. Although they may have been obvious to us, they're not necessarily obvious to other people. Since different people view the same data and filter it through their own, different, personal cognitive filters, they can make different assumptions and draw different conclusions. And having drawn different conclusions they can take totally different and sometimes opposing actions based on those conclusions. This explains why we so often get into conflict and fail to agree on issues.

3.2.4.1 Uses of the Ladder of Inference The model gives us an understanding of the way we, and other people, think. Consequently, we ought to be able to see where our thinking process is in error or, rather, where errors can creep in to our thinking process, and why other people draw different conclusions from the same information. For example:

- In Step 2 we filter the information. Once we realize this we are doing this, we can compare our filtered information with the filtered information from somebody else. When we look at the findings, we might identify blind spots due to cognitive filters, where we missed something that somebody else found and vice versa.
- In Step 3 the model helps us realize (*Continuum* HTP) that other people can add different meanings to the data and so the output of this step can be different again.
- In Step 4 the model helps us realize that other people may have different perspectives, different cognitive filters and different assumptions. This is the perception (*Continuum* HTP) that allows us to develop win-win situations in negotiations by applying the "Don't Care" situation (Section 3.2.2). This is because other people may desire different things from the negotiation and at the same time not care about other things. The result being we get something that we care about and the other party doesn't care about while the other party get something they care about that we don't care about.
- In Step 5 we draw conclusions (*Scientific* HTP). We recognize that other people may draw different conclusions.
- Step 6 is a learning process where, based on our experience in the previous steps, we change the contents of our internal database. And so the next time we observe something we will adjust our cognitive filters to take into account the new knowledge and belief we gained in Step 6 of this iteration of climbing the ladder.

Perceptions from the *Continuum* HTP indicate that we need to document our assumptions and make them clearly visible whenever we make assumptions. That's the old adage that, "when you assume, you make an ass out of you and me". By documenting the assumptions you skip making the asses.

3.2.5 Miller's Rule

Miller's Rule (Miller 1956):

- Is a Critical Thinking tool.
- States the human brain cannot comprehend more than 7±2 items at a time.
- Is mostly overlooked in presenting information, which leads to artificial complexity (Section 13.3.1.1).
- Is an instance of the KISS principle (Section 3.2.3).

3.2.5.1 Using Miller's Rule in Idea Generation Situations The ideas generated when thinking about a situation or issue are often initially linked together in a complex figure. This figure is presumably understood by the person who drew it since the information is in their long-term memory.* However, when the figure is presented to other people their eyes tend to glaze over and they start to tune out the explanation.† These figures lead to artificial complexity (Section 13.3.1.1). To prevent this occurrence, the originator of the figure shall comply with the KISS principle requirements (Section 3.2.3.1) to convert the original figure into a hierarchical set of drawings. There should be one high-level drawing and a separate drawing for the contents of each block in the high-level drawing with no more than nine objects in the figure most of the time. The number nine should be used as a guide, not as an absolute maximum.

3.2.6 Occam's Razor

Occam's Razor:

- Is a problem-solving approach.
- Is stated in several ways, but they all mean the following. In a situation where several explanations equally provide a probable solution to whatever issue, situation, or problem is being examined, the simplest explanation, namely the one with the fewest assumptions or guesses, is probably the right one. Note how this sentence might have been simplified.

---

* Of course, this may be an assumption.

† As noted in the classroom prior to using Miller's Rule to simplify the presentation graphics.

- Is attributed to William of Occam, an English Franciscan friar who lived around 1287 to 1347.
- Is an example of inductive reasoning (Section 3.1.3.1.2).

Over the centuries, Occam's Razor has been expanded to contain the following two principles:

1. *The principle of plurality*: plurality should not be posited without necessity, or don't make things more complex than they need to be.
2. *The principle of parsimony*: don't do with more what can be done with less. This principle might also be considered as the basis for designing reliability into electronic systems, namely performing a function with the fewest components makes a more reliable implementation of the function; fewer parts to fail.

3.2.7 The Principle of Hierarchies

The Principle of Hierarchies in systems (Spencer 1862) cited by (Wilson 2002) is a Critical Thinking tool that humanity has used to manage complexity for most of its recorded history and is defined in the following three quotations:

1. "All complex structures and processes of a relatively stable character display hierarchical organisation regardless of whether we consider galactic systems, living organisms and their activities or social organisations" (Koestler 1978: p. 31).
2. "Once we adopt the general picture of the universe as a series of levels of organisation and complexity, each level having unique properties of structure and behaviour, which, though depending on the properties of the constituent elements, appear only when those are combined into the higher whole,* we see that there are qualitatively different laws holding good at each level" (Needham, 1945) cited by (Koestler 1978: p. 32).
3. "The English philosopher Herbert Spencer appears to be the first to set out the general idea of increasing complexity in systems (Spencer 1862). The term itself was first used by the English biochemist (and scholar of Chinese science) Joseph Needham

---

* Namely emergent properties (author).

(Needham 1937). The following quotation from a Web source provides an insight into the fundamentals of the theory (UIA 2002):

1. The structure of integrative levels rests on a physical foundation. The lowest level of scientific observation would appear to be the mechanics of particles.
2. Each level organizes the level below it plus one or more emergent qualities (or unpredictable novelties). The levels are therefore cumulative upwards, and the emergence of qualities marks the degree of complexity of the conditions prevailing at a given level, as well as giving to that level its relative autonomy.
3. The mechanism of an organization is found at the level below, its purpose at the level above.
4. Knowledge of the lower level infers an understanding of matters on the higher level; however, qualities emerging on the higher level have no direct reference to the lower-level organization.
5. The higher the level, the greater its variety of characteristics, but the smaller its population.
6. The higher level cannot be reduced to the lower, since each level has its own characteristic structure and emergent qualities.
7. An organization at any level is a distortion of the level below, the higher-level organization representing the figure which emerges from the previously organized ground.
8. A disturbance introduced into an organization at any one level reverberates at all the levels it covers. The extent and severity of such disturbances are likely to be proportional to the degree of integration of that organization.
9. Every organization, at whatever level it exists, has some sensitivity and responds in kind" (Wilson 2002).

3.2.8 Process for Critical Analysis of an Argument

One way of using Critical Thinking to create or analyse an argument is to use the following process adapted from Tittle (Tittle 2011: p. 17):*

1. Determine the point of the argument (claim/opinion/conclusion).
2. Identify the reasons and the evidence.

---

* This process can be used to examine an argument or to create one (*Continuum* perspective).

3. Check the validity of the reasons and evidence.

4. Articulate as many unstated premises and connections in the reasoning (assumptions) as you can.

5. Check the validity of the unstated premises and connections in the reasoning.

6. Define the terms used in the argument.

7. Clarify all imprecise language (*Quantitative* HTP).

8. Differentiate between facts and opinions (*Continuum* HTP).

9. Eliminate or replace "loaded" language and other manipulations.*

10. Assess the reasoning/evidence:
   * If deductive reasoning, check for truth (facts), acceptability and validity.
   * If inductive reasoning, check for truth (facts), acceptability, relevance and sufficiency.

11. Determine ways to strengthen the argument† by:
   * Providing and incorporating additional reasons and/or evidence.
   * Anticipating objections and providing adequate responses to the objections.

12. Determine ways to weaken the argument‡ by:
   * Considering and assessing counterexamples, counterevidence and counterarguments.
   * Determining if the argument should be modified or rejected because of the counterarguments.
   * If appropriate, identify and provide any additional information required before the argument could be accepted or rejected.

Perceived from the *Continuum* HTP, this process can be used both to examine an argument as well as to create a stronger one.

---

* Words which have emotional significance or contain implied judgments.
† And do so.
‡ If writing the paper and ways are found, then strengthen the argument to remove those weaknesses.

3.2.9 The STALL Technique

STALL is an original acronym and a mnemonic tool to help you remember how to deal with situations that range from being asked a question to avoiding panicking in a crisis. STALL stands for:

- *Stay calm*: don't panic; wait until you understand what's going on. Then you can either panic or deal with the situation in a logical manner (*Continuum* HTP).
- *Think*: think about what you're hearing, experiencing, being told, or seeing. You're generally receiving symptoms; you need to understand the cause.
- *Analyse and ask questions*: gain an understanding what's going on. This can be considered as the first stage of the problem-solving process. And when you're asking questions and thinking, use idea generating tools such as Active Brainstorming (Section 7.1) to examine the situation.
- *Listen*: you learn more from listening than from talking yourself.
- *Listen*: you learn more from listening than from talking yourself. Listening, analysing, and asking questions are done iteratively until you feel you understand the situation. You have two ears and one mouth, that's the minimum ratio in which they should be used. Namely, that means do at least twice as much listening as talking.

3.3 Evaluating Critical Thinking

Since there are diverse opinions on the nature of Critical Thinking, perceptions of the skills and abilities used to evaluate Critical Thinking can also provide insights as to the nature of Critical Thinking, and so are discussed in this section. Faced with the problem of evaluating the degree of critical the first step in developing the solution was to ask the question, "Has anyone already done it?" in accordance with the Process for Tackling a Problem (Section 11.5). A literature review showed that the problem of assessing the degree of Critical Thinking in students seemed to have already been solved. Consider the following approaches:

1. Wolcott and Gray's five levels, discussed in Section 3.3.1.
2. Paul and Elder's student profiles, discussed in Section 3.3.2.

3. Facione and Facione's four levels, discussed in Section 3.3.3.
4. Perry's nine-level approach, discussed in Section 3.3.4.
5. Ability to detect similarities and differences, discussed in Section 3.3.5.
6. The updated Bloom's taxonomy, discussed in Section 3.3.6

3.3.1 Wolcott and Gray's Five Levels

Wolcott and Gray aggregated lists of Critical Thinking abilities by defining five levels of Critical Thinking by students based on the words they used in written assignments (Wolcott and Gray 2003). In evaluating the findings, perceptions from the *Generic* HTP noted that Wolcott's method for assessing a Critical Thinking level was very similar to that used by Biggs for assessing deep learning in the education domain (Biggs 1999). Wolcott's five levels (from lowest to highest) are:

1. Confused fact finder.
2. Biased jumper.
3. Perpetual analyzer.
4. Pragmatic performer.
5. Strategic revisioner.

Consider each of them.

3.3.1.1 Confused Fact Finder   A confused fact finder is a person who is characterized by the following:

- Looks for the "only" answer.
- Doesn't seem to "get it".
- Quotes inappropriately from textbooks.
- Provides illogical/contradictory arguments.
- Insists professor, the textbook, or other experts provide "correct" answers even to open-ended problems.

3.3.1.2 Biased Jumper   A biased jumper is a person whose opinions are not influenced by facts. This person is characterized by the following:

- Jumps to conclusions.
- Does not recognize own biases; accuses others of being biased.

- Stacks up evidence for own position; ignores contradictory evidence.
- Uses arguments for own position.
- Uses arguments against others.
- Equates unsupported personal opinion with other forms of evidence.
- Acknowledges multiple viewpoints but cannot adequately address a problem from viewpoint other than own.

3.3.1.3 Perpetual Analyzer   A perpetual analyser is a person who can easily end up in "analysis paralysis". This person is characterized by the following:

- Does not reach or adequately defend a solution.
- Exhibits strong analysis skill, but appears to be "wishy-washy".
- Write papers that are too long and seem to ramble.
- Doesn't want to stop analysing.

3.3.1.4 Pragmatic Performer   A pragmatic performer is a person who is characterized by the following:

- Objectively considers alternatives before reaching conclusions.
- Focuses on pragmatic solutions.
- Incorporates others in the decision process and/or implementation.
- Views task as finished when a solution/decision is reached.
- Gives insufficient attention to limitations, changing conditions, and strategic issues.
- Sometimes comes across as a "biased jumper", but reveals more complex thinking when prompted.

3.3.1.5 Strategic Revisioner   A strategic revisioner is a person who is characterized by the following:

- Seeks continuous improvement/lifelong learning.
- More likely than others to think "out of the box".
- Anticipates change.
- Works toward construction of knowledge over time.

3.3.2 Paul and Elder's Student Profiles

Paul and Elder also assessed student performances in four levels but in a different manner (Paul and Elder 2006: pp. 74–77), namely:

1. *Exemplary students*: (grade of A) who display excellent reasoning and problem-solving skills.
2. *High-performing students*: (grade of B) who display sound reasoning and problem-solving skills.
3. *Mixed-quality students*: (grade of C) who display inconsistent reasoning and problem-solving skills.
4. *Low-performing students*: (grades of D or F) who display poor reasoning and problem-solving skills.

3.3.3 Facione and Facione's Four Levels

Peter A. Facione and Noreen C. Facione also provide a holistic Critical Thinking scoring rubric for evaluating Critical Thinking in four levels according to the treatment of the skills and abilities applied to actions as "Strong", "Acceptable", "Unacceptable" and "Weak", where:

- *Level 4*: evaluates as consistently doing all or almost of the actions as "Strong".
- *Level 3*: evaluates as consistently doing most or many of the actions as "Acceptable".
- *Level 2*: evaluates as consistently doing most or many of the actions as "Unacceptable".
- *Level 1*: evaluates as consistently doing all or almost all of the actions as "Weak".

3.3.4 Perry's Nine-Level Approach

Perry evaluated student's cognitive capabilities in nine levels of increasing ability to see multiple potentially correct solutions (acceptable solutions) and the degree of self-learning as opposed to seeing single correct solutions and being spoon-fed with knowledge by the instructor (Perry 1981) where students:

- Progressed through nine-stages of Critical Thinking starting from viewing truth in absolute terms of right and wrong (obtained from "good" or "bad" authorities) to recognizing multiple, conflicting versions of "truth" representing legitimate alternatives; namely using the *Continuum* HTP.

• Improved the way they understood their own thinking.

3.3.5 *Ability to Detect Similarities and Differences*

Gordon et al. provided a way to identify the difference in cognitive skills between innovators, problem formulators, problem solvers and imitators (Gordon G. et al. 1974). The difference is based on:

• Ability to find *differences* among objects which seem to be *similar.*
• Ability to find *similarities* among objects which seem to be *different.*

The differences in the "ability to find ...", namely competence in *Generic* and *Continuum* perspective observation skills lead to systems thinking and beyond as performed by the different type of personalities shown in Figure 3.2 which is based on (Gordon G. et al. 1974). For example:

• *Problem formulators*: score high in ability to find differences among objects which seem to be similar, namely they are good at using the *Continuum* HTP.
• *Problem solvers*: score high in ability to find similarities among objects which seem to be different, namely they are good at using the *Generic* HTP.

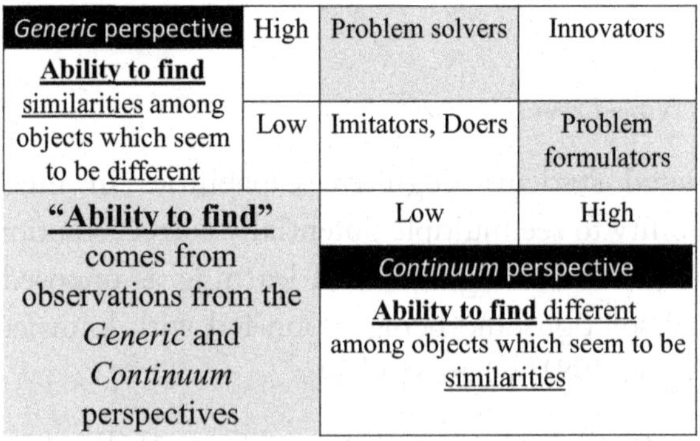

Generic perspective **Ability to find** similarities among objects which seem to be different	High	Problem solvers	Innovators
	Low	Imitators, Doers	Problem formulators
"Ability to find" comes from observations from the *Generic* and *Continuum* perspectives		Low	High
		Continuum perspective	
		Ability to find different among objects which seem to be similarities	

Figure 3.2   Systems thinking and beyond as related to problems and solutions.

From a slightly different perspective, Gharajedaghi discussed four personality types based on the same abilities in the context of separating the problem from the solution (Gharajedaghi 1999: pp. 116–117) where:

- *Leaders and pathfinders*: (innovators in Figure 3.2) have a holistic orientation to seeing the bigger picture and putting issues in the proper perspective.
- *Problem solvers*: are scientifically oriented with a tendency to find similarities in things that are different. They are concerned with immediate results.
- *Problem formulators*: are artistically oriented having a tendency to find differences in things that are similar. They are concerned with the consequences.
- *Doers* are practitioners producing tangible results.

Both Gordon et al. and Gharajedaghi discuss the same abilities in the context of separating the problem from the solution, however they do not provide a way to evaluate a person's skills in those areas which overlap with the *Generic* and *Continuum* HTPs which is something done by many IQ tests.

3.3.6 The Updated Bloom's Taxonomy

Bloom's taxonomy (Bloom et al. 1956) was created in order to promote higher forms of thinking in education. It is a six-level hierarchy where the highest level in the hierarchy represents the highest level of cognitive activity (thinking and Critical Thinking). The updated Bloom's taxonomy (Overbaugh and Schultz 2013) is a modified version and its six levels (lowest to highest) are:

1. *Remembering*: recalling information.
2. *Understanding*: interpreting and modifying the information.
3. *Applying*: using the information to perform a task.
4. *Analyzing*: seeing similarities and differences.
5. *Evaluating*: drawing conclusions.
6. *Creating*: hypothesizing and uncovering new information.

I noticed that in some postgraduate courses between 1996 and 2004 it was possible for students to gain high grades in a course without

Table 3.1 Grading Criteria

GRADE	COGNITIVE SKILLS DEMONSTRATED
A+	Student is able to reflect on what they have learned and demonstrates the ability to generate novel, quality insights for the problems assigned. The student is able to conceptualize at a level extending beyond what has been covered in the module/session materials.
A/A-	Student has mastered a functional understanding of the knowledge derived from the module/session and substantial additional reading. Student demonstrates the ability to integrate the concepts presented and to uncover useful insights.
B+/B	Student demonstrates a clear understanding of how and when to apply the knowledge and can explain, analyze, and solve issues using the concepts presented in the module/session together with some external extensions from their own reading.
B-	Student is able to apply the content from the module/session within the conceptual framework presented. Work demonstrates a solid, procedural level of understanding of principles and practice.
C	Student knows the terminology and can apply the knowledge to solve a problem but the work is shallow, mechanistic, and lacks insight.

demonstrating a grasp of the application of the subject matter in the in-class exercises. Students could even fail to complete the assignment and still pass the course (albeit with a minimum passing grade). This was due to the type of knowledge assessed by the assignment. For example, in a class on software maintenance, the focus of the assignment was to produce a maintenance plan. The assignment focused on remembering and using the knowledge gained in class, and while easy for the instructor to grade, the assignment did not allow an assessment to be made as to the student's understanding of the knowledge. When the assignments were changed from asking the students to remember (reference) and use (apply) the knowledge taught in a class to asking the students to comment and reflect on the knowledge taught in the class, as shown in Table 3.1, the grades fell into line with the student's in-class demonstrated abilities.

3.4 Creating Assignments to Encourage and Evaluate Critical Thinking

Part of the problem with assessing cognitive skills of students is that we are not asking them the right questions, so that they're not using their higher-level cognitive skills. The traditional approach to creating assignments tends to focus on the first three levels. For example, consider the following scenario. Federated Aerospace has developed the prototype for a new fighter aeroplane. It has one major flaw; it has an ejector seat that will kill the pilot 100% of the time it is used. The budget to fix the undesirable situation is $3 million. Two conceptual designs were produced to fix the ejector seat:

1. Design A which would take one year to develop, cost $2.5 million dollars, and would give the pilot a 50% probability of surviving.
2. Design B which would take two years to develop, cost $4 million but would give the pilot a 95% probability of the pilot surviving.

In most classes, the question posed would be something like, "Which conceptual design should be chosen and why (all other things being equal)?" Students dealing with this question would tend to use some kind of Multi-attribute Variable Analysis (MVA) (Section 4.6.2) weighting the development time, cost, and probability of the pilot surviving, because that was the tool they learnt in class. They are remembering, understanding, and applying their knowledge.

In order for the students to exercise the higher cognitive thinking levels, a different question needs to be asked, something like, "What additional knowledge is required to make the acceptance decision (and why)?" This question leads to a wider discussion on the use of the ejector seat before invoking the solution. The discussion might include the probability that the ejector seat would be used within the two years that it would take to develop design B, the value of a human life, and the cost of training a replacement pilot, all of which would have an effect on the weighting.

The teaching also needs to be changed. In the traditional classroom the students are only taught to deal with the first question. In order to exercise the cognitive skills, the students have to be taught to deal with the second question. Ways of dealing with this change include:

1. Working through the first question in class, pose the second question as a homework question asking the students to re-evaluate the decision based on the additional information they discover. This is where they will exercise their higher level cognitive skills.
2. Changing the focus of the assignment as discussed in Section 3.4.1.
3. Introducing Knowledge Readings as discussed in Section 3.4.2.

When the students begin to exercise their higher-level cognitive skills, they are initially uncomfortable because there is no single correct solution or model answer, instead there may be a number of acceptable solutions.

3.4.1 Changing the Focus of the Assignment

The focus of the assignment also has to be changed and it can be changed in a similar way in which the focus of the assignment in the class on software maintenance was changed (Section 3.3.6). For example, in a class on:

- *Project development* – instead of being asked to produce a Project Development Plan, students are asked to "describe, compare, and contrast the way project development is performed in Government and Private Industry."
- *Requirements engineering* – instead of being asked to produce a requirements document students are asked to "discuss the nature of requirements, their use in the acquisition life cycle by the customer and developer, and …."

Changing the focus of the question:

- Required the students to do research and identify knowledge that was not taught in the classroom.
- Taught the student how to avoid plagiarism by citing references.
- Mostly overcame the situation in which students in one class were able to obtain copies of the documents produced by students in previous classes and make use of their content in their assignment.
- Made the assignments harder to grade.

3.4.2 Knowledge Readings

Knowledge Readings (Kasser 2013):

- Are classroom presentations that go beyond just summarising the content of the knowledge in a chapter of the textbook or an assigned reading.

- Allow students to exercise cognitive skills at Levels 3-6 of the upgraded version of Bloom's taxonomy.
- Provide a better learning experience, since learning for the purposes of presentation is a good way of ensuring retention of the knowledge.
- Easily identify if students understand the knowledge being taught in the session.
- Demonstrate that different people perceive information differently.
- Enable the instructor to correct misinterpretations as they arise.
- Provide students with the opportunity to practice presentation skills and obtain feedback on content and style.

The requirements for the Knowledge Readings have evolved to the following:

1. *Summarize content of reading (<1 minute).* The requirement is to facilitate developing the skills to condense the information in the reading and hide (abstract out) details.
2. *List the main points (<1 minute).* This requirement requires the students to analyze and evaluate the knowledge (Taxonomy Levels 4 and 5) to identify and prioritize the main points.
3. *Prepare a brief on two main points.* Requirement 4 is for the team to brief on one main point. However, once a team has made a briefing, there is the probability that another team will want to brief the same main point. This requirement requires the students to read two main points in the text and allows the option for the instructor to bypass some of the potential repetition.
4. *Brief on one main point (<1 minute per point).* This requirement helps to limit the time for the presentation and minimizes repetition.
5. *Reflect and comment on reading (<2 minute).* This requirement invokes the higher level cognitive skills by requiring the students to apply, analyse, evaluate and create knowledge (Taxonomy Levels 3 to 6).

6. *Compare content with other readings and external knowledge.*
   This requirement:
   1. Invokes the higher level cognitive skills by requiring the students to apply, analyse, evaluate and create knowledge (Taxonomy Levels 3 to 6).
   2. Encourages students to research similar material to the assigned readings and compare and contrast the material.
   3. Encourages students to make connections between the various readings allocated to a session, developing their ability to see similarities and differences in the assigned and external readings (*Generic* and *Continuum* HTPs).
   4. Helps to identify and develop students with problem solving and problem formulating skills by requiring the student to apply holistic thinking to the content especially the *Generic* and *Continuum* HTPs. This is where the students can develop and apply their (Section 3.3.5):
      – Ability to find differences among objects which seem to be similar,
      – Ability to find similarities among objects which seem to be different.

7. *State why you think the reading was assigned to the session.* This requirement also invokes the higher level cognitive skills by requiring the students to apply, analyse, evaluate and create knowledge (Taxonomy Levels 3 to 6). The similarities and differences in this part of the presentation illustrate to the students that different people can draw similar and different conclusions from the same data. In a number of instances students have drawn innovative applicable conclusions.

8. *Summarize lessons learned from the session and indicate source of learning, for example, readings, exercise, experience, etc. (<2 minutes).* This requirement also invokes the higher level skills by requiring the students to apply, analyse, and evaluate knowledge (Taxonomy Levels 3 to 5).

9. *Use a different team leader for each session.* This requirement minimizes the workload on students who tend to be perfectionists and undertake to do most of the team

work themselves to compensate for poor performance by individuals.

10. *Presentation to be less than 15 minutes.* This requirement puts an upper limit on the length of the entire presentation.

The requirements also simplify the grading. The explanation for each requirement also identified the Taxonomy Level of the students thinking. Grading was based on the rubric shown in Table 3.2 adapted from Overbaugh and Schultz (Overbaugh and Schultz 2013).

3.4.2.1 Student Reaction to the Knowledge Readings The requirements have evolved as a result of experience in both the synchronous face-to-face and the online distance learning postgraduate classroom. Consider some of the results.

Table 3.2 Grading Based on Cognitive Skills

GRADE	TAXONOMY LEVEL		ABILITY BEING TESTED	DEMONSTRATING SKILL BY …
A+	6	Creating	Can the student create a new product or point of view?	Assembling, constructing, creating, designing, developing, formulating
A	5	Evaluating	Can the student justify a stand or decision?	Appraising, arguing, defending, judging, selecting, supporting, valuing, evaluating
B+/B	4	Analysing	Can the student distinguish between the different parts?	Comparing, contrasting, criticizing, differentiating, discriminating, distinguishing, examining, experimenting, questioning, testing
B-	3	Applying	Can the student use the information in a new way?	Choosing, demonstrating, illustrating, interpreting, operating, scheduling, sketching, solving, using, writing
C+	2	Understanding	Can the student explain ideas or concepts?	Classifying, describing, discussing, explaining, identifying, locating, recognizing, reporting, selecting, translating, paraphrasing
C	1	Remembering	Can the student recall or remember the information?	Defining, duplicating, listing, memorizing, recalling, repeating, reproducing, stating

3.4.2.1.1 Results by Requirement   Perceptions from the results by requirement include:

1. **Summarize content of reading.** Results have shown that quite often different teams present different verbal summaries; even when the lists of items on the PowerPoint slide are the same. This illustrates to the students that different people pick up on different things in documents and the need to make sure that the reader indeed gets the message the writer intends to convey. Smarter students have also realized that an abstract and summary of an assigned reading and the introduction and summary of a book chapter contain all the information that needs to be presented in this part of their presentation. Sometimes some students brief the whole reading at this point demonstrating the inability to abstract the information.*

2. **List the main points.** The differences in the presentations help to illustrate that different people will pick out different main points and rank them in different orders of importance. Often items that one team will list as a main point will be ignored by another team. Sometimes some students try to brief the whole reading at this point demonstrating the inability to abstract the information.*

3. **Prepare a brief on two main points.** This requirement allows the student to demonstrate remembering and understanding (Taxonomy Levels 1 and 2). Experience and student feedback have shown that too many presentations on the same topic tend to become boring very quickly so attention wanders and the students do not focus on the similarities and differences in the presentations. Requirements 3 and 4 were added to minimize repetition.

4. **Brief on one main point.** This requirement helps to limit the time for the presentation and minimizes repetition. Before limiting the brief to one main point each team would brief on the entire reading which resulted in repetition as even

---

* This generally happens at the beginning of the semester and improves as a result of experience.

when the students were instructed not to repeat information that had already been presented they tended to do so. Too much repetition defeats the purpose as discussed above in Requirement 3.

Experience has also shown that at least one brief in each semester will contain material based on misinterpreting or misunderstanding the knowledge in the reading. The instructor can correct the error in the session and reflect on how to present the material in the following iteration of the class in a better way.

At the beginning of the semester most students tend to brief on the knowledge without reflection and comment understanding (Taxonomy Levels 1 and 2). After receiving feedback from the instructor many students can then reflect and comment on the reading which exercises the higher level cognitive skills and minimizes repetition.

Some students appear to be repeating the knowledge without understanding it. They stick to a prepared script, so even if another team has already presented the material, they restate it, and most of the time do not refer to the same knowledge already covered in a previous presentation.

Some students don't seem to be able to tell the difference between "knowledge" and "applying the knowledge" (Section 10.2). The Knowledge Readings help the instructor to point out which goes where; in other words, knowledge in the Knowledge Readings and application of the knowledge in the session exercise.

5. *Reflect and comment on reading.* Some students can do this right away, others have to learn and apparently some never manage to learn how to do this.

6. *Compare content with other readings and external knowledge.* This requirement makes the presentations more interesting. The students sometimes invoke web sites, journal articles, and books, some of which are new to the instructor. The pertinence of the external knowledge also indicates the degree of understanding of the session knowledge. Students often relate anecdotes from their own experience in this part of their presentation.

7. *State why you think the reading was assigned to the session.* The similarities and differences in this part of the presentation illustrate to the students that different people can draw similar and different conclusions from the same data. In a number of instances students have drawn innovative applicable conclusions.

8. *Summarize lessons learned from the session and indicate source of learning.* Often the students state that a lesson was learnt during the team discussion; sometime the lessons learnt come from applicable prior experience and most often from the literature. The requirement to add the source of the lesson learnt was a modification because originally it was difficult to tell from the presentation if the lesson had actually been learnt or was just something being repeated from the text.

9. *Use a different team leader for each session.* This requirement minimizes the workload on students who tend to be perfectionists and undertake to do most of the team work themselves to compensate for poor performance by individuals. Some detail oriented dedicated team leaders have had to be counselled that sometimes people should be allowed to fail in a controlled environment, so that they hopefully will learn from the failure. Better to fail in the classroom than on the job.

10. *Presentation to be less than 15 minutes.* This requirement also helps the students develop time management skills when the instructor allows the presentations to go over time and the class lasts an hour longer than scheduled. The students often seem surprised when the instructor points out that he is not their timekeeper. Most teams learned to manage the time and keep the presentation down to 15 minutes. In one class when the students could not manage the time, and consistently went overtime for three sessions, the time limit was set to 5 minutes at the beginning of the session and the students were given 30 minutes to modify their presentation. This change received positive comments from a number of the students.

3.4.2.1.2 Other Perceptions Include:

- The Knowledge Readings provide the following three of the five top aspects of the engineering design process that best equip secondary students to understand, manage, and solve technological problems (Wicklein, Smith Jr., and Kim 2009):*
  - Multiple [acceptable] solutions to a problem/requirement.
  - Oral communications.
  - Graphical/pictorial communication.
- Each class is different containing students with a different mixture of cognitive skills. The grading performed according the information in Table 3.2 tends to reflect the behaviour of the students observed in the knowledge and exercise presentations and interaction in the question and response dialogues.
- Each team presentation in each session differs; illustrating that there can be more than one acceptable solution to a problem and there can be more than one way to satisfy a requirement.
- These presentations provide excellent "learning opportunities" based on the mistakes the students make in content, style and format.
- Students like feedback on what was good and what was bad, but the bad has to be framed in a positive manner. So the instructor must provide positive feedback pointing out where things were done well, and when providing negative feedback, must not only state that something was bad or wrong, but also add how to correct it or make it better.[†]
- Presentations evolve as the better techniques for presenting information get picked up by other teams. The instructor can point this out to the students, showing that learning has taken place.
- Students misuse Bar Charts (Section 2.1), Trend Charts (Section 2.15) and Pie Charts (Section 2.13) and need to be

---

[*] The remaining top two, ability to handle open-ended/ill-defined problems and systems thinking, are covered in the session exercise not described in this section.
[†] Which is good practice.

shown when to use which type of chart. By comparing the information presented in the different charts students soon pick up on when to use which chart.

- In spite of all the feedback, some students don't seem to be able to make connections between the different elements of the knowledge they are learning. They don't seem to be able to see connections between readings on the same topic, or between readings from the current session and readings from earlier sessions.

- Students who are used to classes where they are lectured at need to be shown why the Knowledge Readings have been introduced. This is generally done in the introductory session to the semester.

- Student feedback is that, while the classes incorporating Knowledge Readings are a lot of work, they feel that they have learned a lot and the classes are changing the way they think.

3.5 Summary

Chapter 3 discussed Critical Thinking, a ubiquitous tool that should be, but often isn't, used in project management, systems engineering, and most facets of our daily life. This chapter viewed Critical Thinking from a Perspectives Perimeter based on the HTPs and discussed applications of Critical Thinking, including some that are not often thought of as being Critical Thinking, such as the KISS principle, Miller's Rule, and Occam's Razor. Two new applications of Critical Thinking were introduced, the "Don't Care" situation and the STALL technique. This chapter then discussed six different ways of evaluating critical thinking and discussed the challenge of creating student assignments to encourage critical thinking and the application of their cognitive skills in the higher levels of the updated Bloom's taxonomy. One way of doing this is via Knowledge Readings which were introduced to postgraduate students at the National University of Singapore (NUS) with encouraging results and student feedback. Lastly, this chapter closed with some of the student feedback and the Lessons Learned from using the Knowledge Readings.

References

Argyris, C. 1990. *Overcoming Organizational Defenses: Facilitating Organizational Learning*. 1st Edition ed. Boston: Allyn and Bacon.

Arons, A. B. 1990. *A Guide to Introductory Physics Teaching*. New York: John Wiley & Sons.

Biggs, J. 1999. *Teaching for Quality Learning in University*. Reprinted 2000 ed. Maidenhead, England: Society for Research into Higher Education and Open University Press.

Bloom, B. S., M. D. Engelhart, E. J. Furst, W. H. Hill, and D. R. Krathwohl. 1956. *Taxonomy of Educational Objectives: The Classification of Educational Goals. Handbook I: Cognitive Domain*. New York: David McKay Company.

Chacko, G. K. 1989. *The Systems Approach to Problem Solving*. New York: Prager.

Crossman, A. 2017. "Hypothetico-Deductive Method." Accessed 26 February 2018. https://www.thoughtco.com/hypothetico-deductive -reasoning-3026351.

Gharajedaghi, J. 1999. *System Thinking: Managing Chaos and Complexity*. Boston: Butterworth-Heinemann.

Gordon, Gerald, Ann E. MacEachron, and G. Lawrence Fisher. "A Contingency Model for the Design of Problem-Solving Research Programs: A Perspective on Diffusion Research." *The Milbank Memorial Fund Quarterly. Health and Society* 52, no. 2 (1974): 185–220. doi:10.2307/3349545.

Juthe, A. 2005. "Argument by Analogy." *Argumentation*, no. 19 (1):1–27.

Kasser, J. E. 2008. *Luz: From Light to Darkness: Lessons Learned from the Solar System*. In the 18th INCOSE International Symposium, at Utrecht, Holland.

Kasser, J. E. 2013. "Introducing 'Knowledge Readings': Systems Engineering the Pedagogy for Effective Learning." In *Asia-Pacific Council on Systems Engineering (APCOSE) Conference*. Yokohama, Japan.

Koestler, A. 1978. *JANUS: A Summing Up*. New York: Random House.

Miller, G. 1956. "The Magical Number Seven, Plus or Minus Two: Some Limits on Our Capacity for Processing Information." *The Psychological Review*, no. 63:81–97.

Needham, J. 1937. *Integrative Levels: A Revaluation of the Idea of Progress*. Oxford: Clarendon Press.

Overbaugh, R. C., and L. Schultz. 2013. *Bloom's Taxonomy*. Old Dominion University, accessed 13 March 2013. http://ww2.odu.edu/educ/roverbau /Bloom/blooms_taxonomy.htm.

Paul, R., and L. Elder. 2006. *Critical Thinking: Learn the Tools the Best Thinkers Use – Concise Ed*. Pearson Prentice Hall.

Paul, R. W. 1991. *Developing Minds*. Revised edition, Volume 1.

Perry, W. 1981. "Cognitive and Ethical Growth: The Making of Meaning." In *The Modern American College: Responding to the New Realities of Diverse Students and a Changing Society*, edited by A. W. Chickering, pp. 76–116. San Francisco: Jossey-Bass.

Rodkinson, M. L., ed. 1903. *The Babilonian Talmud*. Boston New Talmud Publishing Company.

Ruggiero, V. V. 2012. *The Art of Thinking. A Guide to Critical and Creative Thought*, 10th ed. Boston: Pearson, Education, Inc.

Spencer, H. 1862. "First Principles." In *A System of Synthetic Philosophy*, Williams and Norgate. London.

Tittle, P. 2011. *Critical Thinking: An Appeal to Reason*. New York: Routledge.

UIA. 2002. *Integrative Knowledge Project: Levels of Organization*. Union of International Associations, accessed 28th May 2002. http://www.uia.org/uialists/kon/c0841.htm.

Wicklein, R., P. C. Smith Jr., and S. J. Kim. 2009. "Essential Concepts of Engineering Design Curriculum in Secondary Technology Education." *Journal of Technology Education*, no. 20 (2):66–80.

Wilson, T. D. 2002. "Philosophical Foundations and Research Relevance: Issues for Information Research" (Keynote address). In *Fourth International Conference on Conceptions of Library and Information Science: Emerging Frameworks and Method*, July 21 to 25, 2002, at University of Washington, Seattle, USA.

Wolcott, S. K., and C. J. Gray. 2003. *Assessing and Developing Critical Thinking Skills*. Accessed 21 May 2013. http://www.wolcottlynch.com/Downloadable_Files/IUPUI%20Handout_031029.pdf.

4

DECISIONS AND
DECISION-MAKING

Decision-making is the part of the problem-solving process, where the candidate solutions, options, or choices are evaluated against predetermined selection criteria and a decision is made to select one or more of the options. The decision may be easy or difficult, simple or complicated. Some decisions can be made instantaneously; some decisions may require weeks or even years of study to gather the relevant information necessary to make the decision. Some people have problems making decisions (Section 3.3.1.3); others make decisions instantaneously or intuitively. This chapter:

1. Begins by discussing qualitative and quantitative decision-making in Section 4.1.
2. Discusses decision traps that produce bad decisions in Section 4.2.
3. Discusses decision outcomes including how to avoid unanticipated consequences in Section 4.3.
4. Discusses sources of unanticipated consequences in Section 4.4.
5. Discusses the four key elements in making decisions with several anecdotal examples in Section 4.5.
6. Discusses some decision making tools in Section 4.6.

4.1 Qualitative and Quantitative Decision-Making

Perceptions from the *Continuum* HTP indicate, "We need to differentiate between the quality of the decision and the quality of the outcome" (Howard 1973: p. 55). A good decision can lead to a bad outcome and conversely a bad decision can lead to a good outcome. The quality of the decision is based on doing the best you can to increase the chances of a good outcome hence the development and use of decision-making tools to assist the decision maker to make the best decisions possible under the circumstances existing at the time the decision is to be made. Decisions can be made using quantitative and qualitative methods where:

- *Qualitative*: decision-making tends to be subjective being based on feelings about the selection criteria. Since the selection criteria are often not expressed, it can make use of unarticulated selection criteria. However:
  - Qualitative decisions are difficult to justify since they are subjective and based on unarticulated selection criteria.
  - The decision maker can focus on a subset of the selection criteria and ignore others.
- *Quantitative*: decision-making tends to be reductionist being based on predetermined selection criteria so it seems to provide an objective justification for the decision since the reasoning behind the decision is explicit. However:
  - Determining the weighting functions for the selection criteria is often subjective.
  - The decision is limited to the articulated predefined selection criteria.

The literature tends to discuss each tool and decision-making approach as being used in an either-or case, namely use one tool or the other to make a decision. However, in the real world we use perceptions from the *Continuum* HTP to develop a mixture of tools or parts of tools as appropriate. For example, determination of selection criteria is often a subjective approach, even when those criteria are later used in a quantitative manner.

4.2 Decision Traps

Russo and Schoemaker provided ten decision traps, or factors that lead to bad decisions (Russo and Schoemaker 1989), mainly due to poor Critical Thinking, and need to be avoided. In summary, they are:

1. *Plunging in*: beginning to gather information and reach conclusions without taking the time to think though the issue.
2. *Frame blindness*: defining the wrong problem.

3. ***Lack of frame control***: failing to define the problem in more than one way or being unduly influenced by other people's frames.*

4. ***Overconfidence in your judgment***: failing to collect key facts because you are sure of your assumptions and opinions.[†]

5. ***Short-sighted shortcuts***: relying inappropriately on "rules of thumb" such as implicitly trusting the most readily available information or anchoring too much on convenient facts.

6. ***Shooting from the hip***: believing that you can keep all the information in your head and therefore "winging it" rather than following a systematic procedure when making the final choice.

7. ***Group failure***: assuming that with many smart people involved, good choices will follow automatically, and therefore failing to manage the group decision-making process.[‡]

8. ***Fooling yourself about feedback***: failing to interpret the evidence from past outcomes for what it really is,[§] either because you are protecting your ego or because you are tricked by hindsight.

9. ***Not keeping track***: assuming that experience will make its lessons available automatically, and therefore failing to keep systematic records to track the results of your decisions and failing to analyse these results in ways that reveal their key Lessons Learned (Section 13.1.3.1).

10. ***Failure to audit your decision-making process***: failing to create an organized approach to understanding your own decision-making, so you remain constantly exposed to the previous nine mistakes.

---

* Also known as cognitive filters.

[†] Perceptions from the *Generic* perspective perceive the similarity to the "imperious immediacy of interest" source of unanticipated consequences discussed in Section 4.4.

[‡] The assumption is the group has the appropriate domain knowledge to make a good decision.

[§] It is never the decision-maker's fault; it is always someone else's fault.

4.3 Decision Outcomes

Perceiving decision outcomes from the *Continuum* HTP:

- Outcomes lie on a probability of possibilities continuum ranging from 0% to 100% where an outcome with a probability of occurrence of 100% is a certain outcome and an outcome of 0% is one that is never going to happen (negative certainty). Anything in between is an uncertain outcome. The difference between certain and uncertain outcomes is:
  - *Certain*: is deterministic since you can determine what the outcome will be before it happens. For example, if you toss a coin into the air, you are certain that it will come down* and come to rest with one side showing if it lands on a hard surface.
  - *Uncertain*: is non-deterministic since while you know there may be more than one possible outcome from an action, you can't determine which one it will be. For example, if you toss a coin, the outcome is non-deterministic or uncertain because while you know that the coin will show one of two sides when it comes to rest, you cannot be sure which side will be showing. However, you could predict one side with a 50% probability of being correct.†
- Outcomes can be anticipated and unanticipated where:
  - *Anticipated* can be:
    - *Desired*: where the result is something that you want. For example, you want the coin to land showing "heads" and it does.
    - *Undesired*: where the result is something that you don't want. For example, you don't want the coin to land showing "tails" and it lands showing "tails".
    - *Don't care*: where you have no preference for the result. For example, if you have no preference as to which

---

* Unless you toss it so fast that it escapes from the Earth's gravity.

† So how can tossing a coin be certain and uncertain at the same time? It depends on the type of outcome you are looking for. Which side it will land on is uncertain, but that it will land on a side is certain. It is just a matter of framing the issue from the proper perspective.

side is showing when the coin lands, you have a "Don't Care" situation (Section 3.2.2).

- *Unanticipated* once discovered, can also be desired, undesired, and "Don't Care".

• There can also be more than one outcome from an action; for example, each of the outcomes may be:
  • Dependent on, or independent from, the other outcomes.
  • Acceptable or not acceptable.
  • Desired, undesired or "Don't Care" (Section 3.2.2).
  • Unanticipated the first time that the action is taken.
  • A combination of the above.

4.4 Sources of Unanticipated Consequences or Outcomes

Unanticipated consequences or outcomes of decisions need to be min-imized.* In the systems approach, if we can identify the causes of unanticipated consequences we should be able to prevent them from happening. A literature search found Merton's analysis of unintended consequences in social interventions which discussed the following five sources of unanticipated consequences (Merton 1936):

1. Ignorance.
2. Error.
3. Imperious immediacy of interest.
4. Basic values.
5. Self-defeating predictions.

These sources may be generalized as discussed below.

• *Ignorance*: this deals with the type of knowledge that is miss-ing or ignored. Ignorance in the:
  • *Problem domain* may result in the identification of the wrong problem.
  • *Solution domain* may produce a solution system that will not provide the desired remedy.
  • *Implementation domain* may produce a conceptual solu-tion that cannot be realized.

---

* This also applies to unanticipated emergent properties (*Generic* perspective).

- *Error*: there are two types of errors, errors of commission and errors of omission (Ackoff and Addison 2006) where:
  1. *Errors of commission* do something that should not have been done. There are also two types of errors of commission; design errors and implementation errors.
     a. *A design error* is an error which produces an undesired outcome. For example a logic error in a computer program.
     b. *An implementation error* is where a mistake was made in creating the design. For example, a syntax error in a computer program, a failure to test something under realistic operating conditions, the wrong part was installed, or a part was installed backwards.
  2. *Errors of omission* fail to do something that should have been done such as in instances where only one or some of the pertinent aspects of the situation which influences the solution are considered. This can range from the case of simple neglect (lack of systematic thoroughness in examining the situation) to, "pathological obsession where there is a determined refusal or inability to consider certain elements of the problem" (Merton 1936).
     Errors of omission are more serious than errors of commission because, among other reasons, they are often impossible or very difficult to correct. "They are lost opportunities that can never be retrieved" (Ackoff and Addison 2006: p. 20). Merton adds that a common fallacy is the too-ready assumption that actions, which have in the past led to a desired outcome, will continue to do so. This assumption often, even usually, meets with success. However, the habit tends to become automatic with continued repetition so that there is a failure to recognize that procedures, which have been successful in certain circumstances, need not be successful under any and all conditions.*
- *Imperious immediacy of interest*: the paramount concern with the foreseen immediate consequences excludes the

---

* This assumption also applies to component reuse.

consideration of further or other consequences of the same act, which does in fact produce errors.*

- *Basic values*: there is no consideration of further consequences because of the felt necessity of certain action enjoined by certain fundamental values. For example, the Protestant ethic of hard work and asceticism paradoxically leads to its own decline in subsequent years through the accumulation of wealth and possessions.
- *Self-defeating predictions*: the public prediction of a social development proves false precisely because the prediction changes the course of history. Merton later conceptualized the "the self-fulfilling prophecy" (Merton 1948) as the opposite of this concept.

Perceptions from the *Generic* HTP show the similarity with the decision traps (Section 4.2).

4.5 The Four Key Elements in Making Decisions

Since the decision-making process overlaps the problem-solving process up to the point where the decision is made, the decision-making process provides a different perspective on the grouping of the activities performed in problem-solving and decision-making. Since different perspectives provide different insights, perceive the process from the perspective of the following four key elements[†] in making decisions (Russo and Schoemaker 1989: p. 2):

1. *Framing the problem*: considering what must be decided. This is the most critical part of the process because if the problem is framed incorrectly, then the wrong problem will be considered, the wrong questions will be asked, and the wrong solution will be realized. A Problem Formulation Template for framing the problem is presented and discussed in Section 14.3.

---

* Perceptions from the *Generic* HTP perceive the similarity to the decision traps in Section 4.2.

[†] Perceptions from the *Generic* perspective indicate that this is the generic problem-solving process with the addition of a process improvement element.

2. *Gathering intelligence*: determining what factors are pertinent in the situation and what factors can be safely ignored. The pertinent factors relate to determining the solution options and the selection criteria for making the decision. The Five Whys (Section 7.5) is one way of determining what intelligence needs to be gathered.

3. *Coming to conclusions*: a sound systemic and systematic approach considering all the parameters generally results in a better decision. This is the application of Critical Thinking (Chapter 3).

4. *Learning (or failing to learn) from previous decisions*: the application of the principles of Lessons Learned (Section 9.3) pattern matching, feedback, and improvement. You need to compare the expected outcomes of the decision with the actual outcomes and learn from the differences and understand the reasons for the differences. Pattern matching allows you to compare the current situation in which you are making the decision with other similar situations where the patterns in the data match and facilitate the decision. Feedback is the principle of closing the loop and learning from the effects of the decision (the good and the bad results) and not making the same mistake in the future. Not making the same mistake in the future leads to improvements in your decision-making which will result in better decisions.

4.6 Decision-Making Tools

This section discusses the following decision-making tools:

1. Decision Trees in Section 4.6.1.
2. Multi-attribute Variable Analysis (MVA) in Section 4.6.2.
3. Ordering and Ranking in Section 4.6.3.
4. Pair-wise Comparison in Section 4.6.4.
5. The Perfect Score Approach in Section 4.6.5.
6. Prioritization in Section 4.6.6.
7. The Pugh Matrix in Section 4.6.7.

4.6.1 Decision Trees

Decision Trees are:

- A decision-making tool for making a choice between several options and combinations of options and allows for weighted preferences at each decision point.
- Concept Maps (Section 6.1.2) showing all the pertinent factors to a decision in the form of a network of branches, hence the term Decision Tree.

This chapter describes Decision Trees in the context of the following examples:

1. Travelling home from class discussed in Section 4.6.1.1.
2. Travelling from Vivo City to Kent Vale discussed in Section 4.6.1.2.

4.6.1.1 Travelling Home from Class Fred is an adjunct professor at Hypothetical University who is teaching an evening class and needs to make a decision as to how he will get home afterwards. This is an example where:

- All the outcomes of the decision are certain since Fred will be selecting from one or more known options.
- The decision may be different if circumstances change.

4.6.1.1.1 Framing the Problem The problem framed in accordance with the Problem Formulation Template (Section 14.3) is:

1. **The undesirable situation** that Fred is at the class location. He needs to get home after class and has to decide how to accomplish this objective.
2. **The assumptions** being that:
   a. Fred does not own, or did not bring, a car or other vehicle to the classroom that day.
   b. He will be going straight home after class.
3. **The FCFDS**. Fred has made the decision.

4. *The problem* is to:
   a. Identify a number of ways of travelling home.
   b. Decide which way to travel home.
5. *The solution*: perform the decision-making process and make the decision.

4.6.1.1.2 Gathering Intelligence Having framed the problem, Fred has to identify the options and the selection criteria, namely the controlled variables associated with the decision. The list of five options to choose from, shown in Figure 4.1 in the form of a simple Decision Tree, is:

1. Taxi.
2. Bus.
3. Subway.
4. Walk.
5. Get a ride from one of the students.

The intelligence or pertinent information associated with each of the options to be used as selection criteria are:

- *Taxi*: the most expensive option but the fastest way home. Fred can telephone for a taxi from his cell phone and it should arrive at the front of the building within 15 minutes.
- *Bus*: the cheapest and slowest option apart from walking. The bus stop is within 100 meters of the building but he'll have to wait for the bus and he has no idea if it will be crowded or if he'll get a seat.
- *Subway*: faster and slightly more expensive than the bus, but the station is about 500 meters from the building. It has similar waiting and crowding considerations to the bus option.

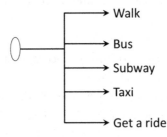

Figure 4.1 Options for getting home from class.

- *Walking*: the cheapest and slowest option but the journey will take about three or four times as long as the bus/subway options with maximum waiting time for the vehicles. On the other hand, he has the time and walking is good exercise.
- *Getting a ride from a student*: will depend on the students and whether one or more is going or willing to go in his direction.

The selection criteria should include the weather since the decision may be different on a sunny day to that of a rainy day.

The traditional approach to building Decision Trees is to list out the paths though the Decision Tree and work out the preferences for each decision point. The systems approach is to use smart thinking to simplify the tree before starting to draw it. For example, in this situation the basic or root decision is between walking and the other options, all of which can be aggregated into riding in a vehicle of some kind as shown in Figure 4.2 where:

- The first level decision is between walking and riding; a choice between two options, an easier decision than choosing from one of the five options directly which shows up clearly in Figure 4.2.
- The second level of decision making is deciding between the various riding options.

4.6.1.1.3 Making the Decision Each option has advantages (good points) and disadvantages (bad points). The preference for walking is 0.7 and the combined preference for the ride decision is 0.3. But where do the preferences come from? The preferences come from a number of subjective and objective factors associated with the option

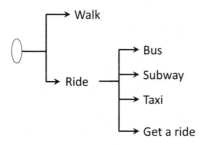

Figure 4.2 Smarter Decision Tree.

as discussed below with reference to making the decision on a sunny day and a rainy day. Fred chooses to use a different simple Decision Tree for each decision instead of one large tree in accordance with the KISS principle (Section 3.2.3).

4.6.1.1.3.1 The Sunny Day Decision   Fred's subconscious mind produces the subjective preference numbers shown in Figure 4.3 for a sunny day for the following reasons:

- *Walking* scores 0.7, the highest, because it is a sunny day, the weather will be good when class ends and he is in no rush to get home.
- *Taxi* scores 0.09 because while it is the fastest, it is also the most expensive and he's not really in a hurry and so is willing to let the journey take longer.
- *Bus* scores 0.12 which is a little more than the taxi because he's not in that much of a hurry and can read a book while waiting for the bus and riding in it. Fred doesn't feel comfortable reading while riding the taxi; he feels that he has to watch that the driver is indeed taking the shortest and cheapest route.
- *Subway* scores 0.06 which is lower than the taxi because while the same factors as for the bus option apply, there is a longer walk to the subway station.
- *Getting a ride from a student* scores 0.03, the lowest, because he feels that getting a ride from someone in that bunch of students is unlikely.

The decision is the option with the highest preference number namely 0.7 for walking.

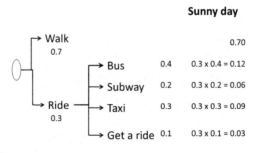

Figure 4.3   Decision Tree for sunny day preferences.

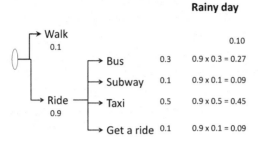

Figure 4.4 Decision Tree for rainy day preferences.

4.6.1.1.3.2 The Rainy Day Decision   Figure 4.3 shows the preferences for a sunny day, but how does rain affect the decision? The
Decision Tree for the rainy day is shown in Figure 4.4. Riding now
gets 0.9 because while Fred doesn't mind walking in the rain, he'd
rather not. The decision as to which ride to select becomes:

- *Taxi* scores the 0.5, highest, as it is the best way to keep dry
  in the rain.
- *Bus* scores 0.3, less than the taxi, because he has to walk about
  a 100 meters in the rain.
- *Subway* scores 0.1, lower than the bus because there is a longer walk to the subway station.
- *Getting a ride from a student* also scores 0.1 because he feels
  that getting a ride from that bunch is unlikely rain or sun.

When the numbers are multiplied the decision to go home via taxi is
the preferred decision at 0.45.

4.6.1.2 Travelling from Vivo City to Kent Vale   Figure 2.33 is a Rich
Picture (Section 6.1.5) showing the information that could be used
for creating the options for returning home from Vivo City to Kent
Vale.* A Decision Tree can be set up based on the options and could
appear as shown in Figure 4.5 where each of the options has been
assigned a number based on weighting the preferences (the weighting
numbers are shown before the option). The weighting numbers for the

---

* Two locations in Singapore.

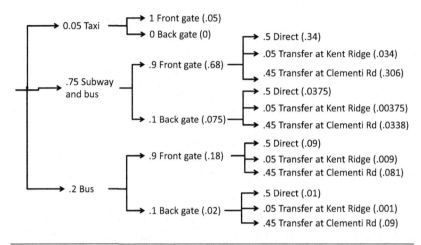

Figure 4.5   Decision Tree for return from Vivo City by transport mode.

preferences at each decision point always add up to 1 to simplify the process (Section 3.2.3). Figure 4.5 has been set up for three sequential decisions:

1. The root or first decision is to choose between taxi, subway-bus combination, and bus without the subway.
2. The second decision is to choose between the front gate and the back gate at the destination.
3. The third decision is to choose between the options of a direct bus or transferring at either Clementi Road or Kent Ridge.

The numerical value for the outcome of each option is the value of the preference number assigned to the option multiplied by the corresponding numbers for all previous decisions in that path and is shown after the option. For example, the preference for subways and bus is 0.75 and the preference for the front gate is 0.9, so the preference for front gate via subway and bus is (0.75x0.9) or 0.68 (0.675 to be exact, but perspectives from the *Quantitative* HTP indicate that two decimal places is sufficient accuracy). When the results are ranked the preferred decision is subway and a direct bus to the front gate (0.34), and the second preference is for subway and bus to the front gate via a transfer at Clementi Road (0.338).

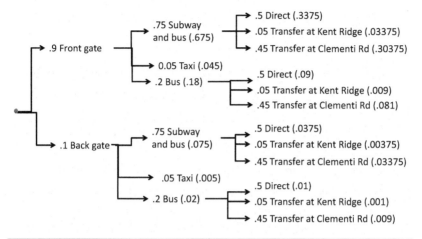

Figure 4.6   Decision Tree for return from Vivo City by destination.

An alternate Decision Tree set up for a different sequence of decisions is shown in Figure 4.6 where:

- The root decision is between the front gate and the back gate at the destination.
- The second decision is between taxi, subway bus combination and bus without the subway.
- The third decision is between the options of a direct bus or transferring at either Clementi Road or Kent Ridge.

The outcome is the same, which is not surprising since the same preferences are used, but the actual numbers are slightly different.

4.6.1.3 Smartening Up the Decision Tree   Setting up the Decision Tree requires some thought which can simplify the decision making in a number of ways including:

- The preference numbers should add up to 1.0 for each decision point as shown in the examples in Figure 4.3 and Figure 4.4. This simplifies the allocation of numbers to the branches.
- Using the approach of breaking a large complex problem into a number of small problems, group the factors involved in the decision in the same way as the factors in

Figure 4.1 were grouped in Figure 4.2. This allows the tree to be pruned before working out all the preferences. For example,

- In the getting home from class situation, if the Decision Tree is to be used once for a single decision, then once the 0.7 preference for walking is stated, there is no need to determine the branches for any of the other options since the 0.7 overrides all the others.
- In the returning home from Vivo City situation, since the Front Gate option is 0.9 if the Decision Tree is to be used once for a single decision, there is no need to work out the values and variations of the alternatives leading to the back gate.

However, in all situations, if the Decision Tree is to be used on more than one occasion in which the preferences may change for any reason, all the branches do need to be identified.

So when making the decision about getting home from Vivo City, should the Decision Tree start with the decision between a route that ends up at the front gate or at the back gate, or should the Decision Tree start with the choice between taking a taxi or not taking a taxi? It depends; this is where a sensitivity analysis on the effect of changing the weighting of the factors could influence the structure of the Decision Tree. On the other hand, Fred should decide if the "Don't Care" situation (Section 3.2.2) applies. For example, if he doesn't care which gate he uses, the front gate – back gate decision is eliminated from the Decision Tree.

4.6.2 *Multi-Attribute Variable Analysis*

Multi-attribute Variable Analysis (MVA) is:

- A tool used by the decision maker who needs to select an option based on how well it meets a number of selection criteria with different degrees of preferences.
- A generic term for a quantitative decision making approach which comes in several shapes and sizes.

- Complex and complicated.
- Based on a subjective foundation in most instances due to the way the weighting is set up.
- A complicated way to use a computer to justify the decision you were told to make.*

The process for using this version of MVA is as follows:

1. Determine the options discussed in Section 4.6.2.1.1.
2. Determine the selection criteria discussed in Section 4.6.2.1.2.
3. Create the MVA matrix for the decision discussed in Section 4.6.2.1.3.
4. Work out the importance of each of the selection criteria discussed in Section 4.6.2.1.4.
5. Develop utility curves for the selection criteria discussed in Section 4.6.2.1.5.
6. Evaluate each option against the selection criteria discussed in Section 4.6.2.1.6.
7. Weight the evaluations by the importance discussed in Section 4.6.2.1.7.
8. Read off the decision discussed in Section 4.6.2.1.8.
9. Determine if a sensitivity analysis is necessary and if so perform it discussed in Section 4.6.2.1.9.

The process is described in the following two examples:

1. Travelling from Vivo City to Kent Vale in Section 4.6.2.1.
2. Finding his perfect mate in Section 4.6.2.2.

4.6.2.1 Travelling from Vivo City to Kent Vale Section 4.6.1.2 described how Fred used a Decision Tree to select the route to travel from Vivo City to Kent Vale. This example uses one type of MVA to make the same decision. Each step of the process is described below.

4.6.2.1.1 Determine the Options The options are the bus routes 10, 30, 143, 188, and a combination of subway and bus as shown in Figure 2.33. Taxi is not to be considered in this instance as Fred has found

---

* I write this semi-seriously.

out that generally there is a long waiting time at the taxi queue and a taxi is perceived as being too expensive.

4.6.2.1.2 Determine the Selection Criteria With respect to getting home from Vivo City, the selection criteria might be:

- **Starting location**: the shortest distance to the starting location would score the highest. The bus stop for the 188 is the furthest to walk; the subway station is closest and is air-conditioned, while the bus stop for the 10, 30, and 143 is slightly further than the subway station.
- **Destination**: can be the front gate or the back gate.
- **Transfers**: the minimum number of transfers needed would score the highest.
- **Transfer points**: combining the three transfer points into a single selection criterion would be complex so they can be left separately as
  - Haw Par Villa.
  - Clementi Road.
  - Kent Vale Terminal.
- **Travel time**: The length of time for the journey including estimates of waiting times at the bus stops and subway stations. The shorter the travel time, the higher the score.

4.6.2.1.3 Create the MVA Matrix for the Decision The first step in the process is to create the blank MVA matrix for the decision as shown in Table 4.1 in its completed form. The process is:

1. Create a column in which to list the criteria.
2. Add a column for the importance of the criteria.
3. Insert a set of columns for each option to be evaluated.
4. Label that set as "Evaluation".
5. Create a second set of columns for each option.
6. Label that set as "Weighted".
7. Lastly add a row at the bottom to contain the totals.

If a spreadsheet is used, then the row column should contain a formula to sum the contents of the values in the column. The blank data is to be inserted into the appropriate position in each of the subsequent steps in the process.

Table 4.1 Completed MVA Matrix for Returning from Vivo City

CRITERIA	IMPORTANCE	EVALUATION					WEIGHTED (EVALUATION * IMPORTANCE)				
		10	30	143	188	Subway	10	30	143	188	Subway
Starting location	0.8	0.8	0.8	0.8	0.3	1	0.64	0.64	0.64	0.24	0.8
Destination	1	0	0.5	0.5	0.8	1	0	0.5	0.5	0.8	1
Transfers	0.3	0.8	1	1	1	0.8	0.24	0.3	0.3	0.3	0.24
Transfer points											
Haw Par Villa	0.9	1	1	1	1	1	0.9	0.9	0.9	0.9	0.9
Clementi Rd	1	0.5	0.5	0.5	0.5	0	0.5	0.5	0.5	0.5	0
Kent Vale	0.1	0.1	0	0	0	0	0.01	0	0	0	0
Travel time	0.5	0.1	0.5	0.5	0.5	1	0.05	0.25	0.25	0.25	0.5
Total		3.8	5.3	5.3	5.1	5.3	2.49	3.39	3.39	3.29	3.59

4.6.2.1.4 Work Out the Importance of Each of the Selection Criteria Work out the importance of each of the selection criteria on its own on a scale of 0 to 1. This is an evaluation of each of the criteria on its own without attempting to compare and rank the criteria. So in thinking about each of the criteria, they might be weighted as:

- *Starting location*: gets 0.8 because is somewhat important.
- *Destination*: gets 1 because is very important.
- *Transfers*: gets 0.3 because it is not really important.
- *Transfer points*: is broken out into the individual transfer locations to be considered separately. This is simpler than trying to work out the value of various combinations of transfer locations.
- *Transfer locations*:
  - Clementi Road gets 1 because it has the most transfer options.
  - Haw Par Villa gets 0.9 because it has a large number of transfer options.
  - Kent Vale gets 0.1 because Fred doesn't really want to transfer there due to limited bus connections.
- *Travel time*: gets 0.5 because it is not that important, as there should be a difference of less than 15 minutes between the slowest and fastest travel times.

When you evaluate the importance of the attributes, if one of the selection criteria is allocated a 0 then it has no importance and can be removed from the table which will simplify the table (Section 4.6.8). That is why this step is performed before performing the evaluations. However, there should be a note somewhere to the effect that the criterion was considered as not being important (not influencing the decision) since when something is not listed, perceptions from the *Continuum* HTP indicate that we do not know if it was (a) forgotten or (b) considered and discarded.

NGT (Section 7.9) and the Perfect Score Approach (Section 4.6.5) are useful tools to use to determine the importance of the selection criteria in situations where a group is making the decision and opinions differ at the start of the discussion.

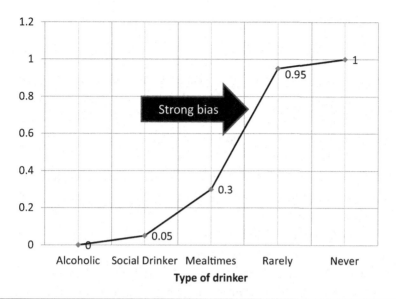

Figure 4.7   Fred's utility curve for Alcohol (type of drinker).

4.6.2.1.5 Develop Utility Curves for the Selection Criteria   A utility curve such as the one shown in Figure 4.7 is the graphical representation of the weighting of the attributes of the variable depending on the utility of that attribute which means that they may have any shape such as binary (yes–no), linear, curved, exponential or some specific custom shape for that specific situation. NGT (Section 7.9) and the Perfect Score Approach (Section 4.6.5) are useful tools to use to determine the values of the attributes in the utility curves in situations where a group is making the decision and opinions differ at the start of the discussion. Consider the selection criteria and the curves that can be developed.

- *Starting location* has three attributes:
  - The subway station gets 1 because is close and air-conditioned.
  - The bus stop for the 10, 30, and 143 gets 0.8 because is slightly further than the subway station.
  - The bus stop for the 188 gets 0.3 because is the furthest to walk.

- *Destination* has three attributes:
  - Front gate gets 1 because it is most desirable.
  - Back gate gets 0.5 because it is less desirable.
  - A "does not connect to the destination" gets 0 because there is no point in taking that bus with the expectation of not transferring.
- *Transfers* has two attributes:
  - A direct connection gets 1 because is the most desirable.
  - At least one transfer gets 0.8 because is less desirable.
- *Transfer points* has two attributes even though there are three transfer points or locations:
  - A transfer at that location gets 1.
  - No transfer at that location gets 0.
- *Travel time*: this one is more subjective than the others.
  - The subway bus combination gets 1 because it is perceived to be fastest since the subway covers half the distance with no traffic congestion.
  - A direct bus to either gate gets 0.5 because it is perceived to be slightly slower than the subway.
  - A choice that requires a transfer gets 0 because the waiting time will increase the journey time.

In this example each selection criterion only has two or three fixed points on its utility curve. In the "finding his perfect mate" (Section 4.6.2.2) some of the criteria have real curves.

4.6.2.1.6 Evaluate Each Option Against the Selection Criteria This step is when each option is considered in turn against each criterion using the utility curve for that criterion. So, commencing with "starting location", the first criterion, the 10, 30 and 143 each receive a 0.8 because the bus stop is slightly further than the subway station.* The subway will get a 1. When evaluating the options against the "destination" criterion, the 10 will get a 0 because it does not go to the destination, the 30 and 143 will get a 0.5 because they go to the back

---

* This is where the evaluation is subjective since it is based on some intuitive subjective process which converts "slightly further" to a value of 0.8.

gate while the 188 will get a 1 because it goes to the front gate. After evaluating all the options against all the criteria and adding up the totals, it can be seen that the 30, 143 bus and subway options received the highest score of 5.3.

4.6.2.1.7 Weight the Evaluations by the Importance Each evaluation is weighted by relative importance on a scale of 0 to 1. The weighted values for each of the criteria are then multiplied by their individual scores to produce the final score.

4.6.2.1.8 Read Off the Decision The subway option has the highest score of 3.59 which makes it the preferred route.

4.6.2.1.9 Determine if a Sensitivity Analysis is Necessary and if So, Perform It This is where you look at the difference in the value between the preferred option and the next best option. If the numbers are small then you have a choice between:

- Accepting that you have identified a "Don't Care" situation (Section 3.2.2) where either option can be selected as being acceptable solutions.
- Going back to the matrix and slightly adjusting the importance of the selection criteria and evaluations that contribute to the decision to see if the adjustments change the decision. If they do, then you need to rethink the numbers and the decision. If the adjustments have no effect on the decision then the decision is probably correct and you may proceed to implement it.
- Adding a new selection criterion to decide between the options.

4.6.2.2 Finding His Perfect Mate As another example of using MVA, consider the situation in which Fred, a divorced male person, wants to set up an objective decision process to find his perfect female mate. This is another example where all the outcomes are certain since Fred will be selecting from one or more known or yet to be identified options. However, this situation provides an example that illustrates some other aspects of MVA and decision-making which were not brought out in Section 4.6.2.1. Fred used the Problem Formulation Template (Section 14.3) to frame the problem as:

1. ***The undesirable situation***: the need for an objective decision-making process to make the decision as to which of the candidates is his perfect mate.*
2. ***The assumptions*** are:
    a. All selection criteria have been identified.
    b. The decision will be made in a logical manner.
    c. Fred has defined the characteristics of a perfect mate.
3. ***The FCFDS***: he has an objective decision-making process to find his perfect mate.
4. ***The problem***: to create the objective decision-making process to find his perfect mate.
5. ***The solution***: create the objective decision-making process.

Fred decides to try MVA because he perceives it as an objective decision-making process and begins with the four key elements as follows. Once he has the objective decision-making process his subsequent problem will be to carry it out. As in this situation, the solution to one problem generally tends to create a subsequent problem. Note, from the *Generic* HTP what Fred is actually doing is similar to acquiring a ready-built or Commercial-off-the-Shelf (COTS) product. The same process applies in both situations.

4.6.2.2.1 Determine the Options   The options or candidates are the women Fred will meet. However, in this example they (the number of options) are not known at the start of the process.

4.6.2.2.2 Determine the Selection Criteria   Fred establishes a set of (subjective) selection criteria† that includes the following in alphabetical order:

- *Alcohol*:‡ a range of attributes from "never touches a drop" to "alcoholic" with intermediate stages of "occasional glass of wine" and "social drinker".

---

* He did not frame the problem as the need to find the perfect mate, just the need for the process.
† Someone else would probably have a different set of selection criteria with different weightings.
‡ Fred has used solution language; he should have used "type of drinker" in functional language.

- *Beauty*: a range of attributes from "cannot bear to look at" to "turns all heads when she enters a room".
- *Cigarettes*:* a range of attributes from "non-smoker" to "100 or more cigarettes per day".
- *Character*: a range of attributes from "honest" to "dishonest".
- *Children (current)*: a range of attributes from "no children" to "four or more".
- *Children (future)*: a range of attributes from "don't want any" to "want up to four or more".
- *Education*: a range of attributes from "high school dropout", through "high school graduate", "undergraduate degree", and "graduate degree" to "doctorate".
- *Financial independence*: a range of attributes from "needs to be supported" to "multi-millionaire".
- *Hobbies and interests*: where the desirable hobbies match Fred's and the undesirable hobbies are ones that he does not want to get involved with. Others would be "Don't Cares" (Section 3.23).
- *Integrity*: a range of "cannot tell the truth" to "always tells the truth".
- *Intelligence*: a range of attributes from "completely dumb" to "smarter than him".
- *Profession*: a list of desirable professions, undesirable professions and Don't Care (Section 3.23) professions.
- *Religion*: a list of desirable religions, undesirable religions and Don't Care religions.
- *Tolerance for differences*: a range of attributes from "completely intolerant" to "tolerant" passing though degrees of tolerance on specific items. For example, she may not play golf but would be tolerant of her partner's need to play.
- *Others*: include how they handle emotions and intimacy.

4.6.2.2.3 Create the MVA Matrix for the Decision At this point in time, Fred has identified a number of selection criteria he cares about based on his life experience, knows that he is going to evaluate the importance of those criteria and will evaluate an unknown number of candidates against those selection criteria so he creates an initial MVA matrix table.

---

* Another example of solution language, he should have used "smoker" in functional language. What happens if she smokes a pipe?

4.6.2.2.4 Work Out the Importance of Each of the Selection Criteria   Fred then works out the importance of each of the selection criteria on a scale of 0 to 1 and enters the information in the MVA matrix as shown in Table 4.2. He is determining how important they are on a stand-alone basis. The table shows that some criteria such as non-smoking, children, and education are very important, while others have different degrees of importance. As in the previous example, Fred evaluates each criterion on its own and does not attempt to compare and rank them. Note, Fred did not preselect the most important criteria to simplify the table (Section 4.6.8).

4.6.2.2.5 Essential and Optional Selection Criteria   Fred also has to make a decision as to whether each of the selection criteria is essential or optional. The difference being:

- ***Essential***: a candidate becomes ineligible for selection if she does not get above a certain value on the utility curve for this criterion. For example, if Fred is looking for a non-smoker and he considers non-smoking as essential, if a candidate

Table 4.2   Initial MVA Matrix Table for Perfect Mate Decision

CRITERIA	IMPORTANCE	CANDIDATE 1	CANDIDATE 2	CANDIDATE 3
Alcohol	1			
Beauty	0.3			
Cigarettes	1			
Character	1			
Children (Current)	0.8			
Children (Future)	1			
Education	1			
Emotions – likes intimacy	0.8			
Emotions – quick to anger	0.6			
Financial independence	0.6			
Hobbies and interests	0.8			
Integrity	1			
Intelligence	1			
Profession	0.25			
Professional	0.75			
Religion	0.5			
Tolerance for differences	1			
Total	N/A			

smokes, then she becomes ineligible and can be removed from the decision matrix.

- *Optional*: a candidate can be selected even if she does not get above a certain value on the utility curve for this criterion. For example, a candidate can still be selected even if she gets 0 for these criteria.

In general, assigning an importance of 1 to a selection criterion makes it an essential criterion. Fred could have eliminated the optional selection criteria to simplify the table (Section 4.6.8) for his first round of decision-making. Should he not be able to make a decision using the essential criteria, he could then add the most important optional criterion to facilitate the decision

4.6.2.2.6 Develop Utility Curves for the Selection Criteria Fred then develops the utility curves for each of the selection criteria as follows.

4.6.2.2.6.1 Alcohol (Type of Drinker) The attributes for the alcohol selection criterion range from "never touches a drop" to "alcoholic" with intermediate stages of "occasional glass of wine" and "social drinker". These attributes can be assigned values on a scale of 0 to 1 depending on Fred's preferences,[*] where for example:

- Never touches a drop gets 1.
- Occasional glass of wine gets 0.8.
- Social drinker gets 0.5.
- Alcoholic gets 0.

The assigned weighting shows that Fred is not interested in an alcoholic. Fred decides that this is an essential selection criterion and a candidate must score an attribute of more than 0.1 (not be an alcoholic) to be eligible. When the values assigned to the attributes are plotted as a graph as shown in Figure 4.7, the graph is known as a utility curve. The curve shows his bias towards selecting someone who does not drink very much. The usefulness of the untidily curve is for assigning a number to an in-between observation of the candidate.

---

[*] Subjective.

For example, a candidate who occasionally drinks gets something between 0.3 and 0.95 depending on the occasions.

4.6.2.2.6.2 Education   The attributes for the education selection criterion range from "high school dropout", through "high school graduate", "undergraduate degree", and "graduate degree" to "doctorate". These attributes can be assigned values on a scale of 0 to 1 depending on Fred's preferences, where for example:

- Doctorate gets 1.
- Graduate degree gets 0.8.
- Undergraduate degree gets 0.6.
- High school diploma gets 0.1.
- High school dropout gets 0.

This weighting shows that the preference:

- Is not linear.
- Biased towards women who have completed tertiary education.

Fred also decides that this is an essential selection criterion and a candidate must score an attribute of at least 0.6 (have an undergraduate degree at a minimum) to be eligible.

4.6.2.2.6.3 Profession   The attributes for the profession selection criterion range from "unemployed" though "practitioner" and "manager" to "owner or boss" where Fred's preferences are:

- Unemployed gets 0.
- Professional practitioner gets 0.5 (nurse, mechanic, computer programmer, etc.).
- Manager or university professor gets 0.9.
- Owner or boss gets 1.

Fred decides that this is an optional selection criterion.

4.6.2.2.6.4 Religion   This is a similar situation to the "transfer points" selection criterion in Section 4.6.2.1.2. Here, the attributes for the religion selection criterion range from "same religion", "no religion", "don't care about the other person's religion" or list specific religions with a yes/no evaluation. For example, if Fred is a Christian and only wants a mate who is a Christian, then the selection criterion for religion becomes essential. In this instance, Fred decides that this is an optional criterion, and the attitude for differences is covered in the "tolerance for differences" criterion.

4.6.2.2.6.5 Tolerance for Differences   This is also a similar situation to the "transfer points" selection criterion in Section 4.6.2.1.2 where the tolerance for specific differences selection criterion are listed separately. The attributes are:

- Tolerant of differences gets 1.
- Grumbles but tolerant gets 0.1.
- Not tolerant gets 0.

Fred also decides that this is an essential selection criterion and after some further thought decides that a candidate must score a 1 to be eligible because those grumbles will become annoying in time.

4.6.2.2.6.6 The Remaining Selection Criteria   Fred then determines the values for the attributes of the remaining selection criteria in a similar manner. At this point Fred has his objective process and implements it. He does not need a new Problem Formulation Template (Section 14.3) at this time.

4.6.2.2.7 Evaluate Each Option against the Selection Criteria   Fred must now find his candidates and evaluate them. So for example, Fred goes to a party where he meets Sandra who interests him. They talk and he evaluates her as follows:

- As far as the alcohol variable is concerned, Fred watches* how much she drinks and figures out that she seems to be a social drinker so he evaluates her as 0.5 for this criterion.
- As far as the education variable is concerned she has a high school diploma so he evaluates her as 0.1 for this variable.

---

* Fred uses his eyes to verify that her behaviour supports her words.

At the same party Fred meets Gillian, talks with her and evaluates her as follows:

- As far as the alcohol variable is concerned she does not stop drinking so Fred evaluates her as 0.
- As far as the education variable is concerned she has an undergraduate degree so Fred evaluates her as 0.6.

As Fred talks with Sandra and Gillian, he evaluates them on other some of the other criteria as well. Fred then meets Mary, Jessica, and one or two others at the party, at other parties or via various means of introduction and goes out on dates with some of them. After some time he might picture his perfect mate as a little bit of Jessica, a little bit of Mary, a little bit of Sandra and a little bit of some of the others (Bega 1999). However in the real world of today,* he has to make a decision between the candidates so he completes the evaluations for each candidate. When he notices that a candidate does not meet an essential selection criterion he shades the cell in grey to facilitate identification of ineligible candidates.

4.6.2.2.8 Weight the Evaluations by the Importance After performing the evaluations, Fred then multiplies the individual evaluations against the importance of the criteria and produces the weighted selection matrix shown in Table 4.3.

4.6.2.2.9 Read Off the Decision Fred looks at the bottom line in Table 4.3 and sees that while Gillian has the highest score, she and all the other candidates are ineligible because they fail to meet at least one of the essential criteria. Fred is now faced with a further choice. He can:

1. Continue to identify new candidates and evaluate them. Fred is then faced with a further problem of how much time to spend identifying new candidates and evaluating (Section 11.1.4).
2. Change his mind and downgrade essential selection criteria to optional and re-evaluate the current candidates to see if an eligible winner will emerge.

---

* Perceptions from the *Temporal* perspective indicate that while something is impossible today, there may come a time in the future when he will be able to create his perfect mate from a little bit of each of the candidates.

Table 4.3 Weighted Selection Matrix for a Perfect Mate

CRITERIA	IMPORTANCE	EVALUATION					WEIGHTED				
		SANDRA	GILLIAN	MARY	JESSICA	JANE	SANDRA	GILLIAN	MARY	JESSICA	JANE
Alcohol	1	0.5	0	0.2	0.7	0.8	0.5	0	0.2	0.7	0.8
Beauty	0.3	0.9	1	0.4	1	1	0.27	0.3	0.12	0.3	0.3
Cigarettes	1	1	1	0.5	0	1	1	1	0.5	0	1
Character	1	0.3	0.8	0.9	0.9	0.9	0.3	0.8	0.9	0.9	0.9
Children (Current)	0.8	1	1	0.2	0.6	0.5	0.8	0.8	0.16	0.48	0.4
Children (Future)	1	0.5	0.5	1	0.1	1	0.5	0.5	1	0.1	1
Education	1	0.1	0.6	0.8	1	0.6	0.1	0.6	0.8	1	0.6
Emotions – likes intimacy	0.8	1	1	1	1	0.2	0.8	0.8	0.8	0.8	0.16
Emotions – quick to anger	0.6	0.8	0.8	0.4	1	0.1	0.48	0.48	0.24	0.6	0.06
Financially independence	0.6	0.8	0.7	0.8	1	0.1	0.48	0.42	0.48	0.6	0.06
Hobbies and interests	0.8	1	0.9	0.5	0.4	0.2	0.8	0.72	0.4	0.32	0.16
Integrity	1	0.5	0.7	0.9	0.8	0.8	0.5	0.7	0.9	0.8	0.8
Intelligence	1	0.2	0.8	0.8	0.8	1	0.2	0.8	0.8	0.8	1
Profession	0.25	1	1	1	1	0.2	0.25	0.25	0.25	0.25	0.05
Professional	0.75	1	1	1	1	0.4	0.75	0.75	0.75	0.75	0.3
Religion	0.5	0.4	0.6	0.3	0.7	0.9	0.2	0.3	0.15	0.35	0.45
Tolerance for differences	1	0.4	0.6	0.8	0	1	0.4	0.6	0.8	0	1
	13.4	11.4	13	11.5	12	10.7	8.33	9.82	9.25	8.75	9.04

3. Identify additional selection criteria. However, this will not help him to overcome the failure of these candidates to meet the essential selection criteria.
4. Perform all of the above.

Fred also noted that Mary moved up into second place after the weighting but at the moment since the candidate in the first place remains in the first place, second place position is not relevant.

4.6.2.2.10 Determine if a Sensitivity Analysis is Necessary and if So, Perform It   Fred determines that a sensitivity analysis is not necessary and decides to continue looking for his perfect mate.

4.6.2.2.11 The Emotional Factor   A few days later he meets Lily and his heart goes thump. He falls in love at first sight and moves the MVA decision-making matrix spreadsheet into the trash bin. This ending to the anecdote illustrates two important but often-unmentioned aspect of decision-making discussed below:

1. Some decisions tend to be made emotionally, discussed in Section 4.6.2.2.11.1.
2. Modifying the selection criteria, discussed in Section 4.6.2.2.11.2.

4.6.2.2.11.1 Decisions Tend to Be Made Logically and/or Emotionally The literature on decision-making and problem-solving identified two opinions on decision-making. We make decisions:

1. Logically and/or rationally.
2. Emotionally rather than logically and then use the logic to justify the emotional decision.

Perceptions from the *Continuum* HTP indicate that it is not an either-or situation. We don't make all decisions either rationally or emotionally, rather we make some decisions rationally and some decisions emotionally. Some problems can be decided emotionally on one day and logically the next. For example, once upon a time when my children were very young, Susie said to me that she had noticed that some days they were told off for doing something that they were not told off for doing on other days. She asked me why that was the case.

I thought about it for a moment and then I came up with the concept of a "tolerance level". I explained what a tolerance level was and how it could go up and down depending on what was going on in my life that had nothing to do with the children. So on days when my tolerance level was high they could get away with doing stuff, and on days when my tolerance level was low they were told off for doing the same thing. She accepted that explanation. A few days later I was working in my home office when a little head stuck itself around the corner of the doorway and a little voice asked, "Daddy, what's your tolerance level today?"*

4.6.2.2.11.2 Modifying the Selection Criteria   As Fred evaluates prospective mates he could change the values associated with the attributes of the criteria/variables in the utility curves. His first set of attributes was based on remembered experience. However when he meets other women he may find that the reality is different to the expected and something is not really as important as he thought it was or something might be more important. Should that happen he could adjust the values in the table and re-evaluate the result. That is why he should complete the entire evaluation for a candidate even if the candidate fails an essential criterion. In addition, Fred can also identify a new selection criterion while performing his search and add it to the MVA decision-making matrix. For example, when he met Lily he felt an immediate attraction that he did not feel when meeting any of the other candidates. Consequently, he could add an essential "felt attraction" or "chemistry" selection criteria with attributes of "yes" = 1, "no" = 0 and "perhaps" = 0.5 to the MVA decision-making matrix where a minimum score is 0.5. If he then decides to override his emotions and do the logical thing, if Lily does not meet the other essential selection criteria he will be faced with an interesting situation if he chooses to document the decision logically.

---

* Is that or is that not risk management? I burst out laughing and my tolerance level was high for the rest of the day.

4.6.3 Ordering and Ranking

Ordering and Ranking is:

1. A tool for Prioritization Section (4.6.6) that works as long as the scope of the ranking is limited to just the most and least important items.
2. Explained by means of the following example (Kasser and Williams 1998).

The data is provided in full because the results have ramifications on the way software is developed and projects are managed. These risk-indicators could form the basis for a project audit to identify and prevent problematic projects as a result of the flags raised by unfavourable CRIP Charts (Section 8.1) and ETL Charts (Section 8.16.2).

The formulated problem (Section 14.3) in 1997 was:

1. *The undesirable situation.* Given a set of 34 items identified as risk-indicators that could cause project failures there was a need to find out:
   a. If people agreed that those risk-indicators were indeed potential causes of project failures.
   b. To rank those people them in order of priority.
2. *Assumptions.* The assumptions were:
   a. The 34 risk-indicators had been identified by students in a post-graduate class on Independent Validation and Verification (IV&V) in 1997.
   b. The non-systems thinking ordering and ranking approach was the traditional approach, namely a survey which would ask the survey respondents to perform Pair-wise Comparison (PWC) on each of the 34 risk-indicators one pair at a time.
3. *The FCFDS*: the knowledge (i), that people agreed or disagreed that each of the items were risk-indicators, and (ii), the risk-indicators ranked in order of importance.
4. *The problem*: to create and perform a survey that would return a statistically significant sample.
5. *The solution* was creating and performing the survey which was not straight forward.

When viewing the survey from a Perspectives Perimeter (Chapter 10) based on the HTPs (Section 10.1):

- Perceptions from the *Operational* HTP indicated that since it took the problem owner just over an hour to perform the PWC, it was unlikely that many survey respondents would complete the ranking table in a thoughtful manner if they even tried to complete it.
- Perceptions from the *Quantitative* HTP produced this innovative alternative to PWC. The initial concept was to ask the survey respondents to rank all of the risk-indicators in order of priority using PWC. Yet was that the real need? Perceptions from the *Quantitative* HTP produced two key questions:
  1. "Do we need to know the ranking of **all** of the risk-indicators or are we only interested in the most and least important?" The answer was, "just the most and least important".
  2. "How many most and least important risk-indicators?" The answer invoked Miller's Rule (Section 3.2.5), resulting in the need to only identify the top and bottom seven risk-indicators in the rankings.

4.6.3.1 The Survey A survey questionnaire was constructed and sent to systems and software development personnel via the Internet. The survey asked respondents to:

1. State if they agreed or disagreed that the student provided risk-indicators were causes of project failure.*
2. List the top seven risk-indicators they thought were causes of project failures.
3. List the seven risk-indicators they thought contributed the least to project failures.
4. Write in an additional cause of project failure that was not on the list if they could think of one.

---

* The author recognized that there were other causes of (risks) project failure and added an "other" category to the survey questionnaire for "write-in" risks.

One hundred and forty-eight responses were received. The initial findings are summarized in Table 4.4. Not every survey respondent agreed or disagreed with every risk-indicator. In Table 4.4:

- The first column contains an identification number (ID) identifying the risk-indicator.
- The second column lists the name of the risk-indicator.
- The third column lists the number of students that identified the risk-indicator. The maximum number is 19 because 19 students provided information for the study.
- The fourth column contains the percentage of agreement from the survey.
- The fifth column contains the percentage of disagreement from the survey.
- The sixth column is the ranking of the risk-indicator by the number of agreements in the survey results where a 1 represents a high agreement that the risk-indicator is a contribution to project failure.

4.6.3.2 Survey Results   The survey results were surprising, especially for risk number 31. Total Quality Management (TQM) holds that the Quality Assurance Department is not responsible for the quality of the software; everybody shares that responsibility. Thus, while it was expected that most respondents would agree with this risk-indicator, only 40% of the respondents agreed and 60% disagreed. It was also anticipated that most respondents would agree with the other risk-indicators, yet the overall degree of agreement was:

- 0.7% (one respondent) agreed with all 34 risk-indicators.
- 8.1% agreed with at least 30 risk-indicators.
- 51% agreed with at least 20 risk-indicators.
- 93% agreed with at least 10 risk-indicators.

As for the degree of disagreement:

- 0.7% (one respondent) disagreed with 25 risk-indicators.
- 4.7% disagreed with at least 20 risk-indicators.
- 52% disagreed with at least 10 risk-indicators.
- 88% disagreed with at least one risk-indicator.

Table 4.4   Initial Survey Findings

RISK ID	RISK-INDICATORS	STUDENTS	SURVEY AGREE %	SURVEY DISAGREE %	RANK
1	Poor requirements	19	97	3	1
2	Failure to use experienced people	7	79	1	13
3	Failure to use IV&V[1]	6	38	62	31
4	Lack of process and standards	5	84	16	11
5	Lack of or poor plans	4	95	5	2
6	Failure to validate original specification and requirements	3	91	9	3
7	Lack of Configuration Management	3	66	34	19
8	Low morale	2	51	49	24
9	Management does not understand the System Development Lifecycle	2	59	41	22
10	Management that does not understand technical issues	2	56	44	23
11	No single person accountable/ responsible for project	2	69	31	18
12	Client and development staff fail to attend scheduled meetings	1	42	58	28
13	Coding from high level requirements without design	1	75	25	14
14	Documentation is not produced	1	63	38	21
15	Failure to collect performance & process metrics and report them to management	1	48	52	25
16	Failure to communicate with the customer	1	88	12	5
17	Failure to consider existing relationships when replacing systems	1	85	15	10
18	Failure to reuse code	1	27	73	34
19	Failure to stress test the software	1	75	25	15
20	Failure to use problem language	1	34	66	30
21	High staff turnover	1	71	29	16
22	Key activities are discontinued	1	74	26	17
23	Lack of a Requirements Traceability Matrix (RTM)	1	67	33	19
24	Lack of clearly defined organizational (responsibility and accountability) structure	1	82	18	11

(*Continued*)

Table 4.4 (Continued)   Initial Survey Findings

RISK ID	RISK-INDICATORS	STUDENTS	SURVEY AGREE %	SURVEY DISAGREE %	RANK
25	Lack of management support	1	87	13	6
26	Lack of priorities	1	85	15	8
27	Lack of understanding that demo software is only good for demos	1	47	53	26
28	Management expects a CASE Tool to be a silver bullet	1	45	55	27
29	Political considerations outweigh technical factors	1	86	14	9
30	Resources are not allocated well	1	92	8	4
31	The Quality Assurance Team is not responsible for the quality of the software	1	40	60	29
32	There are too many people working on the project	1	36	64	32
33	Unrealistic deadlines – hence schedule slips	1	86	14	7
34	Hostility between developer and IV&V	1	33	67	33

4.6.3.3 Further Analysis The top seven (high priority) risk-indicators were identified using the following approaches:

1. *The Tally*, discussed in Section 4.6.3.3.1.
2. *The Priorities*, discussed in Section 4.6.3.3.2
3. *The Top Seven*, discussed in Section 4.6.3.3.3.

4.6.3.3.1 The Tally An "agree" was allocated a value of +1, a "disagree" a value of -1. The answers to each survey statement were then tallied. The seven risk-indicators that received the highest positive values (most agreement) as causes of project failure are shown in Table 4.5.

Table 4.5 Top Seven Causes of Project Failures (Tally)

RISK	RISK-INDICATOR	RESPONSES
1	Poor requirements	134
5	Lack of or poor plans	125
6	Failure to validate original specification and requirements	113
30	Resources are not allocated well	109
16	Failure to communicate with the customer	106
25	Lack of management support	98
33	Unrealistic deadlines – hence schedule slips	97

4.6.3.3.2 The Priorities The survey asked respondents to rank the top seven risk-indicators in order of priority. The weighted results are shown in Table 4.6 (top priority first):

4.6.3.3.3 The Top Seven Since the actual position may be subjective, the number of times a risk-indicator showed up in any position in the top seven priority list was also counted. The results for the top seven items are as shown in Table 4.7. The results show a high degree of consensus on these risk-indicators as causes of project failures.

4.6.3.4 Sensitivity Analysis on Project Management Risk-Indicators The sample size for respondents without management experience was 99. The raw tallies for the risk-indicators associated with project management shown in Table 4.8 were examined to see if there was a difference between non-managers and managers with various years of experience. No differences of more than 10% were noted.

Table 4.6 Priority Causes of Project Failure

RISK	RISK-INDICATOR	WEIGHT
1	Poor requirements	864
16	Failure to communicate with the customer	683
5	Lack of or poor plans	574
4	Lack of process and standards	361
25	Lack of management support	350
6	Failure to validate original specification and requirements	329
29	Political considerations outweigh technical factors	304

Table 4.7 Top Seven Causes

RISK	RISK-INDICATOR	COUNT
1	Poor requirements	99
16	Failure to communicate with the customer	86
5	Lack of or poor plans	77
4	Lack of process and standards	51
25	Lack of management support	51
29	Political considerations outweigh technical factors	45
6	Failure to validate original specification and requirements	44

Table 4.8   Project Management Related Risk-Indicators

RISK	RISK-INDICATOR
5	Lack of or poor plans
8	Low morale
15	Failure to collect performance and process metrics and report them to management
25	Lack of management support
27	Lack of understanding that demo software is only good for demos
29	Political considerations outweigh technical factors
32	There are too many people working on the project
33	Unrealistic deadlines – hence schedule slips

4.6.3.5 The "Other" Category   The "other" category was added to perform risk management and avoid Simpson's paradox (Section 10.1.5.6.12). Several respondents added one or two additional risk-indicators in the "other" category of the questionnaire. These were:

- Failure to control change.
- Rapid rate of change of technology.
- Low bidding.
- Poor management.
- Lack of a technical leader.

Thus, the small student sample size of 19 seems to have identified most of the important risk-indicators. However, applying some Critical Thinking, the question remains as to what these items would have scored had they been in a list of 39 risk-indicators. This is why the survey results needed validating by comparison with an independent similar study (Section 4.6.3.8).

4.6.3.6 The Risk-Indicators with Most Disagreements   Part of the analysis of the survey results was to determine which risk-indicators received the most disagreement as well as the least agreement as causes of project failure (*Continuum* HTP). This was to validate the results by ensuring that the same risk-indicator did not show up in the top seven agreements as well as in the top seven disagreements and was done by determining the:

- Most disagreements by the recipients.
- Least agreements by the recipients.

The risk-indicators receiving the most disagreements are shown in Table 4.9.

Table 4.9 Risk Indicators with Most Disagreements

RISK	RISK-INDICATOR	RESPONSES
18	Failure to reuse code	88
3	Failure to use IV&V	80
32	There are too many people working on the project	75
12	Client and development staff fail to attend scheduled meetings	74
34	Hostility between developer and IV&V	70
31	The Quality Assurance Team is not responsible for the quality of the software	68
15	Failure to collect performance & process metrics and report them to management	67

4.6.3.7 The Risk-Indicators Receiving Least Agreement The risk-indicators receiving the least agreement as causes of project failure are shown in Table 4.10.

The seven risk-indicators receiving the least agreement as causes of project failure showing up in Table 4.9 and Table 4.10 were:

1. *Failure to reuse code*: a major advantage of the object-oriented approach is said to be the ability to lower costs by reusing code. Yet 73% of those surveyed did not agree with this risk-indicator.
2. *Hostility between developer and IV&V*: this risk-indicator shows a team problem and results in less than optimal costs due to the lack of cooperation.
3. *There are too many people working on the project*: this risk-indicator is based on the mythical man-month (Brooks 1982) which describes the problems associated with assigning additional people to projects.

Table 4.10 Risk Indicators with Least Agreements

RISK	RISK-INDICATOR	RESPONSES
20	Failure to use problem language	30
18	Failure to reuse code	32
34	Hostility between developer and IV&V	34
32	There are too many people working on the project	43
31	The Quality Assurance Team is not responsible for the quality of the software	45
3	Failure to use Independent Verification and Validation (IV&V)	49
28	Management expects a CASE Tool to be a silver bullet	53
12	Client and development staff fail to attend scheduled meetings	54
27	Lack of understanding that demo software is only good for demos	55

4. *Failure to use problem language*: the use of problem language was promoted as one of the major advantages by Ward and Mellor published ten years before the survey (Ward and Mellor 1985). Yet, only 34% of the respondents agreed that it was a risk-indicator. Several did not know what the term meant.

5. *The quality assurance team is not responsible for the quality of the software*: as discussed above, this was the only risk-indicator that should have shown agreement, not disagreement.

6. *Client and development staff fail to attend scheduled meetings*: this is a symptom of poor communication between the client and the developer. In addition, while there are other communication techniques available, if meetings are scheduled, and not attended, negative messages are sent to the project personnel.

7. *Failure to collect performance and process metrics and report them to management*: if measurements are not made and acted upon, how does management know what is going on and can the process be improved? Yet 52% of the respondents disagreed that this was a risk-indicator!

4.6.3.8 Validating the Survey Results The approach used to validate the survey results was to use the Chaos study as a reference (CHAOS 1995). The study had recently (at that time) identified a number of major contributors to project failure. Five risk-indicators in this study that were chosen as the most important causes for project failure also appear on the Chaos list of major reasons for project failure. The correlation between the findings of this study and the Chaos study is shown in Table 4.11. While "resources are not allocated well" did not show up in the top seven lists of this study, it was fourth in the tally. "Changing requirements and specifications" which showed up in the Chaos study as a contributor to project failure was not identified by the students as such but was written in to the survey results as an "other" by a few of the respondents.* Thus, the findings of this study support the findings of the Chaos study.

---

* Which brings us back to the question posed in Section 4.6.3.5.

Table 4.11 Comparison of Results with Chaos Study

RISK	THIS STUDY	CHAOS STUDY
1	Poor requirements	Incomplete requirements
16	Failure to communicate with the customer	Lack of user involvement
30	Resources are not allocated well	Lack of resources
–	No equivalent	Unrealistic expectations
25	Lack of management support	Lack of executive management support
–	No equivalent	Changing requirements and specifications
5	Lack of or poor plans	Lack of planning

4.6.4 Pair-Wise Comparison

The Pair-wise Comparison (PWC) technique is a decision-making tool recommended in the literature when the decision has to be made from a large number of choices. PWC can be used on its own, and is used as a part of Interpretive Structural Modelling (ISM) (Warfield 1976) and Analytical Hierarchy Process (AHP) (Saaty 1980). The assumptions behind PWC include:

- In general, while people have difficulty selecting between large numbers of options, they can choose between two alternatives.
- Each decision is being made under conditions of certainty where the preference is for either one of the alternatives or the other.
- The preference is based on selection criteria that may or may not be defined, namely can be subjective or objective.

4.6.4.1 The PWC Process The process for making a decision using PWC is as follows.

1. Create a matrix table in a spreadsheet with the options listed in both the rows and the columns. If the matrix is large, label the columns with the row numbers rather than the text just like in an N^2 chart (Section 2.10).
2. Block out the cell common to each row and column with a "-" since there is no point in comparing an option with itself.
3. Block out the lower half of the table, it is because the choices in it duplicate the top half but in reverse and would cancel out.

4. Add one row below the list of choices. This additional row will contain the total number of 0s in the column after the table has been completed so label it "number of 0s".

5. Add four columns following the list of choices and label the additional columns as:

   a. *1s*: these cells will contain the total number of 1s in the row for that option as explained below.

   b. *0s*: these cells will contain the total number of 0s for that option transposed from the column count as explained below.

   c. *Total*: these cells will contain the sum of the 1s and 0s columns as explained below.

   d. *Rank*: these cells contain the ranking of the option in the totals. If a spreadsheet is used, then the cells would contain the formula for the ranking function.

6. At this point in the process, the table should look like Table 4.12.

7. Starting with row 1, column 1,

   a. For each decision in the row, figure out the preference.

   b. If the row option is preferred to the column option, place a "1" in that square else place a "0" in the square and move on to the next decision square in the row.

   c. Make the decision for the alternatives in the square.

   d. After the last decision in the row is made, move down to the start of the next row.

8. Once the decisions part of the table is completed the decisions are processed as follows:

   a. Add together the number of 1s in each row and store the result in the corresponding cells in the column labelled "1"s.

Table 4.12   PWC Matrix for Decision Between Five Choices

	1	2	3	4	5	1S	0S	TOTAL	RANK
1	–								
2	–	–							
3	–	–	–						
4	–	–	–	–					
5	–	–	–	–	–				
0s in Rows									

b. Add together the number of 0s in each column and store the result in the corresponding cells in the row marked "0"s in Rows.

c. Transpose the values in the "0"s in the Rows row into a 0s column located next to the column labelled 1s.

9. The last step is to add up the values in the 1s and 0s columns and store the combined value in the column labelled "Total".

The row with the highest number in the "Total" column represents the decision.

4.6.4.2 Using PWC to Make a Decision Fred used a Decision Tree to make a decision as to which mode of transportation to use to return home from class in Section 4.6.1. Consider how he could have used PWC to make the same decisions. So using PWC for the sunny day situation, Fred compares the choice between taxi (row) and bus (column).

- The preference is for a bus so the common cell gets 0.
- Moving along the row, the preference between taxi and subway is subway so the common cell gets 0.
- Moving along the row, the preference between taxi and walking is walking so the common cell gets 0.
- Moving along the row, the preference between taxi and getting a ride is taxi so the common cell gets 1.
- Fred then moves down to the next row and compares the preferences for the bus with the remaining options in that row, and so on down the rows.

Fred ends up with the table shown in Table 4.13. In this instance, the Walk option received a 4 so it is the preferred choice. The decisions

Table 4.13 PWC Matrix for Decision on a Sunny Day

	TAXI	BUS	SUBWAY	WALK	RIDE	1S	0S	TOTAL	RANK
Taxi	–	0	0	0	1	1	0	1	4
Bus	–	–	1	0	1	2	1	3	3
Subway	–	–	–	0	1	1	1	2	2
Walk	–	–	–	–	1	1	3	4	1
Get a ride	–	–	–	–	–	0	0	0	5
0s in Rows	0	1	1	3	0				

Table 4.14   PWC Matrix for Decision on a Rainy Day

	TAXI	BUS	SUBWAY	WALK	RIDE	1S	0S	TOTAL	RANK
Taxi	–	1	1	1	1	4	0	4	1
Bus	–	–	1	1	1	3	0	3	2
Subway	–	–	–	1	1	2	0	2	3
Walk	–	–	–	–	1	1	0	1	4
Get a ride	–	–	–	–	–	0	0	0	5
0s in Rows	0	0	0	0	0				

would be different on a rainy day where the preference is for the taxi as shown in Table 4.14.

4.6.4.3 The Downside of PWC

PWC:

- Is fine in theory and when the number of factors involved in the decision is small.
- Assumes there is a preference between each pair, when in some situations there is no preference.
- Takes too long when the number of factors is large.*

Consider the following situation discussed in Section 4.6.3. A survey was designed to determine if the respondents agreed or disagreed with the hypothesis that each of 34 different risk-indicators was a contributor to project failure. However, we also wanted to know the relative importance or ranking of the risk-indicators. Asking for a "yes/no" agreement was simple but would not provide a ranking. A Lickert scale would be more subjective,† more complicated and complex and not produce a ranking. If we were to follow the standard process and apply the traditional approach to ranking 34 items, we would have had to ask the respondents to perform a PWC on all 34 items. The PWC approach was scoped by taking the time to complete a full sized PWC matrix which took just over an hour. Consequently, it was felt that while the full sized matrix would provide lots of information, few respondents would actually take the time to perform the PWC so it was time to rethink or redefine (dissolve) or reformulate the problem.

---

* Which is exactly the situation it was designed for.
† The whole survey was subjective anyhow.

The key question was, "Do we really need to know the ranking of all 34 items?", or, "Do we just need to know the most important?" The answer from the *Quantitative* HTP was that we just needed to know the most important. This reformulation or re-scoping of the problem allowed us to forget PWC and use a simpler Ordering and Ranking tool (Section 4.6.3). This is an example of scoping the problem. In facing similar situations, use the *Quantitative* HTP to perceive the situation and understand the need. Ask the stakeholders, the following two questions:

1. The key question from the previous paragraph, "Do we really need to know the ranking of all 34 items?", or, "Do we just need to know the most important?"
2. "Do we need the PWC approach given that it does not allow for no-preference situations and the sample size is limited?"

Depending on the answers you may also be able to use the simpler Ordering and Ranking tool (Section 4.6.3), the Perfect Score Approach (Section 4.6.5), the Pugh Matrix (Section 4.6.7), Interpretive Structural Modelling (ISM) (Warfield 1976) or Analytical Hierarchy Process (AHP) (Saaty 1980).

4.6.5 The Perfect Score Approach

The Perfect Score Approach is a variation of MVA. The advantages of the Perfect Score Approach include:

- It can be used when there are more than a few alternatives. In this situation there were 12 alternatives.
- It can be used when the stakeholders are geographically distributed and cannot attend a meeting. Its first successful use was at the NASA Goddard Space Flight Center (Kasser and Mirchandani 2005).
- It helps with getting the stakeholders involved in the choice so that they buy into the result. We met with the stakeholders and discussed the options and the criteria several times during the course of establishing the requirements for the system. The stakeholders were satisfied with the decision and accepted the decision without any further comment or discussion.

The disadvantages of the Perfect Score Approach include:

- The stakeholders get to make three evaluations in series over a time span of several days, instead of settling the matter in a single meeting.

The Perfect Score Approach process is as follows:

1. Determine the alternatives. This can be done by discussing the situation with the stakeholders.
2. Determine the selection criteria.
3. Rank the criteria in absolute order of importance on a scale of 1 to 10. The ranking can be done by providing all the stakeholders with a survey and asking them to complete the form.
4. For each criterion, add up the values from each stakeholder and divide by the number of stakeholders.
5. If there are more than nine selection criteria, remove the least important.
6. Rank the remaining criteria on their relative importance also on a scale of 1 to 10. The relative ranking can be done by providing all the stakeholders with a PWC table and asking them complete it. Since there are nine or less items in the table, it should not take them too long.
7. For each criterion add up the values from each stakeholder and divide by the number of stakeholders.
8. Add together the absolute order of importance values and the relative importance numbers for each criterion.*
9. The result is the perfect score for each alternative choice.
10. Create the Perfect Score Approach table.
11. Evaluate each alternative against the perfect score for each selection criterion. This can be done by passing the table to each stakeholder and averaging the results as before. The completed table will look something like Table 4.15.

Table 4.15 contains some interesting information including:

- The absolute and relative columns are not linear and some criteria have equal values. This is because they contain the averages of the stakeholder survey responses. For example,

---

* Multiplying them will produce larger numbers but will not change the result.

Table 4.15   A Perfect Score Approach Matrix

CRITERIA	RELATIVE	ABSOLUTE	PERFECT SCORE	ALTERNATIVES											
				1	2	3	4	5A	5B	6	7	8	9	10	11
A	7	10	17	3	9	2	17	17	1	5	5	14	0	10	11
B	6	9	15	3	8	6	15	15	14	14	14	15	15	17	17
C	5	8	12	1	6	1	12	12	11	10	10	12	0	15	15
D	4	8	12	12	12	12	12	12	12	12	12	12	12	12	12
E	4	7	12	12	12	12	12	12	12	12	12	11	10	12	12
F	4	7	11	9	11	10	6	10	10	8	8	8	8	8	10
G	4	5	9	9	8	6	9	9	9	9	9	9	9	1	9
H	3	5	8	6	3	5	1	8	8	6	5	5	6	4	5
Total			96	55	69	54	84	95	77	76	75	86	60	79	91

Criterion A did not score a perfect 8 in relative order of importance, showing lack of consensus, but did score a 10 on absolute order of importance showing consensus.

- The consensus and lack of consensus can clearly be seen where some rows have almost the same numbers and others have very different numbers in the corresponding columns.
- Alternatives 5a and 5b were two variations of a single alternative, yet received very different scores.

4.6.6 Prioritization

Prioritization is a decision-making tool for determining which of the items on a list to deal with and which items to ignore. The basic concept is to deal with the items that have the highest priority, then deal with the items with the next highest priority and so on down the list until resources have been exhausted. These limited resources include:

- *Time*: there may be a limited amount of time to deal with the items.
- *Money*: they might not be enough money to deal with or provide every item on the list.
- *People*: there may not be enough people to deal with the items on the list.

The key part of prioritization is to prioritize the items. When the number of items is small it is relatively easy. Where the number of items is large, it is more difficult. Accordingly, a number of tools been developed to prioritize large numbers of items. The tools can be sorted into two types, rank every item on the list by priority, or just select those with the highest priority. So when faced with the problem of prioritising a list, the first question that needs to be answered is, "Do we need to prioritize the whole list, or are we just concerned with the most important?" The answer will tell us which of the types of prioritization tools to choose, such as:

1. Decision Trees discussed in Section 4.6.1.
2. MVA discussed in Section 4.6.2.
3. Ordering and Ranking discussed in Section 4.6.3.
4. PWC discussed in Section 4.6.4.
5. The Pugh Matrix discussed in Section 4.6.7.

Perceptions from the *Continuum* HTP point out that there is a difference between important and urgent (Covey 1989) where:

- *Urgent*: means of something requires immediate attention. We react to urgent events of having little choice but to perform the activity to attend to the urgent item.
- *Important*: has to do with results, something is important if it contributes to high priority goals. We often have a choice as to when to perform the activity.

Perceptions from the *Temporal* HTP point out that priorities can change depending on circumstances and a priority list needs to be evaluated periodical. The preparation activities for major and minor milestone reviews in a project (Section 14.9.2) should include re-evaluation of priorities, the updated list of priorities and reason for any change to be included in the milestone document documentation.

4.6.7 The Pugh Matrix

The Pugh Matrix (Pugh 1992):

- Is a cross between MVA (Section 4.6.2) and PWC (Section 4.6.4).
- Was developed by Stuart Pugh, who was a professor and head of the design division at the University of Strathclyde in Glasgow.
- Is a weighted decision matrix in which the criteria are weighted in order of importance where the more important the criteria the higher the weighting.
- Is used to select a single best option from several options in a situation in which there is insufficient resources to select more than one option.
- Is used to evaluate various alternatives against a baseline. For example, evaluating potential alternatives to an existing product or process.
- Is used to select the best of several alternatives, when none of the alternatives can meet the full specification.
- Is used in new product development to decide which features to include in a product

The matrix is constructed with the criteria in the rows and the baseline and alternatives in the columns as shown in Table 4.16 for selecting between three options and used in the following manner.

1. The number of selection criteria is reduced to the essential or must have criteria leaving out the optional criteria to simplify the table.
2. Create the matrix for the remaining criteria and options as in the format shown in Table 4.16.
3. Evaluate the baseline against the criteria.
4. The first alternative is evaluated against the baseline. When the alternative is
   - Better, it gets a +1.
   - The same it gets a 0 (and sometimes an "S" for same).
   - Worse it gets a –1.
5. The remaining alternatives are evaluated against the baseline in the same way and the table completed. There is no need to total the unweighted columns.
6. Each criterion is then weighted.
7. The individual evaluations are then multiplied by the weighting factor for the selection criteria.
8. Sum the weightings for each alternative (column).
9. The option with the highest weighted evaluation is the preferred choice.

Table 4.16 looks very similar to Table 4.1. Unlike PWC in which each candidate is assessed against all of the others, the comparisons in the Pugh Matrix are made against a single baseline or preselected target candidate. From the *Continuum* HTP, the evaluation against a single baseline or preselected target candidate opens up the evaluation to misrepresentation because it is equivalent to a single line in the PWC matrix and judicious pre-selection of the baseline can influence the result.

4.6.8 Screening, Reducing or Preselecting the Criteria

The previous examples have contained a reasonable number of selection criteria. In a situation where there are a large number of selection criteria, smart thinkers determine the importance the criteria

Table 4.16 Empty Example of a Pugh Matrix

CRITERIA						WEIGHTED		
	BASELINE	OPTION1	OPTION 2	OPTION 3	WEIGHTING	OPTION1	OPTION 2	OPTION 3
Criterion 1								
Criterion 2								
Criterion 3								
Criterion 4								
Criterion 5								
Criterion 6								
Totals								

first using Ordering and Ranking (Section 4.6.3), and then apply the Pareto principle (Section 2.11) and use the most important ones similar to the reduction in the Pugh Matrix (Section 4.6.7). If this reduction gives rise to a situation where the decision isn't clear, then one or two additional criteria, namely the next in importance, should be added to the matrix and the decision should be re-evaluated. Fred failed to remove the optional selection criteria when he was trying to select his perfect mate (Section 4.6.2.2). He was probably too emotionally involved to think clearly about his actions.

4.7 Class Exercise

Using the information in Table 4.3, select any one candidate as the baseline and convert the information in the table into to a Pugh Matrix (Section 4.6.7). Discuss the results using Critical Thinking (Chapter 3).

4.8 Summary

Chapter 4 discussed decision-making, a critical part of the problem-solving process. This chapter began by discussing qualitative and quantitative decision-making, decision traps that produce bad decisions, decision outcomes, and how to avoid unanticipated consequences, as well as sources of those unanticipated consequence. This chapter then discussed the four key elements of decision-making and provided some anecdotal examples. The major part of this chapter discussed seven decision-making tools. Three of the tools are well-known: Decision Trees, MVA and PWC. The Pugh Matrix is a cross between MVA and PWC but can also be misused to bias the decision. After discussing Prioritization, this chapter showed how the other tools can be used to perform Prioritization. Lastly, this chapter introduced the Perfect Score Approach; an original tool first used at the NASA GSFC that works very well when there is a plurality of opinions among the stakeholders and can also be successfully used when geographically separated stakeholders need to be involved in the decision.

References

Ackoff, R. L., and H. J. Addison. 2006. *A Little Book of f-Laws: 13 Common Sins of Management*. Axminster: Triarchy Press Limited.

Bega, L. 1999. "Mambo Number 5". In *A Little Bit of Mambo*. RCA.

Brooks, F. 1982. *The Mythical Man-Month Essays on Software Engineering*. Reprinted with corrections. Reading, Mass: Addison-Wesley Publishing Company.

CHAOS. 1995. *The Chaos Study*. The Standish Group, accessed March 19, 1998. http://www.standishgroup.com/chaos.html.

Covey, S. R. 1989. *The Seven Habits of Highly Effective People*. New York: Simon & Schuster.

Howard, R. A. 1973. "Decision Analysis in Systems Engineering." In *Systems Concepts*, edited by R.F. Miles Jr., pp. 51–85. New York: John Wiley & Son, Inc.

Kasser, J. E., and C. J. Mirchandani. 2005. "The MSOCC Data Switch Replacement: A Case Study in Elicitating and Elucidating Requirements." In the 15th International Symposium of the International Council on Systems Engineering (INCOSE). Rochester, NY.

Kasser, J. E., and V. R. Williams. 1998. "What Do You Mean You Can't Tell Me if My Project Is in Trouble?" In First European Conference on Software Metrics (FESMA 98). Antwerp, Belgium.

Merton, R. K. 1936. "The Unanticipated Consequences of Social Action." *American Sociological Review* no. 1 (6):894–904.

Merton, R. K. 1948. "The Self-Fulfilling Prophecy." *The Antioch Review*, no. 8 (2):193–210.

Pugh, S. 1992. *Total Design: Integrated Methods for Successful Product Engineering*. Harlow, Essex, England: Pearson Education Ltd.

Russo, J. E., and P. H. Schoemaker. 1989. *Decision Traps*. New York: Simon and Schuster.

Saaty, T. 1980. *The Analytic Hierarchy Process*. New York: McGraw Hill.

Ward, P. T., and S. J. Mellor. 1985. *Structured Development for Real-Time Systems*. Englewood Cliffs, N. J.: Yourdon Press Computing Series. Yourdon Press.

Warfield, J. N. 1976. *Societal Systems: Planning, Policy and Complexity*. New York: John Wiley & Sons, Inc.

5
FRAMEWORKS

In this book, frameworks are tables used as tools that illustrate where and how things fit together. This chapter discusses the following frameworks:

1. The 2x2 format generic framework in Section 5.1.
2. The Hitchins-Kasser-Massie Framework (HKMF) in Section 5.2.
3. The Problem Classification Framework in Section 5.3.
4. The Risk Rectangle in Section 5.4.

5.1 The 2x2 Format Generic Framework

The 2x2 format is a widely used framework format which presents a framework or table consisting of two rows and two columns that form the axis of an X-Y chart (Section 2.16) and then plots information in that framework instead of a graph. The 2x2 framework consists of two items each having two subitems. One example of the use of the 2x2 framework is as follows. A researcher notices that in society some people are homosexual and others are heterosexual, and might develop a theory to provide a reason as to why some people are homosexual and others are heterosexual. The theory uses an observation, an assumption, and an inference.

1. *Observation:* there are male and female bodies.
2. *Assumption:* bodies contain souls about which theologians speculate.
3. *Inference:* just as there are male and female bodies (*Generic* HTP); there are male and female souls (Inference from the *Scientific* HTP).

		Soul	
		Male	Female
Body	Male	Heterosexual	Homosexual
	Female	Homosexual	Heterosexual

Figure 5.1 Match (and mismatch) of souls to bodies.

The researcher develops the 2x2 matrix shown in Figure 5.1. The zero line is at the change between male and female, the axes then extend out to positive and negative values. The theory postulates that:

- A homosexual male person is one where the body is male and the soul is female. The degree of homosexuality will depend on how far along each axis that person is positioned.
- A heterosexual person is where the body is one sex, and the soul is of the same sex.
- A bisexual person is one where the body and soul are at the centre of the table.
- A heterosexual woman is one where the body is female and the soul is female. A strictly heterosexual woman has a female body and a female soul at the end of each axis. A homosexual male is the reverse.

Of course at the present time, you'd have to wait until the afterlife to test the theory.

Another example of the 2x2 matrix in this book is the SWOT table (Section 14.2.1).

5.2 The Hitchins-Kasser-Massie Framework

The Hitchins-Kasser-Massie Framework (HKMF) (Kasser and Massie 2001) is:

- A tool for locating boxes used in the process for finding out-of-the-box solutions (Section 11.6).
- A tool for discussing various aspects associated with workflows.
- Shown in Figure 5.2.*

---

* Based on a format created by Dr Xuan Linh Tran.

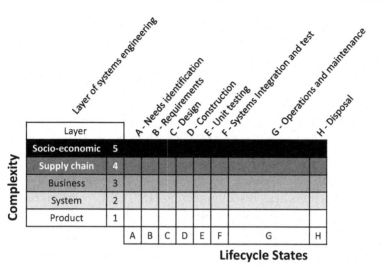

Figure 5.2 The HKMF for understanding systems engineering.

- Is not a process model. While the horizontal axis corresponds to the states on the Waterfall Chart (Section 14.9) representation of the System Lifecycle (SLC), projects may not pass through the areas in a linear sequence.

The HKMF was developed when trying to determine the requirements for what should be taught in postgraduate systems engineering coursework at the SEEC. The research attempted to develop a Systems Engineering Body of Knowledge (SEBOK) based on the role of the systems engineers in the different states of the SLC and in the different Hitchins' layer (Hitchins 2000). In its early days, the framework has:

- Provided one of the reasons why systems engineers can't agree on the nature of systems engineering.
- Identified the "A" and "B" paradigms in systems engineering (Kasser 2012b).
- Identified that systems engineers operating in one layer use a different vocabulary to those operating in another layer. For example, the term "capability" has different meanings in Layers 1 and 3.

- The multitude of definitions of systems engineering; some of which are based on internal perspectives from the different areas of the HKMF.
- Identified that systems engineers perform different functions in the different areas of the HKMF.
- Facilitated traceability of requirements; requirements on a system in Layer 2 can be traced back to the undesirable socio-economic situation in a higher layer.
- Shown that systems engineering, at least the International Council on Systems Engineering (INCOSE) version, resides in Layer 2 while Operations Research resides in Layer 3, mainly in area 3G.
- Systems engineering when performed in Layer 5 is known as political science.

The two dimensions of the framework plot the system or product layer of complexity and process (lifecycle) state on different axes where:

1. *The vertical or product axis* is the five layers of systems engineering (Hitchins 2000) in accordance with the Principle of Hierarchies (Section 3.2.7). Hitchins proposed the following five-layer model for systems engineering (Hitchins 2000) where:
   - *Layer 5 is socioeconomic:* the layer of regulation and government control.
   - *Layer 4 is industrial systems engineering or engineering of complete supply chains/circles:* many industries make a socio-economic system. A global wealth creation philosophy.
   - *Layer 3 is business systems engineering:* many businesses make an industry. At this level, systems engineering seeks to optimize performance somewhat independent of other businesses.
   - *Layer 2 is project or system level:* many projects make a business. Western engineer-managers operate at this level, principally making complex artefacts.
   - *Layer 1 is the product level:* many products (subsystems) make a system; the tangible artefact level.

- This model can be extended downwards to add:
- *Layer 0:* the component layer where many components make a product.
- *Layer –1:* the parts level where many parts make a component.

2. *The horizontal or timeline axis* is the states in the SLC. Perceptions from the *Continuum* and *Quantitative* HTPs identified nine different states of the SLC. While these states have been stated in various ways in the literature, they are defined in generic terms in Section 14.9.1.

The out-of-the-box idea for the HKMF came from the *Generic* HTP (the chemistry box). Mendeleev published a framework based on increasing atomic weight in 1869; the Periodic Table of Elements, and populated it with the known elements, leaving gaps which represented then unknown elements. In a similar manner, the HKMF forms a framework for studying activities in the workplace in the different layers and states of the SLC.

The HKMF provides:

1. A set of boxes to search in a systemic and systematic manner to find an out-of-the-box solution to a problem (Section 11.6).
2. An anchor point, page or viewpoint when thinking about and discussing activities in the workplace.

5.3 A Problem Classification Framework

This framework for classifying problems (Kasser 2012a) shown in Figure 5.3 is a tool:

- To assist on deciding which strategy to use to find a remedy for a complex problem
- Based on distinguishing between subjective and objective complexity (*Continuum* HTP) where the axes are:
  - *Level of difficulty:* (subjective complexity) discussed in Section 5.3.1.
  - *Structure of the problem:* (objective complexity) discussed in Section 5.3.2.

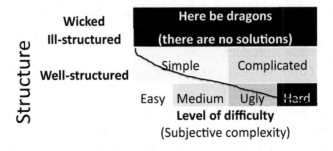

Figure 5.3   A Problem Classification Framework.

5.3.1 The Four Levels of Difficulty of the Problem

The level of difficulty of a problem is subjective.* Ford introduced four categories of increasing order of difficulty for well-structured mathematics and science problems: easy, medium, ugly, and hard (Ford 2010). These categories may be generalized and defined as follows:

1. *Easy problems:* which can be solved in a short time with very little thought.
2. *Medium problems:* which can be solved after some thought, may take a few more steps to solve than an easy problem and can probably be solved without too much difficulty, perhaps after some practice.
3. *Ugly problems:* which will take a while to solve. Solving them involves a lot of thought, many steps and may require the use of several different concepts.
4. *Hard problems:* which usually involve dealing with one or more unknowns. Solving them involves a lot of thought and some research and may also require iteration through the problem-solving process as learning takes place (as knowledge that was previously unknown becomes known).

Note how the learning curve maps into Figure 5.3. The curve shown in the figure is at the zero of the horizontal axis of the table when the problem is hard. As the learning increases, the problem moves towards the zero on the vertical axis, namely the problem becomes easy.

---

* A problem that is easy for one person to solve may be a difficult problem for someone else.

Classifying problems by level of difficulty is difficult in itself because difficulty is subjective since one person's easy problem may be another person's medium, ugly, or hard problem. For example, consider an undesirable situation faced by Fred who arrives in a foreign country for a visit and lodges in an apartment where he has to do his own cooking. As Fred cannot speak the local language, he is in a number of undesirable situations. Consider the one in which the kitchen has a gas cooker, but he has no way to ignite the gas. The corresponding FCFDS is that Fred has something to ignite the gas.* Assuming Fred has local currency or an acceptable credit card, is the difficulty of the problem of purchasing something that will ignite the gas easy, hard, or something in between? The answer is "it depends". Classifying the difficulty of the problem depends on a number of issues including:

- If Fred has faced this problem before in the same country? If so, what did he do then?
- If Fred knows where to purchase matches or a gas lighter.
- If Fred even knows how to say "matches" or "gas lighter" in the local language. If he does not know the words, he may not be able to ask anyone to provide the items.

Thus as far as Fred is concerned, the problem is:

- *None existent*: if Fred already has matches, a gas lighter, a cigarette lighter or another instrument with which to light the gas.
- *Easy*: if Fred knows where to purchase matches or a gas lighter and knows the local words.
- *Medium*: if Fred knows where to purchase matches or a gas lighter and does not know the local words. After all, he can go to the store or relevant location and look around until he sees matches or lighters on a shelf and then purchase them.
- *Hard*: if Fred does not know where to purchase matches or a gas lighter and does not know the local words. The problem is hard because two unknowns have to become knowns for a solution to be realized.

---

* Note the use of functional language instead of "matches" in solution language.

5.3.2 The Structure of the Problem

Perceived from the *Continuum* HTP, problems lie on a continuum which ranges from [1] "well-structured" through [2] "ill-structured" to [3] "wicked" as shown in Figure 5.3 where the solution to each type of structured problem is achieved by a different version of the problem-solving process. Consider each of them.

5.3.2.1 Well-Structured Problems Well-Structured Problems are problems where the existing undesirable situation and the FCFDS are clearly identified. These problems may have a single solution or sometimes more than one acceptable solution. Examples of Well-Structured Problems with single correct solutions are:

- Mathematics and other problems posed by teachers to students in the classroom. For example, in mathematics, $1 + 1 = 2$ every time.
- Making a choice between two options. For example, choosing between drinking a cup of coffee and drinking a cup of tea. However, the answer may be different each time the problem is faced.

Examples of Well-Structured Problems with several acceptable but different solutions are:

- What brand of coffee to purchase? Although the solution may depend on price, taste, and other selection criteria, there may be more than one brand (solution) that meets all the criteria.
- Which brand of automated coffee maker to purchase?
- What to have for dinner this evening?
- What type of transportation capability to acquire?
- Finding the cheapest airfare between Singapore and Jacksonville, Florida. If two airlines charge the same fare, each would be an acceptable solution if there were no other selection criteria such as the time for the journey.

Well-Structured Problems with single solutions tend to be posed as closed questions, while Well-Structured Problems with multiple acceptable solutions tend to be posed as open questions.

5.3.2.2 Ill-Structured Problems Ill-Structured Problems, sometimes called "ill-defined" problems or "messy problems"* (Ackoff 1974), are problems where either or both the existing undesirable situation and the FCFDS are unclear (Jonassen 1997). Examples of ill-structured complex problems are:

- The initial feeling that something is wrong and needs to be changed which triggers the problem-solving process.
- Where to dispose of nuclear waste safely? This is where the FCFDS is unclear.
- How to combat international terrorism? This is where different stakeholders perceive different causes of the situation and different ways of dealing with the causes.

5.3.2.3 Wicked Problems Wicked Problems are extremely Ill-Structured Problems[†] first stated in the context of social policy planning (Rittel and Webber 1973). Wicked Problems (Shum 1996):

- Cannot be easily defined so that all stakeholders cannot agree on the problem to solve.
- Require complex judgements about the level of abstraction at which to define the problem.
- Have no clear stopping rules (since there is no definitive "problem", there is also no definitive "solution" and the problem-solving process ends when the resources, such as time, money, or energy, are consumed, not when some solution emerges).
- Have better or worse solutions, not right and wrong ones.
- Have no objective measure of success.
- Require iteration – every trial counts.
- Have no given alternative solutions – these must be discovered.
- Often have strong moral, political, or professional dimensions.

---

* When complex.
[†] Technically there is no problem since, while the stakeholders may agree that the situation is undesirable, they cannot agree on the problem.

5.3.3 Positioning Problems in the Matrix

Different people may position the same problem in different places in the framework. This is because as knowledge is gained from research, education, and experience a person can reclassify the subjective difficulty of a problem down the subjectivity continuum from "hard" towards "easy". Note how the learning curve maps into Figure 5.3.

In the systems approach, there are no solutions to Ill-Structured Problems (Simon 1973) and Wicked Problems; they must be converted to one or more Well-Structured Problems before the remedial part of the problem-solving process can begin.

5.4 The Risk Rectangle

The Risk Rectangle:

- Is a tool for deciding which risks should be mitigated.
- Is a framework. The Y or vertical axis or rows represent the severity of the impact of the risk, and the horizontal or X axis or columns represent the probability.
- Is used in Risk Management (Chapter 12).

There is no single uniform standard metric for the probability of the occurrence of the event. The US Department of Defense (DOD) qualitative levels of probability are: Frequent (A or 5), Likely (B or 4), Occasional (C or 3), Seldom (D or 3), and Unlikely (E). Similarly, there is no single standard metric for severity of impact of the outcome of the occurrence of the risk. The DOD qualitative levels of severity are:

- *Catastrophic (I):* Loss of ability to accomplish the mission or mission failure. Death or permanent total disability (accident risk). Loss of major or mission-critical system or equipment. Major property (facility) damage. Severe environmental damage. Mission-critical security failure. Unacceptable collateral damage
- *Critical (II):* Significantly (severely) degraded mission capability or unit readiness. Permanent partial disability, temporary total disability exceeding three months' time (accident risk). Extensive (major) damage to equipment or systems.

Significant damage to property or the environment. Security failure. Significant collateral damage.

- **Marginal (III):** Degraded mission capability or unit readiness. Minor damage to equipment or systems, property, or the environment. Lost days due to injury or illness not exceeding three months (accident risk). Minor damage to property or the environment.
- **Negligible (IV):** Little or no adverse impact on mission capability. First aid or minor medical treatment (accident risk). Slight equipment or system damage, but fully functional and serviceable. Little or no property or environmental damage.

The DOD multiplies the probability by the severity to come up with a single number that represents the risk. These are:

E: extremely high risk (A*IV)
H: high risk (B*III)
M: moderate risk (C*II)
L: low risk (D*I)

In the commercial world we can define the levels as:

- **Probability:** Almost certain (5), Likely (4), Possible (3), Unlikely (2), and Rare (1).
- **Severity of impact:** Extreme (5), Major (4), Moderate (3), Minor (3), and Insignificant (1).

The Risk Rectangle based on these values of severity and probability is shown in Table 5.1 where:

E: *extremely high:* 25 (5*5) is coloured red.
H: *high risk:* greater or equal to 20 (4*4) is coloured orange.

Table 5.1 Risk Rectangle

	PROBABILITY				
SEVERITY	CERTAIN (5)	LIKELY (4)	POSSIBLE (3)	UNLIKELY (2)	RARE (1)
Extreme (5)					
Major (4)					
Moderate (3)					
Minor (2)					
Insignificant (1)					

M: *moderate risk:* between 5 and 20 is coloured yellow.

L: *low risk:* less than or equal to 4 (2*2) is coloured green.

In order for the Risk Rectangle to be a practical tool, the qualitative descriptive terms must be quantified into specific numbers which is not an easy thing to do. For example numbers need to be assigned to the terms significant and severe. These ought to be specified in terms of percentages for example a significant loss might be 90% of functionality and a severe loss might be 75%. Once these levels have been specified, the loss for a specific event can then be estimated and placed in the appropriate category. Perceptions from the *Generic* HTP show that this is the same process that is used to determine the values of the ranges for each of the categories in a CRIP Chart (Section 8.1). Section 5.4.2 contains an example of using the Risk Rectangle.

5.4.1 *The Fallacy in the Risk Rectangle*

The Risk Rectangle is generally used to decide which risks need to be mitigated based on multiplying the probability of occurrence by the severity of the effect; that single number. Accordingly risks with high severity and low probability of occurrence tend to be ignored because the single number is low. With an understanding of probability theory, ignoring these risks is not a good idea. Just because the probability is low does not mean the risk is not going to materialize and turn into an event.

For example, if the risk probability of a failure of a component is one in 100, what that means is out of a large number of sets of 100 components one component in each set is probably going to fail. The theory does not predict which one. So if 100 people are going to make a parachute jump, and the parachutes have been poorly prepared, there is a risk of failure of one in a 100; they have no way of knowing whose parachute is going to fail. Any risk with a high severity, even with an extremely low probability of occurrence, must be mitigated. Some are, for example, the risk of assassination of a national president or prime minister is normally very low. Yet a lot of effort is made to protect the person occupying the position, even though there is usually a process in place for the succession.*

---

* Don't misunderstand that statement, I am not advocating that the effort should not be made. I am advocating that all such low probability–high severance risks should be mitigated.

Table 5.2 Options Trading Risk Rectangle

	PROBABILITY OF LOSS IN TRADE				
SEVERITY OF LOSS	>90% (5)	>80%(4)	80–20% (3)	<20% (2)	<10% (1)
>$500 (5)					
<=$500 (4)					
<$300 (3)					
<$100 (2)					
<$10 (1)					

5.4.2 Setting Up and Using a Risk Rectangle

Consider the following example of setting up and using a Risk Rectangle. Fred has been looking at his investments. He has read a little bit about the stock market and the difference between owning shares and owning options. He has opened an account with an online broker and has been learning about the options market. He sees the leverage that options can provide but is concerned about the risk. He's noticed in his paper-trading page that every time he looks at trading an option, the software shows him the potential gain and loss in the trade as well as the probability of the trade being successful, losing money and being breakeven.* He thinks about the amounts he can afford to lose on trades, having learned that even the best brokers do not win on every trade. He copies out a Risk Rectangle (Table 5.1) and enters amounts equal to the severity of the loss in the rows. So, for Fred, a loss of more than $500 would have a severity of 5 while a $10 loss would be almost negligible with a severity of 1. He fills in the other numbers with intermediate values. He then looks at the probabilities and decides what values to put into those in the columns. So he ends up with Table 5.2. When he looks at any trade, he can plot it in the table. The software will show him what the gain on the trade is and what the probability of the loss and the amount of the loss are. He feels comfortable using the table irrespective of the amount he stands to gain from the trade. He feels that there is no point in entering a trade for which he stands to gain $10,000, if there is a 90% probability that he will lose $500. Using the table to make the decision based on the criteria he set up for the rows in the columns takes the emotion out of the trade. He is using the Risk Rectangle as a decision tool.

---

* This is a discussion on risks, not options trading.

5.5 Summary

Chapter 5 discussed four frameworks used to illustrate where and how things fit together. The generic 2x2 format table is basically a four-area table used to show the relationship between four different items. This chapter used an example of the 2x2 table to present a theory that could explain why some people are homosexual and others are heterosexual based on the observation that bodies can be male or female and the inference from the *Generic* HTP that souls can also be male and female. The HKMF is a framework for understanding the activities performed in systems engineering and project management and is also useful in finding out-of-the-box solutions by looking into the other areas of the framework (boxes). The Problem Classification Framework classifies problems by their structure and the degree of subjective complexity (difficulty). Lastly, the Risk Rectangle, a framework for identifying which risks to manage was discussed, and this chapter provided an example of how you can use the Risk Rectangle to set up an objective decision-making rule for deciding if you should or should not purchase a particular option when playing with the stock market.

References

Ackoff, R. L. 1974. *Redesigning the Future: A Systems Approach to Societal Problems*. New York: John Wiley & Sons.

Ford, W. 2010. "Learning and Teaching Math." Accessed 8 April 2015. http://mathmaine.wordpress.com/2010/01/09/problems-fall-into-four-categories/.

Hitchins, D. K. 2002. *World Class Systems Engineering – The Five Layer Model* [Website], accessed 3 November 2006. http://www.hitchins.net/5layer.html.

Jonassen, D. H. 1997. "Instructional Design Model for Well-structured and Ill-structured Problem-solving Learning Outcomes." *Educational Technology: Research and Development*, no. 45 (1):65–95.

Kasser, J. E. 2012a. "Complex Solutions for Complex Problems." In Third International Engineering Systems Symposium (CESUN). Delft, Holland.

Kasser, J. E. 2012b. "Getting the Right Requirements Right." In The 22nd Annual International Symposium of the International Council on Systems Engineering. Rome, Italy.

Kasser, J. E., and A. Massie. 2001. "A Framework for a Systems Engineering Body of Knowledge." In 11th International Symposium of the INCOSE. Melbourne, Australia.

Rittel, H. W., and M. M. Webber. 1973. "Dilemmas in a General Theory of Planning." *Policy Sciences*, no. 4:155–169.

Shum, S. B. 1996. "Representing Hard-to-formalise, Contextualised, Multidisciplinary, Organisational Knowledge." In Workshop on Knowledge Media for Improving Organisational Expertise, 1st International Conference on Practical Aspects of Knowledge Management. Basel, Switzerland.

Simon, H. A. 1973. "The Structure of Ill Structured Problems." *Artificial Intelligence*, no. 4 (3–4):181–201. doi: 10.1016/0004-3702(73)90011-8.

6
GRAPHICS

Graphics are:

- Thinking and communications tools.
- Any kind of visual image.

Good graphics are graphics that are:

- Easy to understand by someone who understands the topic.
- Intuitive. They need very little explanation to be understood by newcomer to the topic, where "very little" is defined as not being a verbal repletion of the contents of the graphic.
- Compliant with Miller's Rule (Section 3.2.5).

Bad graphics are graphics containing too many items, usually the first draft of a graphic that violates the KISS principle (Section 3.2.3), again usually because the author hasn't thought about what's in the graphic and arranged the elements to facilitate comprehension.

6.1 Different Types of Graphics

There are many different types of graphics, this chapter discusses the following:

1. Causal Loops in Section 6.1.1.
2. Concept Maps in Section 6.1.2.
3. Graphs in Section 6.1.3.
4. Mind Maps in Section 6.1.4.
5. Rich Pictures in Section 6.1.5.

Other types of graphics include photographs and the other charts used in this book.

6.1.1 Causal Loops

Causal Loops are:

- Tools used for thinking about and communicating relationships.
- Often identified with systems (systemic) thinking (e.g. Senge 1990) because they show the functional and operational relationships (behaviour) between various parts of a system.
- Feedback loops.
- Usually drawn as circles containing the items and arrows between the circles showing the relationships.

As an example, the relationships between the population of predators and prey in a given area can be drawn in form of the Causal Loop, shown in Figure 6.1, which shows:

- ***How a change in each element affects another element.*** For example, consider the change in the population of predators and prey. As the number of predators increase (indicated by the up arrow), the number of prey deceases (presumably, the predators consume more prey). However when the number of prey decreases the number of predators also decrease (presumably because the food supply becomes limited and the

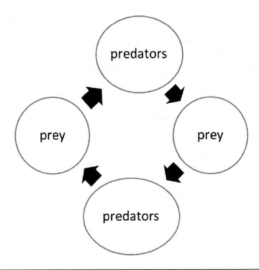

Figure 6.1 Predator - prey relationship.

predators starve or move out of the area). When the number of predators decreases, the number of prey increases (presumably because the prey can multiply in the absence of predators). When the number of prey increases, the number of predators also increases (presumably their food supply has increased) and the loop enters another cycle.

- *The relationship between the change in size of the predator and prey population.* The causes are presumed due to observation of the behaviour of the predators and prey. This loop does not help in thinking about the time delays involved in the change of population states or include the effect of any other element on the populations.

Another type of Causal Loop is shown in Figure 6.2. This one shows the effect on water temperature of (1) heating the water and (2) adding ice to cool the water. There are two feedback loops:

1. *The positive feedback loop*: indicating that as the water is heated the temperature rises.
2. *The negative feedback loop*: indicating that as the ice is added to the water, the water temperature decreases.

Causal Loops:

- Have limitations. For example, the figure just shows the effect on the relationship between the elements in the loop when an element changes. Each loop does not help in thinking about any steady state conditions or the rate of change of temperature.

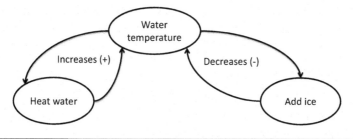

Figure 6.2 Effect of heating and cooling on water temperature.

- Exist in several variations. Sometimes they are drawn as in Figure 6.1, sometimes as in Figure 6.2, and sometimes in a different format. The relationships may be shown as arrows, words, or symbols. There is no standard way of drawing these loops, just pick a way that makes the drawing easy to understand by everyone who will use the drawing.

6.1.1.1 Creating a Causal Loop   Since a Causal Loop is a Concept Map (Section 6.1.2), the generic process in Section 6.1.2.1 may be modified for creating Causal Loops. Accordingly, the more detailed specific process for creating a Causal Loop is as follows:

1. Identify the elements in the Causal Loop.
2. Store the elements in a List (Section 9.4). This step is done in an iterative manner with the previous step.
3. Identify relationships between elements in the list. If a new element shows up in the thought process in this step, add it to the list.
4. Draw the individual loops showing the relationships between two or more elements. If a new element shows up in the thought process, add it to the list.
5. Combine the loops into a larger loop.
6. If the number of elements in the loop exceeds nine, then in accordance with Miller's Rule (Section 3.2.5) aggregate elements of the loop into a more complex element to reduce the complexity of the loop as in the conversion from eight elements in Figure 2.38 to four elements in Figure 2.30. There will then be two loops at different levels in the hierarchy.

Consider the following example of creating a Causal Loop describing the relationships between the elements used in making a cup of coffee to be served:

1. At the right temperature.
2. With the correct amount of sweetener.
3. With the correct amount of milk.
4. With the desired strength of coffee.

6.1.1.2 The Process for Creating a Causal Loop Describing the Relationships between the Elements in a Cup of Coffee

1. The process starts with identifying the elements in the process.
2. The elements which are then written down as a list of candidate items for being in the loop are:
   a. Water.
   b. Heating device.
   c. Cup.
   d. Sweetener.
   e. Milk.
   f. Coffee.
3. Relationships between the strength and temperature of the water and the items are identified.
4. Some of the relationships between the items are then drawn, including:
   a. The effect of heating and cooling the water or mixture of coffee, milk, and sweetener shown in Figure 6.2.
   b. Four other relationships that affect the temperature of the mixture of coffee, sweetener, and water are shown in Figure 6.3. In drawing the relationships it was discovered that the mix could be cooled by adding ice as well

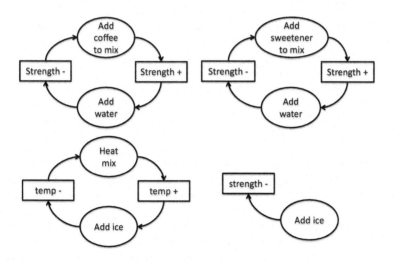

Figure 6.3   Some of the relationships in making a cup of coffee.

as water, and adding ice also reduced the strength of the mix. Accordingly, "ice" is added to the list of elements in the process.

c. The other relationships would then be determined, such as:

- The effect of adding milk to the mix, left out of this example for the sake of keeping the figures simple.
- A cup contains the mixture. Since the absorption of heat by the cup is assumed to be negligible, the cup is not mentioned in any of the relationships.

5. The various individual relationship loops drawn in the previous step are combined into the initial draft Causal Loop shown in Figure 6.4.

6. The complexity in the loop should be masked by combining the "add sweetener" and "add coffee" from the mix elements into a more complex "add ingredients" element, as shown in Figure 6.5 in accordance with the KISS principle (Section 3.2.3). When you draw the figure, you realize that adding ingredients can reduce the temperature of the mix and add the relationship arrow. Another advantage of creating a higher-level Causal Loop such as Figure 6.5 is that it will probably not change if there is a change in the elements inside one of the activities.

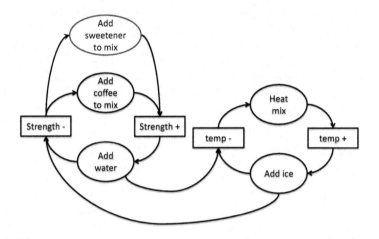

Figure 6.4　Combining the relationships into a Causal Loop.

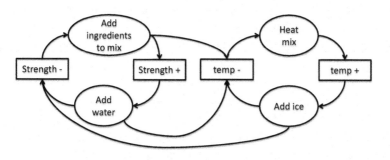

Figure 6.5 Higher-level Causal Loop.

The Causal Loop does not:

- Describe the process for making the cup of coffee to be served; it only shows the relationships between the elements used in the process. The process should be designed once the relationships are understood.
- Assign any value to the strength of the relationship between elements. It only shows that a relationship exists.

6.1.1.3 Causal Loops and Flowcharts Causal Loops show relationships; Flowcharts (Section 2.7) show dependencies. For example, Figure 11.1 shows the problem-solving process as a Causal Loop relating the undesirable solution, the problem-solving process, and the solution as a continuous loop. Figure 11.5 shows the same loop in more detail as a process Flowchart implicitly identifying the decision that causes the loop to iterate or terminate. Figure 11.5 shows that a single pass around the loop may remedy some problems while others will need more than one pass.

6.1.1.4 Common Errors in Causal Loops A common error when drawing Causal Loops is to ignore the KISS principle (Section 3.2.3) and include too many details (items) in a single diagram which introduces:

- Subjective complexity, discussed in Section 5.3.1, making the figure difficult to understand.
- Objective complexity, discussed in Section 5.3.2, by inserting extraneous details.

6.1.2 Concept Maps and Relationship Diagrams

A Concept Map sometimes called an affinity diagram or a relationship diagram is:

- The tool most often used to connect ideas.
- The generic name for a diagram that shows the association or connections between ideas or things.
- A tool that has been used for thousands of years.

Concept Maps:

- Consist of blocks containing the concepts connected by arrows. The type of relationship or connection between the concepts is often included in the drawing as text associated with the arrow as shown in Figure 6.2.
- Show up in many guises, including subway and city maps, Causal Loops (Section 6.1.1), N^2 Charts (Section 2.10), the Waterfall Chart (Section 14.9) view of the System Development Process (SDP), and process and software Flowcharts (Section 2.7).

Concepts may be associated in many ways, including the following:

- *Linear*: such as in Figure 6.6 and in a process Flow Chart such as Figure 2.11. In Figure 6.6, the first concept is "thinking" which leads to "innovation" via two parallel paths.
- *Circular*: such as the predator-prey relationship shown in Figure 6.1 showing that an increase in predators:
  - leads to a decrease in prey because more predators are consuming more prey, which

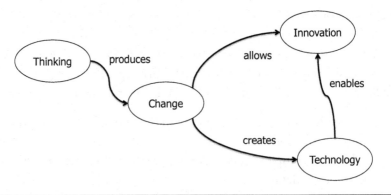

Figure 6.6   Typical Concept Map connecting ideas about thinking.

- leads to a decrease in predators because there is fewer prey to consume, which
- leads to an increase in prey because there are fewer predators consuming prey, which
- leads to an increase in predators, and the circle repeats.
- *Hierarchical*: such as in an organization chart.
- *Spider or centre outwards*: such as in Figure 6.7.

Figure 6.6 and Figure 6.7 are both Concept Maps that show a relationship between "thinking", "change", "innovation", and "technology". Figure 6.6 infers that there is a linear relationship, and while the activity kicks off with some thinking, once a change has taken place, no further thinking takes place. Figure 6.7, on the other hand, infers that the act of thinking is central to the relationship between the other items on the Concept Map. Each type of Concept Map has something to contribute to the thinking and communications processes.

When asked to draw a Concept Map of how they relate "thinking", "change", "innovation" and "technology", students invariably produce variants of Figure 6.6 and Figure 6.7. Each figure is correct since it depicts the way the student relates the concepts. Accordingly, when communicating concepts, you should use the type of Concept Map that clearly communicates the desired relationship between the concepts. For example, if you want people to see:

- A linear relationship between the concepts, use a variant of Figure 6.6.
- How thinking pervades the other activities, use a variant of Figure 6.7.

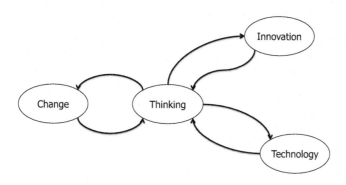

Figure 6.7   Spider format Concept Map.

6.1.2.1 Creating a Concept Map   Create a Concept Map by using the following process.

1. Create a List of the concepts (Section 9.4).
2. Think about the relationships between two or more concepts and draw those relationships.
3. Once you have a few Relationship Charts combine them into a single Concept Map. If there is something in the List (Section 9.4) that does not show up on the Concept Map, it may be an indication that:
   a. Something else is missing from the List.
   b. It is not pertinent to the issues under consideration.
4. If there are more than nine items in the Concept Map, combine or aggregate concepts to reduce the number to comply with Miller's Rule (Section 3.2.5).

Note: the act of drawing the relationships can also identify additional concepts to add to the List. For example, consider a classroom. The Concept Map developed is:

1. Based on the assumption that the items in the classroom are related by the activities that take place in the classroom.
2. Determined by what aspect of the classroom is being thought about.

   Accordingly, the initial thoughts about a classroom might generate a List containing a mixture of the items in a classroom and the activities that take place in the classroom. When the ideas have stopped flowing, the list may be split into two lists:
3. The items in the classroom (*Structural* HTP) including:
   • Chairs
   • Clock
   • Desks
   • Electrical lighting

- Electrical power
- Emergency alarm
- Internet access
- Rubbish bin
- Students
- Teacher
- Whiteboard
- Whiteboard eraser
- Whiteboard markers

4. The desired (*Operational* and *Functional* HTPs) and undesired (*Continuum* HTP) activities or functions take place in a classroom including:
   - Accessing emails
   - Eating
   - Drinking
   - Learning
   - Listening
   - Sleeping
   - Spilling drinks
   - Talking
   - Watching videos

The list of activities may be further split into desired and undesired if appropriate. The Concept Maps that will follow will depend on what aspect of the classroom is being thought about. For example when thinking about:

- *How the students and teacher respond to an emergency alarm*: you might draw a linear Concept Map beginning with the emergency alarm sounding off.
- *Aspects of teaching and learning*: you might draw Concept Maps containing the relationships between the students and the teacher in the instructor-based classroom such as the one in Figure 6.8 (Zhao, Kasser, and Hitchins 2009).

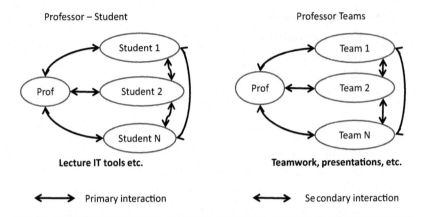

Figure 6.8 Two of the relationships in the instructor-based classroom system.

6.1.2.2 The Two Most Common Mistakes Made When Creating and Presenting Concept Maps The two most common mistakes made when presenting Concept Maps are:

1. ***Showing too many items in the concept map***: namely, the author did not remove the clutter by grouping the concepts into a hierarchy of ideas so as to make the final version of the drawing conform to Miller's Rule (Section 3.2.5). Section 2.10 explains how to use an N^2 Chart as an alternative to a Concept Map when the relationships between a large number of items are being considered.

2. ***Showing a mixture of ideas or objects at different levels in the hierarchy***: such as in Figure 2.22 which contains the ingredients block and the details of the ingredients, namely information in more than one level in the hierarchy.

6.1.3 Graphs

Graphs:

- Are tools to help think about, understand and communicate relationships between items.
- Have been used for many years.
- Show what happens to one or more variables plotted on the Y-axis (vertical) when compared to the variable plotted on the X-axis (horizontal).

Common types of graphs discussed in this book include:

- Control Charts, discussed in Section 2.5.
- Polar Charts, discussed in Section 2.13.
- Trend Charts, discussed in Section 2.15.
- XY Charts, discussed in Section 2.16.

Each type of graph shows information in a different way. Select the graph that helps you think about the information or presents the information you want the viewer to see in a way that is familiar to the viewer.

6.1.4 Mind Maps

A Mind Map is another word for a Concept Map (Section 6.1.2).

6.1.5 Rich Pictures

Rich Pictures are:

- Graphics that contain sketches, as well as symbols and images. The term was popularized in Checkland's Soft Systems Methodology (SSM) (Section 13.1).

Examples of Rich Pictures are:

- Figure 1.1, which depicts the most widely used cognitive psychology information processing model of the brain based on the work of Atkinson and Shiffrin (Atkinson and Shiffrin 1968) cited by Lutz and Huitt (Lutz and Huitt 2003) which likens the human mind to an information processing computer. Both the human mind and the computer ingest information, process it to change its form, store it, retrieve it, and generate responses to inputs (Woolfolk 1998). These days we can extend our internal memory using paper notes, books, and electronic storage as shown in Figure 1.1.
- Figure 2.33, a Rich Picture that provides the context for the problem of determining the fastest route for travelling from Vivo City to Kent Vale by showing the factors involved in making the decision.

6.2 Summary

Chapter 6 discussed five different types of graphics that were not discussed in Chapter 2. The graphics discussed in this chapter are Causal Loops, Concept Maps, Graphs, Mind Maps, and Rich Pictures. These tools may be used for thinking and communicating and include any type of visual image not mentioned in this book. This chapter also invoked the KISS principle to guide you into creating good understandable graphics.

References

Atkinson, R., and R. Shiffrin. 1968. "Human Memory: A Proposed System and Its Control Processes." In *The Psychology of Learning and Motivation: Advances in Research and Theory (Vol. 2)*, edited by K. Spence and J. Spence. New York: Academic Press.

Lutz, S., and W. Huitt. 2003. *Information Processing and Memory: Theory and Applications*. Valdosta State University. Accessed 24 February 2010. http://www.edpsycinteractive.org/papers/infoproc.pdf.

Senge, P. M. 1990. *The Fifth Discipline: The Art and Practice of the Learning Organization*. New York: Doubleday.

Woolfolk, A. E. 1998. "Chapter 7: Cognitive Views of Learning." In *Educational Psychology*, pp. 244–283. Boston: Allyn and Bacon.

Zhao, Y.-Y., J. E. Kasser, and D. K. Hitchins. 2009. "Systems Engineering in the Conceptual Stage: A Teaching Case Study". In the 3rd Annual Asia-Pacific Conference on Systems Engineering (APCOSE). Singapore.

7

IDEA GENERATION TOOLS

This chapter discusses the following idea generation tools:

1. Active Brainstorming in Section 7.1.
2. Association of Ideas in Section 7.2.
3. Brainstorming in Section 7.3.
4. Constraint Mapping in Section 7.4.
5. The Five Whys in Section 7.5.
6. The Kipling Questions in Section 7.6.
7. Lateral Thinking in Section 7.7.
8. Letter and word manipulation in Section 7.8.
9. The Nominal Group Technique (NGT) in Section 7.9.
10. Slip Writing in Section 7.10.

7.1 Active Brainstorming

Active Brainstorming (Kasser and Mackley 2008, Kasser 2013):

- Is a thinking tool that increases the number of ideas produced in Brainstorming (Section 7.3).
- Sessions are organized in the same way as Brainstorming sessions.
- Should only be used after the initial flow of ideas from Brainstorming dry up.
- Produces additional ideas relating to the problem or issue in a systemic and systematic manner. Table 7.1 contains data from seven teams in the first postgraduate classroom Brainstorming/Active Brainstorming exercise at the National University of Singapore (NUS) showing the increase in the number of ideas. Later exercises provided similar results.*

---

* The actual number depended on how well the students understood the concept of Active Brainstorming. The "too many to count" is probably "too lazy to count".

Table 7.1   Improvement in Number of Ideas Generated

TEAM	TOTAL NUMBER OF IDEAS AFTER BRAINSTORMING	TOTAL NUMBER OF IDEAS AFTER ACTIVE BRAINSTORMING	IMPROVEMENT (%)
1	20	40	100
2	9	89	889
3	22	66	200
4	31	64	106
5	39	79	103
6	28	89	218
7	20	"Too many to count"	Large

- Achieves these increases in the number of ideas generated by examining the issue from each of the HTPs (Section 10.1) and triggering ideas by asking the Kipling Questions (Section 7.6) "who", "what", "where", "when", "why", and "how" in a systemic and systematic manner.

7.1.1 Using Active Brainstorming

While Active Brainstorming can be performed by an individual, it is best used in a workshop or session in the context of the following three-stage process.

1. Before the session begins.
2. The session or workshop.
3. Post workshop idea sorting and storing.

7.1.1.1 Before the Session Begins   Before the session begins:

1. Identify who needs to be present.
2. Invite them, providing a reason for them to attend, and tell them what issue or problem the session will be discussing to give them time to think up ideas before the session.
3. Determine who is to be:
   a. The facilitator to pose the questions.
   b. The scribe to write the ideas on the whiteboard or other recording medium.

7.1.1.2 The Session or Workshop The requirements for the session or workshop are the same as the requirements for a Brainstorming session (Section 7.3.1). When the session begins, the facilitator should remind the participants as to why the meeting was called and what the initial question was. There will be a natural tendency to generate spontaneous ideas in an unstructured Brainstorming manner, particularly in a session containing newcomers to the technique. The ideas will include answers, further questions, names of people to contact for more information, and the need for further analysis.

The facilitator should:

- Not attempt to stem the flow of ideas and ask the participants to wait for the appropriate question.*
- Just make sure the ideas are recorded by the scribe in whatever media is being used for the purpose (white board, flip charts, mind mapping software, etc.)

Once the initial flow of ideas stops, the facilitator starts the true Active Brainstorming process. Using the Active Brainstorming idea-triggering template shown in Table 7.2 to perceive the situation from a Perspectives Perimeter (Chapter 10) based on the HTPs (Section 10.1), the facilitator begins by posing the Kipling Questions (Section 7.6) from the *Big Picture* HTP. The initial cues for the Active Brainstorming questions can come from the ideas generated from the regular Brainstorming (Section 7.3) session performed just prior to commencing the Active Brainstorming session. For example, if one of the ideas produced by regular Brainstorming was "she plays the flute", then Active Brainstorming can focus on that idea and expand it beginning with questions such as:

- Why is she playing the flute?
- Who is she playing with?
- Where is she playing it?

When starting the questioning sequence for the *Operational* HTP, it often helps to draw a Flowchart (Section 2.7) or a similar Concept

---

* Which is one reason the ideas are not documented in the idea triggering template shown in Table 7.2.

Table 7.2   Active Brainstorming Idea Triggering Template

	WHO?	WHAT?	WHERE?	WHEN?	WHY?	HOW?
Big Picture						
Operational						
Functional						
Structural						
Generic						
Continuum						
Temporal						
Quantitative						
Scientific						

Map (Section 6.1.2) to provide a focus for questioning. After posing a question:

- The ideas should be recorded by the scribe in the same place that the initial flow of ideas was stored. The scribe should not store the responses in the Active Brainstorming idea triggering template shown in Table 7.2 during the session since doing so tends to divert the session into a discussion (dispute) as to the area in which to store the idea, and interferes with the flow of ideas.
- If no ideas come forth immediately, and sometimes they don't because not all areas are pertinent to every issue, the facilitator should skip to the next question or even the next row or column. However, the question should be noted by the scribe so that it can be assigned as an action item to be answered following the workshop.

At the end of the flow of ideas from the last question in a row, the facilitator moves down to the first column in the subsequent row. Expect a question posed in one area of Table 7.2 to sometimes generate ideas that pertain to other areas. Examples of typical questions posed from the HTPs are provided below in Section 7.1.2. The facilitator should ensure that the discussions triggered by each question are terminated when the flow dries up or starts generating redundant ideas. The workshop is terminated once the ideas stop flowing.

7.1.1.3 Post-Workshop Idea Sorting and Storing

- The ideas are sorted into the Idea Storage Templates (IST; Section 14.2) or even the HTPs used as an IST.
- Action items are assigned to specific personnel to research answers to the questions that were unanswered during the workshop.
- These findings are then stored in the appropriate IST.

7.1.2 Typical Active Brainstorming Questions

The following questions based on the Association of Ideas (Section 7.2) are intended as a starting point for you to add your own follow-on thoughts and questions. The list is not intended to be complete, and not all questions may be appropriate to specific situations. In addition, the questions posed in Lateral Thinking (Section 7.7) can also be used in Active Brainstorming.

7.1.2.1 Typical Questions from the Big Picture Perspective

1. What is the purpose of the…?
2. Why this system is there in the first place?
3. Why is it performing these activities?
4. What problem is this system remedying?
5. Where is this system in the context of things?
6. What is this next to?
7. Why is this next to…?
8. What are the assumptions underlying the system?

7.1.2.2 Typical Questions from the Operational Perspective

9. What are the operational scenarios? (open system view)
10. Who is going to operate/administer it?
11. What do they need to operate/administer it?
12. Under what conditions will it be operated/administered?
13. Where will they operate/administer it?
14. When will they operate/administer it? (redundant to *Temporal* perspective)
15. Why will they operate/administer it?

16. How will they operate/administer it?
17. How will they gain access to it?

7.1.2.3 *Typical Questions from the* Functional *Perspective*

18. What activities does/will it perform? (closed system view)
19. How does it perform those activities?

7.1.2.4 *Typical Questions from the* Structural *Perspective*

20. What parts does it have?
21. What are they interchangeable with?
22. What can the parts be replaced with?

7.1.2.5 *Typical Questions from the* Generic *Perspective*

23. What does this remind you of?
24. What functions does this system inherit from its class of systems?
25. What does it have in common with...?
26. Who has had a similar problem?
27. What is this similar to?
28. What applies to both situations?
29. Where can I find a similar situation?
30. When was there a similar situation?
31. When will there be a similar situation?
32. Why is this similar?
33. How is this similar?

7.1.2.6 *Typical Questions from the* Continuum *Perspective*

34. What is an alternative way of...?
35. What is the opposite of?
36. Why is this different?
37. How is this different?
38. In what way can we change ... – it depends, see Table 7.3.
39. Should we try to change ... – it depends, see Table 7.3.
40. How could we reduce the...?
41. How could we increase the...?
42. What happens if ... breaks or fails?

Table 7.3 Attribute of a Change Mapped to HTP

CHANGE	HTP
Cheaper	*Quantitative*
Stronger	*Structural*
Easier to use	*Operational*
Lighter	*Structural*
Safer	*Operational*, *Functional*, and *Structural*

7.1.2.7 Typical Questions from the Temporal Perspective

43. What happens before, after, at the same time?
44. What part of the … limits the useable lifetime?

7.1.2.8 Typical Questions from the Quantitative Perspective

45. How well does it work?
46. Why is this larger/smaller than…?
47. What is the cost of…?
48. How can this be made cheaper?
49. What part is the most expensive and why?
50. How much money do we have to spend?

7.1.2.9 Typical Questions from the Scientific Perspective

51. What could we use…?
52. What kind of vehicle could we use to…?
53. How will you know when the problem no longer exists or is remedied?

7.1.3 Key Questions

As you gain experience in Active Brainstorming, you will learn which type of questions from the areas provide the pertinent insight to the various types of issues being discussed and focus on those areas. These questions are known as key questions. The answers to the key questions provide the pertinent information and insight to achieve the goal such as defining the correct problem and identifying the correct feasible solution. Key questions will depend on the situation.

7.1.4 Questions to Focus on Problems and Situations

You can frame questions to focus on problems and situations with the appropriate wording (Ruggiero 2012: p. 129). For example, questions starting with:

- "How can …?" tend to produce problems.
- "Is …?", "Does …?" or "Should …?" tend to produce situations.

7.1.5 Using Active Brainstorming as an Individual

You can do Active Brainstorming in a regular Brainstorming (Section 7.3) meeting or you can do this on your own when examining a situation. You ask the same questions silently to yourself and act as your own facilitator. If you are in a meeting, then as you answer your own questions, call out the ideas (answers you thought of). If you can't think of an idea to your own question, then call out the question as an idea to be researched later. If you use Table 7.2 reduced to business card size as a memory prompt, and don't let other people see what you are doing, you will quickly develop a reputation for being full of ideas and asking good questions.

7.2 Association of Ideas

Association of Ideas is a tool for generating ideas by individuals or by groups. When ideas appear in succession, there is a relationship or association between an idea and the following one. This relationship can be expressed in the traditional three laws of association which go back to the time of Aristotle (384 to 322 BC) (Osborn 1963: p. 114), namely:

1. *Contiguity*: nearness, the association is something that reminds you of something else.
2. *Similarity*: the idea is similar to something.
3. *Contrast*: the idea is opposite or a contrast to something.

Other types of association include:

- *Functional*: the ideas are about something that does the same thing, even if the implementations are different. For example, travelling by bus and airplane; two different implementations of the travelling function.

- *Temporal*: the ideas are about things that happen at the same time.
- *Procedural*: the ideas always follow in a certain sequence.
- *Operational*:* the ideas are about things that operate on the same item. For example, a brush and a comb both operate (are used) on hair.
- *Coincidental*: there does not seem to be any association between the ideas in the minds of the people to whom the ideas are communicated.

Association can work through sounds, pictures, aromas as well as words; in fact through any sense you have.

7.2.1 Using Association of Ideas

Association of Ideas can be used as a Perspectives Perimeter (Chapter 10) by asking questions from the perspective of each type of association during Active Brainstorming (Section 7.1) and other ideation sessions using the modified version of Table 7.2 shown in Table 7.4. For example:

1. *Contiguity*: what does this remind you of? (*Generic* HTP).
2. *Similarity*: what is this similar to? (*Generic* HTP).
3. *Contrast*: how is this different from …? (*Continuum* HTP).
4. *Functional*: what does the same thing as this, even if the implementations are different? (*Functional/Continuum* HTPs).
5. *Temporal*: has this happened before?
6. *Procedural*: what is done in the same sequence as this? (*Functional/Generic* HTPs).
7. *Operational*:* what is this also used on …? (*Generic* HTP).

---

* Not to be confused with the *Operational* HTP.

Table 7.4   Active Brainstorming Idea Triggering Template for Association of Ideas

	WHO?	WHAT?	WHERE?	WHEN?	WHY?	HOW?
Contiguity						
Similarity						
Contrast						
Functional						
Temporal						
Procedural						
Operational						

7.3 Brainstorming

Brainstorming (Osborn 1963):

- Is a tool for generating ideas (ideation) in small groups.
- Is based on the Association of Ideas (Section 7.2) where one idea triggers the next.
- Has many variations.

In Brainstorming and other ideation techniques, the number of ideas generated will be greater if the participants are notified ahead of time as to the:

1. Purpose of the ideation meeting.
2. Problem to be addressed.
3. Need to bring some ideas with them.

Osborn's four original basics for Brainstorming were (Osborn 1963: p. 156):

1. No criticism of ideas.
2. Encourage wild and exaggerated ideas.
3. Go for large quantities of ideas.
4. Build on each other's ideas.

Brainstorming can be performed by an individual or by a team. In team sessions, a group of people get together, are given a problem statement and ideate (produce ideas). The Brainstorming team contains:

- A leader/facilitator who guides the session and enforces the rules.
- A scribe who records the ideas.
- A small number of people who will do the ideation.

7.3.1 Requirements for Brainstorming Sessions

Brainstorming sessions shall conform to the following requirements:

1. The facilitator shall introduce the session by stating a specific problem rather than a general situation.*
2. The scribe shall record all of the ideas.
3. The participants shall state their ideas.
4. The participants shall suggest modifications of ideas previously stated to improve the idea or combine two or more ideas into another idea.
5. The participants shall not self-censor their ideas before stating them. This is because other people may like those ideas or see them from a different perspective and subsequently build on those ideas to produce something better.
6. There shall be no criticism of ideas during the session.
7. The ideas shall be evaluated and sorted after the Brainstorming session.
8. There shall be no limit on the scope of the ideas. Wild ideas can be tamed down later if appropriate.
9. The only discussion on ideas shall be for the purpose of clarification.
10. The facilitator shall not allow the session to break up into groups.
11. The composition of the participants shall be mixed in age, sex, and experience and domain knowledge.
12. Participants shall ideally be at the same level in the organizational hierarchy to minimize the intimidation effect where people lower in rank in the hierarchy are unwilling to disagree with people higher up.
13. If rank is mixed, lower ranks shall speak first.

While a number of variations of Brainstorming have been described in the literature, they all tend to suffer from a number of defects including:

- Being a generally passive approach because they are based on waiting for the ideas to be generated before writing them down.†

---

* The situation might be summarized to provide the context of the problem.
† There are variations which trigger ideas using 'what' and 'why' questions.

- Team sessions being prone to capture by the most opinionated person in the Brainstorming session.
- Being unstructured, while allowing free range of ideas, Brainstorming tends to fail to focus on issues pertinent to the session.

Other ideation techniques such as Active Brainstorming (Section 7.1), the Nominal Group Techniques (NGT) (Section 7.9) and Slip Writing (Section 7.10) overcome these defects to various degrees in various manners.

7.4 Constraint Mapping

Constraint Mapping (Dunn 2012):

- Is a systematic tool for identifying and classifying limitations and obstacles that stand in the way of achieving any goal.
- Is useful for identifying selection criteria for selecting between candidate choices as part of the problem-solving process.
- Is a Perspectives Perimeter (Chapter 10) for discussing the constraints on a situation.

7.4.1 Categories of Constraints

Constraints generally fall into the following six categories (Dunn 2012):

1. **Physical**: the technology, equipment, or other physical resources may not be available, or the decision may have to use or be compatible with existing equipment.
2. **Legal**: there may be laws and regulations such as property rights that constrain the choice of actions. For example, shooting uncooperative personnel is not allowed under many modern legal codes (even if they deserve it).
3. **Organizational**: the organizational culture, poor management, and processes may preclude certain choices because "we don't do things that way in this organization".
4. **Political**: the boss or the stakeholders may not like this choice.

Table 7.5 Active Brainstorming Template for Constraint Mapping

	WHO?	WHAT?	WHERE?	WHEN?	WHY?	HOW?
Physical						
Legal						
Organizational						
Political						
Distributional						
Budgetary						
Other						

5. ***Distributional***: the benefits of selecting an option need to be distributed equitably amongst the stakeholders.
6. ***Budgetary***: since budgets are generally limited, the choice of options may be limited by affordability.

7.4.2 How to Perform Constraint Mapping

An effective way of performing Constraint Mapping is to use an Active Brainstorming (Section 7.1) session from a Perspectives Perimeter (Chapter 10) containing the six perspectives listed in Section 7.4.1 and adding an "Other" category. The process would be based on the modified Active Brainstorming table in Table 7.5 starting by focusing on perceptions of the Physical constraints. When the ideas have dried up, the second iteration would focus on perceptions of the Legal constraints and so on until all of the categories of constraints have been considered. The last iteration would perceive the issue of constraints from the "Other" constraints category and consider any other aspects that may come to mind. It is likely that during the Active Brainstorming session the ideas generated will range over the constraints and include factors that affect the weighting of the constraints in subsequent decisions.

7.5 The Five Whys

The Five Whys is a systematic approach to examining a symptom and determining the root cause. The technique was originally developed by Sakichi Toyoda and was used within the Toyota Motor Corporation to deal with problems. Conceptually, it's a simple process; just ask a series of questions each beginning with the word "why". The answer to the question always begins with the word "because". So the sequence is to ask the question note the response and ask the question again, And so on, until there is no point in asking another "why" question. On average you can get to the root cause by asking the question "why" five times. That's why the technique is known as the Five Whys.

Perceptions from the *Continuum* HTP have identified three different situations in which the Five Whys is a useful tool. They are:

1. Simple situations discussed in Section 7.5.1.
2. Complex situations discussed in Section 7.5.2.
3. Failure prediction and prevention situations discussed in Section 7.5.3.

7.5.1 Simple Situations

The vast majority of descriptions of the technique apply in simple situations and linearly focus on a single "why" question followed by a single "because" answer. For example, a medieval history teacher might provide the students with the following example of Five Whys which gets down to the root cause:

1. Why was the kingdom lost? Because the battle was lost.
2. Why was the battle lost? Because the knight did not show up to lead the charge.
3. Why did the knight not show up to lead the charge? Because he didn't have a horse.
4. Why didn't he have a horse? Because the horse didn't have a shoe.
5. Why didn't the horse have a shoe? Because there were no nails for the blacksmith to attach the shoe to the horse.

So according to this logic, the reason the battle was lost was simply a supply problem and that the blacksmith didn't have any nails. This sequence is based on an ancient poem from the Middle Ages. It shows a one-dimensional chain of cause and effect, or symptom and problem. The one-dimensional chain of cause and effect may be valid for simple problems such as "Why did the machine fail?", or "Why wasn't breakfast served on time?"

The reason the technique is taught in this one-dimensional way is because it was developed in a simple situation and it is simple to explain.

7.5.2 Complex Situations

When using the Five Whys to deal with complex problems we need to take into account that there probably will be more than one possible reason for something happening or not happening at each level and each reason has to be investigated by itself. Because when we need to consider the branches namely there is more than one "because" answer to a "why" question the process description becomes complex and complicated and that's where the Cause and Effect Chart (Section 2.2) such as the one shown in Figure 2.2 helps to illustrate the flow. With reference to Figure 2.2 the undesirable situation is that someone wants to make a cup of instant coffee and there is no hot water.

7.5.2.1 The First "Why" The first why asks the question, "Why is there no hot water?" which kicks off the process. The initial one-dimensional answer is, "Because there is no electricity" which leads straight into asking, "Why is there no electricity?" And it might miss a different cause. And if that missed cause was the true reason for there not being any electricity, the wrong problem would be solved. Someone thinking about why there is no hot water might come up with reasons that include, "there is no electricity", "the kettle is broken" or even "the kettle wasn't plugged in and switched on". Each of these reasons has to be checked out.

7.5.2.2 The Second "Why" The questioning now has to follow two paths.

The first path asks, "Why is there no electricity?" Again there are two answers.

1. Because there is a power failure
2. Because there is a broken circuit breaker or fuse.

7.5.2.3 The Third "Why" So the first path in the third level of questioning is, "Why is there a power failure?"

The answer might be, "Because nobody paid the electricity bill and the power supply has been cut off". The answer might also be, "There is a failure in the network and the electricity company is taking care of it". For this second answer the corrective action in either case is pretty much obvious: pay the bill or wait for the power company to restore power. If the situation occurs frequently enough to be really annoying, then an alternative emergency backup power supply or an alternative method of heating water such as gas could be installed.

Returning to the alternate broken kettle path, at this point the question is not why, the question is, "Do we want to repair or replace the kettle?" If the answer to the question is replace the kettle, then the questioning stops at this point and the corrective action is to repair replace the kettle. If the answer to the question is repair the kettle, then the "why" question picks up asking, "Why is the kettle broken?"

Answers include, "Because the heating element has failed", or "Because the switch on the kettle is inoperative".

While the sequence can drill down examining why the heating element failed or why the switch failed, in this instance it's probably going to be cheaper to replace the kettle, and the process ends with a recommendation to replace the kettle.

When using the Five Whys, it's probably not advisable to drill down through all levels at one time. Because at each level, the "because" may be a guess or a hypothesis and would need to be verified before going down to the next lower level. And if the hypothesis is wrong, there is no reason to go down to the next level in that branch. Two situations where we would want to explore every branch and every reason and drill down to the lowest level for each reason are:

1. In risk management when we are discussing potential failure symptoms and the probable causes of those failures so we can design them out.
2. In failure analysis in a situation where we cannot access the equipment but need to plan some remote tests to determine the nature of the failure.

7.5.3 *Failure Prediction and Prevention*

The traditional use of the Five Whys is to examine the situation after the fact, the form of the question being "why did" or "why is"?

However, the approach can be used to predict and prevent failures of things going wrong. In this second approach, a symptom is assumed to have occurred, and the Five Whys will generally have more than one answer at each level as described in Section 7.5.2.

7.6 The Kipling Questions

The Kipling Questions are a systematic way of triggering ideas when examining a situation or discussing a problem. Rudyard Kipling introduced them in a poem:

> I have six honest serving men
> They taught me all I knew
> I call them What and Where and When
> And How and Why and Who

(Kipling 1912)

These questions are used in Active Brainstorming (Section 7.1) to pose questions from each of the HTPs (Section 10.1). Active Brainstorming contains examples of questions beginning with "who", "what", "where", "when", "why", and "how". For example when discussing an incident, the six questions may be used to start examining situation in the following manner.

1. *WHO* was involved?
2. *WHAT* happened?
3. *WHERE* did it take place?
4. *WHEN* did it take place?
5. *WHY* did it happen?
6. *HOW* did it happen?

Consider each of them.

- *"Who" Questions*: generally view a situation from the *Operational* and *Functional* HTPs and personalize the issues. Traditionally the "who" includes stakeholders:
  - Who are ultimately responsible and have the authority to authorize any action will be taken in the situation.
  - Who are unhappy with the undesirable situation.

- Who will bear the costs of converting the situation to a desirable situation.
- Who will benefit from the new situation.
- Who will carry out the work or process of converting the situation from an undesirable situation to a desirable situation.
- Who caused the undesirable situation may not actually be stakeholders, but they should be identified. They should not be blamed in most instances.
- *"What" questions*: ask for descriptions of purposes, things or events. "What" questions include:
  - What are you doing?
  - What is it?
  - What if …?
  - What do you want?
  - What is stopping you from…?
  - What do you think the solution is?
  - What do you think the problem is ?
- *"Where" questions*: are used to locate an action or event in space.
- *"When" questions*: are used to locate an action or event in time.
- *"Why" questions*: generally seek to understand the reason for an observation. It's used in cause-and-effect analysis to try and understand the root cause of a failure or some other undesirable situation. It was popularized in the Five Whys (Section 7.5).

From the *Continuum* HTP, changing the "why" question to a "why not" question challenges people. For example, if during the course of the discussion somebody says that something can't be done, posing the "why not" question in the form of "why can't it be done", may lead to a discussion that determines that it actually can be done it just wasn't thought through enough.

- *"How" questions*: are generally answered with a verb or a description of a process: they are good for probing into details of what has happened or what will happen. In systems analysis, "how" questions are useful in figuring out how to design something that will make a scenario possible. In requirement solicitation, a standard question ought to be, "How will you know when this requirement is met?" The answer to the question becomes the acceptance criterion.

7.7 Lateral Thinking

Lateral Thinking is a tool for handling insight and the generation of new ideas (de Bono 1973: pp. 10–11). De Bono claims that Lateral Thinking is different from traditional "vertical" thinking which moves from idea to idea in a sequential manner to reach a conclusion. The difference being that traditional vertical thinking focuses on a solution and the details associated with the solution, while Lateral Thinking produces a set of alternative solutions. Lateral Thinking:

- Takes place before, during, and after the ideation session.
- Separates creation of ideas and judgment of ideas.
- Uses the metaphor of six coloured thinking hats.

The six different thinking hats, used when planning, during and after the ideation meeting are:

1. Blue Hat thinking, discussed in Section 7.7.1.
2. White Hat thinking, discussed in Section 7.7.2.
3. Green Hat thinking, discussed in Section 7.7.3.
4. Yellow Hat thinking, discussed in Section 7.7.4.
5. Black Hat thinking, discussed in Section 7.7.5.
6. Red Hat thinking, discussed in Section 7.7.6.

7.7.1 Blue Hat Thinking

Blue Hat thinking:

- Generally takes place before the ideation session.
- Is used when planning ideation sessions or meetings.
- Identifies the:
  - Focus of the meeting.

- Agenda.
- Participants who need to be at the meeting.

Questions to trigger Blue Hat thinking include:

- What roles will the attendees play?
- How long will the meeting last?
- How much time will be spent on each part of the agenda?
- How to make sure everyone participates?
- How to summarize the results?
- Who will take what action after the meeting?

7.7.2 White Hat Thinking

White Hat thinking:

- Generally takes place before the ideation session.
- Assesses the relevance and accuracy of information:
  - Supplied to the meeting participants.
  - Produced as ideas.
- Separates facts from speculation.
- Notes both views when there is conflicting information.

Questions to trigger White Hat thinking before the ideation meeting include:

- What do we know?
- What do we need to know?
- How will we get the missing information?

7.7.3 Green Hat Thinking

Green Hat thinking:

- Generally takes place during the ideation session.
- Generates the ideas.
- Is used in the ideation meeting to look for:
  - New ideas and alternatives.
  - Modify and remove faults in existing ideas.

7.7.4 Yellow Hat Thinking

Yellow Hat thinking:

- Generally takes place after the ideation session.
- Is used when processing ideas generated by Green Hat thinking.
- Helps to determine the benefits of the ideas.

Questions to trigger Yellow Hat thinking include:

- What benefit/value/return on investment does the idea offer?
- Why do we think the idea might/might not work?

7.7.5 Black Hat Thinking

Black Hat thinking:

- Generally takes place after the ideation session.
- Is used when processing ideas generated by Green Hat thinking.
- Is the compliment to Yellow Hat thinking, dealing with the disadvantages of, or concerns about, the ideas.

Questions to trigger Black Hat thinking include:

- What problems are associated with this idea?
- What might go wrong if it is implemented?
- Why do we think the idea might fail?

7.7.6 Red Hat Thinking

Red Hat thinking:

- Generally takes place before and during the ideation session.
- Is concerned about the feelings, intuition, and emotion of the participants in a meeting.

- Is used:
  - When planning the meeting.
  - By the meeting facilitator during the meeting itself, since participant's feelings can change over time as the result of some action taken by another participant.

Questions to trigger Red Hat thinking include:

- What are the concerns of each participant?
- How can those concerns be addressed?
- How does/will each participant feel about the agenda?
- How does/will each participant feel about particular ideas?
- How does/will each participant feel about the decisions to be taken/during or after the meeting?
- Should a participant receive special treatment?
- How does/will each participant feel about the steps to be taken after the meeting?

7.8 Letter and Word Manipulation

Letter manipulation is a tool to create ideas by transposing letters in words and removing or adding or removing letters to trigger ideas. For example, change:

- Bundle to bungle.
- Create to crate.
- Deploy to destroy.
- Draft to daft.
- Expensive to expansive or extensive.
- Explore to explode.
- Feel to fuel.
- Fuming to fusing.
- Guest to ghost.
- Last to lost.
- Point to pint.

In word manipulation change one word for another word to trigger ideas. For example, change a word to one:

- With an opposite meaning: for example, change "good" to "bad" or change "cheap" to "expensive".
- Of the same generic type: for example, change "dog" to "cat".
- Which sounds almost the same: for example, change "illuminate" to "eliminate".

7.9 Nominal Group Technique

The Nominal Group Technique (NGT) (Delbecq, Van de Ven, and Gustafson 1975) is a methodology designed to allow every member of the group to express their ideas while minimizing the influence of other participants (the capture effect by the most opinionated that tends to occur in Brainstorming). NGT should be used when:

- You want to generate a lot of ideas and want everyone to participate freely without influence from other participants.
- You want to identify priorities of proposed solutions or select a few alternatives for further examination.
- When you want to avoid heated conflict because the issue is controversial.

NGT has a number of variations, but the basic process is something like the following:

1. The facilitator poses the focused question stating the problem or issue.
2. The participants write down their ideas just like in Slip Writing (Section 7.10).
3. After the ideation process has dried up, the facilitator asks each participant in turn to state one idea. The idea is written down on the whiteboard. No comments or discussion of each idea is allowed. After everybody has expressed an idea,

the cycle repeats as long as someone has an idea to share. Participants may "pass" on their turns and may then add an idea on a subsequent turn providing for hitchhiking of ideas generated by association.

4. The ideas are discussed in turn and clarified as necessary. Combination and discarding does not take place at this time.

5. Each participant is then asked to privately list his or her top ten ideas in order of priority and give the list to the facilitator. If there are a large number of ideas this may be a done as a two-step process, first listing the top ten ideas and then prioritising the ideas.

6. The facilitator then records the rankings and averages the scores. This may be done during a coffee or tea break or as a group, thereby adding an element of fun. The facilitator may write the ideas on the whiteboard, flip charts, or projected spread sheets and add stars next to each idea as they show up on subsequent lists, and the participants can watch the idea rankings change in a similar manner to watching election results on television.

7.10 Slip Writing

The Crawford Slip Method (CSM) was developed by Dr C. C. Crawford, a professor of education at the University of Southern California in the 1920s (Mycoted 2007), as a tool for ideation in very large groups (Ballard and Trent 1989). The five-step Slip Writing process is as follows.

1. The participants are given slips of paper and pens or pencils.

2. The facilitator poses the focused question (problem) in the same manner as in Brainstorming.

3. The participants write down the ideas that come to mind.

4. When the writing slows down, the slips are collected and ideas collated.

5. In many instances, summaries of the ideas are provided to the participants after the session.

In some variations such as classroom sessions, the ideas are written on Post-it Notes, one idea per sticky slip. When ideation has stopped, the participants step up to a wall or a whiteboard in turn and read out their ideas, posting the slips as one column to one idea. After the first person has finished, each subsequent person who has a similar or identical idea to a previous one posts the idea below the original idea. When everyone has posted their ideas, the breadth of the columns represent the number of ideas and the depth of a column represents the number of participants who thought of the same idea. The breadth will generally reflect the diversity of the participants.

Slip Writing only collects the initial ideas. As Slip Writing does not include the hitchhiker effect of Association of Ideas experienced in Brainstorming, Slip Writing should generally only be used as an ideation tool in large groups.

7.11 Visualization

Visualization is a tool to help create and manage scenarios. It may be used to:

- Conceptualize a non-existing scenario such as a FCFDS.
- Examine the effect of hypothetical or postulated changes in the scenario such as the result of the failure. For example visualization is often used to answer the question "what if...?" In this case you visualize the event as having occurred and then examine the consequences.
- Work backwards from the solution (Section 11.8).
- Do Risk Management (Chapter 12) in real-time by visualizing what can go wrong in specific scenarios and then checking to make sure nothing that was visualized will go wrong. One of the basic uses of this technique is called a site survey. It is used in a situation where something has to be delivered or installed in a remote location. So somebody is sent out to use Visualization to make sure that there no impediments to the delivery and there is enough space for whatever is going to be installed as well as convenient AC power sockets and ventilation. There are stories about equipment being delivered to submarines that would not fit through the hatch, and so the contractor had to cut a hole in the side of the submarine and then repair the hole. I saw one example in 2016 at NUS. I was coming into

the office one morning and I saw a group of people standing around a large packing case on a pallet. It was obvious
that the packing case would not go into the door of the building. I smiled and took a photograph. About an hour later, I
went out to get a cup of tea from the kiosk (Figure 11.12).
This time I saw that packing case in mid air on the end of a
rope being hoisted to somewhere. I took another photograph
and now use these pictures when I teach risk management. A
site visit would have prevented that undesirable situation from
happening because there should then have been an installation
requirement on whatever equipment was in the packing case
that would have set a maximum size limit on assemblies.

- Visualize improvements in situations in real-time. For example, I have often taught in various classrooms. Before teaching
in a new classroom, I usually try to go look at the classroom
and visualize myself teaching in that room. I then compare
the visualization with the reality of the facilities in the classroom. I then realize, for example, there is no clock at the back
of the room, so I won't be able to monitor the time in my usual
way. So I either have to ask for a clock to be installed or modify the way I teach to do that time check in a different way.

7.11.1 How to Visualize

The following generic process is suggested as a starting process. Feel
free to modify to suit yourself.

1. Put yourself in a location where there are no distractions. This
   means turn off the television, the phone, and the music player,
   and make sure nobody will interrupt you for the duration of
   the visualization.
2. Assume a comfortable position.
3. State what it is you want to visualize and why. One useful tool
   to do this is a Mission Statement (Section 8.9).
4. Conceptualize the scenario in the present tense. Watch it taking place in your mind. It must be a specific scenario or a
   number of scenarios; it must not be a state. For example:
   - "Being rich" is a state (of being), it's not a scenario.

- "Not smoking" or "not drinking" are states. The scenarios are the situations in which someone is not smoking or is not drinking.
- "Being improved" or "doing something better" are states not scenarios. The scenarios are situations in which something is done in a quantifiable improved or better manner.

5. Examine the scenario from different HTPs (Section 10.1) including the *Big Picture*, *Operational*, *Functional*, *Quantitative*, and *Structural* HTPs.
6. Document what you see; use whatever tools suit you, such as Lists (Section 9.4), Concept Maps (Section 6.1.2), and Flowcharts (Section 2.7).
7. Now visualize how you arrived into the situation that has just been documented working backwards from that future situation to where you are in the present time (Section 11.8).
8. Visualize the major milestones (Section 14.9.2) along the way.
9. Visualize the activities between each pair of major milestones in the same way that you conceptualized the future scenario and examined it in Steps 4 and 5.
10. Document the milestones and the pairs of activities; the tool to use is a Project Plan (Section 8.11).

Perceptions from the *Generic* HTP will show that this process is identical to the planning process (Section 8.11.2). Perceptions from the *Continuum* HTP will show where and how this process has to be customized for different situations. For example, visualising making a cup of instant coffee is simple. Perceiving the scenario from the:

- *Operational* HTP, one gets the ingredients, puts them in the cup of hot water and the results as a cup of instant coffee.
- *Structural* HTP indicates a cup, a kettle, a spoon or other stirring instrument, coffee, sweetener, milk or cream, and the electricity.
- *Functional* HTP, one performs a number of functions, putting water into the kettle, turning on the electricity, heating the water, putting the coffee into the cup, putting the sweetener into the cup, putting the milk or cream into the cup, adding the hot water, and stirring the mixture.

Perceptions from the *Functional* HTP also examine the sequence in which the functions are performed. This identifies functions which can be performed in parallel and which must be performed in series. For example, the ingredients can be placed into the cup while the water is heating. But the hot water cannot be poured into the mixture of ingredients until (1) the water is hot and (2) the ingredients are in the cup. Other activities may be done in parallel or in series depending on how many people (the resources available) are involved in making that cup of instant coffee. If two people are making that coffee, one person can heat the water at the same time as the other person puts the ingredients in the cup. If only one person is making the coffee then the person first starts the water heating task and then inserts the ingredients into the cup.

7.11.2 A Visualization Exercise

Think about your present situation, and modify the generic visualization process to visualize where you'd like to be in five years time and how you got there from the present situation. Then do the visualization. You now have an action plan to make that desirable future happen.

7.12 Summary

Chapter 7 discussed ten idea generating tools and introduced Active Brainstorming, which extends the Brainstorming process by asking the Kipling Questions in a systemic and systematic manner. Other tools discussed in this chapter include Association of Ideas, Brainstorming, Constraint Mapping, the Five Whys, Lateral Thinking, letter and word manipulation, the NGT, and Slip Writing. Some of these tools are useful in groups, others are suitable for individuals. Although this chapter discussed the tools individually, they may be used in combination. Accordingly, this chapter showed how Active Brainstorming could be used while performing Constraint Mapping.

References

Ballard, J. A., and D. M. Trent. 1989. "Idea Generation and Productivity: The Promise of CSM." *Public Productivity Review*, no. 12 (4):373–386.

de Bono, E. 1973. *Lateral Thinking: Creativity Step by Step*. New York: Harper & Row.

Delbecq, A. L., A. H. Van de Ven, and D. H. Gustafson. 1975. *Group Techniques for Program Planning: A Guide to Nominal Group and Delphi Processes*. Edited by Alan C. Filley, *Management Applications Series*. Glenview, IL: Scott, Foresman and Company.

Dunn, W. N. 2012. *Public Policy Analysis*. 5th Ed. Upper Saddle River, NJ: Pearson Education, Inc.

Kasser, J. E. 2013. *Holistic Thinking: Creating Innovative Solutions to Complex Problems*. Createspace Ltd.

Kasser, J. E., and T. Mackley. 2008. "Applying Systems Thinking and Aligning It to Systems Engineering." In the 18th INCOSE International Symposium. Utrecht, Holland.

Kipling, J. R. 1912. "The Elephant's Child." In *The Just So Stories*. Garden City, NY: The Country Life Press.

Mycoted. 2007. *Crawford Slip Writing*. Mycoted, accessed 18 January 2011. http://www.mycoted.com/Crawford_Slip_Writing.

Osborn, A. F. 1963. *Applied Imagination Principles and Procedures of Creative Problem Solving*. 3rd Rev. Ed. New York: Charles Scribner's Sons.

Ruggiero, V. V. 2012. *The Art of Thinking: A Guide to Critical and Creative Thought*. 10th Ed. Boston: Pearson, Education, Inc.

8
MANAGEMENT TOOLS

The traditional use of management tools is as standalone tools. In the systems approach to project management, they are used interdependently as described in this chapter. Each tool is described for those who are not familiar with it, and embedded in the description are the interdependencies with the other tools. The tools discussed in this chapter are:

1. Categorized Requirements in Process (CRIP) Charts in Section 8.1.
2. Earned Value Analysis (EVA) in Section 8.2.
3. Financial Budgets in Section 8.3.
4. Gantt Charts in Section 8.4.
5. The Golden Rule in Section 8.5.
6. Just-in-time (JIT) decision-making in Section 8.6.
7. Management by Exception (MBE) in Section 8.7.
8. Management by Objectives (MBO) in Section 8.8.
9. Mission Statements in Section 8.9.
10. PERT Charts in Section 8.10.
11. Project Plans in Section 8.11.
12. The Technology Availability Window of Opportunity (TAWOO) in Section 8.12.
13. The "Thank You" in Section 8.13.
14. The Three Streams of Activities in Section 8.14.
15. Timelines in Section 8.15.
16. Traffic Light Charts and Enhanced Traffic Light (ETL) Charts in Section 8.16.
17. The Waterfall Chart introduced in Section 8.17 and discussed in Section 14.9.
18. Work Breakdown Structures in Section 8.18.
19. Work Packages in Section 8.19.

8.1 Categorized Requirements in Process (CRIP) Charts

The Categorized Requirements in Process (CRIP) Chart (Kasser 1999) is a project management, systems, and software engineering tool that:

- Is used in monitoring and controlling projects.
- Provides a way to think about and measure technical progress.
- Identifies potential problems in near real-time so as to be able to prevent or mitigate the problems before they occur (risk management).

While simplistic approaches of tracking the realization activities of all the requirements or features such as Feature Driven Development (FDD) (Palmer and Felsing 2002) can inform about the state of the realization activities, they cannot be used to estimate the degree of completion since each requirement or feature has a different level of complexity and takes a different amount of effort to realize. The need is for a measurement approach that can:

- Roll up the detailed information into a summary that can be displayed in one or two charts.
- Readily relate to the existing cost and schedule information.

The CRIP approach (Kasser 1999) meets that need by looking at the change in the state of a summary of the realization activities which convert requirements into systems during the System Development Process (SDP) from several HTPs. The summary information is presented in a table known as a CRIP Chart which:

- Covers the entire SDP.
- Uses a technique similar to FDD Charts.
- Provides simple summaries suitable for upper management uninterested in details.
- Indicates variances between plan and progress but not the causes of the variance. It is up to management to ask for explanations of the variances.
- Is based on the use of WPs (Section 8.19) in planning a project, hence have to be integrated into the SDP at the planning stage of a project.
- Is designed to be used in association with EVA (Section 8.2) budget and schedule information as shown in Figure 8.1.

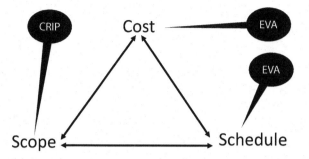

Figure 8.1 The relationship between CRIP Charts and EVA in the Triple Constraints.

This section first describes the CRIP Chart and then gives examples of how it can be used.

8.1.1 The Five-Step CRIP Approach

The five-step CRIP approach is to:

1. Identify categories for the requirements.
2. Quantify each category into ranges.
3. Categorize the requirements.
4. Place each requirement into a range in each category.
5. Monitor the differences in the state of each of the numbers of requirements in a range at the SDP formal and informal reporting milestones.

The first four steps take place before the System Requirement Review (SRR). The last step which takes place in all the states of the SDP following the SRR is the key element in the CRIP approach because it is a dynamic measure of change rather than a static value. Consider each of the five steps.

8.1.1.1 Step 1: Identify Categories for the Requirements Identify categories for the requirements. Typical categories are:

- **Complexity**: of the requirement.
- **Estimated cost**: to implement the requirement.
- **Firmness**: the likelihood that the requirement will change during the SDP.
- **Priority**: of the requirement.
- **Risk**: probability of occurrence, severity if it occurs, etc.

Each of the different categories may be considered as points on a Perspectives Perimeter of categories (Chapter 10).

8.1.1.2 Step 2: Quantify Each Category into Ranges   Quantify each category into no more than ten ranges. Thus, for:

- **Priority**: requirements may be allocated priorities between one and ten.
- **Complexity**: requirements may be allocated estimated complexities of implementation between "A" and "J".
- **Estimated cost to implement**: requirements may be allocated estimated costs to implement values. For example less than $100, between $100 and $500, between $500 and $1000, etc.
- **Risk (schedule completion)**: requirements may be awarded a value between one and five.

The ranges are relative, not absolute. Any of the several quantitative decision-making techniques for sorting items into relative ranges may be used (Section 4.6). The buyer/customer and supplier/contractor determine the range limits in each category.

A requirement may be moved into a different range as more is learned about its effect on the development or the relative importance of the need changes during the SDP. Thus, if the priority of a specific requirement or the estimated cost to implement changes between SDP reporting milestones changes, the requirement may be moved from one range to another in those categories. However, the rules for setting the range limits, and the range limits must not change during the SDP.

8.1.1.3 Step 3: Categorize the Requirements   Every requirement shall be placed in each category.

8.1.1.4 Step 4: Place Each Requirement into a Range in Each Category   Place each requirement into one range slot for each category. The information used to place the requirements into the ranges for the categories comes from the WP (Section 8.19) in the Project Plan (PP) (Section 8.11). If all the requirements end up in the same range slot, such as all of them having the highest priority, the range limits should be re-examined to spread the requirements across the full set of range slots. If most of them end up in a single range slot, then that slot should be expanded into several slots. There is no need for the ranges to be linear. For example, ranges could be 1–10, 11–20, 20–30, etc., or 1–10, 11–15, 16–20, 21–30, etc. In the second case it just means that the range 11–20 has been split into two ranges.

Once the requirements have been categorized in ranges, an Attribute Profile (Section 9.1) for each category can be drawn in the form of a Histogram (Section 2.9) as shown in Figure 9.2 for the Priority category and Figure 9.1 for the Risk category.

8.1.1.5 Step 5: States of Implementation At any time during the SDP, each requirement shall be in one, and only one, of five CRIP states. The CRIP states of implementation of each requirement during the project are:

1. *Identified*: a requirement has been identified, documented and approved.
2. *In-process*: the supplier has begun the development activities to realize the requirement.
3. *Completed*: the supplier has completed development activities on the equipment that will perform the requirement.
4. *In test*: the supplier has started to test compliance to the requirement.
5. *Accepted*: the buyer has accepted delivery of the part of the system (a Build) containing the implementation of the requirement.

The summaries of the number of requirements in each state are reported at project milestones and reporting meetings.

8.1.2 Populating and Using the CRIP Chart

An unpopulated CRIP Chart is shown in Table 8.1 where:

- The vertical axis of the chart is split into the ten ranges in the category (1–10).
- The horizontal axis of the chart is split into five columns representing the CRIP states of a project.

Table 8.1   An Unpopulated CRIP Chart

RANGE	IDENTIFIED			IN PROCESS			COMPLETED			IN TEST			ACCEPTED		
	P	E	A	P	E	A	P	E	A	P	E	A	P	E	A
1															
2															
3															
4															
5															
6															
7															
8															
9															
10															
Totals															

Each CRIP state contains three cells; planned "P", expected "E" and actual "A", where:

- *[P] Planned for next reporting period*: the number of requirements planned to be in the CRIP state before the following reporting milestone.
- *[E] Expected*: the number of requirements expected to be in the CRIP state, based on the number planned in the previous reporting milestone. This is a copy of the "P" value in the CRIP Chart for the previous milestone.
- *[A] Actual*: the number of requirements actually in the CRIP state.

For the first milestone-reporting period, the values for:

- *"Expected"* "E" are derived from the Project Plan (PP) (Section 8.11) for the time period.
- *"Actual"* value "A" is the number actually measured at the end of the reporting period.
- *"Planned* for next reporting period" value "P" is a number derived from the PP and the work done during the current reporting period.

As of the first milestone following the start of a project, the numbers in the "P" column of a CRIP state of the chart at one milestone are always copied into the "E" column of the same CRIP state in the chart for the next milestone. The "A" and "P" values reflect the reality. As work progresses the numbers flow across the CRIP states from "Identified" to "Accepted".

At each reporting milestone, the changes in the CRIP state of each of the requirements between the milestones are monitored. The numbers of each of the requirements in each of the categories are presented in tabular format in a CRIP Chart at reporting milestones (major reviews or monthly progress meetings). Colours can be used to draw attention to the state of a cell in the table. For example the colours can be allocated* such that:

- *Violet* shows realization activities for requirements in that range is well ahead of estimates.
- *Blue* shows realization activities for requirements in that range is ahead of estimates.
- *Green* shows realization activities for requirements in that range is close to estimates.
- *Yellow* shows realization activities for requirements in that range is slightly below estimates.
- *Red* shows realization activities for requirements in that range is well under the estimates.

The range setting for the colours in the CRIP Charts should be the same as the range settings using in the ETL Charts (Section 8.16.2) for the project.

CRIP Charts show that a problem might exist. Any time there is a deviation between "E" and "A" in a CRIP State, the situation needs to be investigated just as a deviation in an EVA Chart (Section 8.2) has to be explained. A comparison of the summaries from different reporting milestones can identify progress and show that problems may exist. On its own however, the CRIP Chart cannot identify the actual problem; its purpose is to trigger questions to determine the nature of the actual problem.

The CRIP Charts when viewed over several reporting periods can identify other types of "situations". While the CRIP Chart can be

---

* The quantitative numbers for the ranges would be agreed upon between the stakeholders, specified in the contract prior to the commencement of the project, and not changed during the SDP.

used as a stand-alone chart, it should really be used together with EVA (Section 8.2) budget and schedule information. For example, if there is a change in the number of:

- *Identified requirements and there is no change in the budget or schedule.* There is going to be a problem. Thus:
  - If the number of requirements goes up and the budget does not, the risk of failure increases because more work will have to be done without a change in the allocation of funds.
  - If the number of requirements goes down, and the budget does not, there is a financial problem. However, if it is in the context of a fixed price contract it shows additional profit.
- *Requirements being worked on and there is no change in the number being tested.* There is a potential supplier management or technical problem if this situation is at a major milestone review.
- *Requirements being tested and there is no change in the number accepted.* There may be a problem with the supplier's process or a large number of defects have been found and are being reworked.
- *Identified requirements at each reporting milestone.* The project is suffering from requirements creep if the number is increasing. This situation may reflect controlled changes due to the change in the customer's need, or uncontrolled changes.

Since projects tend to delay formal milestones until the planned work is completed, the CRIP Charts are more useful in the monthly or other periodic meetings between the formal major milestones.

8.1.3 *Advantages of the CRIP Approach*

The advantages of the CRIP approach include:

- Can be used in both the "A" and "B" paradigms of systems engineering (Kasser 2012).
- Links all work done on a project to the customer's requirements.
- May be used at any level of system decomposition.
- Provides a simple way to show progress or the lack of it, at any reporting milestone. Just compare the "E" and "A" numbers and ask for an explanation of the variances.

- Provides a window into the project for top management (buyer and supplier) to monitor progress (Micromanagement by Upper Management (MBUM)).
- Can indicate if lower priority requirements are being realized before higher priority requirements if priority is a category.
- Identifies the probability of some management and technical problems as they occur, allowing proactive risk containment techniques.
- May be built into requirements management, and other computerized project and development management tools.
- May be incorporated into the progress reporting requirements in system development contracts. Falsifying entries in the CRIP Chart to show false progress then constitutes fraud.
- Requires a process. Some organizations don't have one, so they will have to develop one to use CRIP Charts.
- Requires Configuration Management (CM) which tends to be poorly implemented in many organizations. The use of CRIP Charts will enforce good CM.

8.1.4 Disadvantages of the CRIP Approach

The CRIP Chart approach has the following disadvantages, it:

- Is a different way of viewing project progress.
- Requires categorization of the requirements.
- Requires sorting of the requirements into ranges in each category.
- Requires prioritization of requirements if priority is used as a category, which it should be.

8.1.5 Examples of Using CRIP Charts in Different Types of Projects

The following sections of this chapter show how CRIP Charts can indicate the technical progress of a project and identify potential problems using the following stereotype examples:

1. An ideal project discussed in Section 8.1.5.1.
2. A project with requirements creep in Section 8.1.5.2.
3. A challenged project in Section 8.1.5.3.
4. A "make up your mind" project in Section 8.1.5.4.

The projects are all identical until completion of SRR.

Since projects tend to delay formal milestones until the planned work is completed, the CRIP Charts are more useful in the monthly or other periodic meetings between the formal major milestones. However, for the example of these stereotype projects, the CRIP Charts are provided for the formal milestones since their names are widely known.

As an example, consider Federated Aerospace, a major government contractor with multiple simultaneous project and contracts. One of Federated Aerospace's projects provides examples of the use of CRIP Charts as follows. Federated Aerospace organized a proposal team to bid on a Request for Proposal (RFP) issued by a Government agency. Upon receipt of the RFP the project team identified 279 requirements in the document and created CRIP Charts for several categories of requirements including cost. The proposal team estimated the costs to realize those requirements as part of the proposal effort. Once the costs were estimated, the proposal team defined ten ranges of costs and allo-cated each requirement into the appropriate range. The CRIP Chart at the completion of the proposal shown in Table 8.2 indicates that:

- The RFP contained 279 requirements.
- The requirements have been grouped into 10 cost ranges. There are 86 requirements in Range 1, 73 in Range 2, 23 in Range 3, and so on.

Table 8.2   CRIP Chart at RFP Time (Cost Category)

RANGE	IDENTIFIED			IN PROCESS			COMPLETED			IN TEST			ACCEPTED		
	P	E	A	P	E	A	P	E	A	P	E	A	P	E	A
1	0		86	0											
2	0		73	0											
3	0		23	0											
4	0		34	0											
5	0		26	0											
6	0		15	0											
7	0		8	0											
8	0		7	0											
9	0		5	0											
10	0		2	0											
Totals	0		279	0											

- No further work is planned at this time as shown by the zero values assigned to the "P" columns of the "Identified" and the "In process" States.*

Federated Aerospace's proposal was accepted, and the government awarded a contract to Federated Aerospace for the project. This example provides typical CRIP Charts for the following six notional major milestones in the project (Section 14.9):

1. Systems Requirements Review (SRR).
2. Preliminary Design Review (PDR).
3. Critical Design Review (CDR).
4. Test Readiness Review (TRR).
5. Integration Readiness Review (IRR).
6. Delivery Readiness Review (DRR).

The Federated Aerospace development stream of activities in the project started by confirming that all the requirements in the RFP:

- Were understood by the Federated Aerospace project team.
- Had not changed since the RFP had been issued.
- Were complete; there were no additional or deleted requirements which would change the scope and cost of the contract.
- Were tagged with acceptance criteria.†

The CRIP Chart at the start of the ideal project shown in Table 8.3, based on the information in the RFP CRIP Chart in Table 8.2 indicated that there would be no planned change between the number of requirements identified at SRR and those identified in the RFP since:

- The numbers in each row of the "E" column in Table 8.3‡ match those in the corresponding rows of the "A" column in Table 8.2.
- The number in each row in the "P" column in the "Identified" State of in Table 8.3 has been set to zero since there are no planned additional requirements.

---

* This would change if Federated Aerospace wins the contract award.

† Not used in CRIP Charts, but needed elsewhere.

‡ This is the only time in a project when 'A' column numbers are copied from one CRIP State in a CRIP Chart at one reporting period to the CRIP Chart of the following CRIP State.

Table 8.3   CRIP Chart at the Start of the Project

	IDENTIFIED			IN PROCESS			COMPLETED			IN TEST			ACCEPTED		
RANGE	P	E	A	P	E	A	P	E	A	P	E	A	P	E	A
1	0	86	0												
2	0	73	0												
3	0	23	0												
4	0	34	0												
5	0	26	0												
6	0	15	0												
7	0	8	0												
8	0	7	0												
9	0	5	0												
10	0	2	0												
Totals	0	279	0												

Note, as of the first milestone following the start of a project, the numbers in the "P" column of a State of the CRIP Chart at one milestone are always copied into the "E" column of the same State in the CRIP Chart for the next milestone as shown in Table 8.2.

The CRIP Chart at SRR shown in Table 8.4 indicates that the project has deviated from the baseline plan since:

- There are differences between the expected numbers and the actual numbers of identified requirements since there are differences between the numbers in several rows of the "A"

Table 8.4   The CRIP Chart at SRR

	IDENTIFIED			IN PROCESS			COMPLETED			IN TEST			ACCEPTED		
RANGE	P	E	A	P	E	A	P	E	A	P	E	A	P	E	A
1	0	86	81	81											
2	0	73	78	78											
3	0	23	35	35											
4	0	34	30	30											
5	0	26	26	26											
6	0	15	20	20											
7	0	8	8	8											
8	0	7	7	7											
9	0	5	5	5											
10	0	2	2	2											
Totals	0	279	292	292											

column and the "E" column of the "Identified" State. For example, in Range 1 an "E" number of 86 became an "A" of 81 and in Range 2 an "E" number of 73 became an "A" of 78. Changes can also be seen in Ranges 4 and 6.*

- The total number of identified requirements has increased from 279 to 292.†
- The project development team plans to work on all the requirements to put them into development following the conclusion of the SRR since the numbers from the "A" column in the "Identified" State have been copied into the "P" column of the "In process" State.
- The project does not plan to identify any new requirements between SRR and PDR since all the rows in the "P" column of the "Identified" State have been reset to zero.

The stereotype projects diverge after SRR. Consider how the CRIP Charts provide early identification of the technical progress or lack of progress (an indication of a potential problem) in the milestone reviews of the stereotype projects using the ideal project as a reference.

8.1.5.1 The Ideal Project The ideal project is the one in which everything happens according to the plan and there are no changes in the requirements during the SDP, such as in a short duration project or an educational example.

8.1.5.1.1 The Ideal Project CRIP Chart at PDR The ideal project CRIP Chart at PDR shown in Table 8.5 indicates that the project is proceeding according to plan since:

- No additional requirements were levied on the system as indicated by the zero value in all the rows in "A" column in the "Identified" State.
- The System Design State activities commenced as expected since the "A" numbers in the "In process" State match the "E" numbers.

---

* Upon investigation it was found that the changes in the number of requirements are due to the clarifications that occurred during the requirements elicitation and elucidation process, a typical project happening.
† The cost and schedule was renegotiated as a result and is reflected in the updated cost and schedule summaries also presented in the SRR (not included herein).

Table 8.5   The Ideal Project CRIP Chart at PDR

RANGE	IDENTIFIED			IN PROCESS			COMPLETED			IN TEST			ACCEPTED		
	P	E	A	P	E	A	P	E	A	P	E	A	P	E	A
1	0	0	0	0	81	81	0								
2	0	0	0	0	78	78	0								
3	0	0	0	0	35	35	0								
4	0	0	0	0	30	30	0								
5	0	0	0	0	26	26	0								
6	0	0	0	0	20	20	0								
7	0	0	0	0	8	8	0								
8	0	0	0	0	7	7	0								
9	0	0	0	0	5	5	0								
10	0	0	0	0	2	2	0								
Totals	0	0	0	0	292	292	0								

- The project does not plan to complete the development of any requirements by CDR since there is a zero value in all of the rows in the "P" column in the "Completed". This is because the CDR will be held before the end of the "In process" CRIP State.
- The project does not plan to identify any new requirements between PDR and CDR since all the rows in the "P" column of the "Identified" CRIP State remain at zero.

8.1.5.1.2 The Ideal Project CRIP Chart at CDR The ideal project CRIP Chart at CDR shown in Table 8.6 indicates that the project is still proceeding according to plan since:

- No additional requirements were levied on the system as indicated by the zero value in all the rows in the "A" column of the "Identified" State.
- The plan is for all the development activities to be completed by TRR since all the numbers in the "A" column of the "In-process" State have been copied into the "P" column of the "Completed" State.
- The project does not plan to identify any new requirements between CDR and TRR since all the rows in the "P" column of the "Identified" State remain at zero.

Table 8.6 The Ideal Project CRIP Chart at CDR

	IDENTIFIED			IN PROCESS			COMPLETED			IN TEST			ACCEPTED		
RANGE	P	E	A	P	E	A	P	E	A	P	E	A	P	E	A
1	0	0	0	0	81	81	81								
2	0	0	0	0	78	78	78								
3	0	0	0	0	35	35	35								
4	0	0	0	0	30	30	30								
5	0	0	0	0	26	26	26								
6	0	0	0	0	20	20	20								
7	0	0	0	0	8	8	8								
8	0	0	0	0	7	7	7								
9	0	0	0	0	5	5	5								
10	0	0	0	0	2	2	2								
Totals	0	0	0	0	292	292	292								

8.1.5.1.3 The Ideal Project CRIP Chart at TRR The ideal project CRIP Chart at TRR shown in Table 8.7 indicates that the project is still proceeding according to plan since:

- No additional requirements were levied on the system as indicated by the zero value in all the rows in the "A" column of the "Identified" State.
- The development activities for the system have been completed since the numbers in the "A" column of the "Completed" State match those in the "E" column.

Table 8.7 The Ideal Project CRIP Chart at TIRR

	IDENTIFIED			IN PROCESS			COMPLETED			IN TEST			ACCEPTED		
RANGE	P	E	A	P	E	A	P	E	A	P	E	A	P	E	A
1	0	0	0	0	0	0	0	81	81	81					
2	0	0	0	0	0	0	0	78	78	78					
3	0	0	0	0	0	0	0	35	35	35					
4	0	0	0	0	0	0	0	30	30	30					
5	0	0	0	0	0	0	0	26	26	26					
6	0	0	0	0	0	0	0	20	20	20					
7	0	0	0	0	0	0	0	8	8	8					
8	0	0	0	0	0	0	0	7	7	7					
9	0	0	0	0	0	0	0	5	5	5					
10	0	0	0	0	0	0	0	2	2	2					
Totals	0	0	0	0	0	0	0	292	292	292					

- Testing of all the requirements is expected to begin immediately following TRR since the numbers in the "A" column of the "Completed" State have been copied into the "P" column of the "In test" State.
- The project does not plan to identify any new requirements between TRR and the following milestone since all the rows in the "P" column of the "Identified" State remain at zero.

8.1.5.1.4 The Ideal Project CRIP Chart at IRR   The ideal project CRIP Chart at IRR, shown in Table 8.8 indicates that the project is still proceeding according to plan since:

- No additional requirements were levied on the system as indicated by the zero value in all the rows in the "A" column of the "Identified" State.
- Testing has begun to verify that the system meets all the requirements since all the numbers in the "A" column of the "In test" State match those in the "E" column.
- The project is planning to integrate the system for successful acceptance by the customer before the DRR since the values in the "A" column of the "In test" State have been copied into the "P" column of the "Accepted" State.
- The project does not plan to identify any new requirements between IRR and the following milestone since all the rows in the "P" column of the "Identified" State remain at zero.

Table 8.8   The Ideal Project CRIP Chart at IRR

RANGE	IDENTIFIED			IN PROCESS			COMPLETED			IN TEST			ACCEPTED		
	P	E	A	P	E	A	P	E	A	P	E	A	P	E	A
1	0	0	0	0	0	0	0	0	0	0	81	81	81		
2	0	0	0	0	0	0	0	0	0	0	78	78	78		
3	0	0	0	0	0	0	0	0	0	0	35	35	35		
4	0	0	0	0	0	0	0	0	0	0	30	30	30		
5	0	0	0	0	0	0	0	0	0	0	26	26	26		
6	0	0	0	0	0	0	0	0	0	0	20	20	20		
7	0	0	0	0	0	0	0	0	0	0	8	8	8		
8	0	0	0	0	0	0	0	0	0	0	7	7	7		
9	0	0	0	0	0	0	0	0	0	0	5	5	5		
10	0	0	0	0	0	0	0	0	0	0	2	2	2		
Totals	0	0	0	0	0	0	0	0	0	0	292	292	292		

Table 8.9   The Ideal Project CRIP Chart at DRR

RANGE	IDENTIFIED			IN PROCESS			COMPLETED			IN TEST			ACCEPTED		
	P	E	A	P	E	A	P	E	A	P	E	A	P	E	A
1	0	0	0	0	0	0	0	0	0	0	0	0	0	81	81
2	0	0	0	0	0	0	0	0	0	0	0	0	0	78	78
3	0	0	0	0	0	0	0	0	0	0	0	0	0	35	35
4	0	0	0	0	0	0	0	0	0	0	0	0	0	30	30
5	0	0	0	0	0	0	0	0	0	0	0	0	0	26	26
6	0	0	0	0	0	0	0	0	0	0	0	0	0	20	20
7	0	0	0	0	0	0	0	0	0	0	0	0	0	8	8
8	0	0	0	0	0	0	0	0	0	0	0	0	0	7	7
9	0	0	0	0	0	0	0	0	0	0	0	0	0	5	5
10	0	0	0	0	0	0	0	0	0	0	0	0	0	2	2
Totals	0	0	0	0	0	0	0	0	0	0	0	0	0	292	292

8.1.5.1.5 The Ideal Project CRIP Chart at DRR   The ideal project CRIP Chart at DRR shown in Table 8.9 indicates that the project is still proceeding according to plan since:

- No additional requirements were levied on the system as indicated by the zero value in all the rows in the "A" column of the "Identified" State.
- The integrated system has been accepted by the customer as having met all its requirements as indicated by the match between each of the values of the rows in the "A" column and the corresponding rows in the "E" column in the "Acceptance" State.

8.1.5.2 A Project with Requirements Creep   This section shows how the CRIP Charts can indicate that a project has requirements creep. Assume that the project has completed the SRR shown in Table 8.4 and that the changes in the number of requirements identified occur during the System Design State and the Subsystem Construction States between the SRR and TRR milestones.

The project has chosen to hold the milestone reviews as scheduled even though the work on the additional requirements may be out of phase with the original requirements. This is fine when the additional requirements can be realized without impacting the original planned work such as when the additional requirements are for additional functionality which can be provided independently and integrated into the system as a separate plug in.

8.1.5.2.1 The CRIP Chart for a Project with Requirements Creep at PDR Twenty-six unexpected* additional requirements were identified between SRR and PDR resulting in the total number of requirements increasing from 292 to 318. The CRIP Chart for the project with requirements creep at PDR shown in Table 8.10 indicates:

- Twenty of the unexpected requirements were identified in Range 1 shown by the 20 in the "A" column of the "Identified" State.
- Development activities have begun on these 20 requirements since the value of 81 in the "A" column of the "In process" State has become 101, namely the original 81 and the additional 20.
- Two of the unexpected requirements were identified in Range 5 shown by the 2 in the "A" column of the "Identified" State.
- Development activities have begun on these 2 requirements since the value of 26 in the "A" column of the "In process" State has become 28, namely the original 26 and the additional 2.
- Four of the unexpected requirements were identified in Range 7 shown by the 4 in the "A" column of the "Identified" State.
- Development activities have begun on these 4 requirements since the value of the "A" column of the "In process" State has become 12, namely the original 8 and the additional 4.
- Three of the additional requirements in Range 8 are expected to be identified after PDR as indicated by the 3 in row 8 of the "P" column of the "Identified" State.
- The project does not plan to identify any new requirements in any of the other ranges between PDR and CDR since all the rows in the "P" column of the "Identified" State in those ranges remain at zero.

The impact of the additional work should also show on the schedules (Section 8.4) and EVA Charts (Section 8.2).

---

* These were unexpected as far as the contractor was concerned.

Table 8.10 The CRIP Chart for a Project with Requirements Creep at PDR

	IDENTIFIED			IN PROCESS			COMPLETED			IN TEST			ACCEPTED		
RANGE	P	E	A	P	E	A	P	E	A	P	E	A	P	E	A
1	0	0	20	0	81	101	0								
2	0	0	0	0	78	78	0								
3	0	0	0	0	35	35	0								
4	0	0	0	0	30	30	0								
5	0	0	2	0	26	28	0								
6	0	0	0	0	20	20	0								
7	0	0	4	0	8	12	0								
8	3	0	0	0	7	7	0								
9	0	0	0	0	5	5	0								
10	0	0	0	0	2	2	0								
Totals	3	0	26	0	292	318	0								

8.1.5.2.2 The CRIP Chart for a Project with Requirements Creep at CDR Shown in Table 8.11 indicates:

- Two additional requirements were identified between PDR and CDR resulting in the total number of requirements increasing from 318 to 320.
- No additional requirements were levied on the system as indicated by the zero value in all the rows in the "A" column of the "Identified" State.

Table 8.11 The CRIP Chart for a Project with Requirements Creep at CDR

	IDENTIFIED			IN PROCESS			COMPLETED			IN TEST			ACCEPTED		
RANGE	P	E	A	P	E	A	P	E	A	P	E	A	P	E	A
1	0	0	0	0	101	101	101								
2	0	0	0	0	78	78	78								
3	0	0	0	0	35	35	35								
4	0	0	0	0	30	30	30								
5	0	0	0	0	28	28	28								
6	0	0	0	0	20	20	20								
7	0	0	0	0	12	12	12								
8	0	3	2	2	7	7	9								
9	0	0	0	0	5	5	5								
10	0	0	0	0	2	2	2								
Totals	0	3	2	2	318	318	320								

- Only two of the three requirements in the "E" column of Range 8 were actually identified as indicated by the 2 in row 8 of the "A" column of the "Identified" State.*
- The Project Plans to start and complete the development activities on these additional 2 requirements in Range 8 as indicated by the "2" in the "P" column of the "In process" State and the 9 (7+2) in the "P" column of the "Completed" State in row 8.
- The development activity on the remaining requirements is progressing according to plan as shown by the entries in the "In process" and "Completed" States.
- The project does not plan to identify any new requirements between PDR and CDR since all the rows in the "P" column of the "Identified" State remain at zero.

8.1.5.2.3 The CRIP Chart for a Project with Requirements Creep at TRR   Shown in Table 8.12 indicates:

- Ten unexpected additional requirements were identified between CDR and TRR resulting in the total number of requirements increasing from 320 to 330.
- Four of the unexpected requirements were identified in Range 4 shown by the 4 in row 4 of the "A" column of the "Identified" State.
- The Project plans to start the development activities on the additional 4 requirements in Range 4 as indicated by the "4" in row 4 of the "P" column of the "In process" State.
- Six of the unexpected requirements were identified in Range 5 shown by the 6 in row 5 of the "A" column of the "Identified" State.
- Development activities actually began on these 6 requirements as shown by the 6 in row 5 of the "A" column in the "In process" State.
- The Project plans to complete the development activities on these 6 requirements as shown by the 6 in row 5 of the "P" column of the "Completed" State.

---

* It is possible that a change request was made for the third requirement and the request was rejected for some reason. The CRIP Chart just indicates the change; the CRIP Chart does not provide reasons for the change.

Table 8.12 The CRIP Chart for a Project with Requirements Creep at TRR

RANGE	IDENTIFIED			IN PROCESS			COMPLETED			IN TEST			ACCEPTED		
	P	E	A	P	E	A	P	E	A	P	E	A	P	E	A
1	0	0	0	0	0	0	0	101	101	101					
2	0	0	0	0	0	0	0	78	78	78					
3	0	0	0	0	0	0	0	35	35	35					
4	0	0	4	4	0	0	0	30	30	30					
5	0	0	6	0	0	6	6	28	28	34					
6	0	0	0	0	0	0	0	20	20	20					
7	0	0	0	0	0	0	0	12	12	12					
8	0	0	0	0	2	2	0	9	9	9					
9	0	0	0	0	0	0	0	5	5	5					
10	0	0	0	0	0	0	0	2	2	2					
Totals	0	0	10	4	2	8	6	320	320	326					

- Development work began on two of the additional requirements in Range 8 as shown by the match between the numbers in row 8 of the "E" and "A" columns of the "In process" State of Table 8.12.*
- The development work for the two additional requirements in Range 8 is not expected to be completed by the subsequent milestone since there is a zero in row 8 of the "P" column of the "Completed" State.
- Development work on the remaining requirements is progressing according to plan and the project is expected to commence testing as shown by the matches between the entries in the "A" columns of the "Completed" State and the "P" column of the "In test" State.
- The project does not plan to identify any new requirements between TRR and the following milestone since all the rows in the "P" column of the "Identified" State remain at zero.

8.1.5.2.4 The CRIP Chart for a Project with Requirements Creep at IRR Shown in Table 8.13 indicates:

- For a change, no unexpected additional requirements were identified between CDR and IRR resulting in no change in the total number of requirements.

---

* The reason for only starting work on two of the three could be that one was rejected for some reason, or that the System Design State for meeting that requirement was deferred. The CRIP Chart just indicates the variance without providing a reason.

- No additional requirements were identified since the values of all rows of the "A" column of the "Identified" State are zero.
- Development on the requirements in Range 4 proceeded according to plan by the match between numbers in each of the rows in the "E" and "A" columns of the "In process" State of Table 8.13. The number 4 in the "P" column of the "Completed" indicates that the project development activities are planned to have been completed by the following milestone.
- Development on the requirements in Range 5 proceeded according to plan since the since the number 6 was copied from the "P" column of the "Completed" State in Table 8.12 to the "E" and "A" columns of the "Completed" State of Table 8.13. The number 6 in the "P" column of the "In test" State indicates that the testing activities are planned to have begun by the following milestone.
- Something has stopped the development of activities of the two requirements in row 8 as shown by the zeros in the "E" and the "A" columns of the "In process" State and the zero in the "P" column of the "Completed" State. However, this can only be seen when the two CRIP Charts are compared directly. The CRIP Chart does not provide a reason for the stoppage; it only provides the information that a stoppage has occurred.

Table 8.13 The CRIP Chart for a Project with Requirements Creep at IRR

RANGE	IDENTIFIED			IN PROCESS			COMPLETED			IN TEST			ACCEPTED		
	P	E	A	P	E	A	P	E	A	P	E	A	P	E	A
1	0	0	0	0	0	0	0	0	0	0	101	101	101		
2	0	0	0	0	0	0	0	0	0	0	78	78	78		
3	0	0	0	0	0	0	0	0	0	0	35	35	35		
4	0	0	0	0	4	4	4	0	0	0	30	30	30		
5	0	0	0	0	0	0	0	6	6	6	34	28	34		
6	0	0	0	0	0	0	0	0	0	0	20	20	20		
7	0	0	0	0	0	0	0	0	0	0	12	12	12		
8	0	0	0	0	0	0	0	0	0	2	9	7	9		
9	0	0	0	0	0	0	0	0	0	0	5	5	5		
10	0	0	0	0	0	0	0	0	0	0	2	2	2		
Totals	0	0	0	0	4	4	4	6	6	6	326	318	326		

- Nearly all the requirements that were planned to enter the "In test" State have done so because most of the numbers in the "P" column of the "In test" State in Table 8.12 have been copied to the "E" and "A" columns in Table 8.13.
- There are some problems in starting to test the requirements in rows 5 and 8 since the numbers in the "E" columns do not match those in the "A" columns.
- The Project plans to catch up on these requirements as since there is a 6 in the "P" column of row 5 and a 2 in the "P" column of row 8 in the "In test" State.
- The Project plans for the testing of all the requirements in the "In test" State to be successfully completed and accepted by the next milestone as indicated by the match between the numbers in the "A" column of the "In test" State and the "P" column of the "Accepted" State.
- The Project plans to overcome the delays in testing the requirements in rows 5 and 8 by the next milestone as indicated by the match between the numbers in the "E" column of the "In test" State and the "P" column of the "Accepted" State.

8.1.5.2.5 The CRIP Chart for a Project with Requirements Creep at DRR Shown in Table 8.14 indicates:

- No additional requirements were identified.
- Development activities on the requirements in row 4 have been completed as planned, as indicated by the number 4 in the "P" column of the "Completed" State in Table 8.13 being copied into the "E" and "A" columns of Table 8.14. Moreover, the testing activities on those requirements have not only begun as indicated by the 4 in the "A" column of the "In test" State, they have been completed and accepted by the customer as indicated by the 34 in the "A" column of the "Accepted" State. This is 4 more than the expected 30 in the "E" column of the State.
- The customer accepted all the requirements that had been tested except for two in row 8 as indicated by numbers in the "E" and "A" columns of the "Accepted" State.

Table 8.14   The CRIP Chart for a Project with Requirements Creep at DRR

RANGE	IDENTIFIED			IN PROCESS			COMPLETED			IN TEST			ACCEPTED		
	P	E	A	P	E	A	P	E	A	P	E	A	P	E	A
1	0	0	0	0	0	0	0	0	0	0	0	0	0	101	101
2	0	0	0	0	0	0	0	0	0	0	0	0	0	78	78
3	0	0	0	0	0	0	0	0	0	0	0	0	0	35	35
4	0	0	0	0	0	0	0	4	4	0	0	4	0	30	34
5	0	0	0	0	0	0	0	0	0	0	6	6	0	34	34
6	0	0	0	0	0	0	0	0	0	0	0	0	0	20	20
7	0	0	0	0	0	0	0	0	0	0	0	0	0	12	12
8	0	0	0	0	0	0	0	0	0	0	2	2	2	9	7
9	0	0	0	0	0	0	0	0	0	0	0	0	0	5	5
10	0	0	0	0	0	0	0	0	0	0	0	0	0	2	2
Totals	0	0	0	0	0	0	0	4	4	0	8	12	2	326	328

- The project expected that two requirements in row 8 would go into testing and they did, as indicated by the numbers 2 in the "E" and "A" columns of the "In test" State.

8.1.5.3 The Challenged Project   Consider the challenged project which is the same as the ideal project until the "In test" State begins. Accordingly, the CRIP Charts for the challenged project at SRR, PDR, and CDR are the same as those for the ideal project shown in Table 8.4, Table 8.5, and Table 8.6 respectively. The project diverges from the ideal project after CDR so discrepancies can be seen when the TRR is held on the originally scheduled date.

8.1.5.3.1 The CRIP Chart for the Challenged Project at TRR   Shown in Table 8.15 indicates:

- No additional requirements were identified.
- Development activities in all requirement ranges except Range 6 have not been completed since the "E" and "A" values in row 6 of the "Completed" State do not match.
- The Project plans to catch up on the development activities as shown by the numbers in the "P" column of the "Completed" State.

Table 8.15   The CRIP Chart for the Challenged Project at TRR

RANGE	IDENTIFIED			IN PROCESS			COMPLETED			IN TEST			ACCEPTED		
	P	E	A	P	E	A	P	E	A	P	E	A	P	E	A
1	0	0	0	0	0	0	40	81	41	81					
2	0	0	0	0	0	0	40	78	38	78					
3	0	0	0	0	0	0	5	35	30	35					
4	0	0	0	0	0	0	10	30	20	30					
5	0	0	0	0	0	0	10	26	16	26					
6	0	0	0	0	0	0	0	20	20	20					
7	0	0	0	0	0	0	6	8	2	8					
8	0	0	0	0	0	0	4	7	3	7					
9	0	0	0	0	0	0	1	5	4	5					
10	0	0	0	0	0	0	1	2	1	2					
Totals	0	0	0	0	0	0	117	292	175	292					

- The project is optimistic about commencing testing following the TRR as evidenced by the difference between numbers in the "P" column of the "In test" State and the numbers in the corresponding rows of the "A" column of the "Completed" State. The customer definitely needs to find out the reason for the optimism.

8.1.5.3.2 The CRIP Chart for the Challenged Project at IRR   Shown in Table 8.16 indicates:

- No additional requirements were identified.
- The project should not have transitioned into the Subsystem Testing State of the SDP because of the difference between the numbers in the "E" and "A" columns in the "In test" State.
- The Project plans to catch up as shown by the numbers in the "P" column of the "In test" State.
- The project is still optimistic about completing the testing before DRR because the "P" numbers in the "Accepted" State match the "E" numbers instead of the "A" numbers in the "In test" State. The customer definitely needs to determine the reasons for the optimism.

Table 8.16   The CRIP Chart for the Challenged Project at IRR

RANGE	IDENTIFIED			IN PROCESS			COMPLETED			IN TEST			ACCEPTED		
	P	E	A	P	E	A	P	E	A	P	E	A	P	E	A
1	0	0	0	0	0	0	0	0	0	40	81	21	81		
2	0	0	0	0	0	0	0	0	0	30	78	48	78		
3	0	0	0	0	0	0	0	0	0	5	35	30	35		
4	0	0	0	0	0	0	0	0	0	8	30	22	30		
5	0	0	0	0	0	0	0	0	0	14	26	12	26		
6	0	0	0	0	0	0	0	0	0	0	20	20	20		
7	0	0	0	0	0	0	0	0	0	7	8	1	8		
8	0	0	0	0	0	0	0	0	0	6	7	1	7		
9	0	0	0	0	0	0	0	0	0	4	5	1	5		
10	0	0	0	0	0	0	0	0	0	0	2	2	2		
Totals	0	0	0	0	0	0	0	0	0	114	292	158	292		

8.1.5.4 The "Make Up Your Mind" Project   Consider the typical "make up your mind" project which is the same as the ideal project until SRR and diverges between SRR and PDR because the customer keeps changing their mind.

8.1.5.4.1 The CRIP for the Typical "Makeup Your Mind" Project at SRR   The CRIP Chart at SRR is that same as that for the ideal project shown in Table 8.4.

8.1.5.4.2 The CRIP Chart for the Typical "Make Up Your Mind" Project at PDR   The CRIP Chart for the project at PDR shown in Table 8.17 indicates:

- Fifty-six unexpected additional requirements were identified between SRR and PDR resulting in the total number of requirements increasing from 292 to 348.
- Twenty of the unexpected additional requirements were identified in Range 1 as indicated by the number 20 in the "A" column of the "Identified" State in row 1.
- Development activities have commenced on these requirements as shown by the difference in the numbers in the "E" and "A" columns in row 1 of the "In process" State (20 + 81 = 101).
- Ten of the unexpected additional requirements were identified in Range 2.

Table 8.17 The CRIP Chart for a "Make Up Your Mind" Project at PDR

RANGE	IDENTIFIED			IN PROCESS			COMPLETED			IN TEST			ACCEPTED		
	P	E	A	P	E	A	P	E	A	P	E	A	P	E	A
1	0	0	20	0	81	101	0								
2	0	0	10	0	78	88	0								
3	0	0	14	0	35	49	0								
4	5	0	0	0	30	30	0								
5	9	0	2	0	26	28	0								
6	12	0	0	0	20	0	0								
7	0	0	4	0	8	12	0								
8	3	0	0	0	7	7	0								
9	0	0	6	0	5	11	0								
10	2	0	0	0	2	0	0								
Totals	31	0	56	0	292	326	0								

- Development activities have commenced on these requirements as shown by the difference in the numbers in the "E" and "A" columns in row 2 of the "In process" State.
- Fourteen of the unexpected additional requirements were identified in Range 3.
- The Project plans to identify five additional requirements in Range 4 following PDR.*
- Two unexpected requirements were identified in Range 5 and the Project plans to identify nine additional requirements following PDR.
- The Project plans to identify 12 additional requirements in Range 6 following PDR.
- Four of the unexpected additional requirements were identified in Range 7.
- Development activities have commenced on these requirements.
- The Project plans to identify 3 additional requirements in Range 8 following PDR.
- Six of the unexpected additional requirements were identified in Range 9.
- Development activities have commenced on these requirements.
- The Project plans to identify 2 additional requirements in Range 10 following PDR.

---

* The change requests have been submitted.

- Development activities are proceeding according to plan except for the requirements in Ranges 6 and 10.
- No development activities have started on the requirements in Range 6 as shown by the 20 in the "E" column and the zero in the "A" column of the "In process" State in row 6.
- Development activities have proceeded as planned on the requirements in Range 7 since the values in the "E" column and "A" column of the "In process" State in row 7 are the same.
- No development activities have started on the requirements in Range 10.
- The project does not plan to complete the development activities in process before the following milestone because every row in the "P" column of the "In process" and "Completed States have been set to zero. This could be because the project has been cancelled or for some other reason.

8.1.6 *Comments*

Although written up for use with requirements, CRIP Charts can also be used for Use Cases, scenarios, Technical Performance Measures (TPM) and any other technical measurement that can be tracked across the SDP. When the column in the CRIP Chart is plotted as a Histogram (Section 2.9) it shows an Attribute Profile (Section 9.1) for that attribute.

8.2 Earned Value Analysis

Earned Value Analysis (EVA) is a project management tool for cost control. It is based on comparing the budgeted or planned cost (Section 9.2) and schedule (Section 8.15) with the actual values of money spent and time taken to do the work. It is used to:

1. Determine if the cost is under control.
2. Compare how the actual cost, scope and schedule of a project compares with the planned cost, scope and schedule.
3. Forecast if the project will overrun or under run the planned budget at completion.
4. Forecast if the project will overrun or under run the planned schedule at completion.

The traditional approach to earned value analysis originated in 1966 when the US Air Force mandated Earned Value Management in conjunction with the other requirements on planning and controlling Air Force programs. The requirement was entitled, the Cost/ Schedule Planning Control Specification (C/SPCS). The concept and its requirements have remained basically unchanged since then.

The systems approach integrates EVA into project management. The project manager creates a Project Plan (Section 8.11) prior to the start of the project. The relevant personnel check and then approve the plan. The contents of the plan include the estimated costs and schedules for each activity to be performed in the project as well as the estimated total cost and schedule for the project. The initial estimates provide the baseline costs and schedule. As time passes and each Work Package is completed, the actual, estimated, and forecasted cost and schedule to completion are compared; variances noted and appropriate corrective action taken.

Activities earn value as they are completed; the earned value is the budgeted cost of the activity completed as of the time of the reporting milestone.

8.2.1 The Elements of EVA

In summary the elements of EVA are:

1. *S*cheduling.
2. *A*uthorization of Work.
3. *V*ariance Analysis.
4. *E*stimate at Completion.
5. Baseline Maintenance and Control.
6. Budgeting.
7. Organization.
8. Data Accumulation and Reporting.

8.2.2 EVA Terminology

The terminology generally used with EVA covers planning or estimating, project monitoring and controlling, and providing summaries of the state of the project as described in this section.

8.2.2.1 Planning or Estimating Terminology

- **Budget at Completion (BAC)**: the total authorized budget for the project.

8.2.2.2 Project Monitoring and Controlling Terminology

- **Actual Cost (AC)** also called **Actual Cost of Work Performed (ACWP)**: the cost of all the work that was performed up to and including the reporting period.
- **Earned Value (EV)** also called **Budgeted Cost of Work Performed (BCWP)**: the planned (not the actual) cost of the work that has been performed.
- **Estimate at Completion (EAC)**: the AC plus the ETC.
- **Estimate to Completion (ETC)**: estimated or expected costs of completing the remainder of work on the project as of the reporting period.
- **Planned Value (PV)** also called **Budgeted Cost of Work Scheduled (BCWS)**: the cost of all the work that was scheduled for the reporting period.
- **Schedule Variance (SV)**: the difference between the actual and planned time taken to complete the project or an activity of a project.
- **Cost Variance (CV)**: the difference between the cost actually incurred and the estimated cost.
- **Variance at Completion (VAC)**: calculated as BAC minus EAC.

8.2.2.3 Indices and Summary Terminology

- **Cost Performance Index (CPI)**: an estimate of the projected or actual cost of completing the project based on the performance to date.
- **Schedule Performance Index (SPI)**: an estimate of the remaining time needed to complete the project.

8.2.3 EVA Calculations

The EVA equations are summarized in Table 8.18. In the systems approach, the performance indicators can be used to give an ETL Chart (Section 8.16.2) high-level summary or overview of the state

Table 8.18 EVA Equations

TERM		EQUATION
Cost Performance Index	CPI	EV/AC
Cost Variance	CV	PV - AC
Cost Variance %	CV%	CV/EV
Estimate at Completion	EAC	AC + ETC
Earned Value	EV	BAC * AC/EAC
Schedule Performance Index	SPI	EV/PV
Schedule Variance	SV	EV - PV
Schedule Variance %	SV%	SV/PV
Variance at Completion	VAC	BAC - EAC.

Table 8.19 EVA – TLC

INDEX	VALUE	CONDITION	TLC
CPI	=1	Actual cost = planned cost	Green
	< 1	Over budget	Yellow/red
	>1	Under budget	Blue
SPI	=1	On schedule	Green
	<1	Behind schedule	Yellow/red
	>1	Ahead of schedule	Blue
CV	<0	Over budget	Yellow/red
	>0	Under budget	Blue
SV	<0	Behind schedule	Yellow/red
	>0	Ahead of schedule	Blue
VAC	<0	Projected underrun	Blue
	>0	Projected overrun	Yellow/red

of the project as defined in Table 8.19. The table also shows the suggested colours if the reporting presentation uses ETL Charts (Section 8.16.2) forecast and schedule.

A major difficulty with EVA is making reasonably accurate estimates of the amount of work completed. Perceptions from the *Quantitative* HTP point out that the estimate must be usable but does not necessarily have to be accurate to decimal points. The errors will tend to cancel out as the Work Package elements are rolled up. Ways of making estimates of the amount of work completed depend on the project and include:

- Number of units completed as a percentage of the total number of units that have to be completed.
- Number of Work Packages (Section 8.19) completed.

- Amount charged to an activity. This is not a very good one, but if the budget for an activity is $50,000 and $25,000 has been charged to the activity, one hopes the activity can be estimated as being 50% complete.
- Experience on similar projects.

The systems approach with its focus on products rather than process (activities) avoids many of these difficulties by focusing on tangible results rather than intangible activities.

8.2.4 Requirements for the Use of EVA in a Project

The requirements for the use of EVA in a project are as follows.

1. The project shall have a Project Plan (PP).
2. The work to be performed in the PP (Section 8.11) as of the reporting period shall be split into activities or tasks.
3. The cost for each activity shall be estimated.
4. The project shall have an EVA system.
5. The project shall enter every activity into the EVA system.
6. The project shall enter the estimated cost of every activity into the EVA system.
7. The project shall enter the actual costs incurred during the performance of each task into the EVA system in a timely manner.*
8. The schedule for each activity shall be estimated.
9. The project shall enter the estimated time for each activity into the EVA system in a timely manner.
10. The project shall enter the actual time taken for the performance of each task into the EVA system in a timely manner.
11. The project shall have an EVA system that will allow the actual and estimated costs to be compared.
12. The project shall have an EVA system that will allow the actual and estimated time taken for each project to be compared.
13. The project shall have an EVA system that will allow the costs to be projected forward to the date of completion.

---

* The time shall be determined by the frequency of reporting as agreed to by the project manager and the entity receiving the reports.

14. The project shall have an EVA system that will allow the schedule to be projected forward to the date of completion.
15. The EVA system shall provide the following information as a minimum:
    a. Schedule Variance (SV).
    b. Actual Cost (AC).
    c. Variance at Completion (VAC).
    d. Earned Value (EV).
    e. Budget at Completion (BAC).
    f. Cost Variance (CV).
    g. Estimate at Completion (EAC).
    h. Planned Value (PV).

8.2.5 Advantages and Disadvantages of EVA

EVA has a number of advantages and disadvantages as described in this Section.

8.2.5.1 EVA Advantages The advantage of EVA is proactive project management. By comparing the difference between estimated, actual and projecting cost and schedule to the completion date it is possible to detect problems and compare the effect of different types of corrective action on cost and schedule.

8.2.5.2 EVA Disadvantages The disadvantages of EVA include:

- EVA doesn't take quality into consideration it only considers cost and schedule.
- EVA doesn't seem to take into effect changes to the project requirements and the consequent impact on cost and schedule other than by showing variances without changing the baseline. For example, if there was an approved change to the requirements which impacted the work during a reporting period, then either the additional work was not planned but was performed or planned work was not performed because the change deleted the need to do the work. Accordingly the variance is not real.
- On large projects a lot of data may need to be collected. However these days most projects use some kind of software

and so entering and retrieving information should not be too difficult.

- EVA needs to be integrated into the management planning, organizing, monitoring, and control activities. If it is performed as an add-on for the purpose of meeting a contractual or other requirement, it will add work and accordingly inflate the cost of the project but will not provide any benefit at all.

8.2.6 Examples of the Use of EVA

Consider the following two examples of the use of EVA.

8.2.6.1 The Master's Degree Project   The cost and expenditures for the first five months of the master's degree project described in Section 8.3.2 provide an example of the use of EVA. The data shown in Figure 2.10 are summarized in Table 8.20. In accordance with the rules for EVA the management reserve or contingency of $6,000 is not included in the data. That's why BAC has the value of $44,000. Since there are no additional expenditures, BAC remains stable throughout the duration covered by the table.

8.2.6.2 The Data Centre Upgrade Project   Consider a typical project, a data centre upgrade project that has been proceeding according to the initial schedule estimates until PDR. The project is mostly software but does require the purchase of a new data switch. The day before

Table 8.20   EVA for the First Five Months of a Master's Degree

MONTH	1	2	3	4	5
BAC	$44,000.00	$44,000.00	$44,000.00	$44,000.00	$44,000.00
PV	$15,500.00	$17,000.00	$18,500.00	$20,000.00	$21,500.00
AC	$1,000.00	$17,000.00	$18,500.00	$22,500.00	$23,000.00
VAC	$0.00	$0.00	$0.00	$0.00	$0.00
EAC	$44,000.00	$44,000.00	$44,000.00	$44,000.00	$44,000.00
ETC	$43,000.00	$27,000.00	$25,500.00	$21,500.00	$21,000.00
EV	$1,000.00	$17,000.00	$18,500.00	$22,500.00	$23,000.00
CV	$14,500.00	$0.00	$0.00	−$2,500.00	−$1,500.00
CV%	1450.00%	0.00%	0.00%	−11.11%	−6.52%
SV	−$14,500.00	$0.00	$0.00	$2,500.00	$1,500.00
SV%	−93.55%	0.00%	0.00%	12.50%	6.98%

PDR there was a fire in the building that housed the project. The fire is going to impact the schedule and the cost. Let's take a look and see how that shows up in EVA. Since the fire occurred the day before PDR, there was no impact on the schedule and the cost and so the cost and schedule variances are zero, and the BAC is still the ETC because everything has proceeded according to schedule. However, there will be changes to the cost and schedule of the planned work for the next reporting period because some additional work has to be performed to recover from the fire. Since the project is a small project the project manager was able to do this impact assessment together with the chief system and software engineer so that the management report Section of the PDR will contain updated EVA graphs and CRIP Charts (Section 8.1) reflecting the impact of the fire. The impact assessment is based on the following:

- The building is not useable until repaired.
- There were no backups outside the building.
- Staff can work in temporary accommodation to recreate materials.

The impact assessment estimated that it would take two months to restore the project to the state that it was at PDR. This would require a new Work Package to be inserted in the original schedule between the date of the PDR and the date of the CDR. The estimated cost of the Work Package is $20,000. The project EVA status at PDR is shown in Figure 8.2. The ETC remains at $170,000, but the BAC

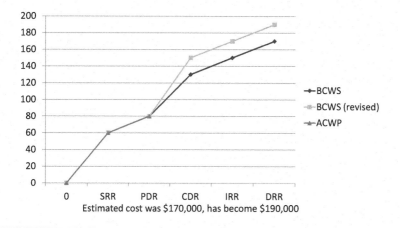

Estimated cost was $170,000, has become $190,000

Figure 8.2   Project EVA status at PDR.

Table 8.21 Notional ETL Chart Colours for Cost and Schedule Component of PDR

SRR	PDR		CDR PLANNED
	Last time	Current	
Green	Green	Yellow/Red	Yellow/Red

has been increased by $20,000 so it's now equal to $190,000. The slope of the PV lines between PDR and CDR are different. This reflects the extra $20,000 estimated cost. However, the work following CDR to DRR is expected to be the same as originally planned so the slope of the two lines remains the same. Accordingly, the project is currently scheduled to go over cost by $20,000 and incur a two-month delay.

The ETL Chart for cost and schedule component of PDR is shown in Table 8.21. The changes due to the fire can show up as green, yellow, or red depending on the cost and schedule variance thresholds set for the colour as shown in Table 8.27.*

Now, the project manager was on vacation at PDR. When she returned from her vacation and found out what had happened, she produced a backup of all the work that she had kept on her personal portable disk drive. She believed in risk management, but had been unable to convince her management to modify the configuration management system, such as it was, to include an off-site backup. Her personal backup reduced the delay by one month and halved the cost of the delay. Accordingly, by the time the project got to CDR, it was only one month behind schedule and $10,000 over cost. The one-month delay was due to the temporary use of furniture, verifying that the backup really was up-to-date, and associated activities with the temporary accommodation and then restoring the fire-damaged accommodation to workable condition. The revised project status at CDR is shown in Figure 8.3. The figure displays information with respect to the start of the project that is the original estimates. The figure does not show that the CDR cost and schedule were reduced

---

* The table is located in Section 8.16 which discusses ETL Charts, hence this forward reference.

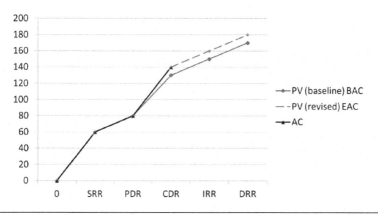

Figure 8.3 Project EVA status at CDR.

by $10,000 and one month from the revised PDR estimates. This improvement could be shown in a number of ways, including:

- Two financial graphs the first showing the status with reference to the start of the project; the second showing the change between PDR and CDR as in Figure 8.3.
- A Compound Line and Bar Chart (Section 2.4), such Figure 2.6 or one made up from Figure 8.3 and two vertical bars, the first one showing the planned costs for the period between the milestones and the second one showing the actual: Figure 2.10 provides an example of such a chart.
- Two ETL Charts, the first with reference to the start of the project; the second showing the change between PDR and CDR.
- A table showing the changes in EAC and ATC.

One of the design elements approved at CDR was the necessary data switch. This was to be a commercial off-the-shelf (COTS) device. The specific device was selected after a comparison of a number of COTS switches based on cost and delivery schedule. However after CDR the proposed vendor went bankrupt. This meant that the selected switch was no longer available for use. As a result the design team performed unplanned activities to locate and procure an alternative switch. These unplanned activities needed a new design WP to make any changes necessary in cable lengths, installation drawings, changes to test plans and procedures, etc., with a corresponding cost and schedule impact on the project.

Table 8.22 EVA Values at Project Milestones

	SRR	PDR	CDR	IRR
BAC	$170,000.00	$170,000.00	$170,000.00	$170,000.00
PV	$60,000.00	$80,000.00	$140,000.00	$150,000.00
AC	$60,000.00	$80,000.00	$130,000.00	$166,000.00
VAC	$0.00	$20,000.00	$10,000.00	$16,000.00
EAC	$170,000.00	$190,000.00	$180,000.00	$186,000.00
ETC	$110,000.00	$110,000.00	$50,000.00	$20,000.00
EV	$60,000.00	$71,578.95	$122,777.78	$151,720.43
CV	$0.00	$0.00	$10,000	–$16,000
CV%	0.00%	0.00%	8.14%	–10.55%
SV	$0.00	–$8,421.05	–$17,222.22	$1,720.43
SV%	0.00%	–10.53%	–12.30%	1.15%

The impact was a new WP for design which had to be inserted into the schedule. This resulted in a delay of one month, and a cost escalation of $6,000, $1,000 for labour and an extra $5,000 for the next cheapest switch that could be delivered with the least amount of schedule delay. Consequently the IRR was delayed by one month because the replacement switch had to be delivered and tested before IRR, and the EAC increased from $170,000 to $186,000 (9.4% increase) as shown in Table 8.22.

The information in Figure 8.2 and Figure 8.3 are also shown in Table 8.22 together with some additional parameters. The value of BAC does not change as the project progresses because it's the original estimate that was forecast before the project began. The project proceeded according to plan from the beginning to the PDR. However the fire at the PDR resulted in additional work. That shows up in the change from $60,000 to $80,000 in the value of PV at PDR. The additional $20,000 shown in the VAC row means that EAC increased from $170,000 to $190,000 and the ETC is now calculated on the difference between the actual AC and the EAC. Similar changes occurred in PV and AV due to the events before CDR and IRR. CV shows up as negative in this table representing an overrun.

8.2.7 The Systems Approach Perspective on EVA

EVA seems to be designed to reduce project cost and schedule data to numbers. The terminology also seems to be confusing when first encountered. EVA however is mandated for use in US government contracts so government contractors have to use it. However in the commercial centre sector a simpler approach could be employed. Use the EVA numbers cost information but keep the schedule information in Gantt Charts (Section 8.4). Only bring them together in an ETL Chart during the management brief in the reporting meeting.

Financial information is only as good as the estimates and is only a part of the story. The systems approach to project management links all the work to requirements, manages change proactively, uses Work Packages (Section 8.19) and presents information in the simplest format and in the customer's language in accordance with the KISS principle (Section 3.2.3) thereby preventing the following top ten reasons as to why EVA does not work (Lukas 2008):

1. No documented requirements.
2. Incomplete requirements.
3. Work Breakdown Structures (WBS) not used or not accepted.
4. WBS incomplete.
5. Plan not integrated (WBS-Schedule-Budget).
6. Schedule and/or budget incorrect.
7. Change management not used or ineffective.
8. Cost collection system inadequate.
9. Incorrect progress.
10. Management influence and/or control.

Perceptions from the *Generic* perspective identify a similarity between these top 10 reasons and the top 7 causes for project failure in Table 4.7.

8.3 Financial Budgets

A financial budget:

- Is a planning tool for estimating and pacing personal and project spending.
- Contains a List (Section 9.4) of the items and services to be purchased and an estimate of the amount and the time when each expense will have to be paid.
- Is prepared in the front-end part of EVA (Section 8.2).

8.3.1 Preparing a Project Financial Budget

The traditional approach to preparing a project budget is activity-based (Section 8.11.1). You start with the people and figure out what they will be doing (the activities) like Sandra Stenson's approach (Section 8.11.1). You then cost each activity associated with the person based on the number of hours they will be working on the project, adding in all the remaining costs.

The systems approach is different; it is product-based (Section 8.11.1). Estimate the work to be done on the project working backwards from the solution (completion) (Section 11.8) using Visualization (Section 7.11), PAM Charts (Section 2.14) and PAM Network Charts (Section 2.14.2) and create the WPs (Section 8.19) capturing as much of the work as possible. Starting with the lowest level activities, assign the work to proposed staff members and identify costs in the following categories. Then roll up the costs into the higher-level activities adding costs appropriate to the high level activities.

1. Personnel
2. Equipment
3. Travel
4. Benefits
5. Consultants
6. Additional
7. Contingencies
8. Indirect costs

There is no need to estimate the cost of every item in each category. You only need to estimate the cost of the high-cost items because they will have a larger impact on the budget. This is an application of the Pareto Principle (Section 2.13). The low cost items may be bundled in various ways, for example:

- Office supplies is a category that covers paper, pencils, pens, stationary, ink cartridges, etc.
- Miscellaneous low-cost spare parts can be bundled together as spare parts.

The estimate for the cost of these bundles should be based on past experience on similar projects.

8.3.1.1 Personnel This category covers the estimates for the following for each task:

- Level of competency required for the activity.
- The cost per hour (hourly rate) for the activity based on the competency level.
- The number of hours to be worked on the task.
- The person(s) at the competency level.

8.3.1.2 Equipment This category covers the estimates for the following for each task:

- The cost of each item of equipment.
- The cost of any tools.

The equipment and tools may be purchased, leased, or borrowed from another project.

8.3.1.3 Travel This category covers the estimates for the following for each task:

- The estimated cost of any travel.

8.3.1.4 Benefits This category covers the estimates for the following for each task:

- Taxes, payroll, etc.
- Health care, retirement plans, life insurance, etc.
- Days not worked (vacation, public holidays, etc.)

8.3.1.5 Consultants This category covers the estimates for the following for each task:

- Internal or/and external consultants (if any).
- Temporary workers.
- Outsourced labour services.
- Other professional services.

8.3.1.6 Additional This category covers the estimates for the following for each task:

- Facilities.
- Telephone.

- Copying and printing.
- Postage.
- Computer discs and drives.
- Any other items which are not listed.

8.3.1.7 Contingencies   While it is nice to think that all costs have been estimated and captured, the theme of risk management is "expect the unexpected". Accordingly, a small contingency amount often called the management reserve should be added to the cost of the project.* The traditional approach is to add it as a line item once all other costs have been estimated. The systems approach adds the contingency cost to each task where it is harder to find making it more difficult to be eliminated by overzealous bean counters. Savvy project managers might incorporate the contingency costs in both ways knowing that when the contingency line item is reduced or even eliminated they will still have some excess in the budget.

8.3.1.8 Indirect Costs   This category covers the estimates for the costs assigned to the entire project for items which cannot be specifically linked to tasks. These might include tea and coffee, drinking water, etc.

8.3.1.9 Validating the Budget   Once the budget has been developed, it needs to be validated to be sure that is realistic and feasible. One way of doing this is applying the generic perspective and comparing the budget with a budget of a previous project of a similar nature. If that previous project took place more than a year or so earlier, the costs may have to be adjusted for inflation.

8.3.2 Creating a Financial Budget for a Master's Degree

As an example of creating a budget consider the estimated budget for studying for a master's degree full-time. The process will take a year.

---

* Not allowed when EVA (Section 8.2) is used in US government contracts.

The first thing to do is list all the costs. In this case, there are only five categories of estimated costs (simple numbers) which are:

1. Tuition fees $24,000.
2. Housing, $500 a month = $6,000.
3. Expenses (books, food, clothes, phone, Internet, etc.) $1,000 a month = $12,000.
4. Travel $2,000.
5. Contingency $6,000.

The expenses are all lumped together. The number is an approximation based on other people's experience. There is little point in wasting time identifying the expenses for the individual items. There probably won't be any greater degree of accuracy. The contingency covers all other expenses, some of which may not be known at planning time.

The estimated payment schedule over 12 months is:

- Tuition paid in two equal instalments in months 1 and 7.
- Travel paid in month 1 (open return ticket).
- Other expenses paid monthly.
- Total estimated expenses are $24,000 + $6,000 + $12,000 + $2,000 + $6,000 = $50,000.

The estimated payment schedule, excluding the contingency payments can be drawn in a table as shown in Table 8.23. The monthly budget column shows how much is to be spent each month, and

Table 8.23 Budget for Studying for a Master's Degree

MONTH	MONTHLY BUDGET	CUMULATIVE BUDGET	MONTHLY SPENT	CUMULATIVE SPENT
1	$15,500	$15,500	$1,000	$1,000
2	$1,500	$17,000	$16,000	$17,000
3	$1,500	$18,500	$1,500	$18,500
4	$1,500	$20,000	$4,000	$22,500
5	$1,500	$21,500	$500	$23,000
6	$1,500	$23,000	$200	$23,200
7	$13,500	$36,500	$13,000	$36,200
8	$1,500	$38,000	$2,000	$38,200
9	$1,500	$39,500	$1,300	$39,500
10	$1,500	$41,000		
11	$1,500	$42,500		
12	$1,500	$44,000		

the cumulative budget column summarizes the cumulative planned expenses. This shows how much cash has to be in hand or in the bank at the beginning of each month without considering the contingency expenses. The last two columns show how much was spent each month and cumulative amount of spending up to that month. For example, in the first month the plan was to spend $15,500 but only $1000 was actually spent. This is probably because a payment was delayed. Sure enough, in the second month we can see that we planned to spend $1500 for a cumulative spending of $17,000, and we actually spent $16,000 that month which brought the cumulative amount spent up to $17,000, so this reflects the delayed tuition payment. The budget can also be shown graphical format as shown in Figure 2.9 by plotting the planned cumulative monthly expenses (vertical axis) against the Timeline (Section 8.15) (horizontal axis). Figure 2.10 shows that the actual amount of funds spent has varied slightly from the planned amount but the project is currently forecasted as finishing within budget. Table 8.23 provides no forecasting information.

EVA (Section 8.2) provides information about how the planned (forecasted) and the actual expenditures of a project relate for each reporting period, shown here as a month, and, over the entire project lifecycle. In general, estimates are based on experience in similar activities, inquiries about costs and from standard cost tables and other relevant sources.

8.4 Gantt Charts

Gantt Charts:

- Are a specialized type of Bar Chart which were invented by Henry Gantt to compare the time planned for activities with the time taken by the activities (promises with performance) in the same chart space (Clark 1922).
- Are thinking and communications tools widely used in project management.
- Are tools with which to view a project from the *Temporal* HTP.
- Provide a visual representation of a project Timeline (Section 8.15) in the form of a matrix of rows and columns in which

the horizontal dimension of the matrix represents time. A Gantt Chart contains activities and milestones:

- *Activities*: horizontal bars and indicate the duration of tasks from a start date to a finish date. The length of the bar represents the length of time an activity takes and the colour or thickness of the bar can be used to represent things about the tasks (completed, level of difficulty, etc.).
- *Milestones*: triangles or diamonds and represent points in time where activities start and end at reporting points during the course of an activity. Milestones can be major or minor (Section 14.9.2) and may take time. For example, a major milestone review for a complex project may take several days and needs to be shown as such in the Gantt Chart.
- Show when activities start and finish and how long they take.
- Do not show dependencies between the tasks.*

8.4.1 How to Create a Gantt Chart

Traditionally, Gantt Charts are created when creating a Timeline (Section 8.15.1) during the project planning process (Section 8.11.2). The adapted traditional process for creating a Gantt Chart is as follows:

1. Identify the starting and ending milestones for the activities to be shown in the Gantt Chart.
2. Working back from the ending milestone, create a List (Section 9.4) of all the major milestones (Section 14.9.2) between the starting and ending milestones.
3. For each pair of milestones:
   a. Create a List (Section 9.4) of all the activities to be shown in the Gantt Chart. Use a PAM Chart (Section 2.12) to minimize missing activities.

---

* Some project management software does provide the capability to draw arrows between the end of one task and the start of another in the Gantt Chart view. I recommend that you do not use that capability if you have more than a few tasks on the chart since the additional lines will cause clutter and may be misinterpreted. PERT Charts (Section 8.10) are designed for the purpose of showing dependencies and can usually be drawn by the same software.

2. Combine low-level activities into higher-level activities, until there is only one high-level activity between that pair of milestones.

For example, consider creating a Gantt Chart for the problem-solving process according to Osborn (Osborn 1963). In this instance:

1. The starting and ending milestones are:
   a. The starting milestone is where the problem-solving activity begins.
   b. The ending milestone is the one in which the solution is working and remedying the problem.
2. The major milestones are:
   a. The starting milestone where the problem-solving activity begins.
   b. The problem has been defined.
   c. Ideas have been developed.
   d. The ending milestone in which the solution is working and remedying the problem.
      Note, the numbers are reversed, to remain in step with the current numbering paradigm.
3. The list (Section 9.4) of activities at some intermediate level, from the starting milestone to the ending milestone, is:
   a. Problem definition tasks
   b. Problem preparation tasks
   c. Idea creation tasks
   d. Idea evaluation tasks
   e. Idea development tasks
   f. Solution evaluation tasks
   g. Solution adoption tasks

A Gantt Chart of the activities drawn at this time would look like Figure 8.4. Each activity has a number associated with the milestone. In the real world if there are a large number of tasks it would be very complex and difficult to understand (complicated). Accordingly, the tasks need to be aggregated, and grouped into higher-level tasks. Recognising that the Gantt Chart is an example of the N^2 Chart (Section 2.10), the activities can be aggregated as shown in Figure 8.5 where the zeros have been inserted for educational purposes and

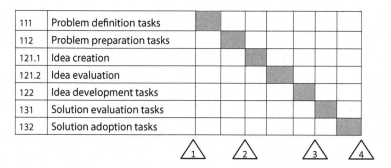

111	Problem definition tasks
112	Problem preparation tasks
121.1	Idea creation
121.2	Idea evaluation
122	Idea development tasks
131	Solution evaluation tasks
132	Solution adoption tasks

Figure 8.4 Initial schedule in a Gantt Chart.

111	Problem definition tasks
112	Problem preparation tasks
121.1	Idea creation
121.2	Idea evaluation
122	Idea development tasks
131	Solution evaluation tasks
132	Solution adoption tasks

Notes:
  'o' is shown for educational purposes, not normally used in Gantt charts

Figure 8.5 Aggregating activities in a Gantt Chart.

are not normally used in project Gantt Charts. The zeros in the N^2 Chart show that when an activity in one row inputs to an activity in a following row and no other, the two activities can potentially be combined. When the activities are combined, and the higher level activities renamed, the resulting simplified Gantt Chart showing the top-level schedule is as shown in Figure 8.6. The top-level chart shall contain no more than nine bars in accordance with Miller's Rule (Section 3.2.5).

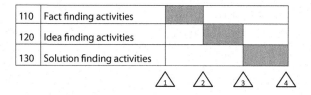

110	Fact finding activities
120	Idea finding activities
130	Solution finding activities

Figure 8.6 Top-level schedule.

In the systems approach to project management, Gantt Charts are a Timeline view of the set of project Work Packages (Section 8.19), they are not created independently.

8.4.2 Showing Schedule Changes in Gantt Charts

Changes in schedules can be shown in various ways depending on the situation. For example:

- Changes at milestones causing iteration should be shown as discussed in Section 8.4.2.1.
- Changes between millstones due to delays should be shown as discussed in Section 8.4.2.2.

8.4.2.1 Changes at Milestones Causing Iteration   Should not be shown from the *Functional* perspective in manner of Waterfall Chart (Section 14.9), they should be shown from the *Temporal* perspective using several Gantt Charts as shown in the following example from the Nuts and Bolts Project (Kasser 2016b). Federated Aerospace is developing the Widget System in which the SDP starts in the Needs Identification State (Section 14.9.1). The project is the first of its kind: there are no similar systems in existence. The Widget system comprises two subsystems, Part A and Part B. The original seven-month Widget project schedule shown in Figure 8.7* was planned in the traditional manner as a single pass through the Waterfall (Section 14.9) assuming there would be no serious problems during the SDP. Note the Subsystem Construction and Subsystem Test States have been combined into a Realization State in the figure. However, "The best laid schemes o' mice an' men gang aft agley, [often go awry]" (Burns 1786).

All went well with the Widget system as it passed through the sequential states of the SDP until a major problem showed up in the System Test State. At this point, the problem impacted the development schedule and the SDP reverted to a second Needs Identification State as shown in the revised schedule in Figure 8.8. The second

---

* The Milestones are omitted to simplify the chart because the purpose of the Figure is to show the task relationships.

Months	1	2	3	4	5	6	7
Needs	▓						
Requirements		▓					
Design			▓				
Realization				▓			
Integration					▓		
Test						▓	
O&M							▓

Figure 8.7 Widget project: original schedule.

Months	1	2	3	4	5	6	7	8	9	10	11	12	13
Needs	▓												
Requirements		▓											
Design			▓										
Realization				▓									
Integration					▓								
Test						▓							
Needs-2							▓						
Requirements-2								▓					
Design-2									▓				
Realization-2										▓			
Integration-2											▓		
Test-2												▓	
O&M													▓

Figure 8.8 Widget project: revised schedule.

iteration of the SDP began in Month 7 and the original O&M State was delayed to Month 13.

While the solution to the original problem demonstrated that the revised design would meet the functional requirements, at the end of the second System Test State in Month 12, the design still needed to be validated for the non-functional and manufacturing requirements. Accordingly, at this point in time the SDP iterated back to the third System Design State as shown in the revised schedule in Figure 8.9 for an additional delay of two months. The third Realization and System Test states were skipped since the changes did not affect the design and the project was so far behind schedule.

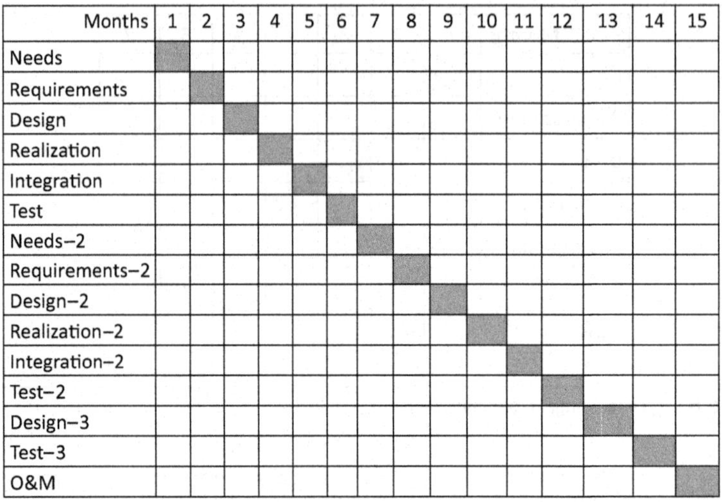

Months	1	2	3	4	5	6	7	8	9	10	11	12	13	14	15
Needs	█														
Requirements		█													
Design			█												
Realization				█											
Integration					█										
Test						█									
Needs–2							█								
Requirements–2								█							
Design–2									█						
Realization–2										█					
Integration–2											█				
Test–2												█			
Design–3													█		
Test–3														█	
O&M															█

Figure 8.9   Widget project: extended revised schedule.

8.4.2.2 Changes due to Delays   When a schedule timeline is first drawn, it is drawn as an ideal or notional schedule. However in the real world events happen that cause delays (Burns 1786). These delays need to be shown in the corresponding Gantt Chart. For example, suppose the original Widget project schedule shown in Figure 8.7 suffered a two-month delay during the Design State which caused the CDR to be delayed and must be shown on the modified project schedule. This is a delay, not a required iteration as shown in Figure 8.8. One way of showing delays is illustrated in Figure 8.10.

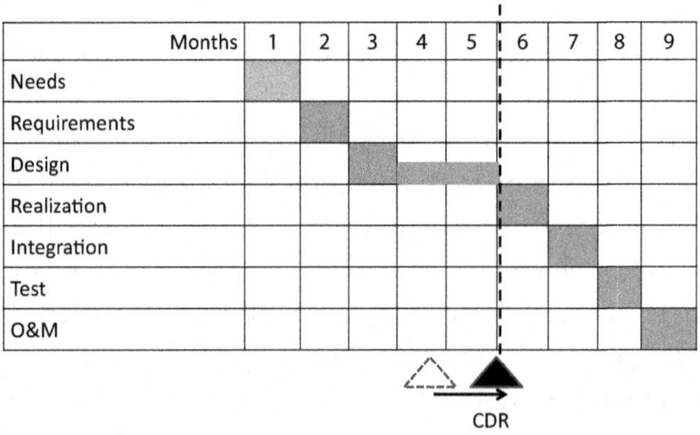

Months	1	2	3	4	5	6	7	8	9
Needs	█								
Requirements		█							
Design			█	▓					
Realization					█				
Integration						█			
Test							█		
O&M									█

CDR

Figure 8.10   Widget project: adjusted schedule.

The two-month delay in Months 4 and 5 is shown as a half-height bar in Figure 8.10. Sometimes delays are shown as red bars on the chart where green bars represent the notional timeline, and blue bars represent activities being performed ahead of schedule. Whichever convention is in use, the prime directive in the Gantt Chart, in fact the innovation that it brought to project management, is to show the original timeline *and* the modified adjusted timeline *on the same* chart.

8.5 The Golden Rules

There are actually two Golden Rules:

1. The Golden Rule governing behaviour discussed in Section 8.5.1.
2. The Golden Rule pertaining to funding discussed in Section 8.5.2

8.5.1 The Golden Rule Governing Behaviour

The Golden Rule governing behaviour is:

- Based on a part of Hillel's response to the pagan who wanted an instant summary of Judaism. As reported in the Babylonian Talmud Tractate Sabbath, Hillel summed up Judaism as, "What is hateful to thee, do not unto thy fellow; this is the whole law" (Rodkinson 1903).
- A systems thinking tool because people are part of the system. It is the fundamental principle of Judaism and should also be a code of behaviour for any manager, leader, or systems engineer. The rule is stated in a negative way. Sometimes the rule has been stated in a positive way. There been many commentaries over the years on the difference between stating the rule in a positive and negative manner. In summary, the negative manner is realistic, the positive manner (treat others as you'd like them to treat you) is idealistic. One of the most important and effective uses of this principle is the "Thank You" (Section 8.13).

Effective leaders often embody this principle by not asking their followers to do something they would not do themselves.

8.5.2 *The Golden Rule Pertaining to Funding*

The Golden Rule pertaining to funding is often stated as, "she who has the gold makes the rules". This rule reflects the real world. Projects exist because they're funded. That means the person who is funding the project makes the rules and is the final authority with responsibility for changes.*

8.6 Just-In-Time Decision-Making

Just-in-Time (JIT) Decision-Making is:

- Based on the *Temporal* HTP.
- A tool for deferring decisions until the last possible moment that the decision has to be made (Kasser 2000a).
- Controlled procrastination (*Continuum* HTP).
- Adapted from the JIT concept for ordering material in manufacturing developed by the Ford Motor Car Company to reduce the amount of capital tied up in raw materials (Ford and Crowther 1922: p. 143).
- A part of Project Planning (Section 8.11) in that the last possible moment to make that decision is calculated by working backwards from the point in time when the effects of the decision will be noted.

For example in the manufacturing industry, a decision has to be made between ordering two parts. They both perform identically but only one of them will be used. The date at which they will start to be used is the milestone. The time from placing the order to the receipt of the parts and the acceptance testing of the parts before they're ready to be used is estimated. An additional buffer time is added, and when the total time is subtracted from the start to be used milestone, the latest date for placing the order is seen. The latest date for making the decision is just before the latest date for placing the order. For

---

* It's a rule that needs to be pointed out to rebellious teenagers and enforced.

example the part needs to be in hand on 1 May. A quick check shows that the ordering process takes four weeks, adding a day or so buffer means that the decision as to which part to purchase has to be made by 25 March.

In other situations, for example when deciding between different designs, different suppliers, and different travel routes, Risk Management (Chapter 12) must be used to ensure that at least one of the choices is feasible. For example, a computer system is going to communicate with another computer system sometime in the future. There is no need to decide how it's going to communicate until the time comes to build or buy the communication interfaces. This is because there are standard COTS Wi-Fi, Ethernet, and other means of connecting computers. When designing and building technological systems, delaying these decisions does not lock designs into technology that may obsolete by the time the design becomes realized and the equipment goes into service.

8.7 Management by Exception

Management by Exception (MBE) is a tool that:

- Allows the span of control to be widened by allowing the manager to ignore projects that are performing to the planned values (the norm).
- Sets tolerance limits on the parameters of an object (process or product being developed) and ignores the object if the limits are not exceeded.
- Allows delegating decisions to the lowest level, giving employees responsibility, as long as the consequences of the decision do not cause the limits to be exceeded.

8.7.1 *The Key Ingredients in MBE*

The key ingredients in MBE are (Bittel 1964):

1. *Selection*: pinpoints the criteria that will be measured. In the systems approach these are the objectives determined by MBO (Section 8.8).

2. *Measurement*: assigns value to past and present performance.
3. *Projection*: analyses the measurements and projects future performance.
4. *Observation*: informs management of the state of performance.
5. *Comparison*: compares performance with limits or boundaries and reports the variances to management.
6. *Decision Making*: prescribes the action to be taken to:
   a. Bring performance back within the limits.
   b. Adjust the limits or expectations.
   c. Exploit opportunity.

8.7.2 Advantages and Disadvantages of MBE

The advantages include:

- Reduces the amount of monitoring and controlling performed by upper management.
- Upper management need not spend time on projects that are progressing normally.
- Undesirable situations are indicated by the limits being exceeded so that upper management can intervene.

The disadvantages include:

- Open to Micromanagement by Upper Management (MBUM) once a parameter exceeds the limit threshold.
- Mistakes in setting limits may cause problematic situations to be unnoticed until it is too late to take corrective action, or may flag too many alarms.
- Can be confused with "management without caring" resulting in low morale in organizational units that do not raise exceptions as in the C3I Group Case (Section 13.1.2).
- It is based on the assumption that only upper management can deal with a problematic situation. However, this disadvantage may be overcome if the local personnel can produce a plan for dealing with the problem that satisfies upper management.

8.7.3 Using MBE

There are two states in MBE, namely:

1. *The planning state* in which the limits are set. When the objectives of each Work Package (Section 8.19) are set using MBO (Section 8.8) and the upper and lower level tolerances for each objective are determined. The limits may be set by investigating each task or by using a number of standard deviations. However, as with most other things, there is a trade-off: the smaller the limit, the more exceptions will need to be investigated. The larger the limit, the fewer investigations, but there will be a greater chance that a serious situation will be missed.

2. *The monitoring and controlling states* in which the limits should not be exceeded. Tools used in MBE in this state include process control Trend Charts (Section 2.15) such as the one shown in Figure 2.7, CRIP Charts (Section 8.1) and ETL Charts (Section 8.16.2) such as Figure 8.21 and Figure 8.22 used in project status reporting.

8.8 Management by Objectives

Management by Objectives (MBO) (Mali 1972) is a compound tool:

- For planning a project.
- For monitoring the progress towards completion.
- That was popular as a management approach in the 1960s.

MBO as introduced was unnecessarily complex and complicated. However, the core concepts in MBO are simple and manageable, namely:

1. Set realistic objectives or goals for every activity.
2. Monitor progress towards those objectives as the project proceeds.
3. Take corrective action if the objectives are not going to be met.

These core concepts are actually embodied in standard project management and EVA (Section 8.2) and built into the SDP Waterfall Chart template (Section 14.9). The SDP is divided into a number of states, each of which has to accomplish predefined objectives by the milestone at the end of the state. For example, the objectives of the System Requirements State are to produce the System Requirements Document (SRD) at the SRR which takes place at the end of the state.

MBO was originally introduced by Peter Drucker as a systems approach to managing an organization (Drucker 1954) where the objectives one layer in the hierarchy are set to accomplish and support the objectives of the higher level of the organization, a similar concept to the "Do Statement" (Section 3.2.1). In the language of systems, when setting objectives, the objectives of the subsystem shall support the objectives of the system.

8.8.1 MBO in the Planning State of a Project

MBO relates to activities and objectives, it does not involve schedules and timelines. The process for using MBO in the planning state of a project is as follows:

1. Determine the states and milestones appropriate to the project for the project (Section 14.9.2). There are no uniformly agreed-to names for milestones. Milestones can be major and minor, formal and informal.
2. If the project is complex use the Waterfall Chart (Section 14.9) as a template. Since the scope of projects varies, the mixture of major and minor, formal and informal, milestones also vary. Each project will have its own mixture, similar to those of similar projects.
3. Determine the objectives to be completed by the last major milestone (the last state) in the project. These may include events to be achieved and products to be produced.
4. Determine the objectives for each previous state of the SDP.
5. Determine the sub-objectives for each objective. A useful tool for doing this is the "Do Statement" (Section 3.2.1).
6. Create the Work Packages (Section 8.19) and project network of activities that will produce each objective and sub-objective in a sequential orderly manner. Useful tools for doing this standard planning process are PAM Charts (Section 2.12), PAM Network Charts (Section 2.12.2), and PERT Charts (Section 8.10).

8.9 Mission Statements

A Mission Statement is a communications tool; it communicates the organization's intended purpose.

- Perceptions from the *Operational* HTP indicate that:
  - Mission Statements can be used at all levels within the organization as well as for the entire organization, since every department, division, or other organizational element should have a purpose.
  - Mission Statements are used as a reference to remember what to do, and when ideas come up concerning what the organization might do, the Mission Statement is used as a reference to determine if the idea should be adopted. For example, if an employee within a company selling food and beverages comes up with an idea to sell airplanes, expanding into the airplane market is not part of the company's mission. Accordingly, the employee should be thanked for the idea (Section 8.13) and encouraged to submit more ideas in the future, but this specific idea should not be adopted. Of course, there is always an exception. If the idea is really good and the return on investment is high and there is expertise within the organization, the organization might consider setting up a new department to implement the idea.
- Perceptions from the *Functional* HTP indicate that the Mission Statement defines the functions performed by the organization in pursuit of a goal.
- Perceptions from the *Quantitative* and *Structural* HTPs indicate that:
  - A Mission Statement often has at least two parts, namely:
    - *The goal or purpose*: for example, "To provide the best service possible".
    - *How that goal or purpose will be achieved*: for example, "by … (a specific quantifiable statement).

- Each of the Mission Statements within an organization should align with the Mission Statement of the element of the organization at the next higher level in the hierarchy.
- Perceptions from the *Generic* HTP indicate that:
  - A Mission Statement is similar to an abstract of a book. The Mission Statement sums up the purpose of the organization in a sentence or small paragraph just like the abstract of a book summarizes the contents of the book in a paragraph or two.
- Perceptions from the *Continuum* HTP indicate that:
  - A mission is different to a vision. A vision is a FCFDS; a mission is the process that is being, or will be, performed to realize the vision by making the transition from the current situation to the FCFDS.
  - The Mission Statement should differentiate the organization from similar organizations at the particular level in the organizational hierarchy.

The "Do Statement" (Section 3.2.1) is a useful tool for deriving Mission Statements for various parts of the organization to ensure traceability to the top-level Mission Statement of the organization.

8.10 PERT Charts

A Program Evaluation Review Technique (PERT) Chart:

- Is a project management tool used to help thinking about scheduling and coordinating tasks within a project.
- Is a specialized version of a Flowchart (Section 2.7).
- Was developed by the US Navy in the 1950s to manage the timing of research activities for the Polaris submarine missile program (Stauber et al. 1959) at about the same time that the Critical Path Method (CPM) was developed for project management in the private sector to perform the same function.
- Presents a Concept Map of the relationship between activities in a project as a network diagram consisting of numbered nodes representing the dates of events or milestones in the project linked together by labelled directional lines (lines

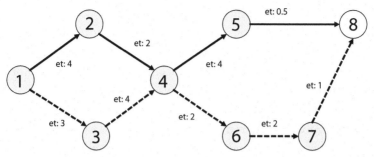

Shows expected completion times (et) for tasks between Milestones 1 and 8

Figure 8.11 Part of a typical PERT Chart.

with arrows) representing tasks in the project. For example, the PERT Chart shown in Figure 8.11 has eight nodes, of which Nodes 1, 4 and 8 are major milestones. The tasks (arrows) are labelled to show expected completion times (et) of the tasks. When tasks are performed in parallel the longest path is known in project management as the critical path and identified in the figure by dotted lines. For example, in the time between Milestones 1 and 4, the critical path is the route formed by Tasks 1–3 and 3–4 because it takes nine time units as opposed to the eight time units for the path formed by Tasks 1–2 and 2–4.

- May be considered as a PAM Network Chart (Figure 2.37) with the product information abstracted out, hidden, or removed (whichever way you care to think about it).

While the PERT Chart is a very effective management tool, it can also be used in its Flowchart (Section 2.7) incarnation as a communications tool to show people:

- How their work relates to the project as a whole.
- Who their input comes from (suppliers).
- Who their output goes to (customers).
- When their output is needed.

For example, I once used a PERT Chart as a communications tool in the following manner. The context was in 1989 in the Systems Engineering and Services (SEAS) contract supporting the National Aeronautics and Space Administration (NASA) Goddard Spaceflight

Center (GSFC) in a multi-tasking environment supporting the upgrading of a number of interdependent data processing and command and control facilities in which the subcontractor who I worked for was responsible for systems engineering while the contractor was responsible for management and software engineering.

At one time I tried to work out how all the tasks were related. So I gathered information from the different groups on what they were doing, who supplied them with inputs and who used their outputs and printed* a PERT Chart and coloured in the system engineering, hardware engineering, software engineering, and test engineering activities in different distinctive colours using highlighters. I also coloured the arrows between the activities in the corresponding colours and highlighted the transfer points (i.e. a point in time where development transfers the system to the test team). I placed the coloured PERT Chart on the wall in the corridor outside the office.†

It didn't take very long for people to come out of their offices and study the chart. For the first time, everyone had a picture of the project as a whole and how their activities were related to those of the other groups working on the project. A few days later similar PERT Charts appeared on the walls of other departments showing other project activities. That was the upside of the situation. A week or so later I received an informal reprimand because I was a systems engineer and PERT Charts were management tools which, as a systems engineer, I should not be using.

8.10.1 How to Create a PERT Chart

Remember:

1. Milestones are dates and are shown as circles; activities take place over time and are represented as the arrows between the circles as shown in Figure 8.11.
2. The PERT Chart focuses on the activities and milestones. The products and resources associated with the activities are not included in the PERT Chart. The schedule, dates, and other time information is also not included, other than the

---

* Using a dot matrix printer and sticking the strips of paper together with clear tape.
† It was too long to go on the wall in the office.

nominal time to perform the activity. This time information is used to depict the critical path.

3. PERT Charts are created during the planning process (Section 8.11.2)

The non-systems activity-based approach for creating a PERT Chart assuming there is no Timeline (Section 8.15) is as follows:

1. Start at the initial milestone.
2. Create the Timeline (Section 8.15).
3. Think of the activities that will commence at that milestone and draw them out to milestones.
4. Repeat Step 2 at those milestones.
5. Repeat Steps 2 and 3 until the activity lines come together at the final milestone.

The intuitive systems approach for creating a PERT Chart assuming there is no Timeline (Section 8.15) is as follows:

1. Start at the final milestone, the last milestone in the project.
2. Create the Timeline (Section 8.15) by working backwards to the initial milestone (Section 11.8).
3. Use a PAM Chart (Section 2.12) to figure out what products are to be delivered at that milestone, and what activities produce the products.
4. Draw the activities leading to the milestone as arrows. Each activity starts at another milestone.
5. For each of these new milestones, use a PAM Chart (Section 2.12) to figure out what products are to be delivered at that milestone.
6. Draw the activities leading to these milestones as arrows in the PERT Chart. Each activity starts at a previous milestone.
7. Repeat steps 5 and 6 until you reach the milestone that kicks off the project.

Applying systems thinking to this process, obvious that repeating Steps 5 and 6 will produce a complex and complicated chart that violates the KISS principle (Section 3.2.3). Accordingly the systems approach creates a set of PERT Charts (mostly abstracting out the activities that create the Work Packages (WP) (Section 8.19)) as follows:

1. Determine the major milestones for the project (Section 14.9.2). This is done as part of the planning process (Section 8.11.2).
2. Create the Timeline (Section 8.15) by working backwards to the initial milestone (Section 11.8).
3. Determine the objectives that have to be met at each milestone from the WP (Section 8.19). These will generally be the products that have to be produced by the date of the milestone. The objective may also include an activity that takes place at the milestone. For example if the activities that take place at the milestone include presentations, then creating and delivering the presentation is also an objective. By determining the objectives for each milestone, the systems approach provides for MBO (Section 8.8) into the management process in a transparent manner.
4. Draw the single line of arrows and milestones starting the kick-off major milestone to the final major milestone. The notional reference major milestones (Section 14.9.2) provide a template which can be adjusted to suit the project.
5. Start at the final milestone, the last milestone in the project. If you don't have a WP (Section 8.19), use a PAM Chart (Section 2.12) to figure out what products are to be delivered at that milestone, and what activities produce the products.
6. Draw the activities leading to the major milestone as arrows. Each activity starts at another milestone. Consider these milestones as minor milestones, or lower level milestones between the major milestone and its previous major milestone. For example if the major milestone is CDR, the previous major milestone will be the PDR. The minor milestones:
    a. Will be milestones where intermediate products are transferred from one part of the organization to another between the two major milestones.
    b. May be in any of the Three Streams of Activities (Section 8.14).
7. Each activity has a component in the Three Streams of Activities (Section 8.14) with the appropriate products and resource requirements.

8. For each of these new milestones, use a PAM Chart (Section 2.12) to figure out what products are to be delivered at that milestone.
9. Draw the activities leading to these milestones as arrows in the PERT Chart. Each activity starts at another, previous in time, milestone.
10. Repeat Steps 8 and 9 until the arrows come together at the previous major milestone.
11. Start at this major milestone. Use a PAM Chart (Section 2.12) to figure out what products are to be delivered at that milestone, and what activities produce the products.
12. Repeat Steps 6 to 10 until the arrows come together at the first or kick-off major milestone.

The systems approach to drawing the PERT Chart has the following advantages:

- It keeps each drawing understandable in accordance with Miller's Rule (Section 3.2.5).
- It ensures that the Three Streams of Activities (Section 8.14) come together at each major milestone.
- It provides for MBO (Section 8.8) in a transparent manner.

In the systems approach to planning, risk and opportunities are considered when estimating times for activities in the planning process (Section 8.11.2). These contribute to the early and late times of the time estimates and allow "what-if?" questions to be asked at planning time to mitigate risks or take advantage of opportunities.

8.11 Project Plans

A Project Plan (PP):

- Is one of the two key documents in a project.
- Is a tool that provides the information contained in the answers to the Kipling Questions (Section 7.6) posed in Active Brainstorming (Section 7.1) the project, namely:
  - Who are the stakeholders in the project?
  - What is the project going to achieve?
  - Where will the activities take place?

- When will the project take place?
- Why is the project being undertaken?
- How will the project be …?

Accordingly, the scope of the Project Plan includes:

- Budget.
- Schedule.
- Needed resources, staff, material, etc.
- Constraints.
- Risks and risk management (i.e., what might go wrong and how to prevent or mitigate the risks).

8.11.1 *The Two Planning Paradigms*

Perceptions from the *Continuum* HTP have identified two planning paragraph paradigms namely:

1. *Activity-based*: concentrates on the activities to be performed using resources as a starting point and then works forwards to the products.
2. *Results-based*: outcomes-based or objectives-based, which concentrates on the results to be achieved (products to be produced) and works backwards to the needed resources.

The difference between these two approaches is illustrated by the following scenario taking place in Federated Aerospace (FA) (Kasser 1995). It was the Monday morning of Task Planning week. Sandra Stenson and Fred met to begin planning the activities to be performed on the facility upgrade contract.

"Let's start with Task 31, the Stage 3 Upgrade/Transition", said Sandra as she spread the task planning forms on the table. "We have systems engineers, software developers, hardware engineers, and test personnel on the task, so we'll make each activity a cost account. This way everybody will know what to charge to" said Sandra, and she began to pencil in cost accounts. "Now let's figure out the deliverables for each cost account".

"Wait a minute", said Fred, "let's look at it from a different perspective and draw a PAM Chart [Section 2.12]. We are going to have an Operations Concept Review [OCR] in four months (the milestone); we'll need a Concept of Operations [CONOPS] and a Transition Plan by then (the products). We'll need the integration and test procedures two months after the review. Let's make each of those deliverables a separate cost account, and who so ever works on them (the activities to produce the product) can charge to the product, not to the engineering activity."

Sandra's approach to planning is activity-based; Fred's approach is results- or product-based. Sandra is using a planning tool that leads her into the activity-based planning mode. She is using the Gantt Chart (Section 8.4) and WBS (Section 8.18) as an input tool instead of as a view of the activities in the project. Using the Gantt Chart as an input tool forces "activity-based planning" which focuses on the activity, rather than on the outcomes of the activity.

The results- or product-based approach:

- Works back from the products produced to determine the activities that produce those activities, rather than trying to think up products for the activities to produce.
- Provides data about the time spent to produce a product. This data may be used to refine models for cost estimating additional activities and for proposal pricing.
- Produces measurable results; namely, the deliverables were or were not delivered.
- Uses PAM Charts (Section 2.12) and WPs (Section 8.19) as input tools instead of WBS (Section 8.18).

Working effectively means working in a cost effective manner. Sandra's activity-based planning is much less effective than Fred's results-based approach, because it is always easier to work back from a known answer (the products in this case) (Section 11.8) than to work forwards towards an unknown one.

8.11.2 *Creating the Project Plan*

1. Find samples of PPs from previous projects or on the Internet.
2. Customize the samples to create a List (Section 9.4) of section headings.
3. Create an Annotated Outline (Section 14.1).
4. Create a List (Section 9.4) of the products that have to be delivered before acceptance. These will be contract specific and may include the final product, spare parts, documentation, training, etc.

5. Identify the major milestones. Work back from the end of the project (Section 11.8). Let the final milestone be the acceptance by the customer.

6. List the products to be produced for each major milestone. If the project uses the Waterfall Chart as a template (Section 14.9), the products are predefined by the appropriate Waterfall milestone review templates.

7. Use PAM Charts (Section 2.12) to identify the activities and resources that produce the products.

8. Split the work into the Three Streams of Activities (Section 8.14).

9. Create top-level WPs (Section 8.19) for each activity.

10. Expand the top-level Work Packages in each stream of work into lower level Work Packages using PAM Charts (Section 2.12).

11. Ensure every management planning activity WP is linked to a development doing activity WP.

12. Ensure every doing activity WP is linked to a testing activity WP.

13. Ensure that every doing and testing activity WP is linked to a management activity WP.

14. Estimate risk, cost, and schedule for the lowest level Work Packages.

15. Roll the information up into the higher level ones.

16. Plan to mitigate risks identified in later WPs by adding risk management activities to earlier activities (Section 12.9). For example, Activity A8-1 in Figure 2.39 might be mitigated by doing something in Activity A3-1 as shown in Figure 8.12.

17. Enter the information into a project management software database.

18. Iterate until performance, cost, risk, and schedule are acceptable (Figure 8.13):
    a. Reduce the length of the critical path.
    b. Remove some of the low priority performance requirements from the final product.

19. Fill in the remaining blanks in the PP Annotated Outline (Section 11.4.4) with the resulting data and other pertinent information.

20. Continue with the rest of the document production process (Section 11.4.5).

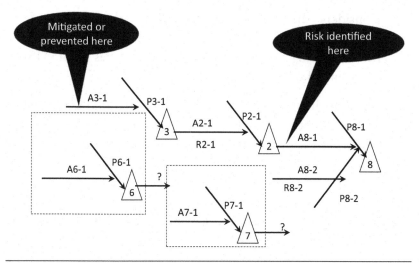

Figure 8.12   Incorporating prevention in the project planning process.

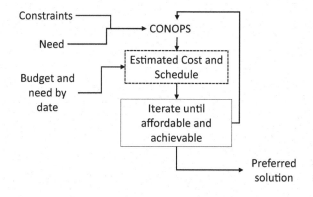

Figure 8.13   Iterate until affordable and feasible.

8.12 The Technology Availability Window of Opportunity

The Technology Availability Window of Opportunity (TAWOO) (Kasser 2016a) is a six-state tool that:

- Allows project managers to determine if a technology is mature enough to integrate into the system under development *as well as* determining if the technology will be available for the operating life of the system once deployed.
- Extends the Technology Readiness Level (TRL) (Mankins 1995).

- Considers the use of the technology over the whole product lifecycle including consideration of Diminishing Manufacturing Sources and Material Shortages (DMSMS) at the end of the technology lifecycle.

This section discusses the tool and the holistic thinking that led to the development of the tool providing examples of the use of a number of the tools discussed in this book.

8.12.1 Framing the Original Problem

This section frames the original problem using the Problem Formulation Template (Section 14.3).

1. *The undesirable situation*: the lack of "a systematic metric/measurement system that supports assessments of the maturity of a particular technology and the consistent comparison of maturity between different types of technology" (Mankins 1995).
2. *Assumptions*: unknown.
3. *The FCFDS*: a situation that contains a "systematic metric/measurement system that supports assessments of the maturity of a particular technology and the consistent comparison of maturity between different types of technology" (Mankins 1995).
4. *The problem*: how to transition between the undesirable situation and the FCFDS, namely first to conceptualize and then to develop a "systematic metric/measurement system that supports assessments of the maturity of a particular technology and the consistent comparison of maturity between different types of technology" (Mankins 1995).
5. *The solution*: creating and deploying the product that will operate in the FCFDS to provide the remedy to the undesirable situation.

8.12.2 The Traditional Non-Systems Approach

This section discusses the traditional non-systems approach employed in the 1990s which produced the TRL to provide a baseline reference in the form of an example.

8.12.2.1 The Undesirable Situation The undesirable situation is articulated in a focused manner as follows:

- It is 1998.
- A system under development is to be deployed in 1999 to meet a projected need.
- There is no current suitable technology that can be employed for realizing that system.
- There is no systemic and systematic way to determine the readiness of a technology for use in a product other than seeing it incorporated in current products (GAO 1999).

8.12.2.2 Assumption The focus is on the acquisition, namely the development of the technology until it is suitable to incorporate in the product or system being acquired ignoring the rest of the lifecycle of the technology following the acquisition.

8.12.2.3 The FCFDS The technology is ready in 1999 when needed and in use in a fully operational deployed product or system.

8.12.2.4 The Problem Create a tool or a methodology (or both), that a project manager can use to determine if a technology is mature enough to integrate into the system under development so that the FCFDS will be created in a timely manner.

8.12.2.5 The Solution The solution in 1998 was the TRL shown in Table 8.24, a tool that was developed in NASA to provide a "systematic

Table 8.24 NASA's TRLs

9	Actual system "flight proven" through successful mission operations
8	Actual system completed and "flight qualified" through test and demonstration (ground or space)
7	System prototype demonstration in a space environment
6	System/subsystem model or prototype demonstration in a relevant environment (ground or space)
5	Component and/or breadboard validation in relevant environment
4	Component and/or breadboard validation in laboratory environment
3	Analytical and experimental critical function and/or characteristic proof-of concept
2	Technology concept and/or application formulated
1	Basic principles observed and reported

metric/measurement system that supports assessments of the maturity of a particular technology and the consistent comparison of maturity between different types of technology" (Mankins 1995). The project manager could assess various technologies and determine which one to use. TRLs = 1, 2, 3, and 4 seem to constitute the research levels, TRL = 5 and 6, the development levels, and TRL = 9, the production level. The TRL was used in NASA and later adopted by the US Department of Defense (DOD) (GAO 1999) to assess a technology and approve it for use if it was above a certain TRL.

Whilst the TRL seems to be well-known, a number of deficiencies in the TRL which reduce its fitness for purpose have been pointed out (*Continuum* HTP). For example:

- Katz et al. wrote, "Program managers underestimate the time and technical effort needed to mature technologies above TRL = 6 to achieve higher levels of maturity" (Katz et al. 2014).
- Sauser et al. wrote,

    It has been stated that the TRL:
    - does not provide a complete representation of the (difficulty of) integration of the subject technology or subsystems into an operational system (Dowling and Pardoe 2005, Mankins 2002, Meystel et al. 2003, Valerdi and Kohl 2004),
    - includes no guidance into the uncertainty that may be expected in moving through the maturation of TRL (Dowling and Pardoe 2005, Mankins 2002, Cundiff 2003, Shishkio, Ebbeler, and Fox 2003, Smith 2005, Moorehouse 2001), and
    - assimilates no comparative analysis technique for alternative TRLs (Dowling and Pardoe 2005, Mankins 2002, Valerdi and Kohl 2004, Cundiff 2003, Smith 2005). (Sauser et al. 2006)

Sauser et al.'s Point 2 which aggregates findings from prior research is very pertinent since the TRL is a single data point. While single data points provide information on the current status of a something they cannot, and should not, be used to predict the future. No wonder "program managers underestimate the time and technical effort needed to mature technologies above TRL = 6 to achieve higher levels of maturity" (Katz et al. 2014). This situation has been recognized and there has been research into historical data and project success and failure to develop ways of reducing the uncertainty in the prediction. However, research into the problem of determining future technology readiness such as seeking ways to reduce the uncertainty in the predictions (Crépin, El-Khoury, and Kenley 2012) still remains focused on the early stages of the technology lifecycle (El-Khoury 2012).

8.12.3 The Systems Approach to Remedying the Undesirable Situation

Now frame the problem holistically as follows.

8.12.3.1 The Undesirable Situation   The undesirable situation is the same as in Section 8.12.2.1. The holistic approach perceives the specific instance of the undesirable situation from each HTP as discussed in this Section.

8.12.3.1.1 Big Picture Perspective   Perceptions from the *Big Picture* perspective include:

- The same perceptions articulated in Section 8.12.2.1.
- A description about need of technology for the system.
- A description of environment in which the system or product incorporating the technology will be used.
- A list and description of the known users of the system.
- A list and description of the adjacent systems interfacing with the system.

8.12.3.1.2 Operational Perspective   Perceptions from the *Operational* perspective include scenarios of the different types of missions the system using the technology will perform. Typical generic scenarios include the use of the system incorporating the technology in different categories of missions such as:

- *One-of-a-kind, single use, short and long term missions* such as the NASA planetary space explorers in the 20th century. NASA generally developed the technology for a spacecraft for a mission. Since the number of spacecraft were small, the technology could be used at TRL = 6. A small number of spacecraft could be crafted and deployed without being placed in mass production.

- *One-of-a-kind military targets of opportunity* such as Operation Chastise, 16 May 1943, which went operational at what would have been TRL = 6. The special purpose dam-busting bombs were crafted and deployed for that specific mission without being placed in mass production and made available for other types of missions.
- Examples of various uses of the technology in considerable numbers of commercial and military products over a long period of time. This type of deployment requires TRL = 9 to guarantee availability of the technology when needed.
- Various in-between scenarios.

8.12.3.1.3 Functional Perspective Perceptions from the *Functional* perspective describe how the technology functions.

8.12.3.1.4 Structural Perspective Perceptions from the *Structural* perspective include limitations of the technology imposed by its physical structure.

8.12.3.1.5 Quantitative Perspective Perceptions from the *Quantitative* perspective indicate:

- The maturity of the technology can be represented in mono-tonically increasing levels of technology readiness ranging from a "concept that needs to be developed" to "being incorporated in significant quantities of production items".
- Nine levels of technical maturity in the TRL shown in Table 8.24 comply with Miller's Rule (Section 3.2.5) for comprehension of an issue.

8.12.3.1.6 Generic Perspective Perceptions from the *Generic* perspective include ways of assessing readiness and capability to do something, including:

- Capability maturity models.
- Competency models.
- ISO 9001.

- Risk assessment rectangles (Section 5.4).
- Temperature thermometers or other meters with useable range markings.
- The "S" curve which illustrates the introduction, growth and maturation of innovations and technology.

8.12.3.1.7 Continuum Perspective Perceptions from the *Continuum* perspective include:

- The differences in the types of operational uses for the technology mentioned in Section 8.12.3.1.2.
- The different types of missions which are described in the *Operational* perspective.
- The differences between:*
  - using a methodology and a tool to assess the *current* state of something, and
  - using a tool to predict the *future* state of the same thing.
- Risks and risk management pertaining to the misuse of the methodology and tool.

8.12.3.1.8 Temporal Perspective Perceptions from the *Temporal* perspective include:

- The technology use cycle which has been shown in the form of the whale diagram (Nolte 2005).
- Technology maturity and obsolescence are currently considered independently in the technology lifecycle. This is a key observation leading to the inference in the *Scientific* perspective to change the problem from "technology readiness" to "technology availability".
- Once ready for use in products, technology is only available during the adulthood and maturity phases of the technology lifecycle.

8.12.3.1.9 Scientific Perspective Inferences from the *Scientific* perspective indicate that while a single TRL can provide information

---

* This is a key difference.

on the current maturity level of the technology, it cannot, and should not, be used to predict the maturity level of the technology at a future date.

8.12.3.2 Assumptions

- Any other assumptions about the technology.

8.12.3.3 The FCFDS
The FCFDS is that the project manager has a tool or methodology to determine if a specific technology will be available when needed for the duration of all categories of missions.

8.12.3.4 The Problem
The inference from the *Scientific* perspective of the FCFDS is to restate the problem as "to create a tool or methodology (or both) to allow the project manager to determine if the technology will be available when needed at some future date for the duration of all categories of missions". The tool or methodology will need to take into account at least the following:

- Time to advance maturity to a level suitable for use in the project which will depend on category of mission (single, one-of-a-kind, use or mass production).
- The period of time in which the technology is available for use in products and systems before it becomes obsolete.
- Obsolescence issues now considered separately as DMSMS.

This rephrasing of the problem statement has altered the scope of the problem in a significant way. It leads the project manager into going beyond systems thinking (Section 1.4.2) and using the *Temporal* HTP to consider:

- The rate of change of technology maturity during its development.
- The wider issues pertaining to the obsolescence of the technology after deployment.

8.12.3.5 The Solution
In the holistic problem-solving process, ideally at least two solutions (tools and/or methodologies) would be conceptualized and a selection would be made to determine the most acceptable solution. For the purposes of this example, consider the conceptualization of one of those solutions.

8.12.4 Perceptions of the TAWOO

The TAWOO is one conceptual solution to the problem. Going beyond systems thinking (Section 1.4.2), consider the TAWOO from the appropriate progressive and remaining HTPs.

8.12.4.1 The Temporal *Perspective*   "Although TRL is commonly used, it is not common for agencies and contractors to archive and make available data on the timeline to transition between TRLs" (Crépin, El-Khoury, and Kenley 2012). The *Temporal* HTP suggests that the data should be archived and used to estimate/predict maturity. If that data were available, one could infer from the *Scientific* HTP that one could consider the rate of change of TRL rather than a single static value at one particular time. Figure 8.14 shows that the technology was conceptualized in 1991 and the development was planned to advance one TRL each year starting in 1993 for production in 1999. However, the development did not go according to plan. The technology did not get to TRL = 2 until 1995 advancing to TRL = 3 two years later in 1997 and jumping to TRL = 6 in 1998. So can the technology be approved for a project due to go into service in 1999? It depends. If the project can use the technology when TRL = 6, then yes. But, if the product using the technology is to go into mass production, the answer cannot be determined because there is insufficient information to predict when the technology will be at TRL = 9. The project will have to obtain more information about the factors affecting the rate of change in TRL to make a forecast as to the future.

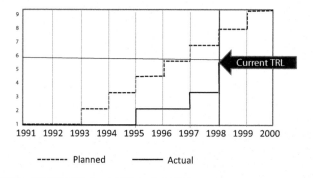

Figure 8.14   The technology TRL 1991–2001.

8.12.4.2 The Generic *Perspective* Perceptions from the *Generic* perspective indicate that projects use EVA (Section 8.2) and display budgeted/planned and actual cost information in graphs such as Figures 2.3 and 2.4 in which future costs are forecast.

8.12.4.3 The Scientific *Perspective* Combine observations from the *Generic* and *Temporal* perspectives and display the rate of change of the TRL in the form of an EVA graph as shown in Figure 8.15. When this is done, one additional significant item of information is obtained. Assuming nothing changes and progress continues at the same rate as in 1997–1998, the technology should reach TRL = 9 by 1999. However, the reason for the rate of change between 1996–1997 and 1997–1998 is unknown. This provides the project manager with some initial questions to ask the technology developers before making the decision to adopt the technology. The static single value TRL has become a dynamic TRL (dTRL) (Kasser and Sen 2013). The dTRL component would make adoption choices simpler. Prospective users of the technology could look at their need by date, the planned date for the technology to achieve TRL = 9 and the past progress through the various TRLs. Then the prospective users could make an informed decision based on the graph in their version of Figure 8.15. If the rate of change projects that the desired TRL will not be achieved when needed and they really needed the technology, they could investigate further and determine if they could help increase the rate of change of TRL.

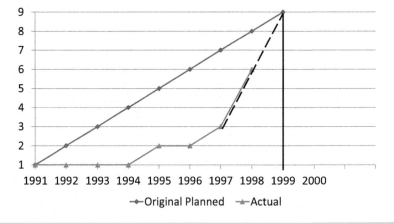

Figure 8.15 The dynamic TRL (dTRL).

Insight from the *Temporal* and *Generic* HTPs has conceptualized the use of a dTRL to help to predict when a technology will achieve a certain TRL. The need for a dTRL has been recognized in practice and there has been research into estimating the rate of change of technology maturity (El-Khoury 2012). The dTRL concept was used for quite a few years in the US aerospace and defense industry beginning in the Strategic Defense Initiative era (early 1990s) and took the form of Waterfall Charts (Section 14.9) that tracked the TRL (Benjamin 2006).

8.12.4.4 Comments   While the dTRL addresses the front end of the technology lifecycle, the issues pertaining to the other states of the technology lifecycle may have to be addressed in a different manner. One framework might be the TAWOO States and Levels shown in Table 8.25 which extend the TRL through the whole technology lifecycle. However, should the dynamic aspect of levels 1-8 be overlooked, the front end of the TAWOO will become just as useless as the TRL, because it will then be a TRL.

While the twelve TRL Levels shown in Table 8.25 do not comply with Miller's Rule (Section 3.2.5), they emphasize that TAWOO

Table 8.25   TAWOO States and Levels

TAWOO STATE	TRL LEVEL	COMMENTS
6. Antique	12	Few if any spares available in used equipment market. Phase out products or operate until spares are no longer available.
5. Obsolete	11	Some spares available, maintenance is feasible.
4. Approaching obsolescence	10	Use in existing products but not in new products. Plan for replacement of products using the technology.
3. Operational	9	Available for use in new products (in general). system "flight proven" through successful mission operations
2. Development	8	Actual system completed and "flight qualified" through test and demonstration
	7	System prototype demonstration in an operational environment
	6	System/subsystem model or prototype demonstration in a relevant operational environment
1. Research	5	Component and/or breadboard validation in relevant operational environment
	4	Component and/or breadboard validation in laboratory environment
	3	Analytical and experimental critical function and/or characteristic proof-of concept
	2	Technology concept and/or application formulated
	1	Basic principles observed and reported

covers more than the birth stages of a technology and relate the TAWOO to the TRL (provide an anchor point). There are only six TAWOO States which do comply with the rule.

8.13 The "Thank You"

The "Thank You":

- Is one of the least used and most useful project management tools because
  - People are part of the system.
  - People have feelings that need to be taken into consideration.
- Provides benefits to the leader, manager, or systems engineer. Just saying thank you for a job well done not only provides recognition but in general it also provides motivation to do well in the future. When using the "thank you", face the person, make eye contact, and smile. Failing to do so is worse than not saying "thank you".
- Is a tool that should be used in every facet of daily life. I am used to saying thank you almost automatically when someone does something for me. And I've noticed that it changes people's behaviour. For example:
  - In Adelaide, Australia, most people say thank you to the bus operator when they get off the bus. I used the "thank you" at NUS. The NUS Clementi campus is so large that it has several bus routes to move faculty and students around the campus. So every time I got off the bus I used to say thank you to the bus driver. I noticed a couple of things:
    a. I was the only person who seemed to be doing it.
    b. After a while, I'd be waiting for the bus with a long line of people, and if I was near the front, many times the bus stopped in such a way that I was able to be the first person to board the bus. It took me awhile to notice it, and then I realized the bus drivers who were allowing me to board the bus first were ones that I'd said thank you to on previous occasions.
  - Saying thank you in a restaurant also provides benefits. The serving staff treat you better than they treat people who don't say thank you.

So not only is the thank you a very useful management tool to show appreciation, it

- Also has a direct benefit for the user.
- Is an example of the Golden Rule governing behaviour (Section 8.5.1) because the people you're saying thank you to have the same feelings as you have.
- Is used in organizations in the form of award plaques and certificates and letters of appreciation.

8.14 The Three Streams of Activities

The Three Streams of Activities (Kasser 1995):

- Is a template for planning a project workflow in conjunction with the PAM Chart (Section 2.12).
- Elaborates the Waterfall Chart (Section 14.9) view where each state of the Waterfall:
  - Begins and ends at a major milestone.
  - Consists of Three Streams of Activities; Management, Development and Test/Quality.
- Is shown in Figure 8.16 where:
  - *Management*: the set of activities which include:
    - Monitoring and controlling the development and test stream activities to ensure performance in the state in accordance with the PP (Section 8.11).

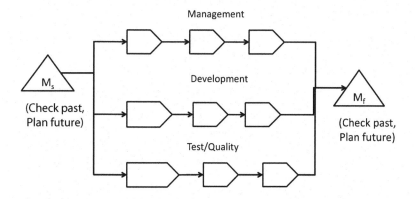

Figure 8.16   The Three Streams of Activities.

- Updating the PP to elaborate the WPs (Section 8.19) for the Three Streams of Activities in the subsequent state in more detail.
- Endeavouring to ensure that needed resources in the subsequent state will be available on schedule.
- Providing periodic reports on the condition of the project to the customer and other stakeholders.
- Being the contractual interface with the customer.
- Performing the appropriate risk management activities on the process.

- *Development*: the set of activities which produce the products appropriate to the state by performing the design and construction tasks and appropriate risk management activities on the product.
- *Test*: the set of activities known as Quality Control (QC) or Quality Assurance (QA), Test and Evaluation (T&E) and Independent Verification and Validation (IV&V). which include:
- Identifying defects in products.
- Verifying the degree of conformance to specifications of the products produced by the development stream in the state by performing appropriate tests or analyses

8.15 Timelines

A Timeline is a tool:

- To quickly visualize a sequence of events, for example, in a project.
- To clearly convey the sequence to interested parties.

A Timeline:

- Consists of a sequence of activities and milestones; in series, parallel, or a combination of series and parallel activities.
- Is often shown from two perspectives:
  - *Gantt Charts* (Section 8.4) show the timing and are often called schedules.
  - *PERT Charts* (Section 8.10) show the dependency between the activities and identify the critical path.

8.15.1 Creating a Timeline

Timelines are created as part of the project planning process (Section 8.11.2) working backwards from the final milestone to the start of the project (Section 11.8).

There are software packages that combine the calendar relationships and the dependencies by showing an arrow from the end of one task to the start of the next task. These are useful when there are a small number of tasks. However when trying to understand the relationships between a large number of tasks in a project unless the combined chart shows nine or less lines in compliance with Miller's Rule (Section 3.2.5), they should not be used; the two separate charts should be used. This is in accordance with the dictum of viewing something from more than one perspective (Chapter 10). In this case the two perspectives are calendar time and task dependencies.

8.15.2 Using PERT and GANT Views as a Cross-Check

Since a PERT Chart (Section 8.10) and a Gantt Chart (Section 8.4) show different views, they can be used to test for errors in planning. This is one reason not to show the dependency flows in a Gantt Chart but to use the PERT Chart as a separate view. For example, consider the Gantt Chart for a project shown in Figure 8.17. The five activities are identified by their starting and finishing milestones. The project starts at Milestone 1, and is at Milestone 6 and has four intermediate milestones. When the same project is viewed in a PERT Chart, it can be seen that

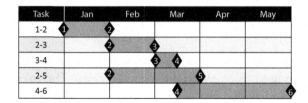

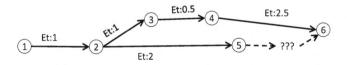

Figure 8.17 Gantt PERT crosscheck.

there is no activity that depends on the completion of Milestone 5. This is probably the symptom of one or more planning errors including:

- Milestone 5 and Milestone 4 should be the same milestone.
- Activity 4–6 is starting at Milestone 4 and should start at Milestone 5.
- There is a missing activity between Milestones 5 and 6.

The activities will need to be examined to determine which of the errors have been made and the appropriate corrective changes made to the Timeline.

8.16 Traffic Light and Enhanced Traffic Light Charts

Traffic Light Charts are tools that summarize progress and project status in a simple easily understood manner. The systems approach to project management enhances the traditional single snapshot Traffic Light Chart by adding the time dimension to enhance the information provided by the chart. Perceptions from the *Generic* HTP indicate that this is similar to CRIP Charts (Section 8.1) and the dTRL (Section 8.12.4.3).

8.16.1 *Traffic Light Charts*

Traffic Light Charts (TLC) are tools that show summaries in the colours of a stoplight or traffic light. For example:

- *Green* represents the data being summarized is good.
- *Red* indicates that something is seriously wrong or broken.
- *Yellow* indicates that something needs to be watched.
- *Blue* is used to indicate that the data being summarized is much better than good.

Table 8.26 provides examples of the types of information Traffic Light Charts can be used to represent different situations. The colours can be added to existing tables, inserted into summary tables, or used to tag other types of graphics. For example, in project management the colours:

- Provide a quick overview of the status of the project.
- Are based on a combination of the status of project schedule, budget, and problems or risks at the reporting milestone where the contribution of each status is defined at the start of

Table 8.26 Information Represented by Colours in Different Types of Traffic Light Charts

SITUATION	RED	YELLOW	GREEN	BLUE
Project management	Behind schedule	On schedule but needs watching	On schedule	Ahead of schedule
Risk management	Very risky	Medium risk	Low risk	No risk
Number of defects being produced	Much more than expected, corrective action needed yesterday (exceeding tolerance limit)	More than expected, corrective action needed soon (approaching tolerance limit)	As expected (within tolerance)	Fewer than expected

Table 8.27 Values for Traffic Lights

COLOUR	SCHEDULE	BUDGET	PROBLEMS
Blue	Ahead of schedule by X%	Well within budget by A%	None
Green	On schedule (±S%)	Within budget (±M%)	None
Yellow	Slightly behind schedule by Y%	Slightly over budget by B%	At least 1 minor problem
Red	Well behind schedule by Z%	Well over budget by C%	At least 1 major problem

project to match cost/schedule Charts. In addition the definition the A, B, C, S, M, X, Y, and Z, values and the definition of a major and a minor problem shown in Table 8.27 need to be clarified at the start of the project. These values shall not change during the lifetime of the project.

- *Blue and Green* signify that combination of (an "and" function) all three items, project schedule, budget, and problems or risks are above the value defined in Table 8.27.
- *Yellow and Red* signify that least one of the three items, project schedule, budget, and problems or risks (an "or" function) is below the value defined in Table 8.5. Note the -P, -B and -S signify which of the items contributed to the colour.

8.16.2 Enhanced Traffic Light Charts

Enhanced Traffic Light (ETL) Charts are a tool that

- Can provide information that is not presently available in most projects.
- Can potentially reduce the time spent in meetings.
- Is based on adding perceptions of the project from the *Temporal* HTP to the basic Traffic Light Charts (Section 8.16.1).

As an example, consider the monthly project status meeting at the SEEC in UniSA scheduled for February 2005, wherein several project managers were to report on the status of their project. I prepared a project status presentation covering 11 projects containing 126 PowerPoint slides of project status information, continuity, and other relevant information. The agenda list of projects is shown in Figure 8.18 as a typical bulleted list. Each project was to be introduced with an overview chart containing a traffic light coloured block as shown in deck of cards style in Figure 8.19. The approach provides the traffic light summary when the project is up for discussion.

Now consider an alternative approach using the systems approach. Present the list of projects as an agenda slide in the form of the table shown in Figure 8.20. That is not much of an improvement until you add the traffic light blocks in a third column as shown in Figure 8.21 and include hot links to each of the projects.

The Traffic Light Chart allows the discussion to immediately focus on the projects in trouble (in red), hence it is ideal for MBE and MBUM. The chart in Figure 8.21 can be enhanced by adding perceptions from the *Temporal* HTP as shown in the ETL Chart in Figure 8.22 in the form of two additional columns, reminding the viewers of the state of the project at the prior reporting period and showing expected state of the project at the following future reporting period

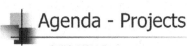

Agenda - Projects

- DMO MPM Degree
- DMO Certification Contract
- DSTO Evaluating Coalition C4ISR Architectures Contract
- DSTO Maritime Support Contract
- Wedgetail TRDC C4ISR Course
- Research student supervision
- Semester 1 Software T&E Course
- PETS
- Research Group Meetings
- SEEC Administrative tasks
- INCOSE Region VI Support

3

Figure 8.18   Typical project status meeting agenda.

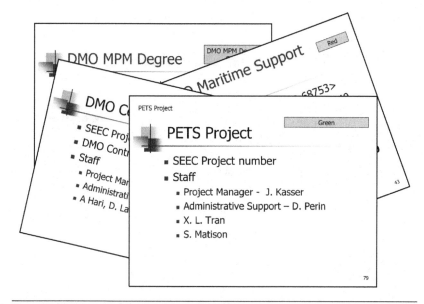

Figure 8.19 Some of the projects with traffic lights.

#	Project
1	DMO MPM Degree
2	DMO Certification Contract
3	DSTO Evaluating Coalition C4ISR Architectures Contract
4	DSTO Maritime Support Contract
5	Wedgetail TRDC C4ISR Course
6	Research student supervision
7	Semester 1 Software T&E Course
8	PETS
9	Research Group Meetings
10	SEEC Administrative tasks
11	INCOSE Region VI Support

Figure 8.20 Agenda in tabular form.

in a similar manner to the CRIP Chart (Section 8.1) (*Generic* HTP). New information that was not previously available can now be seen at the high level summary. For example:

- Projects 1, 6, 8, and 9 are conforming to the planned schedule and budget and are not facing any problems, namely they are proceeding according to the nominal status.

• Hot link the project titles to presentation sections: non-sequential access

#	Project	Status
1	DMO MPM Degree	Green
2	DMO Certification Contract	Yellow -P
3	DSTO Evaluating Coalition C4ISR Architectures Contract	Yellow -P
4	DSTO Maritime Support Contract	Red -BS
5	Wedgetail TRDC C4ISR Course	Blue
6	Research student supervision	Green
7	Semester 1 Software T&E Course	Yellow -P
8	PETS	Green
9	Research Group Meetings	Green
10	SEEC Administrative tasks	Green
11	INCOSE Region VI Support	Yellow -PB

Figure 8.21 Agenda in tabular form with traffic lights.

#	Projects	Last time	Current	Next
1	DMO MPM Degree	Green	Green	Green
2	DMO Certification Contract	Yellow -P	Yellow -P	Red -P
3	DSTO Evaluating Coalition C4ISR Architectures Contract	Yellow -P	Yellow -P	Green
4	DSTO Maritime Support Contract	Red -BS	Red -BS	Red -BS
5	Wedgetail TRDC C4ISR Course	Green	Blue	Green
6	Research student supervision	Green	Green	Green
7	Semester 1 Software T&E Course	Yellow -P	Yellow -P	Green
8	PETS	Green	Green	Green
9	Research Group Meetings	Green	Green	Green
10	SEEC Administrative tasks	Green	Green	Yellow -P
11	INCOSE Region VI Support	Yellow -PB	Yellow -PB	Yellow -PB

Figure 8.22 The Enhanced Traffic Light (ETL) Chart.

- Projects 3 and 7, which have been facing minor problems, are expected to face a major problem during the next reporting period.
- Project 4, which has been facing minor problems, is expected to overcome them and return to a nominal state during the next reporting period.
- Project 5 exceeded expectations during this reporting period and is expected to return to nominal status during the next reporting period.
- Project 11 has been facing problems and they are ongoing.

These perceptions from the *Temporal* HTP can be generalized as shown in Figure 8.23 where:

- *Project 1* is proceeding according to nominal status.
- *Project 2* has identified that a major problem or risk is expected to arise during the next reporting period. The project may need additional resources to remedy the problem.
- *Project 3* seems to be overcoming its problems and returning nominal status.
- *Project 4* has been facing one or more major problems and no change is expected. This could be due to (a) poor management, (b) being underfunded so there is no funding to complete the remaining work, or some other reason to be determined.
- *Project 5* has a very happy customer since it is ahead of the nominal status and is expected to remain so in the next reporting period. This situation may be because the project was overfunded and given more than enough time to complete or has a smart project manager.
- *Project 6* has been nominal and is now complete on schedule and within budget.
- *Project 7* had major problems during the previous reporting period which are being tackled successfully and the project is expected to return to nominal status by the next reporting

#	Projects	Last time	Current	Next
1	Project Ho-hum	Green	Green	Green
2	Project Oh oh	Yellow -PB	Yellow -P	Red
3	Project Catching up	Yellow -P	Yellow -P	Green
4	Project Replace manager	Red -BS	Red -BS	Red -BS
5	Project Very happy customer	Green	Blue	Blue
6	Project Completed	Green	Green	N/A
7	Project Promote manager	Red -P	Yellow -P	Green
8	Project Watch this person	Yellow –BS	Green	Blue
9	Project No risk management	Green	Red -P	Red -P
10	Project Took course in risk management	Green	Green	Yellow -P
11	Project Manager doing risk management	Yellow -P	Yellow -P	Yellow -P

Figure 8.23   Project trends using the ETL Chart.

period. This project manager may be a candidate for promotion or a candidate to take over other projects in trouble and get them back on track.

- **Project 8** has gone from experiencing budget and schedule problems in the previous reporting period to nominal status and the project manager is anticipating exceeding the budget and schedule in the next reporting period. This project manager may be a candidate for promotion.

- **Project 9** was nominal in the last reporting period but is currently experiencing one or more major problems which are expected to continue into the next reporting period. If the major problem was not anticipated in the previous status report then the situation needs to be investigated.

- **Project 10** which has been nominal since the last reporting period (or earlier) is expecting to experience minor problems in the next reporting period. The project manager may have taken a continuing education course and started to practice Risk Management (Section 12.2).

- **Project 11** which has been experiencing minor problems since the last reporting period (or earlier) is expecting to continue to experience such problems. If there is no corresponding adverse budget and schedule impact (shown in the Gantt (Section 8.4) and EVA Charts (Section 8.2) accompanying the status report, the project manager may be practicing Risk Management (Section 12.2) and bringing it to the attention of senior management.

In summary the ETL Chart:

- Provides information that was not currently available.
- Allows MBUM by delving into the reasons for the deviation from the planned status.
- Is an ideal tool for MBE (Section 8.7).

8.16.2.1 Creating an ETL Chart for Use in a Presentation   The process for creating an ETL Chart is as follows:

1. Gain consensus from the stakeholders as to the values of the parameters for the placement of information into the colours shown in Table 8.27 at the start of the project.

2. Create a table listing the projects in an appropriate order (e.g. by cost, by closing date, in alphabetical order) in the format shown in Figure 8.20.
3. Add the traffic light column as shown in Figure 8.21 and label it "current".
4. For each project, determine the traffic light colour according to the specification for the colour in Section 8.16.2.
5. Insert a traffic light column before the "current" column and label it "last time".
6. Copy the information from the "current" column in the ETL Chart presented at the previous status report into the "last" column.
7. Insert a traffic light column after the "current" column and label it "next".
8. For each project, estimate the status of the project at the next reporting period and determine the traffic light colour according to the specification for the colour in Section 8.16.2.
9. Save the table.
10. Copy the table into the status report PowerPoint presentation.
11. Add hot links to the first slide of each of the projects as shown in Figure 8.22.
12. The ETL Chart should look like Figure 8.22 but with different colours in the "last", current" and "next" columns.

8.16.2.2 Adding Even More Information The ETL Chart shown in Figure 8.23 can be improved using an idea from the CRIP Charts (Section 8.1) (*Generic* HTP) to show how the current situation compares with the predicted situation as of the last report presentation as shown in Figure 8.24. The current reporting period has been separated in two parts:

1. *Expected from last time*: copied from the "next" column in the last report presentation.
2. *Actual*: as achieved by the work done during this reporting period.

For example,

- *Project 1* was expected to be green and is green.
- *Project 2* was expected to be in the green but is still yellow (problems).
- Differences can be seen in some of the other projects, which require explanation at the reporting presentation.

#	Projects	Last time	Current		Next
			Expected	Actual	
1	Project Ho-hum	Green	Green	Green	Green
2	Project Oh oh	Yellow -PB	Green	Yellow -P	Red
3	Project Catching up	Yellow -P	Yellow -P	Yellow -P	Green
4	Project Replace manager	Red -BS	Red -BS	Red -BS	Red -BS
5	Project Very happy customer	Green	Blue	Blue	Blue
6	Project Completed	Green	Green	Green	N/A
7	Project Promote manager	Red -P	Yellow -P	Green	Green
8	Project Watch this person	Yellow –BS	Green	Green	Blue
9	Project No risk management	Green	Red -P	Red-P	Red -P
10	Project Took course in risk management	Green	Green	Green	Yellow -P
11	Project Manager doing risk management	Yellow -P	Yellow -P	Yellow-P	Yellow -P

Figure 8.24   Final version of ETL Chart.

8.17 The Waterfall Chart

The Waterfall Chart:

- Shows the phases of a notional project, assuming nothing will go wrong as perceived from a time before the project starts.
- Is discussed in Section 14.9.
- Is a Gantt Chart (Section 8.4) with all the background lines (rows and columns) abstracted out to reduce the complexity.

8.18 Work Breakdown Structures

A Work Breakdown Structure (WBS) is:

- Activity-based, focusing on the work to be done.
- A planning tool to create the work to be done on a project in the non-systems approach to project planning.
- A hierarchical view of the information in a project database which shows how high-level tasks are broken out into lower-level tasks.

8.18.1 Basic Principles for Creating a WBS

In the non-systems approach, the interdependency of the connection between the work and the Timeline tends to be overlooked and the WBS is treated as an independent entity. For example, consider the following seven basic principles for creating a WBS (Cleland 1994):

1. A unit of work should appear at only one place in the WBS.
2. The work content of a WBS item is the sum of the WBS items below it.
3. A WBS item is the responsibility of only one individual, even though many people may be working on it.
4. The WBS must be consistent with the way in which work is actually going to be performed; it should serve the project team first and other purposes only if practical.
5. Project team members should be involved in developing the WBS to ensure consistency and buy-in.
6. Each WBS item must be documented to ensure accurate understanding of the scope of work included and not included in that item.
7. The WBS must be a flexible tool to accommodate inevitable changes while properly maintaining control of the work content in the project according to the scope statement.

There is no direct mention of products that the work produces, and the time that is needed and taken to produce the products. As a result, there are often problems and errors in developing the WBS; problems and errors that are preventable or rather disappear in the systems approach to Project Management.

8.18.2 *Common Errors in Developing a WBS*

Common errors in developing a WBS include the following (Cleland 1994):

- The WBS does not capture all the work.
- The WBS describes functions not products.
- The WBS levels are not consistent with how the WBS elements will be integrated.
- The WBS is inconsistent with the Product Breakdown Structure (PBS).

8.19 Work Packages

The systems approach to Project Management uses Work Packages (WP) instead of a WBS (Section 8.18.2) to create a project by considering the WBS, PBS, and Timeline (Section 8.15) as outputs from a project database. A WP is:

- A tool used in the systems approach to project management to plan the work and identify and prevent risks from happening.
- A set of information associated with an activity.

The WP is based on the Quality System Elements (QSE) (Kasser 2000b) and contains the following information:

1. *Unique WP identification number*: the key to tracking.
2. *Name of activity*: a succinct summary statement of the activity or activities.
3. *Priority*: the priority associated with the task linked back to the source requirement.
4. *Narrative description of the activity*. A brief description of the activity or activities.
5. *Estimated schedule for the activity*: estimated time taken to perform the activities. This item contributes to the baseline schedule for the project.
6. *Accuracy of schedule estimate*: median, shortest and longest times to complete. This item is used to create the initial estimate of the critical path and shows up in the PERT Charts (Section 8.10).
7. *Actual schedule*: filled in as and after the activity is performed. This item is compared with the estimated schedule during the performance of the project.
8. *Products* (outputs) produced by the activities in the WP.
9. *Acceptance criteria for products*: the response to the question, "How will we know that the product is working as specified?", as agreed between the supplier and the customer.
10. *Estimated cost*: the estimated fixed and variable costs of the activities and materiel. This item project contributes to the baseline BAC for the project.
11. *The level of confidence in the cost estimate*: or the accuracy.

12. *Actual cost*: (AC) filled in as and when the activities are performed. This item is compared with the estimated schedule during the performance of the project as part of EVA (Section 8.2).

13. *Reason activity is being done*: important because personnel leave and join and the reasons may be forgotten. Some activities are preventative and the reason may not be immediately obvious. This information is also useful when considering change requests during the Operations and Maintenance States of the SLC (Section 14.9.1).

14. *Traceability*: (source of work) to requirements, the CONOPS, laws, regulations, etc.

15. *Prerequisites*: the products that must be ready before the activity can commence.

16. *Resources*: the people, equipment, material, etc.

17. *Name of person responsible for the activity or task.*

18. *Risks*: description and estimate of probability and seriousness of consequences.

19. *Risk mitigation information*: mitigation WP ID(s) for each risk listed in Item 18.

20. *Lower level work package IDs* (if any).

21. *Decision points* (if any).

22. *Internal key milestones*: if the activity is broken out into lower-level WPs.

23. *Assumptions not stated elsewhere*: so as to be available for checking by cognizant personnel.

A typical WP at planning time is shown in Table 8.28. The actual values of cost and schedule will be inserted into the WP during the performance of the activity and summarized as part of the EVA (Section 8.2). Comments on some of the some of the entries are:

- *Item 1*: The ID is 124D showing it is an activity in the development stream of work in WP 124. With this numbering system, the other two WPs would be 124M for the corresponding management activities and 124T for the corresponding test activities in the Three Streams of Activities (Section 8.14).
- *Item 2*: The name has a verb in it to show that it is an activity.

Table 8.28 Typical (Planned) Work Package (Spreadsheet)

1	UNIQUE WP IDENTIFICATION NUMBER	124
2	Name of activity	Feasibility study
3	Priority	2
4	Narrative of the activity	A systems engineer will perform the feasibility study on the selected CONOPS to verify realization of CONOPS is feasible within project constraints. Cognizant personnel will be identified and interviewed
5	Estimated schedule	2 weeks
6	Accuracy of schedule estimate	± 3 days
7	Products	Feasibility study report
8	Acceptance criteria for products	Consensus that study findings are correct
9	Estimated cost	$3,000
10	The level of confidence in the cost estimate	±10%
11	Reason activity is being done	To ensure feasibility of the CONOPS
12	Traceability	An inherent part in the problem-solving process
13	Prerequisites	Completion of CONOPS (Product ID by task ID)
14	Resources	Task leader (4 hours)
		systems engineer (1 full-time equivalent)
		Engineering specialist (1 full-time equivalent)
15	Person responsible for task	Mark Time
16	Risks	Cognizant personnel not available when needed
17	Risk mitigation	telephone ahead of time to make appointments
		identify alternate candidates for interviewing as part of 124-01
18	Lower level work package ID's (if any)	124-01 Identify cognizant personnel
		124-02 Interview cognizant personnel
		124-03 perform rest of feasibility study
		124-04 write up report
19	Decision points (if any)	None
20	Internal key milestones	End of 124-01
		End of 124-02
21	Assumptions not stated elsewhere	Personnel will be available to perform the activity

- *Item 4*: CONOPS (P123P) is listed to define the product that will be used in the activity.
- *Item 7*: the product produced by activity 124D is 124P to correlate the product to the activity in accordance with PAM Chart numbering (Section 2.12).
- *Item 9*: the fixed and variable costs associated with the activity.

- *Item 10*: the accuracy of cost estimate is same as accuracy of schedule. For example, if the schedule accuracy is ±3 days on 10 days, the cost accuracy is ±30%.
- *Item 13*: the prerequisites that have to be completed before the task can begin are the availability of product 123P.
- *Item 14*: the personnel should be named to avoid overloading them with too many tasks. The amount of time spent on the task should be listed. This information is used to determine the labour costs.
- *Item 18*: must match descriptions in narrative Item 4. Each lower level WP has corresponding activities in the other two streams of activities (Section 8.14).

8.19.1 *The Benefits of Using WPs*

The benefits of using WPs include:

- Collecting information that is interdependent between product and process provides the ability to create and use Attribute Profiles (Section 9.1). For example, the Risk Mitigation Plan would be based on an abstracted view of the risk elements in the WP database.
- New perspectives on the system based on the Attribute Profiles (Section 9.1).
- The project information resides in a single integrated database that contains information from the Three Streams of Activities (Section 8.14) which dissolves the problem of updating separate databases to keep them current in the non-systems approach to project management.

8.20 Summary

Chapter 8 discussed 19 tools used for problem-solving in project management. They range from simple to complex. This chapter includes a number of original tools including CRIP Charts that provide a measurement of technical process as well as the opportunity to prevent impending problems in the project and the ETL Chart which uses a similar time derivative approach to the CRIP Chart to display project process and also indicate that there may be problems in the project. Other tools not thought of as project management tools in the current non-systems approach mentioned in this chapter are the Golden Rule, JIT decision-making, the TAWOO, the Thank You, and the Three Streams of Activities. This chapter introduced WPs as the basis for an integrated project database replacing the WBS used in the current non-systems paradigm. Traditional tools discussed are EVA, Financial Budgets, Gantt Charts, MBE, MBO and how to integrate MBO into the planning process, Mission Statements, PERT Charts, Project Plans, Timelines, and the Waterfall Chart.

References

Benjamin, D. 2006. "Technology Readiness Level: An Alternative Risk Mitigation Technique." In *Project Management in Practice: The 2006 Project Risk and Cost Management Conference*. Boston, MA: Boston University Metropolitan College.

Bittel, L. R. 1964. *Management by Exception: Systematizing and Simplifying the Managerial Job*. New York: McGraw-Hill.

Burns, R. 1786. *To a Mouse*.

Clark, W. 1922. *The Gantt Chart a Working Tool of Management*. New York: The Ronald Press Company.

Cleland, D. I. 1994. *Project Management: Strategic Design and Implementation*. New York: McGraw-Hill Companies.

Crépin, M., B. El-Khoury, and C. R. Kenley. 2012. "It's All Rocket Science: On the Equivalence of Development Timelines for Aerospace and Nuclear Technologies." In the 22nd Annual International Symposium of the International Council on Systems Engineering. Rome, Italy.

Cundiff, D. 2003. *Manufacturing Readiness Levels (MRL)*. Unpublished white paper, 2003

Dowling, T., and T. Pardoe. 2005. *Timpa – Technology Insertion Metrics, Volume 1*. Edited by Ministry of Defence. QinetiQ. Fanborough, Hampshire, UK

Drucker, P. F. 1954. *The Practice of Management*. New York: Harper.

El-Khoury, B. 2012. *Analytic Framework for TRL-based Cost and Schedule Models*. Engineering Systems Division, Massachusetts Institute of Technology.

Ford, H., and S. Crowther. 1922. *My Life and Work*. Reprint Edition, 1987, Ayer Company, Publishers, Inc. ed. New York: Doubleday Page & Company.

GAO. 1999. *BEST PRACTICES Better Management of Technology Development Can Improve Weapon System Outcomes*. Washington DC: United States General Accounting Office.

Kasser, J. E. 1995. *Applying Total Quality Management to Systems Engineering.* Boston: Artech House.

Kasser, J. E. 1999. "Using Organizational Engineering to Build Defect Free Systems, On Schedule and Within Budget." In PICMET. Portland OR.

Kasser, J. E. 2000a. "A Web Based Asynchronous Virtual Conference: A Case Study." In The INCOSE - Mid-Atlantic Regional Conference. Reston, VA.

Kasser, J. E. 2000b. "A Framework for Requirements Engineering in a Digital Integrated Environment (FREDIE)." In the Systems Engineering, Test and Evaluation Conference (SETE). Brisbane, Australia.

Kasser, J. E. 2012. *Getting the Right Requirements Right.* In the 22nd Annual International Symposium of the International Council on Systems Engineering. Rome, Italy.

Kasser, J. E. 2016a. "Applying Holistic Thinking to the Problem of Determining the Future Availability of Technology." *The IEEE Transactions on Systems, Man, and Cybernetics: Systems*, no. 46 (3):440–444. doi: 10.1109/TSMC.2015.2438780.

Kasser, J. E. 2016b. "The Nuts and Bolts of Systems." In the 11th International Conference on System of Systems Engineering. Kongsberg, Norway.

Kasser, J. E., and S. Sen. 2013. "The United States Airborne Laser Test Bed Program: A Case Study." In the 2013 Systems Engineering and Test and Evaluation Conference (SETE 2013). Canberra, Australia.

Katz, D. R., S. Sarkani, T. Mazzuchi, and E. H. Conrow. 2014. "The Relationship of Technology and Design Maturity to DOD Weapon System Cost Change and Schedule Change During Engineering and Manufacturing Development." In *Systems Engineering*, vol. 18, no. 1 pp. 1–15. Wiley Periodicals, Inc.

Lukas, J. A. "2008. Earned Value Analysis – Why it Doesn't Work." In *2008 AACE International Transactions.* 2008 AACE International Transactions AACE International, 2008 Toronto, ONT, Canada. Paper is at http://www.icoste.org/LukasPaper.pdf, accessed 5/14/2018

Mali, P. 1972. *Managing by Objectives.* New York: John Wiley & Sons, Inc.

Mankins, J. C. 1995. *Technology Readiness Levels.* Advanced Concepts Office, Office of Space Access and Technology, NASA.

Mankins, J. C. 2002. "Approaches to Strategic Reseach and Technology (R&T) Analysis and Road Mapping." *Acta Astronautica*, no. 51 (1–9):3–21.

Meystel, A., J. Albus, E. Messina, and D. Leedom. 2003. "Performance Measures for Intelligent Systems: Measures of Technology Readiness." In *PERMIS '03 White Paper*, by Alexander Meystel; Jim Albus; Elena Messina; Dennis Leedom; National Inst Of Standards and Technology Gaithersburg MD

Moorehouse, D. J. 2001. "Detailed Definitions and Guidance for Application of Technology Readiness Levels." *Journal of Aircraft*, no. 39 (1):190–192.

Nolte, W. L. 2005. "TRL Calculator." In AFRL at Assessing Technology Readiness and Development Seminar. https://acc.dau.mil/CommunityBrowser.aspx?id=25811, accessed August 27, 2007

Osborn, A. F. 1963. *Applied Imagination Principles and Procedures of Creative Problem Solving.* 3rd Rev. Ed. New York: Charles Scribner's Sons.

Palmer, S. R., and J. M. Felsing. 2002. *A Practical Guide to Feature – Driven Development*: Prentice Hall.

Rodkinson, M. L., ed. 1903. *Tractate Sabbath in The Babilonian Talmud.* Boston: New Talmud Publishing Company.

Sauser, B., D. Verma, J. Ramirez-Marquez, and R. Gove. 2006. "From TRL to SRL: The Concept of Systems Readiness Levels." In the Conference on Systems Engineering Research. Los Angeles, CA.

Shishkio, R., D. H. Ebbeler, and G. Fox. 2003. "NASA Technology Assessment Using Real Options Valuation." *Systems Engineering*, no. 7 (1):1–12.

Smith, J. D. 2005. "An Alternative to Technology Readiness Levels for Non-Developmental Item (Ndi) Software." In 38th Hawaii International Conference on System Sciences. Hawaii.

Stauber, B. R., H. M. Douty, W. Fazar, R. H. Jordan, W. Weinfeld, and A. D. Manvel. 1959. "Federal Statistical Activities." *The American Statistician*, no. 13 (2):9–12.

Valerdi, R., and R. J. Kohl. 2004. "An Approach to Technology Risk Management." In Engineering Systems Division Symposium. Cambridge, MA.

9
MISCELLANEOUS TOOLS

This chapter discusses the following miscellaneous tools suitable for project managers, systems engineers, and vegetarians:*

1. Attribute Profiles in Section 9.1.
2. Budgets in Section 9.2.
3. Lessons Learned in Section 9.3.
4. Lists in Section 9.4.
5. Tables and matrices in Section 9.5

9.1 Attribute Profiles

Attribute Profiles:

- Are outcomes of systems thinking about different attributes of a system.
- Are plots of the attributes of various parts of the system as a Histogram (Section 2.9). For example, an Attribute Profile for the estimated risks associated with implementing the set of requirements at SRR for a small system can be considered as the "A" column in the Risk CRIP Chart (Section 8.1) for that system is a Histogram as shown in Figure 9.1. This Risk Attribute Profile quantifies the risks (either probability of occurrence or severity) into 50 levels and shows the number of requirements in each risk level.
- Can be plotted for any attribute such as risk probability, risk severity, safety, security, cost, priority, reliability, robustness, and the state of the technology (Section 8.12). For example, a Priority Attribute Profile is one in which the priorities of the requirements for a system, on a scale of

---

* This is a joke from the *Generic* HTP based on the presence of the word "suitable" in the first sentence in this chapter and the same wording appearing on food packages.

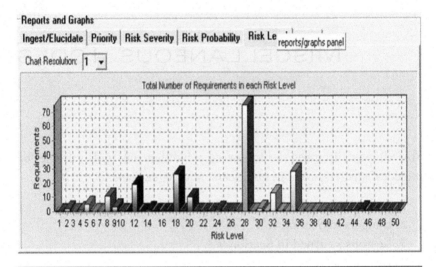

Figure 9.1   Risk Profile.

1 to 10, are collected in a Histogram (Section 2.9) as shown in Figure 9.2. If the profile looks like the one in the figure, then it doesn't seem to have much of a priority and is a candidate for cancellation in a situation where there is a project with a higher Priority Attribute Profile and limited funding. Attribute Profiles of two systems can be compared using a Compound Bar Chart (Section 2.3) such as the

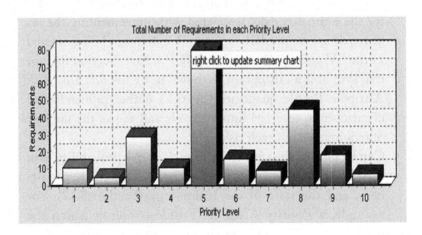

Figure 9.2   Priority Profile.

example in Figure 2.3; Attribute Profiles of more than two systems are best compared using the overlay features of the Kiviat chart (Section 2.14).

- Are used in traditional project management and systems engineering but the word "attribute" is generally missing. For example, we talk about Risk Profiles, not Risk Attribute Profiles.

Creating an Attribute Profile is not very difficult. Begin by deciding which attribute is to be categorized, and then the parts of the system that are going to be categorized against that attribute. Break the attributes into a number of ranges and allocate each part of the system into one of the ranges. The process for creating an Attribute Profile is exactly the same as the process for categorising a requirement when creating a CRIP Chart (Section 8.1).

9.2 Budgets

Budgets:

- Are quantitative tools for defining, or estimating, and then controlling attributes. The most common attribute associated with a budget is financial. Yet perceptions from the *Continuum* HTP indicate that we can use budgets for other attributes of a system or a product being developed; such as power, reliability, safety, time, and weight.
- Consists of the values of the attribute for each WP (Section 8.19) of the system (product or process) integrated into a value for the entire system.
- Can be linked to Attribute Profiles (Section 9.1).
- Are systems because they are made up parts and there is a relationship between the parts.
- Are created during the planning state of the project, monitored and controlled during the implementation states of the project, and reported at major milestones (Section 14.9.2).

9.2.1 Creating a Budget

The following process can be used to create a budget:

1. Create a List (Section 9.4) of all the items that need to be in the budget. If the full planning process (Section 8.11.2) is not being used, use the appropriate idea generating tools (Chapter 7) to generate the list.

2. Estimate the amount of the attribute for each item on the list, for example:

   a. If the budget is for shopping, and there are five items on the shopping list, estimate the individual price of each of the five items. When you add up the price of the five items, you have the total amount of money in your shopping budget.

   b. If the budget is for weight, and there are five items on the list, estimate the individual weight of each of the five items. When you add up the weight of the five items, you have the total weight budget.

3. Determine when the attribute for the element will be needed. For example:

   a. In a financial budget you need to know when the funds will be spent so that they will be available at the time.

   b. If the budget is for another attribute of the system being designed, for example, reliability or weight, the systems engineer needs to know when the designers of the different parts of the system will provide the value for their attribute, so that the systems engineer can integrate all the subsystem values into a total value to make sure that the design of the system will meet the specification for that attribute at the system level. In case there is a problem with one of the subsystems, the systems engineer should then have time to discuss the matter with the relevant designers and adjust the subsystem specifications to ensure that the system specification is not exceeded.

Section 8.3.2 discusses creating a Financial Budget for gaining a master's degree.

9.3 Lessons Learned

The Lessons Learned concept:

- Is a tool to avoid repeating mistakes.
- Is a tool to prevent mistakes made in a project from being repeated in future projects.
- Is based on a profound dictum, "Those who cannot remember the past are condemned to repeat it" (Santayana 1905).
- Consists of five parts:
    1. Identifying Lessons Learned from an activity after the activity has been performed.
    2. Storing the Lessons Learned in a database or repository
    3. Retrieving the appropriate Lessons Learned when faced with a similar task in accordance with The Process for Tackling a Problem (Section 11.5).
    4. Reviewing them before commencing an activity. When reviewing the Lessons Learned, they should be perceived from the *Generic* and *Continuum* HTPs. That means identifying similarities and differences between the situation in which the lesson was learned, and the current situation you are in. Just because something worked or didn't work in one situation does not mean that it will or will not work in a different situation.
    5. Taking the appropriate actions to avoid previous mistakes.

In the non-systems approach, only the first two parts are generally implemented, and usually at the end of the project. That is, the Lessons Learned are stored, but then never retrieved. That's why Lessons Learned archives tend to be known as "write only memory". In the systems approach, the Lessons Learned concept is built in to the process. For example, Lessons Learned are:

- Discussed and documented during reviews especially at major milestones (Section 14.9.2) instead of at the end of the project.
- Retrieved as part of the planning state of the process which determines if anybody has faced that problem before and what they did about it (Section 11.5).

The information associated with a Lesson Learned depends on the situation and shall include:

1. An identification number for the lesson learned.
2. The date and time of the entry into the Lessons Learned database or repository.
3. The name and contact information of the person making the entry into the Lessons Learned database or repository.
4. The situation, issue or event.
5. The symptoms that gave rise to the situation from which the lesson is being learned.
6. The underlying causes the symptom.
7. The action taken to resolve the situation, issue or event.
8. The reasoning as to why the action was chosen.
9. Keywords, if the Lessons Learned are stored in a database, for allow speedy retrieval of pertinent Lessons Learned.

9.4 Lists

A list:

- Is a tool:
  - For thinking about items.
  - For presenting information in an effective manner.
  - To use when identifying entities in a situation.
- Contains a number of items such as in to-do lists, shopping lists, delivery lists, waiting lists and laundry lists.
- Might be an end in itself when thinking about what to purchase at the grocery store or what to send to the laundry.
- Is often the first step in thinking about many things.

9.4.1 Types of Lists

There are a large number of different types of lists including:

- ***Shopping lists***: a list of items that reminds you what to purchase in the shop. An advanced shopping list contains the items sorted in a manner that makes it easy to find the items in the store. For example, the items in category "fruits" are grouped together, those in category "vegetables" are grouped together, etc.

- **Laundry lists**: a list of clothes (and the quantity of each item) being sent to a laundry or dry cleaner. Laundry supplied lists contain the items pre-printed and the user just needs to fill in the amount of each item. Pre-printed lists are useful when the items are relatively few.
- **To-do lists**: a list of tasks to do. Advanced to-do lists not only list the tasks but also identify the priority and deadline (latest completion time) associated with the task.
- **Gift lists**: a list of gifts received on an occasion, or a list of gifts to be purchased for other people, such as a Christmas gift list.
- **Check lists**: a specialized to-do list; a list of things to be done in a specific situation. For example, a pre-flight checklist is a list of tasks for a pilot to perform before the aircraft takes off.
- **Donor lists**: a list of people who have donated to a cause, or a list of people targeted to be approached to donate to the cause.

This book uses the following two types of lists:

1. Bulleted lists or dot points.
2. Numbered lists such as this one.

9.4.2 Creating a List

Creating a list is a matter of thinking about the situation and writing down the ideas that come to mind one after the other in a list. Any idea generating techniques including Brainstorming (Section 7.3), Slip Writing (Section 7.10), and NGT (Section 7.9), may be used to generate the ideas.

9.4.3 Dos and Don'ts for Creating Lists

When creating lists make sure that you:

1. Don't try to sort the items in the list until the ideas stop flowing.
2. Don't forget to capitalize the first word of each item in a list.

3. Sort lists of names of people alphabetically unless the text accompanying the list indicates the sorting method. This is to ensure that nobody feels slighted.

4. Use the word "are" when listing a number of items and every single item in the set is listed. For example, (an implied list of) the names of my children *are* Susie, Lisa and Michael.

5. Use "include" in a list when listing a number of items which are a subset of a larger list of items, namely the list is incomplete. For example, (an implied list of) the parts of a computer *include* a motherboard, a disk drive, and a case.

6. Use numbered lists for:
   - Instructions on how to do something, namely a process.
   - A fixed list of items.

7. Use bulleted lists to:
   - Draw the reader's attention to items that could be missed if the items were embedded in a paragraph or sentence.
   - Highlight key points.

9.5 Tables and Matrices

Tables and matrices are thinking and information communication tools that provide information in tabular format. They come in numerous shapes and sizes. Consider the following examples:

1. Comparison Tables discussed in Section 9.5.1.
2. Compliance Matrices discussed in Section 9.5.2.
3. Data tables discussed in Section 9.5.3.

Other examples of data tables in this book include:

1. The Frameworks discussed in Chapter 5.
2. N^2 Charts discussed in Section 2.10.
3. Traffic Light or Stoplight Charts discussed in Section 8.16.1.

9.5.1 Comparison Tables

A Comparison Table is a tool often used in decision-making when making comparisons between things. It is used in many formats. The parameters to be compared are placed in the rows, and the different

Table 9.1 Comparison of Proposal Efforts

PROPOSAL	NOVA 250	PK45	NSF
Date	Sept 1995	Sept 1995	Dec 1995
Companies	4	2	3
Location	MD/DC	MD/FL	MD/VA
Paradigm	Conventional	Systems approach	Systems approach
Estimated charges	$100,000	$10,000	$20,000

items being compared are in the columns. For example, Table 9.1 mixes numbers and information. This table mixes numbers and information showing how the parameters in the rows were measured in each of the proposal projects in the columns. The important element of information in the table is that whatever was represented by the PK45 and NSF columns was much lower in cost than the Nova 250.

As a second example, in Chapter 10, Table 10.1 shows a mapping between the capability available in a system and the scenarios that use those capabilities. For example, the table shows that capabilities 1, 2, and 4 are used in scenario A; capabilities 3, 4, and 5 are used in Scenario B, and so on. A blank row would indicate a capability that is not used in any scenario and a blank column would show that the system does not have any of the capabilities needed to perform that scenario.

Other examples of Comparison Tables include:

- The Pugh Matrix shown in Table 4.16.
- A Requirements Traceability Matrix (RTM) used in systems and software engineering.

9.5.2 Compliance Matrix

A Compliance Matrix is:

- A Comparison Table (Section 9.5.1) used to demonstrate compliance to requirements or instructions.
- Useful both when performing the task to meet the requirements and demonstrating that the requirements have been met.
- An extremely useful tool to create and include in a proposal response to a RFP. It helps when writing the proposal and assists the agency that filters the proposal for compliance to requirements before passing the proposal on for evaluation.

Table 9.2   Generic Compliance Matrix

WHAT NEEDS TO BE DONE	IN WHICH SECTION IT IS DONE
Item 1	
Item 2	
Item 3	
Remaining items	
Last item	

Table 9.2 shows the format of a generic Compliance Matrix. The first column lists the items that need to be done or requirements, and the second column identifies that the items have been done. If there are a large number of items, the second column should list the section numbers of the document in which the requirement is met.

The first column should be created at planning time and the second column populated before the report is completed. There are several variations of the matrix including those discussed in this section. As one example, during the first session of any class or workshop, I usually ask students to form teams that meet the following requirements:*

1. The team shall contain between 3 and 7 people.
2. At least one member of the team shall be male.
3. At least one member of the team shall be female.
4. At least one member of the team shall have a laptop.
5. At least one member of the team shall be young.
6. At least one member of the team shall be mature.
7. The team shall contain only one person from the same part of company or organization.
8. The team shall contain only one person from the same [birth] country.

After the teams have presented their ways of complying with the requirements, I show them Table 9.3. The table shows very clearly how a typical team complies with the requirements. I put the team member names in the rows because the instructions focused on the

---

* They are a mixture of well-written and poorly-written requirements by design. Dealing with vague requirements is one of the purpose of the exercise.

Table 9.3 Compliance Matrix for Student Instructions

	SEX	LAPTOP	Y/M	ORG	COUNTRY
Joe	M	Y	Y	ADT	Australia
Linda	F	Y	M	QET	UK
Tom	M	Y	Y	RBU	China
Fred	M	Y	Y	ADF	Singapore
David	M	Y	M	DSF	Singapore

team member, and use the columns to demonstrate compliance to the specific requirement. Since the number of team members was small, I chose not to number the rows since the small size is self-evident. Had there been a larger number of students I would have numbered the rows so that the number in the last row would demonstrate compliance to the maximum number requirement. Variations of the table could include the requirements number or use rows where I used columns.

As another example, I ask students in my postgraduate classes to use and include an Assignment Compliance Matrix when turning in essay assignments as an option. The requirements for the essay include "9. The essay shall contain information learnt in each session". I provide the students with Table 9.4 as a guide. The rows contain the sessions and each of the knowledge columns identified which part of the session the knowledge came from. The last column shows in which section of the essay the requirement is met. The gray shading in the Session 0 rows indicates that the requirement does not apply to that session. Other ways of showing that the requirement does not apply include the use of "N/A" or "Not Applicable".

The students are encouraged to use the matrix when writing the essay and to include it in the essay as an option. I also tell them that

Table 9.4 Partial Assignment Traceability Matrix

SESSION	KNOWLEDGE				APPLIED IN
	LECTURE	READING	EXERCISE	EXTERNAL	ASSIGNMENT SECTION
0					
1				X	1.2
2	X	X			2.4
3	X				3.6
4–13					
14					

I cannot grade what is not submitted. Students using the matrix turn in more complete assignments than students who do not.

9.5.3 Data or Information Tables

Data or information tables contain information. There are many examples in this book.

9.6 Summary

Chapter 9 discussed four miscellaneous tools for problem-solving that can be used by project managers and systems engineers. The Attribute Profile is an original tool that profiles a specific attribute of an object or a system by dividing the values of the attributes into a number of ranges and plotting a Histogram of the results. A budget is a tool for calculating a specific attribute, usually in the form of a Financial Budgets, and then maintaining the allocation of resources to that attribute throughout the project. Lessons Learned are a tool to avoid repeating the mistakes of the past and Lists are a useful tool in themselves for identifying and tracking items as well as being the first step in the process of developing Causal Loops or relationship diagrams. This chapter concluded by discussing three different types of tables and matrices. Comparison Tables contain information that allow a set of information for one item to be compared against the equivalent set of information for another item. Compliance Matrices are tables that show how various parts of something comply with the instructions or requirements for that thing. Data tables contain information.

Reference

Santayana, G. 1905. *Reason in Common Sense*, p. 284, Vol. 1 of *The Life of Reason*. New York: Charles Scribner's Sons.

10

THE PERSPECTIVES PERIMETER

The Perspectives Perimeter is a tool for identifying and communicating a set of viewpoints, from which to perceive issues, problems and situations. If you've heard people say, "Let's make sure on the same page", or engineers say, "Let's make sure we are on the same wavelength", you can consider the Perspectives Perimeter as the spectrum of wavelengths, or as the book containing the pages. The use of multiple views multiple views or perspectives provides the systems thinker with an advantage, for example:

> People who learn to read situations from different (theoretical) points of view have an advantage over those committed to a fixed position. For they are better able to recognize the limitations of a given perspective. They can see how situations and problems can be framed and reframed in different ways, allowing new kinds of solutions to emerge. (Morgan 1997)

In summary, the benefits of being able to change perspectives include:

- Opening your mind to new concepts.
- Helping you revise existing concepts.
- Facilitating finding out-of-the-box concepts.
- Making you innovative.

This chapter introduces the Perspectives Perimeter as a tool to help see things from different perspectives and provides examples of the following Perspectives Perimeters:

1. The HTPs discussed in Section 10.1.
2. The "Knowledge – Application of Knowledge" perspectives discussed in Section 10.2.

Other Perspectives Perimeters discussed in this book include:

- The types of association in Association of Ideas discussed in Section 7.2.
- The set of constraints used in Constraint Mapping discussed in Section 7.4.
- The Kipling Questions discussed in Section 7.6.
- The CRIP Chart categories discussed in Section 8.1.1.1.
- The SWOT template discussed in Section 14.2.1.

When examining or discussing something, the perspectives should be listed. In the same way that assumptions should be listed as described in the Problem Formulation Template (Section 14.3). The listing will make it easy to see if a perspective is missing.

Before the discussion part of the meeting starts, agree on which Perspectives Perimeter will be used to view whatever issue is under discussion to ensure everyone is on the same page or rather Perspectives Perimeter. Perceptions from the *Continuum* HTP indicate that the Perspectives Perimeters listed above are not the only ones; use whatever is appropriate to the situation as long as everybody agrees to it. Should a new perspective arise during the course of the discussion, the originator of the idea should state that the idea comes from a perspective not on the perimeter.

10.1 Holistic Thinking Perspectives

The Holistic Thinking Perspectives (HTP):

- Are a systemic tool for gaining an understanding of a problematic situation and inferring both the cause of the undesirability in the situation and a probable solution to the problems posed by removing the undesirability from the situation.
- Provide a standard set of nine perspectives to view a situation.
- Were developed from Richmond's seven streams of systems thinking (Richmond 1993).

The concept that a single perspective may lead to errors in understanding what is being viewed has been known for centuries if not longer. For example the parable of the blind men perceiving a different part of an elephant and inferring what animal they perceive

(Yen 2008). Since each man perceives a different part of the elephant, they each infer that they perceive a different animal. It takes a combination of the perceptions to understand the true nature of the animal being felt.*

These HTPs go beyond systems thinking's internal and external views by adding quantitative and progressive (temporal, generic and continuum) viewpoints. This approach:

- Separates facts from opinion. Facts are perceived from the eight descriptive HTPs; opinion comes from the insights from the *Scientific* HTP.
- Provides an Idea Storage Template (IST) (Section 14.2) for organizing information about situations in case studies and reports in a format that facilitates storage and retrieval of information about situations (Section 10.1.7).

The nine HTP external, internal, progressive, and other anchor points shown in Figure 10.1 are as follows:

1. Two external HTPs, discussed in Section 10.1.1.
2. Two internal HTPs, discussed in Section 10.1.2.
3. Three progressive HTPs, discussed in Section 10.1.3.
4. Two remaining HTPs, discussed in Section 10.1.4.

10.1.1 The External HTPs

The external HTPs are:

1. ***Big Picture***: includes the context for the system, the environment and assumptions.
2. ***Operational***: what the system does as described in scenarios; a black box perspective.

---

* Is this true? Because, without the sense of sight, would someone be able to combine the individual perceptions and infer that the animal was an elephant? Perhaps, but probably only if prior experience had shown that the elephant manifested itself as different animals under different conditions.

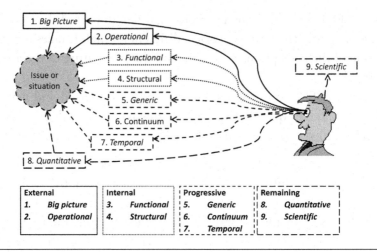

External		Internal		Progressive		Remaining	
1.	Big picture	3.	Functional	5.	Generic	8.	Quantitative
2.	Operational	4.	Structural	6.	Continuum	9.	Scientific
				7.	Temporal		

Figure 10.1 The HTPs.

10.1.2 *The Internal HTPs*

The internal HTPs are:

3. **Functional**: what the system does and how it does it; a white box perspective.
4. **Structural**: how the system is constructed and its elements are organized.

10.1.3 *The Progressive HTPs*

The progressive HTPs, where holistic thinking begins to go beyond analysis and systems thinking are the:

5. **Generic**: perceptions of the system as an instance of a class of similar systems; perceptions of similarity.
6. **Continuum**: perceptions of the system as but one of many alternatives; perceptions of differences. For example, when hearing the phrase "she's not just a pretty face",* the thought may pop up from the *Continuum* HTP changing the phrase to "she's not even a pretty face",† which means the reverse.
7. **Temporal**: perceptions of the past, present and future of the system.

---

* Which acknowledges that she is smart.
† Which means that not only is she not smart, she is also not pretty.

10.1.4 The Remaining HTPs

The remaining HTPs are:

8. **Quantitative**: perceptions of the numeric and other quantitative information associated with the other descriptive HTPs.
9. **Scientific**: insights and inferences from the perceptions from the descriptive HTPs leading to the hypothesis or guess about the issue after using Critical Thinking.

The first eight HTPs are descriptive, while the ninth (*Scientific*) HTP is prescriptive. While the HTPs provide a standard set of perspectives on a Perspectives Perimeter, perceptions from the *Continuum* HTP point out that there are other Perspectives Perimeters including emotional, cultural, personal, the other party's (in a negotiation), etc. These other HTPs should be used as and when appropriate.

10.1.5 Descriptions and Examples of the HTPs

This Section provides descriptions and examples of the HTPs as follows:

1. The *Big Picture* HTP, discussed in Section 10.1.5.1.
2. The *Operational* HTP, discussed in Section 10.1.5.2.
3. The *Functional* HTP, discussed in Section 10.1.5.3.
4. The *Structural* HTP, discussed in Section 10.1.5.4.
5. The *Generic* HTP, discussed in Section 10.1.5.5.
6. The *Continuum* HTP, discussed in Section 10.1.5.6.
7. The *Temporal* HTP, discussed in Section 10.1.5.7.
8. The *Quantitative* HTP, discussed in Section 10.1.5.8.
9. The *Scientific* HTP, discussed in Section 10.1.5.9.

10.1.5.1 The Big Picture *Perspective*   The *Big Picture* perspective incorporates Richmond's forest thinking and:

- Is an external perspective.
- Shows the purpose of the system.
- Provides the bird's eye or helicopter view showing the context of the system providing a view of the forest rather than the trees.

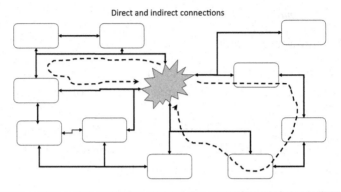

Figure 10.2 The Big Picture perspective - system of interest and adjacent systems.

- Looks down from the meta-level in the hierarchy of systems perceiving the System of Interest (SOI) within the context of its containing system – its environment, the closely coupled adjacent systems with which it interacts and any pertinent loosely coupled more distant systems with which it may indirectly interact as shown in Figure 10.2.
- Shows the external boundary of the system, and the entities that interact with the system. This view is known as a context diagram.
- Contains the assumptions behind the location of the external boundary.

10.1.5.2 The Operational *Perspective* The *Operational* perspective incorporates Richmond's operational thinking and:

- Is an external perspective.
- Corresponds to the traditional black box "closed system" view.
- Provides a view of the normal and contingency mission and support functions performed by a system.
- Tends to be documented in the form of Use Cases, Concepts of Operations (CONOPS) (Section 13.2), "to-be" and "as-is" views, and other appropriate formats.

10.1.5.3 The Functional *Perspective* The *Functional* perspective incorporates Richmond's system-as-a-cause and closed-loop thinking and:

- Is an internal perspective.
- Corresponds to the traditional white box "open system" view.

Table 10.1 Table Showing Mapping between Functions and Scenarios

FUNCTIONS	SCENARIOS				
	TAKEOFF	INFLIGHT	SAFE LANDING	GROUND MOVEMENT	LOLLYGAGGING
Braking	X			X	
Controlling	X	X	X	X	
Lifting	X	X	X		
Navigating		X			
Sideways	X	X	X	X	
Thrusting	X	X	X	X	
Communicating	X	X	X	X	
Thumping					

- Provides a view of the functions or activities (and the relationships between them) performed within the system without reference to which of the physical elements in the system performs those functions.
- Can be a view of what is being done or how it is being done depending on the level of system elaboration.

Each function may or may not be used in an operational scenario. For example, Table 10.1 provides an example of mapping the functions performed in a system (*Functional* HTP) to the scenarios in which the functions are used (*Operational* HTP). In the example, the table shows that none of the functions are used in the Lollygagging Scenario and none of the scenarios use the Thumping function.

10.1.5.4 The Structural *Perspective* The *Structural* perspective is an internal perspective incorporating the traditional physical, technical, and architectural framework views of a system. This perspective provides views of:

- Hierarchies such as the one shown in Figure 2.23. The hierarchy doesn't have to be shown on the vertical format; a horizontal conceptual view such as the Decision Tree in Figure 4.5 is still a hierarchical view.
- Structural elaboration.
- Architectures.
- Internal subsystem boundaries.
- Effects on the system due to its internal structure.

- The organization of the physical and virtual components.
- The interconnections between physical components and subsystems.
- The structure of the information in the system.

10.1.5.5 The Generic *Perspective* The *Generic* perspective:

- Is a progressive perspective.
- Looks at and for similarities.
- Provides information about the class or type of system.
- Considers a system as an instance of a class of systems which leads to the realization that your system inherits desired and undesired functions and properties from the generic class of system.
- Show similarities between the system and other systems in the same or other domains.
- Leads to the:
  - Ability to perceive connections where others do not.
  - Creation of out-of-the-box ideas.
  - Understanding of analogies/parallelism between systems.
  - Adoption of Lessons Learned (Section 13.1.3.1) from other projects and determination if those lessons are applicable to the current project.
  - Adoption of innovative design approaches using approaches from other domains (out-of-the-box thinking).
  - Use of pattern matching.
  - Use of benchmarking.

Consider the two different types of information displays shown in Figure 10.3 and Figure 10.4. One shows aircraft departures, the other train departures. One is electronic, the other electro-mechanical. Yet they both perform the same function namely providing travellers with information as to where to go at what time to catch transportation to specific destinations.*

A reasonably well-known application of the *Generic* HTP is the Theory of Inventive Problem-Solving (TRIZ) (Section 11.8);

---

* Note the use of function language, which describes the function performed by the displays irrespective of the location and physical nature of the display in an airport or railway station.

Figure 10.3 A train departure information board at Munich railway station.

Figure 10.4 A flight information display at Changi airport in Singapore.

a problem-solving process that has evolved over the last 50 years whose underlying concept is, "Somebody someplace has already solved this problem (or one very similar to it). Creativity is now finding that solution and adapting it to this particular problem" (Barry, Domb, and Slocum 2007), namely incorporating Lessons Learned (Section 9.3) from other people into the problem-solving process by definition.

10.1.5.6 The Continuum *Perspective* The *Continuum* perspective is a progressive perspective which looks at, and for, differences and recognizes that:

1. Alternatives exist as discussed in Section 10.1.5.6.1.
2. Any solution or issue is located on at least one continuum of some kind as discussed in Section 10.1.5.6.2.
3. Things are not necessarily "either-or"; there may be states in between as discussed in Section 10.1.5.6.3.
4. Changing conditions may cause movement along a continuum as discussed in Section 10.1.5.6.4.
5. There may be more than one correct solution to a problem, as discussed in Section 10.1.5.6.5.
6. There may be more than one way to achieve an objective, as discussed in Section 10.1.5.6.6.
7. Systems sometimes fail partially as well as completely, as discussed in Section 10.1.5.6.7.
8. There may be more than one objective for a system, as discussed in Section 10.1.5.6.8.
9. Things can and must be seen from different viewpoints, as discussed in Section 10.1.5.6.9.
10. Changes are not necessarily improvements, as discussed in Section 10.1.5.6.10.
11. Different people see things differently, as discussed in Section 10.1.5.6.11.
12. When examining a situation there still may be other unknown variables that may or may not affect the situation, as discussed in Section 10.1.5.6.12.
13. Distinguishing the difference between items, as discussed in Section 10.1.5.6.13.

10.1.5.6.1 Alternatives Exist This insight realizes that alternatives always exist when faced with making decisions. Sometimes the alternatives:

- Are obvious.
- Have to be searched for.
- Identify different solutions.
- Define different problems. For example, Henry Ford wrote,

Our policy is to reduce the price, extend the operations and improve the article. You will notice that the reduction of price comes first. We have never considered costs as fixed. Therefore we first reduce the price to a point where we believe more sales will result. Then we go ahead and try to make the price. We do not bother about the costs. The new price forces the costs down. The more usual way is to take the costs and then determine the price, and although that method may be scientific in the narrow sense, it is not scientific in the broad sense because what earthly use is it to know the cost if it tells you that you cannot manufacture at a price at which the article can be sold? (Ford and Crowther 1922: p. 146)

The usual question was, "What does it cost to produce X?" From the alternative perspective, the question was, "How can X be produced for $Y?" The key is to articulate the correct question, or as it is usually expressed, define the correct problem.

The traditional process improvement approach to cost reductions is to make adaptive changes (Kirton 1994) to slowly reduce the cost as shown in Figure 10.5. This allows the future reduction in cost to be forecast as a continuation of the curve as shown in the figure. Should upper management set a goal way below the curve, as shown in Figure 10.5, the traditional process improvement teams' response is to provide Figure 10.5 to upper management and explain that the goal is unachievable. They may not realize that the goal has been set because a competitor is selling or about to sell a similar product at a price near the goal and if they can't achieve the goal the product will no

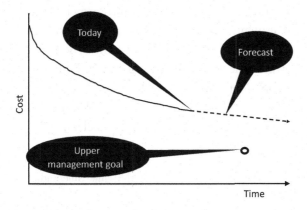

Figure 10.5   Cost targets.

longer be marketable. When faced with an apparently unachievable goal such as the one in Figure 10.5, the process improvement team needs to pose Henry Ford's question and make an innovative change (Kirton 1994).

10.1.5.6.2 Any Solution or Issue Is Located on at Least One Continuum of Some Kind This insight realizes that any problem, solution or issue is located on a continuum or spectrum of some kind, within a spectrum, or on a scale of some kind. Examples include:

1. The spectrum of synchronicity, discussed in Section 10.1.5.6.2.1.
2. The system solution implementation continuum, discussed in Section 10.1.5.6.2.2.
3. The public-private continuum, discussed in Section 10.1.5.6.2.3.
4. The continuum of change, discussed in Section 10.1.5.6.2.4.
5. The continuum of motivation, discussed in Section 10.1.5.6.4.
6. The continuum of solutions, discussed in Section 11.1.10.2.

10.1.5.6.2.1 The Spectrum of Synchronicity In the educational domain, these days technology provides many enhancements to the traditional face-to-face classroom. In fact, there are a large number of possible classes with various mixes of synchronous* and asynchronous[†] techniques. These classes are spread out along a continuum of possibilities, the spectrum of synchronicity shown in Figure 10.6.

The traditional face-to-face classroom lies at the synchronous end of the spectrum. The traditional class can be augmented with a web page, email, and other synchronous and asynchronous techniques. When web augmentation takes place, the web-augmented traditional classroom moves away from the edge of the synchronous end of the spectrum towards the centre. A face-to-face class that uses a web page for proving copies of handouts and readings to the students is not 100% synchronous. However, while the class is not 100% synchronous, it is often referred to as a synchronous class.

---

* Where everybody is in the same place at the same time and things happen in real-time.
† Where people are not in the same place at the same time and things do not happen in real-time.

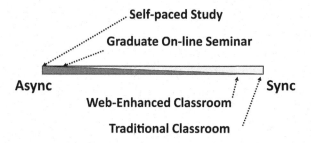

Figure 10.6   The spectrum of synchronicity.

At the other end of the spectrum is the totally asynchronous classroom. This represents the self-paced studies, correspondence schools, and other techniques in which there is no synchronous contact between anyone in the class. A graduate school seminar that is mostly asynchronous does generally allow for synchronous student to instructor and student-to-student communications via the traditional telephone system or via a VOIP system. Therefore, while the graduate seminar is not 100% asynchronous, it has so many of the characteristics of an asynchronous class that it is often referred to as an asynchronous class.

10.1.5.6.2.2 The System Solution Implementation Continuum   The system solution implementation continuum or design space:

- Is shown in Figure 10.7. When considering candidate designs for a system, each candidate will lie on a different point on the implementation continuum with a different mixture of people, technology, and a change in the way something is

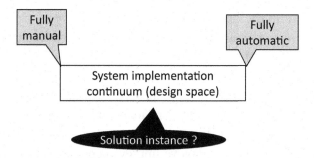

Figure 10.7   Solution system implementation continuum.

done, etc. The concept of designing a number of solutions and determining the optimal solution, which may either be one of the solutions or a combination of parts of several solutions, comes from the *Continuum* HTP. A benefit of producing several solutions is that one of the design teams conceptualizing the solutions may pick up on matters that other teams missed.

- Allows for planning various versions of a product in which the first version lies at the manual and of the continuum and successive releases or upgrades move the product along the continuum in the direction of fully automatic as more is learned about how the system is used.

10.1.5.6.2.3 The Public–Private Continuum   There is a continuum for services rendered in society. Private enterprise lies at one end of this continuum, government lies at the other, with a range of various private and public partnerships in between. There are some public services that should be within the realm of government, some within the realm of private enterprise, and some that can be in either realm. In the non-systems approach, different political systems position services in different parts of the continuum for ideological reasons. Some positions are more problematic than others for specific public services.

10.1.5.6.2.4 The Continuum of Change   Any specific change can be thought of as being located on a continuum ranging from highly adaptive to highly innovative (Kirton 1994). Where:

- Adaptive improvements and changes tend to:
  - Solve and resolve problems by introducing solutions from within the current paradigm.
  - Are more readily implemented than innovative ones.
  - Improve the current paradigm.
  - Face less resistance than innovative changes (Kuhn 1970).
  - Tend to formulate the problem in terms of existing implementation paradigms, then adapt and modify the products and procedures. These remedies result in improvements and "doing better". Adaptive improvements however also lead to the point of diminishing returns (*Quantitative* HTP).

- Reduce costs over a time, as shown in Figure 10.5, yet the rate of reduction slowly reaches the point of diminishing returns. This is the point where an innovative change is the only way to obtain any large degree of improvement.
- Innovative improvements and changes tend to:
  - Dissolve the problem by introducing solutions from outside the current paradigm. These remedies result in breaking moulds and "doing it differently".
  - Introduce a new paradigm.
  - Be perceived as riskier, and consequently tend to be resisted more than adaptive changes (Kuhn 1970).

10.1.5.6.3 Things Are Not Necessarily "Either–Or"; There May Be States in Between   This insight leads to the:

- Replacement of "either-or" questions such as, "Is systems engineering an undergraduate or a postgraduate subject?" by questions in the form of, "To what degree is systems engineering a postgraduate subject?" or better, phrasing the question as, "What is the knowledge needed by a systems engineer, and how much of it can be taught as an undergraduate subject?" This redefining of the nature of the problem statement is a very different perspective to the traditional "either-or", "one right way" perspective.
- The ability to redefine the problem, a key component of the ability to create innovative solutions to problems.

10.1.5.6.4 Changing Conditions May Cause Movement along the Continuum   This insight leads to the realization that systems can exhibit different types of behaviour in different situations rather than always behave in the same way and that the transition conditions causing that change in behaviour may not be known. In the case of human systems, perceptions from the *Continuum* HTP point out that:

- Maslow's hierarchy (Maslow 1970) may not be a pyramid, but may be a pie, and motivating people becomes a matter of figuring out which slices of the pie to offer them (Kasser 1995).

- Theory X and Theory Y (McGregor 1960) behaviour may lie at the two ends of a situational continuum of behaviour rather than be two opposing behaviour patterns. Consequently:
  - Which one to use may be situational. For example, in the military, there are times when an order such as, "everybody down" on the battlefield has to be obeyed instantaneously without any discussion.
  - An individual's need to be motivated may be situational. For example, is there a difference in the way you (1) motivate your children to clean up their rooms and (2) motivate them to come to the table for a dish of ice cream?
  - Theory Z (Ouchi 1982) may lie in the middle of the continuum of behaviour.*

This insight also leads to the recognition that systems have states and can change from one state to another at transition points.

10.1.5.6.5 There May Be More Than One Correct Solution to a Problem   Problem-solvers using the systems approach tend to think in terms of acceptable solutions and optimal solutions, as shown in Figure 10.8, rather than a single correct solution except when faced with mathematical problems where 1 + 1 = 2 in all situations. This aspect of the *Continuum* HTP can be illustrated from Maslow's observation of human behaviour which illustrates the non-systems thinking approach, "I suppose it is tempting, if the only tool you have is a hammer, to treat everything as if it were a nail" (Maslow 1966: pp. 15–16). Applying the *Continuum* HTP you would note that:

- Nails are the solution to one class of problems.
- Nails might be a solution to other classes of problems (although not necessarily optimal).
- The other classes of problems should be monitored while you get the correct tool to tackle those classes of problems.
- There may be times when the need to do something about the problem is so urgent, and in the absence of any other alternative, that nails are the only available solution. As an example, if you need to cut a plank in half, it can be done by hammering

---

* This is a hypothesis; see *Scientific* perspective.

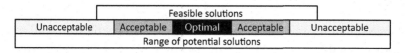

Figure 10.8   The continuum of solutions.

a series of nails along the line to be cut, extracting the nails and then scoring the line of holes until the plank breaks. However, it would be better to get and use a saw to do the job unless you need that plank cut before someone can bring the saw.

10.1.5.6.6 There May Be More Than One Way to Achieve an Objective   This perception indicates that there may be more than one way to achieve the same result leads to:

- Consideration of the use of different technologies in the product or solution domain.
- Consideration of different production or implementation approaches to achieve or realize the objective. In the military domain, this concept would be that objectives could be captured by flanking attacks as well as frontal attacks, or by a combination of both. In the civilian domain this concept means that there may be several roads to a particular destination.
- The realization that an objective may be reached by reformatting the problem statement. For example:

Some years ago. when smoking was permitted in public places, two seminary students were studying together in the library. After a while David said to his partner, "Moshe, I'm dying for a cigarette, do you think the Rabbi will permit me to smoke?"

"I don't know," was the reply, "why don't you ask?"

So David got up and went over to the Rabbi. "Rabbi, is it permitted to smoke while studying?" he asked.

"Certainly not!" the Rabbi replied.

David returned to his seat dejectedly and related what had happened.

"You asked the wrong question", said Moshe, "let me have try".

He got up, went over to the Rabbi, and asked, "Rabbi, is it permitted to study while smoking?"

"Of course", came the response.

10.1.5.6.7 Systems Sometimes Fail Partially as Well as Completely This perception indicates that systems sometimes fail partially or "fail soft" as well as failing completely leads to an analysis of failure modes for the system and each of its components. The analysis may influence the *Structural* and *Functional* HTPs in the design of the system. The concept also leads to a risk analysis of the probability and effect of internal and externally induced failures and ways to mitigate those failures. Internal failures are failures of components due to aging and normal wear and tear (Moubray 1997); external failures are those inflicted from without, such as natural disasters, sabotage and enemy action.

10.1.5.6.8 There May Be More Than One Objective for a System The concept of *Weltanschauung* in Checkland's SSM, CATWOE (Section 13.1.1.3.1) recognizes this perception. For example the objective of a pub or bar as a system could be:

- *A profit making system* from the perspective of the owners.
- *An employment system* from the perspective of the (potential) employees.
- *A recreational system* from the perspective of the customers.
- *A social system* from the perspective of the local residents.
- *A revenue generating system* from the perspective of the taxation authority.

This perception indicates that different stakeholders may have different objectives leads to the win-win principle in negotiation, which recognizes that when different parties to the negotiations want different outcomes, it may be possible to give each party what they want (win-win).

10.1.5.6.9 Things Can and Must Be Seen from Different and Multiple Viewpoints The perception that things can and must be seen from different viewpoints leads to the realization that:

- One man's rubbish may be another man's treasure.
- There are a number of Perspective Perimeters (Chapter 10), each of which should be used in the appropriate situation.
- There may be different perspectives on the nature of something. For example, consider the statement that "heaven and hell are located in the same place". How can that be? Consider the

following anecdote about human behaviour. A preacher who has been thundering away from the pulpit for an hour or so is enjoying giving the sermon; he is in heaven. Now think about the situation from the viewpoint of the congregation suffering through the same sermon. They are both in the same place, but whether they are in heaven or in hell is a matter of perspective.

* The boundary of the system is not fixed for all purposes. This concept is a key insight for tackling complexity (Section 13.3).

10.1.5.6.10 Changes Are Not Necessarily Improvements Changes are not necessary improvements. Sometimes changes are forced on us such as the need to upgrade perfectly good software for a later version simply because the information storage format used by the later version is not compatible with the earlier version.

10.1.5.6.11 Different People See Things Differently The difference can manifest itself in several ways including:

* People can see different things in the same picture and draw different conclusions from the same data. It is important to make sure that you and the person with whom you are having a discussion see the same things in the data you are discussing or at least understand what the other person is seeing; namely, put everyone on the same page or wavelength.
* Different people have different ways of seeing things and belief systems, known as *Weltanschauung* (Section 13.1.1.3.1), worldviews, or paradigms (Kuhn 1970). They may perceive problems, or want different (and perhaps contradictory) remedies (solutions) to an undesirable situation or have different concepts of what the situation is all about.

An understanding of this concept leads to the:

* Recognition of the usefulness of interdisciplinary teams.
* Ability to perceive things from the other person's perspective which is very useful in negotiations and other interactions.
* Understanding that the same words may have different meanings to different people which can be a barrier to communications.

The difference in meanings of words can also be a result of ambiguity since many words have more than one meaning. Perceptions from the *Continuum* HTP allow you to identify humour in situations that non-systems thinkers do not, and make (poor) jokes and puns such as the one about heaven and hell being in the same place. For example:

- *Humour based on ambiguity*: humour in English is often based on ambiguity; the difference in the meaning of words in a different context.
- *Humour based on perceiving opposites*: Gary Larson's *The Far Side* cartoons are excellent examples of this type of humour (Larson 1984).

10.1.5.6.12 When Examining a Situation There Still May Be Other Unknown Variables That May or May Not Affect the Situation   Perceptions from the *Continuum* HTP and Critical Thinking indicate that, as well as the known controlled and uncontrolled variables, there still may be other unknown variables that may affect the situation. This situation is known as Simpson's paradox (Savage 2009). Savage provides the following example of Simpson's paradox. An experiment was performed to measure the amount of weight loss per day due to the addition of a dietary supplement on a number of male and female test subjects. When the results were plotted:

- For the combined male and female test subjects, the results showed an average of 1.5 pounds lost per gram of dose.
- Separately by male and female subjects, the results showed the opposite, both subject groups had a gain in weight.

The contradictory results imply that there are unknown factors at work that need to be determined.

10.1.5.6.13 Distinguishing the Difference between Items   Perceptions from the *Continuum* perspective help to distinguish differences among objects which seem to be similar (Section 3.3.5). For example:

- Perceive the difference between urgency and importance (Covey 1989).
- Perceive the difference between the circle of influence and the circle of concern (Covey 1989).

10.1.5.7 The Temporal *Perspective*   The *Temporal* perspective is a progressive perspective which incorporates Richmond's dynamic thinking and considers the system as it was in the past, is in the present and will be in the future. If the system exists, past patterns of behaviour are examined and future patterns are predicted using this perspective. Insights from this perspective include:

- The consideration of:
  - Availability.
  - Maintenance.
  - Logistics.
  - Obsolescence.
- The concept of prevention of problems.
- Lessons to be learned from the system implementation and improvements for future iterations of the system. Reflecting on the past provides Lessons Learned from the system.
- The concept that past performance may not be a useful predictor of future performance unless the factors contributing to the past performance are understood.
- The concept of unanticipated emergence, namely that even if the implemented solution works it may introduce further problems that may only show up after some period of time. In manufacturing, these problems are known as latent defects. These time delays were grouped as (Kasser 2002):
  1. *First order*: noticeable effect within a second or less.
  2. *Second order*: noticeable effect within a minute or less.
  3. *Third order*: noticeable effect within an hour or less.
  4. *Fourth order*: noticeable effect within a day or less.
  5. *Fifth order*: noticeable effect within a week or less.
  6. *Sixth order*: noticeable effect within a month or less.
  7. *Seventh order*: noticeable effect within a year or less.
  8. *Eight order*: noticeable effect within a decade or less.
  9. *Ninth order*: noticeable effect within a century or less.
  10. *Tenth order*: noticeable effect after a century or more.
- The need to consider change and resistance to change. Paradigm shifts do not occur without a great deal of resistance, especially when people have to unlearn what they know to be correct (Kuhn 1970). Anyone who understands

Kuhn's concept of how paradigm shifts occur could predict the failure of "reengineering" in the 1990s just by looking at the cover of the book that introduced the topic; the key words being, "Forget what you know about how business should work – most of it is wrong!" (Hammer and Champy 1993).

- Understanding the implications of a proposed change in the problem, solution, and implementation (realization process) domains. For example, an undesirable situation due to traffic congestion (problem domain) may be remedied by a subway system (solution domain) that will be constructed by digging tunnels, etc. (implementation domain).

- Learning curves and how systems may improve over time as the personnel become more familiar with its capabilities.

- The need to consider the effects due to aging, the need for upgrades and replacement and the effect of DMSMS and the TAWOO (Section 8.12) state of the technology to be used in the system.

- The need to consider the evolution of adjacent systems so that the solution system being implemented will interface with the adjacent systems (i) as they will be in the future at the time of interface, and (ii) as they will be after being upgraded, which may not be the same as their current state.

- The current paradigm in any discipline is a step in the staircase of history and practitioners need to be open to considering and accepting changes that improve the discipline. This leads to the realization that someday some of today's commonly accepted scientific theories may be as obsolete as the Phlogiston theory* proposed by Johann Joachim Becher in 1667.

- The future will probably be based on technology and inventions yet to be developed. Consider the buildings in central Singapore, shown in Figure 10.9 as an example. The Marina Bay Sands, at the back of the picture, opened in 2010 dwarfs

---

* An obsolete theory that provided an explanation of why different materials burned in different ways.

Figure 10.9 Architecture in the 19th, 20th and 21st centuries.

the Fullerton Hotel, a building opened in 1928 which in turn is taller than the earlier buildings at the front of the photograph. The *Temporal* HTP provides the perception that sometime in the future there may be a construction built using a to-be-developed technology which will dwarf the Marina Bay Sands in the same way in which the Marina Bay Sands dwarfs the Fullerton Hotel.

- All systems eventually come to an end, change states, or fail. Figure 10.10 shows the effect of time on buildings. From this perspective you might want to think if we should care how the structures we build today will appear 2,000 years or so in the future.
- When little boys reach a certain age, they start to wash the dirt *off* their faces. When little girls reach the same age, they start to put dirt *on* to their faces.

10.1.5.8 The Quantitative *Perspective* The *Quantitative* perspective incorporates Richmond's quantitative thinking and:

- Perceives the numbers and measurements associated with the system.
- Indicates that relative comparisons are sometimes more useful than absolute comparisons.

Figure 10.10   Effect of time on buildings.

- Is not about the need to measure everything, "it is more the recognition that numbers must be useful, not necessarily perfect and need not be absolute" (Richmond 1993).
- Is about quantification rather than measurement, and helps to understand relationships and leads to the values of parameters in mathematical relationships in models and simulations. An example of quantification is the Likert scale, named after its originator Rensis Likert. The Likert scale offers a means of determining attitudes across a continuum of choices, such as "strongly agree," "agree", "don't care", "disagree" and "strongly disagree." A numerical value can then be allocated to each statement for further analysis. The numerical values may not necessarily be linear; namely, they may be weighted.
- Provides the concept of the point of diminishing returns, where adding more effort does not produce much of anything in the way of improvement.
- Provides the concept of adding a tolerance value (± something) to a specification.
- Provides the concept that approximate numbers are appropriate in most instances. For example, the well-known value of pi, 3.14, is just an approximation of an infinite number to two significant decimal places.
- Provides the Pareto principle, named after Vilfredo Pareto. Pareto discovered that in many instances, the little things

account for the majority of the results. The commonly used 80:20 ratio just signifies the idea that much of the output comes from just a few inputs, and the 80:20 ratio should not be deemed to be absolute; 80:20 might range from 70:30 to 95:5 in different instances. Examples of the principle include approximations such as:

- 20% of customers account for 80% of sales.
- 20% of the products or services account for 80% of the profits.
- 20% of the sales force generates 80% of sales.
- 20% of staff causes 80% of problems.

- Leads to the question, "How will we know the proposed solution system remedies the undesirable situation or meets our needs?" The ideas generated as responses to this question lead to the quantitative acceptance criteria for the solution system and ways to measure the degree of remediation.

- Can be used to predict and prevent problems by using historical data to make predictions. Capers Jones provided a table of data about software project outcomes as related to the number of Function Points (FP) in the software (Capers Jones 1996). This data plotted in Figure 10.11 can be used to prevent or predict problems in future projects. For example, if the number of FPs in a project at a Software Design

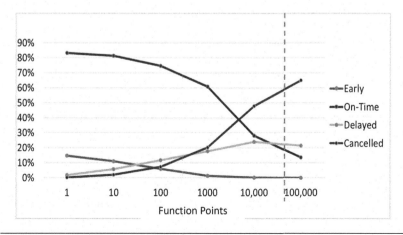

Figure 10.11   Software project outcomes.

Review is more than 50,000 or so, then serious consideration should be given to:

- Managing the project as one with a high probability of failure (serious cost and schedule overrun or cancellation).
- Cancelling the project on the grounds that, while you will not have the software, you will still have the funds, since if the project is cancelled in the future, you will not have the software *and* you will not have the funds.
- Redesigning the software to reduce the number of FPs; however, this will incur a schedule delay and some cost increment for the redesign activity.

- Examples of insight produced by perceptions from the *Quantitative* perspective include:
  - Statistical Process Control (SPC).
  - Six Sigma (Tennant 2001).
  - Miller's Rule that the human brain can only handle 7 ± 2 objects at a time (Section 3.2.5).
  - Brooks' mythical man month (Brooks 1972).

10.1.5.9 The Scientific *Perspective*   Whereas the descriptive perspectives are used to examine (and document) a system, the *Scientific* perspective:

- Incorporates Richmond's scientific thinking and is the output of the analysis process; namely, Lessons Learned (Section 9.3), a statement of the problem, the design of the solution or the guess, etc.
- Is where you infer something that is not there but should be there.
- Is where you infer something that is there but should not be there.
- Generally contains a statement of the findings from the information in the eight descriptive perspectives stated in a manner that can be tested.

For example, Federated Aerospace has just introduced the Widget III into the marketplace. Early sales reports show that the product is not selling as well as projected. Perceptions from the *Quantitative* HTP indicate that the Widget has the same performance as its competitors but has a retail price 20% greater than its cheapest competitor. The sales director develops the hypothesis that "the reason for the poor sales performance is that the price of the product is too high and the price should be reduced". The first problem will be to determine if the hypothesis is valid. If it is (there may be other reasons for the poor sales figures (*Continuum* HTP), then the next problem will be to find a way to reduce the retail price by at least 20% and still make a profit.

Perceptions from the *Operational* HTP indicate that there seems to be a relationship between several items in a system. The hypothesis is then stated in the form of a Causal Loop (Section 6.1.1) by stating "this loop represents the relationship in the behaviour of these components". The problem then becomes to determine if the hypothesis is valid which might be done by using the loop to predict previously unobserved behaviour and then setting up the conditions for that behaviour to occur. If the system behaves as predicted, the hypothesis is supported, if the system behaves differently, then the hypothesis is refuted and the relationships need to be re-examined. This approach is called the Scientific Method and is used to solve research problems (Section 11.1.10.5.1).

- The statement from the *Scientific* HTP can be expressed in terms of the other HTPs. Consider the following examples of making observations from the descriptive HTPs and formulating the *Scientific* HTP:
  1. Learning to recognize Japanese Kanji characters, discussed in Section 10.1.5.9.1.
  2. What's missing from the picture, discussed in Section 10.1.5.9.2.
  3. Where's the coffee, discussed in Section 10.1.5.9.3.
  4. Predictions, forecasts and imagination, discussed in Section 10.1.5.9.4.

10.1.5.9.1 Learning to Recognize Japanese Kanji Characters   Imagine that you are standing on a subway platform in Yokohama, Japan. While waiting for the train you notice a sign in front of you; the one shown in Figure 10.12. The sign shows the linear relationship between three stations on the Yokohama subway system: Motosumiyoshi (previous), Hiyoshi (current), and Tsunashima (subsequent). You can see

Figure 10.12   Station sign at Hiyoshi subway station in Yokohama.

the station name in four alphabets in the centre of the photograph. The top line is written in a Japanese phonetic alphabet (Hiragana) and contains three characters. The second line has the station name in English, Japanese Kanji and Korean.* The Kanji word uses two symbols; one character looks like a square figure 8, and a second is a more complex character. Given that there are three syllables in "Hi-yo-shi", and only two kanji characters, the problem is to work out the syllable represented by each Kanji character.

With two characters the combination could be "Hiyo-shi" or "Hi-yoshi". Systems thinking does not help very much here as the key observation comes from going beyond systems thinking (Section 1.4.2) to the *Generic* HTP. The name of the previous station is Motosumiyoshi. The last[†] Kanji character of Motosumiyoshi is the same as the last Kanji character in Hiyoshi. The hypothesis or guess (*Scientific* HTP) is that the pronunciation of two station names ends with the same sound,[‡] so the syllable represented by the last Kanji character in Hiyoshi is "yoshi". This hypothesis would then have to be tested by asking someone who could read Kanji or by looking at other bilingual signs for the same pattern.

---

* You have prior knowledge that the third alphabet is Korean, although in this example, it could be considered as an unknown alphabet and ignored since the exact alphabet is not pertinent to the problem, a ("Don't Care") language (Section 3.2.2).

† Domain knowledge or an assumption is that the characters should be read from left to right as in English.

‡ Based on the assumption that the direction in which the word is read is the same as in English.

Figure 10.13 What is missing from the picture?

10.1.5.9.2 What's Missing from the Picture? Consider the photograph shown in Figure 10.13 and answer the question, "What is missing from the picture?" Perceptions from the *Big Picture* HTP or context indicate it is a high school. Now perceive the system, the high school, from the *Operational* HTP. Visualize (Section 7.11) the inputs and outputs. Some of the students travel to school by bus. Where do those students cross the road safely? The pedestrian crossing seems to be missing. Or is it? Is the crossing part of the high school, part of the adjacent transportation system, or is it the interface between the high school and transportation systems? In this situation what matters is that the students cross the road safely and the pedestrian crossing is missing, an issue that needs to be addressed at the meta-system level. The photograph does illustrate the point of needing to define the correct system (and subsystem) boundaries to make sure that things are not left out, or, as often stated, "do not fall through the cracks".

10.1.5.9.3 Where's the Coffee? You are at a conference in a foreign country; you don't speak the language but would like to drink a cup of coffee. There are two beverage supply containers on the refreshment table, one containing hot water and one containing coffee such as those shown in Figure 10.14, an image captured at a conference in Israel. While (1) you could ask someone, or (2) let a drop of liquid out of one of the containers and taste the liquid, the point of the exercise is (3) to use holistic thinking to infer which container contains the coffee.

Figure 10.14   Which container contains coffee?

From the *Operational* HTP, one perception might be the packets of powder on the right hand side of the picture. The inference from that perception (*Scientific* HTP) is:

- The hot water is next to the packets so the beverage supply container containing the coffee is the other one.
- Based on the assumptions that:
  - Operationally the packets would be located closer to the hot water container.
  - The containers are marked correctly.

Now perceive the signs next to the beverage containers from the *Generic* HTP. One sign has one word; the other sign has two words. In English, "coffee" is one word and "hot water" is two words. The inference from that perception (*Scientific* HTP) is:

- The hot water is in the container next to the sign with two words so the beverage supply container containing the coffee is the other one.
- Based on the following assumptions:
  - The same vocabulary rule as in English where "coffee" is one word and "hot water" is two words applies in Hebrew.
  - In this instance the reading direction is irrelevant.
  - The containers are marked correctly.

Again the hypothesis or guess would have to be tested to determine if the correct answer was inferred. When inferences from two or more different perspectives indicate the same result there is a greater probability of the result being correct. These types of assumptions are often made implicitly without conscious thought. An invalid assumption invalidates the solution. This is why it is important to document assumptions so that they can be validated at the same time as the solution is being validated.

10.1.5.9.4 Predictions, Forecasts and Imagination Sometimes the test will have to wait if the statement is made as a forecast or prediction or the idea cannot be implemented and tested. For example:

- *Movie stars are a dying breed*: because advances in animation technology are making animated pictures so real that the time will come when realistic artificial characters can be animated under the supervision of the director, doing away with the need for, and expense of, live actors. It is also possible that the software may be set up so that the director can preload several acting styles into the software and allow the character to be played in any of them. Consider how a movie would differ if the hero were to be played by "John Wayne" or by "Charlie Chaplin's tramp". You might even get the choice built into the home distribution medium sometime in the next few years.
- *Leonardo da vinci's imaginative drawings*: some of them, such as the helicopter, could not be tested for five hundred years.

10.1.6 Building Up a Complete Picture or Linking the HTPs

Perceptions from each HTP provide information about part of the situation. For example, consider a car as the system in the context of home family life. When the car is perceived from the HTPs, the perceptions might include:

1. *Big picture*: road network, cars drive the economy, etc.
2. *Operational*: going shopping, taking children to school, etc.
3. *Functional*: starting, stopping, turning, accelerating, decelerating, crashing (undesired but possible function), etc.
4. *Structural*: car with doors, chassis, wheels, and boot.*

---

* Known as a "trunk" in the US.

5. *Generic*: (four-wheeled land vehicle) trucks, vans, etc.
6. *Continuum*: different types of engines and vehicles (land and non-land), etc.
7. *Temporal*: Stanley steamer, Ford Model T, internal combustion, Ford Edsel, hybrid cars, future electric cars, etc.
8. *Quantitative*: miles per hour (mph), engine power, number of passengers, four doors, six wheels, cost, price, etc.
9. *Scientific*: depends on problem/issue.

The information needed will depend on the issue being examined, and not all information may be pertinent in any given situation.

10.1.7 Storing Information in the HTPs

When using the HTPs as an IST (Section 14.2), the methodology for storing information in the HTPs is that in general, with respect to the system or situation, perceptions of:

- *"Who"* belong in the:
    - *Operational* perspective if pertinent to who is performing in a scenario, vignette or Use Case.
    - *Big Picture* perspective if pertinent to an adjacent system or systems.
- *"What"* belong in the:
    - *Big Picture* perspective if it is pertinent to the purpose of the system.
    - *Operational* perspective if pertinent to a scenario, vignette or Use Case.
    - *Structural* perspective if pertinent to technology, a physical or information element of the situation.
- *"Where"* belong in the *Big Picture* perspective or the *Structural* perspective.
- *"When"* belong in the:
    - *Operational* perspective if pertinent to a scenario, vignette, or Use Case.
    - *Temporal* perspective if pertinent to the timeline in the story leading up to the situation.
- *"Why"* belong in the *Big Picture* perspective.
- *"How"* belong in the:

- *Functional* perspective or the *Structural* perspective (how it works).
- *Operational* perspective (how it is used).

In addition:

- If the system goes through different states and there are major differences in its attributes as time passes, then there should be a different set of HTPs for each state.
- Numeric information is stored in the *Quantitative* perspective.
- The cause or reason for the situation is then inferred using inductive or deductive reasoning (Section 3.1.3.1) and stored in the *Scientific* perspective.
- Perceptions stored in the *Operational* and *Functional* perspectives should be written as verbs in the present tense using words ending in "ing", such as reading, writing, and designing.

10.1.8 Documenting Real-World Situations

If you are dealing with a real world situation rather than a case study and writing a situational analysis, perceive your situation from the *Generic* perspective and think of yourself as living a case study. The documentation process becomes:

1. Understand the purpose of what you are doing (why you are doing it and what outcome you hope to achieve).
2. Try to look at the big picture, often called a bird's eye or helicopter view.
3. Think about the "who", "what", "where", "when", "why", and "how" Kipling Questions (Section 7.6).
4. Collect pertinent material.
5. Stop and think about the relationships between items in the material.
6. Make notes, sorting and storing the information in the appropriate HTP, using the rules provided in Section 10.1.7.

10.2 The Knowledge–Application of Knowledge Perspectives Perimeter

When gaining or expressing an understanding about an object, perceptions from the *Continuum* perspective indicate that there is a difference between the knowledge of what an object is, and the knowledge of how it is applied. This difference seems to be something that many students have difficulty in grasping. Accordingly we can define a Perspectives Perimeter for knowledge and application of knowledge, where:

- **Knowledge** is basically "what" something is. It includes perceptions from the *Big Picture, Structural, Generic, Quantitative,* and *Temporal* perspectives.
- **Application of knowledge** is generally "how" it is used. It includes perceptions from the *Operational* and *Functional* perspectives.

For example, consider a car.

- **Knowledge** covers the make, the model, the colour, the performance, and the history. If relevant, it includes the numbers produced each year by the factory in which the car was produced and the day it was produced.
- **Application of knowledge** covers who uses the car under what circumstances, when they use the car, and the scenarios in which the car is used.

10.3 Summary

Chapter 10 discussed the Perspectives Perimeter, a tool for identifying and communicating a set of viewpoints, from which to perceive issues, problems, and situations, and points out the benefits of using a Perspectives Perimeter for examining a situation. If you've heard people say, "Let's make sure on the same page", or engineers say, "Let's make sure we are on the same wavelength", you can consider the Perspectives Perimeter as the spectrum of wavelengths, or as the book containing the pages. This chapter provided two examples of Perspectives Perimeters. The first example was the nine HTPs. The HTPs provide a systemic and systematic tool for applying systems thinking to gain an understanding of the problematic situation and then going beyond systems thinking to determine the nature of the problem and create a solution that will remedy the undesirability in the problematic situation. The second example was the Knowledge – Application of Knowledge Perspectives Perimeter that helps students distinguish the difference between knowledge and the application of knowledge so they can demonstrate their higher-order cognitive skills. This chapter also pointed out where six other Perspectives Perimeters are discussed in this book.

References

Barry, K., E. Domb, and M. S. Slocum. 2007. *TRIZ - What Is TRIZ?* 2007 accessed 31 October 2007. http://www.triz-journal.com/archives /what_is_triz/.

Brooks, F. 1972. *The Mythical Man-Month.* Reading, MA: Addison-Wesley Publishing Company.

Capers Jones. 1996. *Patterns of Software Systems Failure and Success.* London; Boston International Thomson Computer Press.

Covey, S. R. 1989. *The Seven Habits of Highly Effective People.* New York Simon & Schuster.

Ford, H., and S. Crowther. 1922. *My Life and Work.* Rep. Ed. 1987, Ayer Company, Publishers, Inc. ed. New York: Doubleday Page & Company.

Hammer, M., and J. Champy. 1993. *Reengineering the Corporation.* New York: HarperCollins.

Kasser, J. E. 1995. *Applying Total Quality Management to Systems Engineering.* Boston: Artech House.

Kasser, J. E. 2002. "Configuration Management: The Silver Bullet for Cost and Schedule Control." In The IEEE International Engineering Management Conference (IEMC 2002). Cambridge, UK.

Kirton, M. J. 1994. *Adaptors and Innovators: Styles of Creativity and Problem Solving.* London: Routledge.

Kuhn, T. S. 1970. *The Structure of Scientific Revolutions.* Confirming Chicago 2nd Ed., Enlarged. ed. The University of Chicago Press.

Larson, G. 1984. *The Far Side Gallery.* Kansas City, MO FarWorks Inc.

Maslow, A. H. 1966. *The Psychology of Science.* New York, Harper & Row.

Maslow, A. H. 1970. *Motivation and Personality.* New York, Harper & Row.

McGregor, D. 1960. *The Human Side of Enterprise.* New York, McGraw-Hill.

Morgan, G. 1997. *Images of Organisation.* Thousand Oaks, CA: SAGE Publications.

Moubray, J. 1997. *Reliability-centered Maintenance.* 2nd ed. New York: Industrial Press Inc.

Ouchi, W. G. 1982. *Theory Z: How American Business Can Meet The Japanese Challenge.* New York.

Richmond, B. 1993. "Systems Thinking: Critical Thinking Skills for the 1990s and Beyond." *System Dynamics Review,* no. 9 (2):113–133.

Savage, S. L. 2009. *The Flaw of Averages.* Newark, NJ, John Wiley & Sons, Inc.

Tennant, G. 2001. *Six Sigma: SPC and TQM in Manufacturing and Services.* Aldershot, England Gower Publishing Ltd.

Yen, D. H. 2008. "The Blind Men and the Elephant." Accessed 26 October 2010. http://www.noogenesis.com/pineapple/blind_men_elephant.html.

11
PROCESS TOOLS

This chapter discusses the following process tools:

1. The generic problem-solving process in Section 11.1.
2. The Cataract Methodology for systems and software acquisition in Section 11.2.
3. Plan Do Check Act (PDCA) in Section 11.3.
4. A process for creating technical and other project documents in Section 11.4.
5. A Process for Tackling a Problem in Section 11.5.
6. A systemic and systematic approach to finding out-of-the-box solutions in Section 11.6.
7. TRIZ in Section 11.7.
8. Working backwards from the solution in Section 11.8.

11.1 The Generic Problem-Solving Process

The basic tool used in systematic thinking is the generic problem-solving process which provides a template which can be adapted for specific situations in business, project management, and systems engineering, as well as daily life. The traditional non-systems approach considers the problem-solving process as a linear sequence of activities, starting with a problem and ending with a solution. However, the linear problem-solving process really begins when an undesirable situation is recognized and a project is initiated to remedy the undesirable situation. From the *Generic* HTP, this is also the first step in the research process (Section 11.1.10.5.1), namely constructing the problem from the undesirable problematic situation which is puzzling, troubling, and uncertain (Schön 1991). The systems approach is different; it thinks of the problem-solving process as a Causal Loop (Section 6.1.1) relating the undesirable situation, the problem-solving

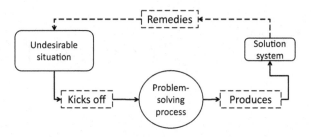

Figure 11.1   The problem-solving process as a Causal Loop.

process and the solution as shown in Figure 11.1 and evolving a solution via iterations of the loop.

When dealing with small problems, the process used to find a remedy is called the problem-solving process or the decision-making process. When faced with large and often complex problems the same generic process is known as the System Development Process (SDP) as shown in Figure 11.2 (Kasser and Hitchins 2013). The words "problem-solving process" in Figure 11.1 have been replaced by the lower-level term, "Series of (sequential and parallel) activities" in Figure 11.2. The figure shows that the lower-level term "Series of (sequential and parallel) activities" is known as:

- The SDP for large or complex systems which breaks up a complex problem into smaller less-complex problems (analysis) then solves each of the smaller problems and hopes that the

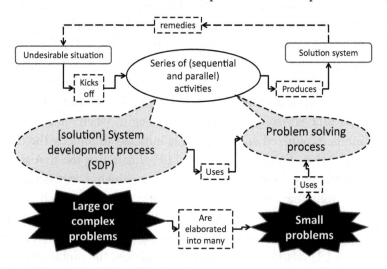

Figure 11.2   Activities in the context of the SDP and problem solving.

combination of solutions to the smaller problems (synthesis) will provide a solution to the large complex problem.

- The problem-solving process for small problems.

The same generic problem-solving process is used to solve simple problems, such as making a cup of coffee or complex problems such as creating world peace. What differs is that the detail and complexity of the process are adjusted to fit the scope of the problem as outlined in Figure 11.2. Some problems can be remedied in seconds; others may take years or even centuries.

Perceived from the *Functional* HTP, an iteration of the generic or notional problem-solving process is a two-part sequential process: planning and doing or implementing. The first part, shown in Figure 11.3, is a modified version of Hitchins' representation of the problem-solving process (Hitchins 2007: p. 173) which depicts the series of activities which are performed in series and parallel that transform the undesirable or problematic situation into the strategies and plans to realize the solution system operating in its context. The process contains the following major milestones (Section 14.9.2) (identified in triangles) and tasks or processes (shown in rectangles):

1. The milestone to provide authorization to proceed, discussed in Section 11.1.1.
2. The process to define the problem, discussed in Section 11.1.2.
3. The process for gaining an understanding, discussed in Section 11.1.3.
4. The process to conceive several solution options, discussed in Section 11.1.4.
5. The process to identify ideal solution selection criteria, discussed in Section 11.1.5.
6. The process to perform trade-offs to find the optimum solution, discussed in Section 11.1.6.
7. The process to select the preferred option, discussed in Section 11.1.7.
8. The process to formulate strategies and plans to implement the preferred option, discussed in Section 11.1.8.
9. The milestone to confirm consensus to proceed with implementation, discussed in Section 11.1.9.

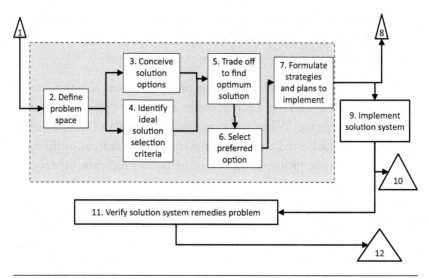

Figure 11.3   Modified Hitchins' view of the problem-solving decision making process.

The second part of the two-part process begins once the stakeholder consensus is confirmed at Milestone 8 at the end of Figure 11.3; the project can move on to the implementation states shown from the *Functional* HTP in Block 9 of Figure 11.3 where the additional following major milestones and tasks are:

1. The process to implement the solution system often using the SDP.
2. The milestone review to document consensus that the solution system has been realized and is ready for validation.
3. The process to validate the solution system remedies the evolved need in its operational context, often known as Operational Test and Evaluation (OT&E) for complex systems.
4. The milestone to document consensus that the solution system remedies the evolved need in its operational context.

Consider each step briefly.

11.1.1 Milestone to Provide Authorization to Proceed

This milestone provides the authorization to proceed with the project.

11.1.2 Define the Problem

This is the sequence of activities in which:

1. The Problem Formulation Template (Section 14.3) for the full project is completed. The completed Problem Formulation Template (Section 14.3) for the project becomes the first draft of the Project Plan (Section 8.11).
2. The undesirable situation is studied.
3. An understanding of the situation is made.
4. The underlying cause is identified.

The activities performed between the milestones constitute their own problem-solving processes. For example, consider the sequence of activities performed between Milestone 1 and Milestone 2. Using the Problem Formulation Template (Section 14.3):

1. *The undesirable situation* is the need to create the process to define the cause or causes of the undesirable situation.
2. *Assumptions*: assumptions about the situation, problem, solution, constraints, etc. that will have an impact on developing the solution.
3. *The FCFDS* is the process to define the problem or problems that are the cause of the undesirable situation.
4. *The problem* is which of the idea generation tools to use to examine the situation and determine the root cause.
5. *The solution* is the selected idea generation tool or tools to use to identify the cause of the undesirable situation such as Active Brainstorming (Section 7.1), etc.

The problem-solving process between Milestone 1 and Milestone 2:

1. Identifies a number of idea generation tools.
2. Examines each of them.
3. Selects which ones would be used to examine the undesirable situation.
4. Examines the undesirable situation.

5. Gains an understanding of the situation.

6. Infers the cause or causes.

Suitable tools for this process depending on the complexity of the problem discussed in this book include the HTPs (Section 10.1), Causal Loops (Section 6.1.1), NGT (Section 7.9), Active Brainstorming (Section 7.1), the ISTs (Section 14.2), and Checkland's SSM (Section 13.1), as well as the appropriate mathematical tools (Section 13.4).

11.1.3 Gaining an Understanding

The key to providing an acceptable remedy to the problem is a true understanding of the situation. This is Covey's Habit 5 (Covey 1989). In the event the situation is complex or complicated, several underlying causes or problems may be identified. In general, this situation is characterized by a failure to obtain stakeholder consensus on the underlying cause of the undesirability in the situation. In such a situation, the complex problem-solving process (Section 13.3) should be followed to evolve the remedy.

Once the variables and constants in the situation have been identified and the relationships determined, the situation is usually deemed to be understood and the underlying cause or causes identified. However, perceptions from the *Continuum* HTP and Critical Thinking (Chapter 3) indicate that there is a risk that there still may be other unknown and uncontrolled variables that may or may not affect the situation. This situation is known as Simpson's paradox (Section 10.1.5.6.12).

11.1.4 Conceive Solution Options

The conception of multiple solutions is one of the differences between the systems approach to problem-solving and traditional problem-solving which identifies one solution and then runs with it. This is the sequence of activities which conceives at least two different solution options. In the SDP each solution is documented in the form of a draft CONOPS (Section 13.2). Thinking tools used include Active Brainstorming (Section 7.1) and the ISTs (Section 14.2). In most instances the options should be generated as if cost and schedule were not an issue. Affordability (cost) and needed-by date (schedule) should be used as selection criteria to select an affordable and achievable option. However there may be situations in which the solution has to use available resources. Such situations tend to occur when the solution system has to comply with specific interface requirements, in training situations, or situations where the budget is limited and cannot be changed or when the solution has to be found within a short period of time.

The number of options to consider will depend on the circumstances (urgency and resources). There are three approaches as to how many options to consider.

1. *Satisficing*: picking first viable feasible solution, which is quick.
2. *Optimizing*: selecting the best solution out of all viable feasible alternative candidates, which can take a long time.
3. *Adaptavizing*: continuing to check all feasible alternatives until the perceived cost of further search equals or exceeds potential benefits of a better solution (Ackoff cited by Athey 1982).

11.1.5 Identify Ideal Solution Selection Criteria

The sequence of activities which identify appropriate solution selection criteria were discussed in the decision-making examples in Chapter 4. Typical selection criteria include:

- Cost.
- Schedule.
- Technology concerns over availability of spares.
- Risks.
- Political considerations.
- Keep stakeholder "A" happy.

If selection criteria are considered as constraints, another useful tool is Constraint Mapping (Section 7.4).

11.1.6 Perform Trade-Off to Find the Optimum Solution

The sequence of activities to perform the trade-offs was discussed in the decision-making examples in Chapter 4.

11.1.7 Select the Preferred Option

Most of these activities were discussed in the decision-making examples in Chapter 4.

11.1.8 Formulate Strategies and Plans to Implement the Preferred Option

The sequence of activities is split into the following two dimensions:

- **Product**: developing a complete set of matched specifications for the solution system and its subsystems that will provide a remedy to the undesirable situation while operating in context. These activities use the ideas stored in OARP (Section 14.2.2) and FRAT (Section 14.2.3) developed during the Brainstorming (Section 7.3) and Active Brainstorming (Section 7.1) activities performed in the previous tasks.
- **Process**: developing the Project Plan (Section 8.11) for realizing the solution system. The plan arranges activities in the Three Streams of Activities (development, test, and management) (Section 8.14) into a solution SDP building on the ideas in SPARK (Section 14.2.4) developed during the Brainstorming (Section 7.3) and Active Brainstorming activities (Section 7.1) performed in the previous tasks. The problem here is defined as creating the Project Plan (Section 8.11); depending on the scope and situation, solution options lie in different points on the system solution implementation continuum (Section 10.1.5.6.2.2) and include various combinations of performing the whole or part of the realization process in-house or outsourcing the work and different mixtures of technology and people. The various conceptual plan options should be developed in the appropriate level of detail to show they are feasible. Then the selection criteria are identified and weighted and a decision made on the optimal implementation approach for that specific project at that specific point in time. Once the decision is made, the selected plan is fleshed out and consensus developed before presentation at the milestone review.

Tools used in the systems approach to planning include CRIP Charts (Section 8.1), Gantt Charts (Section 8.4), MBE (Section 8.7),

MBO (Section 8.8), PAM Charts (Section 2.12), PERT Charts (Section 8.10), Working backwards from the solution (Section 11.8), and WPs (Section 8.19).

11.1.9 Milestone to Confirm Consensus to Proceed with Implementation Phase

This is the milestone that demonstrates stakeholder consensus that the preferred solution will remedy the undesirable situation in an affordable and timely manner by:

* Agreeing that the solution will remedy the undesirable situation when the solution is to be placed into service. Namely the needs have not changed significantly. This mitigation for the effect of change in the undesirable situation is built into project management methodologies such as PRINCE2 (Bentley 1997).
* The Project Plan for realizing the solution system is feasible; namely, the cost estimates are reasonably accurate and affordable, and the schedule estimates are realistic and will provide the solution in a timely manner.

Once the decision is confirmed, the project can move on to the realization phases and this milestone becomes Milestone 1 of the realization states of the project.

11.1.10 Myths and Realities in the Problem-Solving Process

When faced with problems, the best way to approach them is to use the Process for Tackling a Problem (Section 11.5). When faced with complex problems, the best way to deal with them is to understand that the complexity may indicate that there is a defect in the current paradigm* and there is a need to look for an alternative paradigm (Kasser 1995a). The search for an alternative paradigm begins with a change of perspective. Perceptions from the *Generic* HTP indicate that in mathematics, complex numbers consist of a real and an imaginary component. An inference from the *Scientific* HTP in the problem-solving domain using the (*Generic*) similarity to the components

---

* But not necessary the nature of the defect.

of a complex number in mathematics is that the complexity in the problem-solving domain may contain an imaginary or mythical component (Kasser and Zhao 2017). This led to the research question, "Are there myths in the problem-solving process that hinder the solving of complex problems and increase the complexity of the problem-solving process?" This section documents observations of the generic problem-solving process from the *Operational* and *Functional* HTPs which have identified the existence of myths and their corresponding realties.

To clarify the issues discussed in this chapter, the terms myths and realities are defined as follows:

- *Myth*: a popular incorrect assumption widely published or referenced in the literature.
- *Reality*: something that actually exists.*

An understanding of the reality will help to solve problems in a more effective manner. Accordingly, consider the following myths and realities associated with problem-solving, namely:

1. The word "problem" has an unambiguous meaning as discussed in Section 11.1.10.1.
2. The fixation on a single correct solution as discussed in Section 11.1.10.2.
3. The incomplete problem-solving process as discussed in Section 11.1.10.3.
4. A single pass through the problem-solving process leads to an optimal solution to the problem as discussed in Section 11.1.10.4.
5. A single problem-solving approach fits all types of problems as discussed in Section 11.1.10.5.
6. All problems can be solved as discussed in Section 11.1.10.6.
7. The problem-solving process is a linear sequence as discussed in Section 11.1.10.7.

11.1.10.1 The Word "Problem" Has an Unambiguous Meaning The myth is that the word "problem" has an unambiguous meaning. This is an incorrect assumption. The reality is that the word "problem" has at least

---

* Also published in the literature and widely ignored.

three different meanings in the literature since the word "problem" has been defined or used to mean (Dictionary.com 2013):

1. A question proposed for solution or discussion.
2. Any question or matter involving doubt, uncertainty, or difficulty. For example, this type of problem might be formulated as (Section 14.3):
   a. *An undesirable situation.* You might hear someone end a sentence with, "and that's the problem" when they mean, "and that's the undesirable situation".
   b. *The underlying cause of an undesirable situation,* usually a failure of some kind. For example, one may hear someone say, "My phone stopped working. The problem was a discharged battery". In reality, they mean that the cause of the phone stopping working was a discharged battery; the symptom or effect was that the phone stopped working.
3. The need to determine the necessary sequence of activities to transform an initial undesirable situation into a desirable situation.*

11.1.10.2 The Fixation on a Single Correct Solution The myth is that there is always a single correct solution. This is an incorrect assumption. The reality from the *Continuum* HTP is that most of the time there is more than one acceptable solution.

In school, generally, we are taught to solve problems by being given a problem and then asked to find the solution, as shown in Figure 11.4, the assumption being that there is a Well-Structured Problem with a single well-defined correct solution. This is a myth that does not apply in the real world. The reality is that problem-solving deals with problems or undesirable situations that generally have more than one equally acceptable solution. For example, you are hungry, which is generally an undesirable situation. The problem is to figure out a

---

* Once the necessary sequence of activities is determined, the subsequent problem is to plan the process to perform the necessary sequence of activities. Once the plan is created, the subsequent problem is to realize the desirable situation by carrying out the plan.

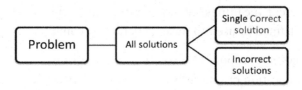

Figure 11.4   The single correct solution.

way to remedy that undesirable situation by consuming some food to satisfy the hunger. There are a number of solutions to this problem including cooking something, going to a restaurant, collecting some takeaway food, and telephoning for home delivery. Then there is the choice of what type of food: Italian, French, Chinese, pizza, lamb, chicken, beef, fish, vegetarian, etc. Now consider the vegetables, sauces, and drinks. There are many solutions because there are many combinations of types of food, meat, vegetables, and methods of getting the food to the table. Which solution is the correct one? The answer is that the correct solution is the one that satisfies your hunger in a timely and affordable manner.* If several of the solution options can perform this function and you have no preference between them, then each of them are just as correct as any of the other ones that satisfy your hunger. The words "right solution" or "correct solution" should be thought of as meaning "one or more acceptable solutions" as shown in the continuum of solutions in Figure 10.8. Examples of the continuum include:

- **Taste**: a cup of coffee can be too sweet or not sweet enough.
- **Contrast**: a picture can be too dark or too light.
- **Tolerances on measurements**: acceptable solutions can be slightly greater or less than the optimal value.

Conventional wisdom based on the mythical need for a single correct solution suggests that when a decision cannot be made because two choices score almost the same in the decision making process, the decision maker should perform a sensitivity analysis by varying the parameters and/or the weighting to see if the decision changes. By recognizing the reality that there may be more than one acceptable

---

* And does not cause any gastric problems.

solution, selecting the "Don't Care" (Section 3.2.2) which solution option is chosen may eliminate the need for the sensitivity analysis.

Figure 10.8 can also be used to explain the dictionary definitions of "satisfy" and "satisfice" where:

- **Satisfy** means provide solutions that are optimal.
- **Satisfice** means provide solutions that are acceptable.*

11.1.10.3 The Incomplete Problem-Solving Process The myth is that the linear problem-solving process starts with a defined problem. In school, generally, we are taught to solve problems by being given a problem and then asked to find the solution as shown in Figure 11.4. The assumption in this situation is that someone has already defined the problem. This is an incorrect assumption. The reality is that the problem or undesirable situation needs to be explored and understood before it can be defined (Fischer, Greiff, and Funke 2012). "Problems do not present themselves as givens; they must be constructed by someone from problematic† situations which are puzzling, troubling and uncertain" (Schön 1991). Accordingly, in reality, the problem-solving process must start with steps that define the problem. The linear problem-solving process accordingly represents the reality by beginning with an undesirable situation which has to be converted to a FCFDS and ending when the undesirable situation no longer exists as shown Figure 11.5. In this problem-solving process, an entity with the authority to take action becomes aware of an undesirable situation. A project is authorized to do something about the undesirable situation.‡ Problem solvers:

1. Collect and analyze the information about the situation.
2. Gain an understanding of the situation.
3. Determine what makes the situation undesirable.
4. Determine if someone has faced a similar problem, what they did about it, and the similarities and differences between the other situation and the current undesirable situation and how those affect the problem and solution in this instance (Section 11.4).

---

* Often stated as "good enough for government work".

† Or undesirable.

‡ Often made up of a number of related factors.

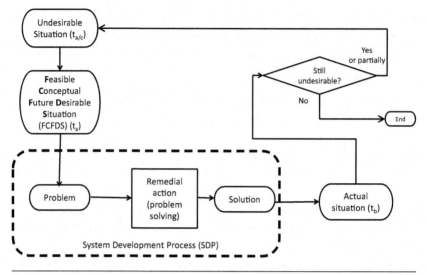

Figure 11.5   The functional perspective of the multi-pass problem-solving process.

5. Ideally, gain stakeholder consensus on the cause or causes of the undesirability of the situation by an understanding of human nature as well as the problem, implementation and solution domains. However, in the current paradigm, this may not be feasible.

6. Conceptualize and then create a vision of a FCFDS, the solution system operating in its context.

7. Plan the transition process from the undesirable situation to the FCFDS based on at least one iteration of the process shown in Figure 11.3.

8. Manage the realization of the solution system operating in the FCFDS by following the process created in Step 7. If the situation is complex, this remedial action transformation process often takes the form of a SDP.

9. Determine how much of the undesirably in the actual situation at the time the solution system is deployed in the FCFDS has been remedied. If the undesirable situation is remedied, then the process ends; if not, the process iterates from the new undesirable situation at t_c.

The person performing the task uses tools described in this book in Steps 1 to 7 to create the transition process performed in Step 8. Step 8 and Step 9 together constitute a process (a series of tasks) that can be performed by junior personnel under the guidance of a senior person.

The descriptions of the linear holistic problem-solving process in Figure 11.5 are notional. That means the description is the way things should be done. Perceptions of the real world indicate that not all projects perform all the activities described in the notional process. Figure 11.5 includes the time dimension, because the remedial action or problem-solving process takes time,* and during that time the original undesirable situation which existed at time t_a may have changed, which means that the solution system operating in the context of the actual situation at time t_b may not have remedied the changed undesirable situation as it exists at time t_b because of one or more of the following:

- The solution system operating in its context does not remedy the entire original undesirable situation.
- New undesirable aspects have shown up in the situation during the time taken to develop the solution system.
- Unanticipated undesired emergent properties of the solution system and/or its interactions with its adjacent systems may produce new undesirable outcomes.

11.1.10.4 A Single Pass through the Problem-Solving Process Leads to an Optimal Solution to the Problem   The myth is that a single pass through the problem-solving process leads to an optimal solution to the problem. This is an incorrect assumption. The reality is that some types of problems require more than one pass to solve (Simon 1973). Figure 11.3 is shown as a linear process with a start and an end. It provides an easy way to teach the problem-solving process and perpetuates the myth that a single pass through the problem-solving process will normally remedy the undesirable situation and that the need for multiple passes are the exceptions.

The reality is that in dealing with complex problems (Section 13.3), the single pass through the problem-solving process is the exception and the multiple pass problem-solving process is the reality as shown from the *Functional* HTP in Figure 11.5. Note in Figure 11.5,

---

* For large scale systems the development process can take years.

the block labelled "Remedial action (problem-solving)" is expanded in Figure 11.3. This is applying Miller's Rule for keeping figures simple (Section 3.2.5) and easy to comprehend.

11.1.10.5 A Single Problem-Solving Approach Fits All Types of Problems The myth is that a single problem-solving problem approach fits all types of problems. The current problem-solving paradigm seems to imply that a single problem-solving approach fits all types of problems as represented in Figure 11.3. This is an incorrect assumption. The reality is different types of problems require different problem-solving approaches. Accordingly, even though the process is identical at the conceptual level, the functions performed in each of the boxes in Figure 11.3 are different. Hence the recommendation for using a Process Architect (Kasser 2005) to design the appropriate process for a specific situation. The Process Architect is a person who is familiar with the following aspects of problems:

1. The level of difficulty of the problem discussed in Section 5.3.1.
2. The structure of the problem discussed in Section 5.3.2.
3. Research problems discussed in Section 11.1.10.5.1.
4. Intervention problems discussed in Section 11.1.10.5.2.
5. Technological uncertainty of the problem discussed in Section 11.1.10.5.3.

11.1.10.5.1 Research Problems This type of problem manifests when the undesirable situation is the inability to explain observations of phenomena or the need for some particular knowledge. In this situation, applying the Problem Formulation Template (Section 14.3):

1. *The undesirable situation* is the inability to explain observations of phenomena or the need for some particular knowledge.
2. *The assumptions* form the basis for the hypothesis to be tested.
3. *The FCFDS* is the ability to explain observations of phenomena or the particular knowledge.
4. *The problem* is how to gain the needed knowledge.

5. *The solution* is to follow the Scientific Method to discover the knowledge often in the form of the supported hypothesis.

The problem-solving process in this instance, is commonly known as the Scientific Method, and works forwards from the current situation in a journey of discovery towards a future situation in which the knowledge has been acquired. The Scientific Method:

- Is a systemic and systematic way of dealing with open-ended problems.
- Has been stated in different variations as the following sequence of activities summarized in Figure 2.16:
  1. Observe an undesirable situation.
  2. Perform research to gather preliminary data about the undesirable situation.
  3. Formulate the hypothesis to explain the undesirable situation.
  4. Plan to gather data to test the hypothesis. The data gathering may take the form of performing an experiment, using a survey, reviewing literature or some other approach depending on the nature of the undesirable situation and the domain.
  5. Perform the experiment or otherwise gather the data.
  6. Analyze the data (experimental or survey results) to test the hypothesis.
  7. If the hypothesis is supported, then the researcher often publishes the research. If the hypothesis is not supported, then the process reverts to Step 2.
- Uses inductive reasoning to create the hypothesis and deductive reasoning (Section 3.1.3.1) to support it.

In the real world, the hypothesis is often created from some insight or a "hunch" in which the previous steps are performed subconsciously. The researcher then designs the data collection method, collects and examines the data to determine if the hypothesis is supported or refuted.

11.1.10.5.2 Intervention Problems This type of problem manifests when a current real-world situation is deemed to be undesirable and needs to be changed over a period of time into a FCFDS. In this situation, applying the Problem Formulation Template (Section 14.3):

1. *The undesirable situation*: may be a lack of some desirable functionality that has to be acquired or created, or some undesirable functionality that has to be eliminated.
2. *The assumptions*: situation specific.
3. *The FCFDS*: one in which the undesirable situation no longer exists.
4. *The problem*: how to realize a smooth and timely transition from the current situation to the FCFDS minimizing resistance to the change.
5. *The solution*: create and perform the transition process to move from the undesirable situation to the FCFDS together with the solution system operating in the situational context.

The problem-solving process first uses the research problem-solving process working forward to visualize (Section 7.11) a number of FCFDS that will remedy the current undesired situation, selects the best one, and then works backwards to the current problematic or undesirable situation visualizing how the transition was implemented by working back from the FCFDS (Section 11.7). The information created in this backwards looking process is then used to document the:

- FCFDS.
- Realization plans documented as a forward process starting from the current situation and ending with the deployment of the FCFDS.

The decision makers or problem-solvers are faced with an undesirable situation: the need to realize the FCFDS. Once given the authority to proceed:

- They use the research problem-solving process to conceptualize a vision of the solution system operating in the FCFDS which becomes the target or goal to achieve.
- Then the intervention problem they face is to create the transition process and the solution system that will be operational in the FCFDS.

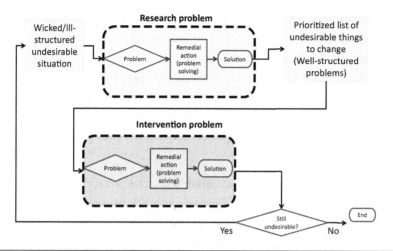

Figure 11.6   Iterative problem-solving.

- They then work backwards from the FCFDS to the present undesirable situation creating the transition process.
- They then document the process as a sequential process working forwards from the present undesirable situation to the FCFDS.

Both the research and intervention problem-solving processes contain a series of sub-problems* each of which have to be solved in turn to arrive at the solution as shown in Figure 11.6.

11.1.10.5.3 The Different Levels of Technological Uncertainty   Shenhar and Bonen characterized projects in the following four-level scale of technological uncertainty (Shenhar and Bonen 1997):

1. *Low technological uncertainty.* Typical projects in this category are construction, road building, and other utility works that are common in the construction industry that require one design cycle or pass through the Waterfall development methodology.
2. *Medium technological uncertainty.* Typical projects of this kind tend to be incremental improvements and modifications of existing products and systems.

---

* Which can in turn be research or intervention.

3. *High technological uncertainty.* Typical projects of this kind tend to be high-tech product development and defence state-of-the-art weapons systems.

4. *Super high technological uncertainty.* These projects push the state of the art and are few and far between in each generation. A typical example from the 20th century is the NASA Apollo program which placed men on the moon and returned them to Earth.

Solving the problems associated with the four types of projects requires a different problem-solving approach as well as the different approaches to systems engineering in each project. For example, the greater the degree of technological uncertainty, the more iterations of the problem-solving process (design cycles) are required and need to be designed into the Project Plan (Section 8.11).

11.1.10.6 All Problems Can Be Solved   The myth is that all problems can be solved. This is an incorrect assumption. The reality is that problems are solved, resolved, dissolved or absolved where only the first three actually remedy the problem (Ackoff 1978: p. 13), namely:

1. *Solving the problem* is when the decision maker selects those values of the control variables which maximize the value of the outcome (optimal solution).

2. *Resolving the problem* is when the decision maker selects values of the control variables which do not maximize the value of the outcome but produce an outcome that is good enough, namely is an acceptable solution that satisfices the need (acceptable solution).

3. *Dissolving the problem* is when the decision maker reformulates the problem to produce an outcome in which the original problem no longer has any meaning. These are generally the innovative solutions or the adoption of a different paradigm such as in the framework for tackling complexity (Section 13.3).

4. *Absolving the problem* is when the decision maker ignores the problem or imagines that it will eventually disappear on its own. Problems may be intentionally ignored because they

are too expensive to remedy or because the technical or social capability needed to provide a remedy is not known, unaffordable or not available.

The word "solve" is often misused to mean "resolved" or "dissolved" as well as "solved", when a better word would be "remedy".

In addition, Ill-Structured Problems cannot be solved; they must first be converted to Well-Structured Problems (Simon 1973). Dealing with Ill-Structured Problems requires multiple passes through the problem-solving process in which the first passes convert the Ill-Structured Problem to a series of Well-Structured Problems which are then solved, resolved, or dissolved in series or in parallel (Section 5.3.2).

11.1.10.7 The Problem-Solving Process Is a Linear, Time-Ordered Sequence   The problem-solving process is taught as a linear process, as shown in Figure 11.3. This is a similar myth to the single pass myth in Section 11.1.10.4. For example, consider what happens if none of the solutions meet the selection criteria in Step 6 of the generic problem-solving process shown in Figure 11.3. If none of the solution options remedies the undesirable situation, or all the solutions are too expensive, or will take too long to realize, or unacceptable for any other reason, then the choices to be made include:

- Absolve the problem for a while until something changes.
- Decide to remedy parts of the undesirable situation, sometimes known as reducing the requirements, until the remedy is feasible. Ways of doing this include:
  - Removing the lower priority aspects of the undesirable situation and determining the new cost/schedule information until the solution option becomes affordable or can be realized in a timely manner as shown in Figure 8.13. This is a holistic approach to the concept of designing to cost.
  - Remedy the causes of undesirability with the highest priorities and absolve the problem posed by the remaining causes.
  - Continue to look for an acceptable feasible solution that will remedy the undesirable situation in a timely manner. This will be Fred's preferred choice in the example in Section 4.6.2.2.

The reality is that the problem-solving process is iterative in several different ways. Consider the SDP as being made up of a number of problem-solving processes. The different types of iteration include:

- *Iteration of the problem-solving process across the SDP.* Each state of the SDP contains the problem-solving process shown in Figure 11.3. Accordingly, if the blocks in the Waterfall Chart (Section 14.9) view of the SDP were visible, the Waterfall Chart would be drawn as in Figure 11.7. Note since the figure contains two levels of the hierarchy, it should only be used to show the repetition of the problem-solving process in each state of an ideal SDP, one in which no changes occur.
- *Iteration of the problem-solving process within a state in the SDP.* Each state in the problem-solving process has two exit conditions:
    1. The normal planned exit at the end of state shown in Figure 11.7.
    2. An anticipated abnormal exit anywhere in the state that can happen at any time in any state and necessitates either a return to an earlier state or a move to a later state and skipping intermediate states (Kasser 2016). The "iterate until achievable and affordable" block in Figure 8.2 is a high-level view of the iteration of blocks 3, 4, 5, and 6 in Figure 11.3.

Figure 11.8 shows two perceptions of iteration in the problem-solving process. The traditional *Functional* HTP shows that the

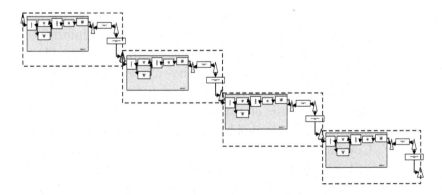

Figure 11.7   Iteration of the problem-solving process across the SDP in an ideal project.

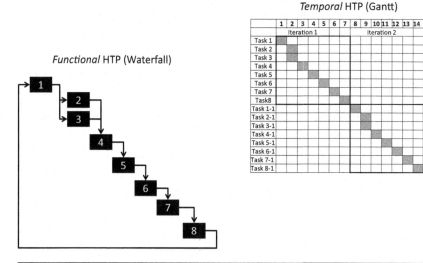

Figure 11.8 Perceptions on iteration in the SDP.

problem-solving process iterates back from the last milestone (not shown) at the end of Task 8 to the first milestone. The *Temporal* HTP shows that the activities are repeated and the second iteration takes place in either the subsequent state of the SDP in the case of a normal exit such as in Figure 8.8. The *Functional* HTP perceives the iteration while the *Temporal* HTP perceives the delay in the schedule. These views are simplistic views for teaching because the process can also iterate inside one of the boxes in Figure 11.8. The abnormal exit from the process and iteration in the waterfall views of the SDP is discussed in Section 14.9.

11.2 The Cataract Methodology for Systems and Software Acquisition

The Cataract* Methodology (Denzler and Kasser 1995):

- Is an implementation of Design to Cost.
- Is a budget-tolerant methodology variant of the problem-solving process as a Causal Loop perspective.

---

* Series of mini Waterfalls.

- Is based on the recognition that the "Build" approach used in the Operations and Maintenance State (Section 14.9.1) of the SLC is also applicable to the SDP.
- With its short iterative lifecycle is well suited for agile systems development.
- Relies on two factors:
  1. The Waterfall (Section 14.9) works very well over a short period of time.
  2. Implementation and delivery of systems and software are often performed in partial deliveries, commonly called "Builds" in which each successive Build provides additional capabilities.

The goal of the Cataract Methodology for systems and software acquisition is to achieve convergence between the customer's needs and the operational system. It does this by using several iterations of the problem-solving process loop to achieve convergence. The generic project planning process (Section 8.11.2) is modified as follows. The initial design is frozen, baselined and presented at a Preliminary Design Review (PDR). In the Cataract Methodology, this particular review differs from the traditional PDR in that lifecycle cost estimates and requirements priorities are included in the design trade studies using the appropriate Work Packages (Section 8.19). The highest priority requirements are selected for inclusion in the early Builds until the sum of their costs to implement is within the appropriate margin of the total allowed cost using the approach shown in Figure 8.13. In this design exercise, the:

- Cost of all selected requirements is computed for the entire lifecycle of the system.
- The most necessary requirements are those selected for implementation.
- Builds are organized so that the highest priority requirements are implemented first.

Once we start building the system, change management becomes more complex because the impact of a change can impact portions already built, as well as cause redesign of yet-to-be-implemented requirements. As the priorities of the requirements and the major cost drivers are known being stored in the WPs (Section 8.19), change management means making informed decisions about the following two types of changes:

1. ***Budgetary changes***: in today's environment, budgets are decreasing while needs are remaining constant or even increasing. Budget changes lead to changes in performance and vice versa. These factors are two sides of the same coin, yet in the non-systems approach, this very simple linkage does not seem to have been made to date. As a matter of fact, the traditional development philosophy tends to keep the cost information isolated from the people who set requirements. Mitigating the risks introduced by a budget decrease tends to be ignored in the SDP. The effect of a budget decrease is change. Some functionality will have to be given up; in other words, requirements will have to be deleted. The change may take two forms:

   1. Cut a certain amount of money from the program, which directly affects the SDP within the organization with ramifications on the staffing and schedule.
   2. Cut some requirements from the system under development, which has a direct impact on the product and an indirect impact on staffing and schedule.

   The budget-tolerant approach to dealing with budgetary changes is to identify the lowest priority requirements. Assess the impact of deleting them since sometimes work already completed may change absolute costs. Then delete the lowest priority requirement(s) consistent with the budget reduction from future Builds. The low priority requirements should have been assigned to the later Builds to facilitate this.

2. ***Requirements changes***: the real world of continuously changing requirements is recognized by the statement that the goal of system engineering is to provide a system that (Kasser 2000):
   - Meets the customer's requirements as stated when the project starts.
   - Meets the customer's requirements as they exist when the project is delivered.

- Is flexible enough to allow cost effective modifications to be implemented as the customer's requirements continue to evolve during the Operations and Maintenance State of the SLC.

This is of course almost impossible with today's technology. However, in many projects it may be possible to come close and achieve a large degree of convergence between the requirements and the capability of the system. The major Lesson Learned (Section 9.3) seems to be not to identify all the requirements at the start of the project, but to identify the (Kasser 2000):

- *Highest priority requirements*: the show stoppers. The risk here is the failure to identify the critical requirements and the failure to set the priority correctly.
- *Real requirements*: as opposed to apparent requirements.

Since the requirements change over time, there is a need for Build planning. The system must be built in such a manner that the requirements are implemented in the order of their priority (Denzler and Kasser 1995). The design path takes one from the domain of where everything is possible to what is actually possible. Thus:

- *Detailed design decisions should be made on a JIT basis*: there is no need to complete the design before starting a Build (Section 8.6). However, the design must be feasible. The risk here is in determining the feasibility of the design. For example, consider a situation where the need is for synchronous voice communications between two places. Since an initial assessment shows that the need can be met using the conventional telephone service or by the use of voice over the Internet (VOIP), there is no need to make that decision early in the design cycle. The characteristics of the telephone link are known. The characteristics of VOIP links are also known. Experiments can take place and the actual decision made JIT to implement the communications links. Since there is a possibility that the requirement for synchronous communications might be deleted in the future, any design effort made earlier would be wasted if the requirement were eliminated. In addition, if the requirement is not eliminated, then advantages can be taken of improvement in technology and/or cost reductions over the time before the decision has to be made.

- *Design decisions must also maximize the "Don't Cares" as well*: the example here is VOIP works (risk minimal) but the actual choice of how to implement the communications subsystem can wait for a while (Section 3.2.2).

Thus the key to an SDP based on the Cataract Methodology is to manage change in a manner that achieves convergence between the needs of the user and the capability of the as-built system in a cost-effective manner. The way to achieve this goal seems to be not to attempt identify all the requirements at the start of the project, but to only identify the highest priority and the riskiest-to-implement requirements. Then to achieve convergence by fleshing out the requirements in a controlled manner and delaying design decisions using a JIT decision-making approach (Section 8.6). The risk of an error of omission (Section 4.4) can be mitigated by using a template for the specific type of system (Section 14.4).

The cataract approach to Build Planning may be likened to a rapid prototyping scenario in which the requirements for each Build are frozen at the start of the Build. This approach, however, is more than just grouping requirements in some logical sequence and charging ahead. Build plans must be optimized for the product, process, and organization to:

- Implement the highest priority requirements in the earlier Builds. Then, if budget cuts occur during the implementation states, the lower priority requirements are the ones that can readily be eliminated because they were planned to be implemented last.
- Make use of the Pareto Principle (Section 2.11) insight that, typically, 20 percent of the application will deliver 80 percent of the capability (Arthur 1992) by providing that 20 percent in the early Builds.

- Allow the Waterfall approach (Section 14.9) to be used for each Build. This tried-and-true approach works on a small project over a short timeframe.
- Produce a Build with some degree of functionality that if appropriate can also be used by the customer in a productive manner. For example, the first software Build should generally, at a minimum, provide the user interface and shell to the remainder of the functions. This follows the rule of designing the system in a structured manner and performing a piecemeal implementation.
- Allow a factor for the element of change.
- Optimize the amount of functionality in a Build (features versus development time).
- Minimize the cost of producing the Build.
- Level the number of personnel available to implement the Build over the SDP to minimize staffing problems during the SDP.

11.2.1 Build Zero

The Cataract methodology incorporates an initial Build, Build Zero, which contains the initial two states, Need Identification and Requirements, of the Waterfall methodology (Section 14.9) with the exception that there is recognition that:

- All the requirements are not finalized at SRR.
- Additional requirements will become known as the project progresses.
- Design and implementation decisions will be deferred so as to
  - Maximize the "Don't Care" situations (Section 3.2.2)
  - Be made in a JIT manner (Section 8.6).

The work in Build Zero is to:

1. Identify the highest priority requirements.
2. Baseline an initial set of user needs and corresponding requirements.
3. Develop the WP database (Section 8.19).
4. Complete the first draft of the
   a. Project Plan (Section 8.11).
   b. CONOPS (Section 13.2).

5. Design the Architecture Framework for the system.

Typically, architectural design involves identifying and exploring several design options at a level of detail consistent with the technical and commercial risks. The options evaluate the performance and attributes of alternative architectural structures. Based on an appropriate level of understanding of candidate components, the feasibility of particular architectures or architectural variants is confirmed and their performance assessed. The trade-off analysis leads to a preferred architecture solution and to confirmation of the requirements for the subsystems/component functions and interfaces necessary to affect that architecture. (DERA 1997)

6. Perform risk assessment to determine the proposed Architecture Framework can meet all of the highest priority requirements.

7. Document the assumptions driving the Architecture Framework and a representation of operational scenarios (Use Cases) that the Architecture Framework prohibits (scenarios for which the system is not suitable). This activity also helps identify missing and non-articulated requirements early in the SDP. The design of the Architecture Framework for the entire system in Build Zero introduces a risk that it may not be suitable for changes years later in its Operations and Maintenance State (or even earlier). This is why part of the Build Zero effort is to determine scenarios for which the system is not suitable. The customer is then aware of the situation. The goal of the Cataract Methodology is to achieve convergence between the customer's needs and the operational system. In the course of time, one can expect that the need will change to something for which the system cannot provide capability. At that time, a revolutionary Build will be needed to replace the system. However, it will be done with full knowledge in a planned manner, rather than the ad-hoc manner of today's environment.

8. Develop the Project Plan (Section 8.11) to level the workload across the future Builds and implement the highest priority requirements in the earlier Builds as described above.

From Build One inclusive, each subsequent Build is a Waterfall (Section 14.9) in itself. The requirements for the Build are first frozen at the Build SRR. Then the design effort begins. Once the design is over, the Build is implemented and when completed turned over for integration. While the design team does assist with the integration, their main effort is to start to work on the design of the next Build. Once the first Build has been built and is working, the requirements freeze, design-integrate-test-transition and operate stages of the SDP commences for the second Build. This cycle will continue through subsequent Builds until the system is decommissioned, although the contract may change from the development organization to the maintenance organization. Each Build is an identical process but time delayed with respect to the previous one. Each successive Build provides additional capability.

A change request, if accepted, is assigned to be implemented in the appropriate future Build. From this perspective, the gap between the user's need and the completed section of the system converges over time. Project personnel move from one Build to the next remaining in their stream of activity (Section 8.14); the development team moves from one Build to the next, as does the testing team. Ideally the Builds are sequential with no wasted time between them. The customers tend to get increasingly involved with the system during later Builds by virtue of being able to use early Builds.

Each Build is placed under configuration control and may be delivered to the customer. Accepted change requests modify the requirements for future Builds, with the sole exception of "stop work" orders for Builds-in-progress if the change is to remove major (expensive to implement) requirements being implemented in a Build-in-progress. The milestone reviews (Section 14.9.2) within a Build are identical to those in the Waterfall methodology (Section 14.9), since the Build is implemented using a Waterfall. All change requests received during any Build are processed and, if accepted, are allocated to subsequent Builds. Freezing of the requirements for each Build at the Build SRR means that when the Build is delivered it is a representation of the customer's needs at the time of the Build SRR. It may not meet the needs of the customer at the time of delivery, but the gap should be small depending on the time taken to implement the Build since the SRR, thus achieving convergence between the needs of the customer and the capability of the as-delivered system.

11.3 Plan-Do-Check-Act

Plan Do Check Act (PDCA):

- Is often thought of as a tool used in process improvement.
- Is often described in the form of the following four stage process:
    1. *Plan*: analyze the process, understand the process, define the process, and determine what needs to be improved, investigate alternative actions and then propose a change or changes that will lead to improvements.
    2. *Do*: try out the proposed improvement on a small scale.
    3. *Check*: measure the results, and verify that an improvement took place.
    4. *Act*: Assuming an improvement took place, upgrade the process to incorporate the improvement, and iterate back to the plan stage for the next improvement.
- Is often drawn as a Causal Loop.
- Was developed by Dr W. E. Deming, who called it the Shewhart cycle after his mentor Alan Shewhart, who gave him the idea.
- Is an instance of the generic problem-solving process (Section 11.1).

Perceptions from the *Generic* HTP indicate that PDCA is an instance of a generic tool used in other activities. For example:

- It is a feedback or Causal Loop (Section 6.1.1).
- The systems approach of evolving solutions to problems shown in Figure 11.1 is an example of PDCA.
- When taking a road trip to a new destination, if you keep checking the map or use the global positioning satellites (GPS) while you're driving, you are using the same concept. In this case you travel a little, check you are going in the

right direction, travel a little more, etc., until you reach the destination.

- In market research, a new product is generally tested in a small market to test consumer response before increasing production to sell the product in the mass market.
- In engineering, prototypes are developed to try out the design on a small scale and verify that the prototype when operated in the proposed environment satisfies its requirements.
- Engineers have often used the concept of "build a little test a little" to construct the first version of a product or system. For example when building the prototype a new design of a radio they first build the audio output subsystem and test it. They then build the subsystem previous to the audio output system and test it by injecting a signal. When that is working, they move on to the next subsystem and test it, and so on, until they have a complete working radio receiver.
- NASA used the tool to develop the system that went to and from the Moon. Each Gemini and Apollo flight tested a critical function that would be required to land a man on the moon and return him safely to Earth. For example, Gemini VIII tested the docking function. Because if it was not possible to dock two spacecraft with the available technology, the concept proposed for the Apollo program would not be feasible and a different concept would have to be developed.
- MBO (Section 8.8) uses the same concept. The methodology sets up a number of objectives that have to be met as the project progresses along its timeline (Section 8.15). The difference is that the objectives are set up at the beginning of the project, and in traditional PDCA, an objective is set for each iteration of the PDCA loop.
- The Observe-Orient-Decide-Act (OODA) loop (Boyd 1995) uses the same concept. However the focus of the OODA loop is on the speed of completing the loop to get inside the opponent's decision-making cycle. In addition, from the *Generic* HTP, the After Action Review which takes place once the outcome of the decision is known is an instance of Lessons Learned (Section 9.3).

- Agile system development uses the same concept and also emphasizes speedy completion of the loop.
- Introducing different versions of the product each one improving the functionality uses the same concept. This can be planned so that for example if a company introduces the Mark I version of a new product, it can create revenue while working on the Mark II. In addition while the competitors are working hard to create their versions of the Mark I, the company, can then release the Mark II version, when the competitors release their Mark I versions. This can also be unplanned in detail for example the company takes feedback on how consumers are using the Mark I and what improvements they would like, and then produces the Mark II.
- The methodology for managing complex problems (Section 13.3) also uses the same concept. In that instance, each iteration of the PDCA loop remedies part of the undesirability in the complex problematic situation.
- PDCA can be observed in risk mitigation and prevention (Section 12.9) as shown in Figure 11.9.

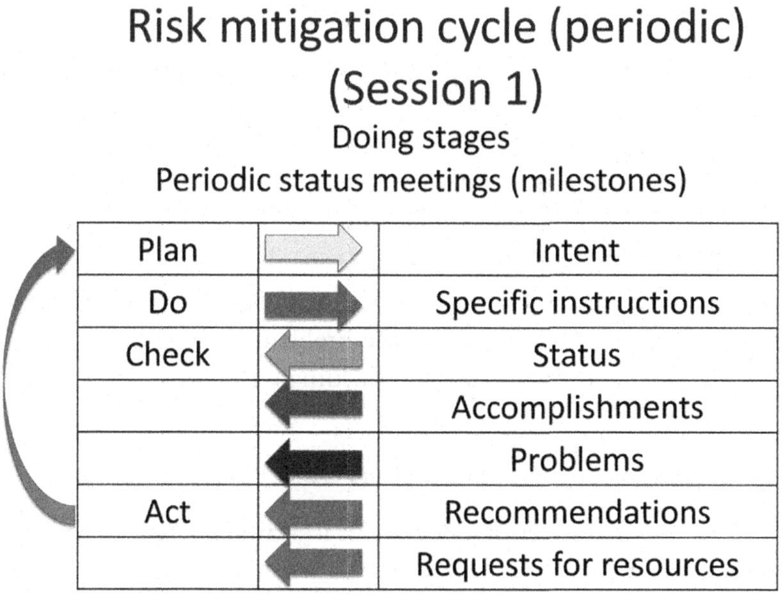

Risk mitigation cycle (periodic) (Session 1)
Doing stages
Periodic status meetings (milestones)

Plan		Intent
Do		Specific instructions
Check		Status
		Accomplishments
		Problems
Act		Recommendations
		Requests for resources

Figure 11.9   Risk mitigation cycle.

Perceptions from the *Continuum* HTP, note that process improvement is commonly drawn as a closed loop and termed "a cycle". The use of the word "cycle" implies that periodically, the entity assumes the same state periodically. This approach leads to "activity-based thinking". It may be true that the process improvement team performs each action in each iteration, and the process is in a constant state of improvement. Hence, once an improvement is incorporated, the process is different. While process improvement should be continuous, it also has to take place in a controlled manner and changes implemented at specific milestones. There should be no moving baselines. A better way to show the process improvement process on its own is to use the process improvement spiral (Kasser 1995a). The process improvement spiral is an iterative loop consisting of four steps with baselines at the start of each iteration. The spiral is more illustrative of this condition and should lead to "results based thinking".

When showing how process improvement is integrated into the organization, the existing process operates in parallel with the modifications being developed, and then there is a transition, when the modified process becomes the operational process.

11.3.1 Using PDCA

Whenever you're in a situation where you try something (perform an intervention) to see if it produces a desired outcome and then examine the outcome and take further appropriate action and so on (in an iterative manner) until the desired objective is reached, you are using the PDCA spiral. The perceptions from the *Generic* HTP listed above provide you with some of those situations.

If, as a systems thinker, you recognize this situation, then you can use appropriate tools such as the Problem Formulation Template (Section 14.3) and the Process for Tackling a Problem (Section 11.5).

11.4 Process for Creating Technical and Other Project Documents

Creating the first draft of a document is a difficult task in itself. It's much easier to edit something that is written than to create what needs to be written. The task can be facilitated by the use of a template and this process for document preparation which avoids later rewrites (minimizes scrap). If a document is written once, and meets these requirements, the result will be a better document at a lower cost, due to the reduced number of changes in the review cycle (Kasser and Schermerhorn 1994). The following list was presented as the requirements for writing documents; actually, they are requirements for the content of documents:

1. The information shall be written in the reader's (customer/ user) language.
2. The information within the document shall be pertinent to the reader.
3. The information in a document shall be complete.
4. All definitions shall be unambiguous.
5. All information shall be organized in a logical manner.
6. All wording shall be clear and concise.
7. Redundant or replicated information shall not be included in the document.
8. All specifications or requirements shall be stated in a manner that makes them verifiable.

The goals of the following document preparation progress are to:

- Produce a useful document that communicates the correct concepts between the writer and the reader.
- Minimize the time spent producing the document.

The following sequence of activities or process based on Kasser (Kasser 1995b) meets those goals:

1. Locate and evaluate a template or similar document, as discussed in Section 11.4.1.
2. Develop metrics for the document, as discussed in Section 11.4.2.
3. Create the abstract, as discussed in Section 11.4.3.
4. Prepare an annotated outline, as discussed in Section 11.4.4.
5. Perform the iterative part for filling in the annotated outline, as discussed in Section 11.4.5. This can be considered as a feedback loop in which sections of the document are created and checked rather than waiting until the entire document has been completed before checking it.

6. Publish a formal draft copy, as discussed in Section 11.4.6.
7. Update document based on reviewer's comments, as discussed in Section 11.4.7.
8. Publish document, as discussed in Section 11.4.8.

11.4.1 Locate and Evaluate a Template or Similar Document

In accordance with the Process for Tackling a Problem (Section 11.5), apply the Lessons Learned concept (Section 9.3) from previous documents before you create a document; use the generic template for a document (Section 14.5) as a start. Look for at least one similar document to use as a basis. Examine them for good and bad points using the process for critical analysis of an argument (Section 3.2.8), and then proceed through the document generation process described below. If you can't find a similar document, then look for reference methodologies, company standards, or anything that will provide you with a first cut at the material the document has to contain.

11.4.2 Develop Metrics for the Document

This step allows you to anticipate how the reviewers will evaluate the document. Metrics for specific types of engineering documents may be generated from Military-Standard 2167A (MIL-STD-2167A 1998) if appropriate and other sources such as the set of categories for evaluating a systems description provided by Teague and Pidgeon (Teague and Pidgeon 1985: p. 197). Their categories are:

- *Completeness*: the presence of all pertinent information and the lack of irrelevant and redundant information. In other words, no errors of omission (Section 4.4).
- *Consistency*: ensuring that the terminology, style and descriptions are identical throughout a specific document and within the whole set of system documents. This category applies to the graphics as well as to the text.
- *Correctness*: the information must be correct. In other words there are no errors of commission (Section 4.4). There are two types of these errors:

1. *Syntax/typographical*: easy to find by means of a spelling checker or visual inspection.
2. *Logical*: difficult to find, since you need an understanding of what is being described in the document to know that the document is incorrect.

- *Communicability*: a measurement of how well the document communicates the pertinent information to the reader. This category relates to the page layout, legibility, terminology, and the use of appropriate wording. Words such as "it", "this", and "these" may be ambiguous and should be avoided unless you are really up against the page size limitation.

11.4.3 Create the Abstract

An abstract is an overview of the document written to entice the reader into reading the whole document. A typical abstract should contain the following three parts:

1. The undesirable situation which triggered the work described in the document.
2. An outline of the anecdote or idea or proposal.
3. The outcome, results, or resulting benefits.

The process for creating the draft abstract is to use bullets or dot points in the form of an outline list. The draft abstract list should only be converted to the prose version of the abstract once the document is complete. This is a time saving process because the content of the document may change as the document is being written and if the full abstract is written in prose at the beginning of the process, the time spent composing that prose will be wasted since the abstract will have to be rewritten at the end of the process.

The following provides an example of a draft and fleshed-out abstract containing all three parts using the [ ] signs to separate the parts.* The abstract is for a paper that discusses improving the way difficult concepts in systems engineering are taught.

---

* The [ ] are for educational purposes only and should be removed from the final version of a real document.

The draft abstract is:

```
1.Relationships difficult to explain
2.Used modified FRAT* in class with positive results
3.Paper uses FRAT for LuZ
4.Lessons Learned
```

The fleshed out abstract is:

Abstract. [In teaching systems engineering the relationship between functions, physical decomposition and requirements during the process of defining, designing and developing the system, has been difficult to get across to the students.] [While trying to improve the learning process, an explanation of the relationship between functions, physical decomposition and requirements during the process of defining, designing and developing the system based on a modification of the Functions Requirements Answers and Test (FRAT) views of a system was tried on undergraduate students at the University of South Australia in 2006-2007 with positive results][This paper uses the adapted FRAT as a frame in which to describe the relationship between functions, physical decomposition and requirements using as an example the definition, design and development of the control and electronics part of the LuZ Solar Electrical Generating System (SEGS-1) in 1981-1983. The paper also provides some Lessons Learned from the project.]

The following is an example of a draft and fleshed-out abstract of a paper on thinking about thinking. This abstract however only contains the first and last parts.

The draft abstract is:

```
1.Thinking about thinking
  Emerging paradigm
  Need for multiple HTPs
```

---

* See Section 14.2.3 for details of FRAT.

3. Proposes a set of HTPs
   Use RAFBADS as example*
   The two flaws
Observations on the state of systems engineering
The fleshed out abstract is:

Abstract. [This is a paper on thinking about thinking. Systems engineering is an emerging discipline in the area of defining and solving problems in the manner of Wymore. The emerging paradigm for problem-solving is "systems thinking". Both systems engineering and systems thinking have recognized the need to view a system from more than one HTP.][This paper proposes a set of HTPs for applying systems thinking in systems engineering and then defines a systems thinking HTP set of views for a system, the use of which will provide one way of aligning systems thinking to systems engineering. The paper then provides an example of applying the set of HTPs to the Royal Air Force Battle of Britain Air Defence System (RAFBADS) and shows that not only does the set of HTPs provide a way to model the system; it also picked up two potentially fatal flaws in the system. The paper then concludes with some observations on the state of systems engineering from a number of the HTPs.]

Both of these examples communicate what their papers are about. Readers who are:

- *Not interested* in the topic will skip the paper, not wasting time reading it and finding it of little value.
- *Interested* in the topic will continue to read the paper. Hopefully the contents will hold their interest.

Opinions are split as to whether abstracts should contain citations to source documents. My preference is to insert them unless the style guide for the publication precludes including the citations. My general rule is when in doubt, cite!

---

* Acronym is allowed in draft abstract since it will only be seen by the author.

11.4.4 Prepare an Annotated Outline

Once the draft abstract is ready, the usual flow in the documentation production process is to begin with an outline. This outline takes the form of a table of contents. The outline is agreed to, and the production of the document proceeds. However, in many instances, a table of contents is not good enough since it does not indicate the proposed content of each section. The author and reviewer can and often do interpret the meaning of the titles differently.

The process can be improved by replacing the table of contents with an annotated outline (Section 14.1), which contains the table of contents, together with a paragraph or two on each section describing the planned contents of the section. The writing process should only begin when the annotated outline is approved.

11.4.5 Perform the Iterative Part, or Filling in the Annotated Outline

The iterative part of the process of writing the document converts the annotated outline to a document. The following iterative part is performed as long as the schedule allows:

1. Obtain and review pertinent literature or source information documents. Mark or extract (copy) all pertinent information or pointers to relevant data. Build a file to refer to when creating your document.
2. Hold informal fact finding meetings. Talk with cognizant personnel who can supply:
   - Source documents.
   - Information that is not written down.
   - Directions for obtaining additional pertinent information.
3. If you borrow documents and you can't extract the information you need in a timely manner scan or photocopy any pertinent information. Return the documents in a timely manner.
4. Document facts received during fact-finding meetings. If possible record the meeting but not without the permission of all the participants. Summarize all pertinent information discussed. Send a copy of the summary to the people you spoke with and get their concurrence that the information

you documented is correct. Find out where to obtain other pertinent information if necessary.

5. Research further source information. If your discussions identify missing information, research the subject and obtain the necessary data. Do not ask others to do your research for you and provide you with the required information.*

6. Write up sections. As you write the document, each section containing "This section will contain ..." is replaced by the true contents. You should:

   a. Use the appropriate style guide or template consistently.
   b. Use a software tool for managing the styles of citations and references: it is a great timesaver.
   c. Use a spelling and grammar checker. Typographical erros [sic] make a document look sloppy and are so easy to fix.
   d. Adhere to the page limit if one is set.
   e. Avoid jargon.
   f. Spell out acronyms the first time they are used.
   g. Write the text to flow logically (to the reader).
   h. Apply Critical Thinking (Chapter 3) to the content and the order of presenting information by following the process for critical analysis of arguments (Section 3.2.8) or equivalent.
   i. Stay focused on the topic.
   j. Avoid irrelevant (and interesting to you) clutter.
   k. Format the document so that pertinent information is readily seen. This book is an example of using the technique. Do this because unlike works of fiction which are usually read in sequential order from start to finish, most people do not read technical documents unless they really need to know the details; they tend to scan the document instead.
   l. Not plagiarize; cite all sources, even conversations with cognizant personnel.

7. Discuss write-ups of sections as they are produced in informal walkthroughs, inspections, and other discussion meetings. These review sessions build the quality into the product

---

* Unless they work for you.

during the production process. It is always cheaper to make changes to draft manuscripts than to signed-off documents. There is a trade-off between upfront costs of doing it right, and generating a draft and revising it after a meeting or review.

The hardest part of creating a document is to produce the first draft. If everyone is responsible for quality, then changes after the first review cycle are part of the process and not due to defects. It is easier at times to use the draft as a focus for discussion or to identify missing but needed information and ask the reviewers to supply same, as compared to spending a lot of time trying to dig out information the reviewer would have instant access to. There is an optimal point for each document, where it is cost effective to review a draft document, and incorporate changes at one time, as compared to spending more time developing the document, then holding the review and making changes.

11.4.5.1 Produce Peer Review Copy of Document   When you have gathered enough information and written up enough sections, produce the peer review copy of the document. It doesn't have to be complete, but it does have to identify the anticipated contents of any missing sections. This could be the original, "This section will contain ..." parts of the annotated outline or new sections written in a similar manner. The peer review copy is the first informal draft of the document.

11.4.5.2 Circulate Document for Comment   Documents have to be checked for style, format and technical content. A peer review process best checks the technical content. Circulating the document at this time provides:

- Early feedback of the correctness of the information.
- Pointers to missing information.

Provide copies of the document to everyone in the project (stakeholders) as well as at least one person outside the project because:

- Project members will tend to catch errors in the document (errors of commission) (Section 4.4).
- Outside personnel will tend to note missing information (errors of omission) (Section 4.4).

Circulate the document to potential customers and users as well (more stakeholders). For example, circulate a requirements document to the designers who will use the document before signing off on the document. This will allow them to:

- Identify the need for clarification of any ambiguous elements.
- Provide an indication of missing information (something they think they will need, that is lacking from the document).

11.4.5.3 Request and Receive Comments There's little point in circulating a draft if you don't get any comments back. Ask for the comments by a specific date which provides enough time for people to read the document and is not too far in the future. If the date is too far in the future, your reviewers may set the document aside in favour of a more urgent task and forget all about the document. Send them a gentle reminder a few days before the document is due. Make it easy for busy people to make constructive comments by providing a way to trigger their thoughts.

Think about what you'd like other people to provide you with, when they ask you to review one of their products. Ask for comments to be marked in the document in red ink (red lined). Don't require formal typed comments at this time. Provide a review form with space for specific comments as well as general comments to be ticked* such as:

- "Great document; couldn't have done better myself".
- "Not bad, but still needs work in the sections listed below".
- "You left out the following points:" ... so leave space for some points.

11.4.5.4 Evaluate and Incorporate Comments When the comments come back, thank the senders[†] (Section 8.13). Evaluate all comments and incorporate any that clarify the contents of the document. There is a good probability that some of the comments will conflict with others. Resolve these conflicts by talking with the people who wrote the comments to try to understand why they suggested their changes.

When you evaluate the comments, see if there is a pattern or trend. You may find the same type of comment occurs on several pages.

---

* Use "checked" in the US.

[†] One way is to thank them while also informing them when the document will be published and where to get copies.

Should this situation be true, you may want to rethink how you are presenting the information.

11.4.5.5 Hold an Informal Document Review/Walkthrough   One good way to ensure that comments are received in a timely manner and to resolve conflicting comments is to schedule a document review meeting. The number of days to wait after the document is sent out for review will depend on the type of document and the urgency of getting it published. The delay should not be too long or people will put the document aside and forget it (Section 11.4.5.3). People should have time to review the document and mark up any comments before the meeting. At the meeting, go through the document section by section and try to obtain consensus on changes. If consensus cannot be achieved on any specific section, agree to disagree and skip to the next section and rethink.

11.4.6 Publish Formal Draft Copy of Document

This is the draft that goes to the reviewer or even to the customer for formal comments. Since you have been working closely with the customer during the iterative phase, this state should just be a formality for contractual purposes.

11.4.7 Update Document Based on Reviewer's Comments

In the event the reviewer desires changes in the document, they may be incorporated into the document at this time.

11.4.8 Publish the Document

Publish the document and distribute a copy to all people with a need to know. Put a copy in the project library and send courtesy copies to outside personnel who provided information or constructive comments.

If you are working with your organization's publications department:

- Agree on what they will do to your text before you authorize any work at all.
- Ensure they are cognizant of the entire process and the date you:
  - Expect to provide them with the manuscript.
  - Need the finished document.

- Feed draft graphics to them according to an agreed schedule. Remember they will be working on other documents, and the artist may only be a part-time member of your team.
- Provide them with machine-readable text that is compatible with their publishing software. Ensure they do not have to retype any text to minimize errors.
- If the publications department makes any errors, you will probably be paying them to make the errors and then paying them again to correct the errors.
- Check all pages carefully, even the ones they were not supposed to touch.
- Return the document to them for publishing. Remember that it takes them time to print the document, and machines tend to break down.

11.5 Process for Tackling a Problem

The Process for Tackling a Problem:

- Is a tool to deal with an undesirable situation, namely there is a problem.
- Is a tool to minimize mistakes and waste.
- Leverages on other people's knowledge and experience.
- Is shown in Figure 11.10.

Formulate the problem using the Problem Formulation Template (Section 14.3). The generic Problem Formulation Template for the problem of formulating a problem is as follows.

1. *The undesirable situation*: is the need to develop a problem statement.
2. *Assumptions*:
   a. There is enough expertise in the group formulating the problem to understand the undesirable situation and specify the correct problem.*

---

* If this assumption is not true, then that expertise needs to be obtained for the duration of the activity. Providers of the expertise include other people within the organization, consultants, and members of the group looking it up on the Internet.

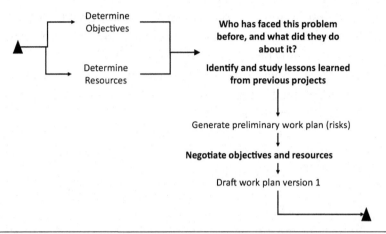

Figure 11.10   Process for tackling a problem.

    b. The problem statement can be developed without concern about constraints because it doesn't actually specify a solution. The constraints will affect the solution.

3. *The FCFDS*: the problem statement has been developed, and has formulated the correct problem.

4. *The problem*: how to create the FCFDS.

5. *The solution*: consists of two parts, the creation of a set of activities and the performance of those activities that produce the FCFDS. The activities make the transition from the undesirable situation to the FCFDS.

The first version of the template generally does not include a solution. The problem is to create the solution that implements the transition to the FCFDS. So, expanding Figure 11.10, the process for developing the solution is as follows:

1. Identify the objectives that have to be met, and the resources that are available.

2. Prioritize the objectives that have to be met.

3. Determine if anybody has faced a similar problem in the past and what they did about it and if what they did about it is applicable to this situation.

4. Locate templates for the products that have to be developed. There is no need to recreate the product structure if a suitable structure already exists.

5. Check the Lessons Learned database (Section 9.3) to avoid making the mistakes of the past.

6. Develop the preliminary Compliance Matrix (Section 9.5.2) that states all the objectives that have to be met.

7. Develop the first or preliminary version of the Project Plan (Section 8.11) that contains all the activities, the estimated schedule and cost, and the necessary resources.

8. Complete the Compliance Matrix to make sure that all the objectives have been covered.

9. Compare the estimates of cost, schedule and resources in the preliminary version of the Project Plan with the schedule resource and cost constraints of the real-world situation.

Since in most situations the estimates will be greater than the available, adjust the plan to remove the lowest priority objectives, until the plan meets the available resources.

If the plan cannot produce the objectives within the available resources, then either the available resources have to be increased, or the project is doomed from the start.

This version of the plan becomes the baseline plan of the project.

11.6 A Process for Finding Out-of-the-Box Solutions

There is a lot of encouragement on the need to think out of the box, but there is very little information on how to think out of the box other than in TRIZ (Section 11.7). This tool:

- Fills that gap by providing an example of how to think out of the box.
- Is a systemic and systematic approach to finding out-of-the-box solutions.

To use the tool, start by formulating the problem of finding an out-of-the-box solution using the Problem Formulation Template (Section 14.3) as follows:

1. *The undesirable situation* is the need to think out of the box in a particular situation.

2. *Assumptions*:
   a. Everyone is working in a box.

b. The out-of-the-box solution to a problem in one box can be found in a different box.

3. *The FCFDS*: thinking out-of-the-box systemic and systematic manner by locating those other boxes and transferring ideas from those boxes into our box.

4. *The problem*: how to convert the FCFDS into reality (the *Scientific* HTP).

5. *The solution* is to be determined.

The process of finding a solution to the problem began with some Active Brainstorming (Section 7.1). The (answers to the) following four key questions led to the solution.

1. *From the Operational HTP*: the question was, "What we are doing in our box?" The answer was, "problem-solving".

2. *From the Generic HTP*: the question was, "Are other people in different boxes doing similar activities?" The answer was "yes".

3. *From the Functional HTP*: the question was, "What do they use when doing those activities?" The answer was, "knowledge and experience".

4. *From the Structural HTP*: the questions were, "Are there any frameworks that arrange the activities in the workplace in an organized manner?", and, "Are there any frameworks that arrange knowledge in an organized manner?" The answers to both questions were, "yes". The HKMF (Section 5.2) shown in Figure 5.2 is a framework that arranges the activities in the workplace. Two frameworks that contain knowledge arranged in an organized manner are The Library of Congress catalogue and the Dewey decimal system.

The process for finding an out-of-the-box solution using these frameworks is as follows:

1. Plot the current activity in the HKMF (Section 5.2) shown in Figure 5.2.

2. Locate information about the current activity or similar activities being performed in other areas (boxes) of the HKMF.

3. Study what's happening in those boxes and determine if there is something useful that will provide a solution to your problem. Use Active Brainstorming (Section 7.1), focusing on the *Generic* and *Continuum* HTPs looking at similarities and differences. For example if you are facing a problem collecting requirements in Area 2B take a look at how policymakers in Area 5B collect requirements for policies, or look at how people involved in integrating and testing the system in Area 2F deal with the same type of problem.

4. If the previous four steps didn't provide a solution, or even if they did and there is time, create another framework, for example, by knowledge as shown in Table 11.1.

5. Look at similar activities in different domains. For example, if you are working railway transportation in Area 2B, look at what people working in road transportation in Area 2B are doing and if there any useful ideas. This is the basic concept behind benchmarking.

6. Locate information about the current activity or similar activities being performed in other areas (boxes) of the framework.

7. Study what's happening in those boxes and determine if there is something useful that will provide a solution to your problem. Use Active Brainstorming (Section 7.1), focusing on the *Generic* and *Continuum* HTPs looking at similarities and differences. For example, if you're facing a problem of designing a kitchen in a very small apartment, take a look and at kitchens in recreational vehicles and small boats. Same problem, three different domains, yet the solutions will be similar.

Table 11.1 Adjacent Boxes by Types of Knowledge in Different Domains

DOMAIN	FICTION	ARTS	ENGINEERING	SCIENCES
Space				
Air				
Surface – land				
Surface – water				
Subsurface – land				
Subsurface – water				

11.6.1 Case Studies

The following two examples or case studies illustrate the use of this approach. They are:

1. The kiosk queue.
2. The long wait at the traffic light.

11.6.1.1 The Kiosk Queue In 2016 there was an undesirable situation at the National University of Singapore (NUS), with respect to the kiosk that provided tea, coffee, and other refreshments during the day. Students used to line up in front of the kiosk to order their refreshment. The average situation with a small student queue is shown in Figure 11.11. However there were times of the day, particularly in between classes, when the line became long and impeded the flow of students travelling across the queue, namely down and up the stairs and towards and away from the camera. These students had to force their way through the kiosk queue or walk around it.

When Active Brainstorming (Section 7.1) the undesirable situation, the key question which came from the *Generic* HTP was, "What is this situation similar to?" The insight provided by the question was that it was a traffic problem. A similar situation in traffic was noted outside NUS that very same evening, as shown in Figure 11.12. There the driveway is kept clear by the box inside the yellow lines. So a

Figure 11.11 Student queue.

Figure 11.12 Traffic flow control.

probable solution to the congestion problem outside the kiosk might be a yellow box that would provide a space the cross traffic with space to pass through the queue.*

11.6.1.2 The Long Wait at the Traffic Light The long wait at the traffic light was an exercise I used to give my students at NUS. The traffic shown in Figure 11.12 is actually waiting at a traffic light. The exercise showed a video which was a 360° view from a pedestrian waiting at the traffic light and informed the students that the waiting time for the pedestrian was often very long and this was an undesirable situation. The exercise was for them to conceptualize a solution to the undesirably long wait at the light. The students used Active Brainstorming (Section 7.1) and came up with a number of suggestions including:

- Dissolving the problem by removing the traffic light and making the pedestrians use the bridge, shown in Figure 11.12.
- Providing various kinds of entertainment to pass the time while waiting for the light to change.
- Providing shopping kiosks.

---

* Unfortunately I left NUS before I could figure out how to bring my proposed solution to the attention of the appropriate authority. There was no suggestion box that I could find. But that's a separate problem.

These suggestions were generated by perceiving the situation from the *Operational* and *Functional* HTPs, but the innovative solutions tend to come from the *Generic, Continuum,* and *Temporal* HTPs. The students never asked the *Generic* HTP question, "Who has faced this problem before and what did they do about it?" (Section 11.4). Had they done so, they would have realized or eventually understood that this was not the first traffic light to face this problem and investigated existing solutions to the problem which did not include entertainment and shopping kiosks. Sometimes by asking this question the team realizes the extent of the lack of domain knowledge in the team and employs the appropriate necessary expertise. The root cause of the undesirability was not the long wait but the uncertainty as to when the light would change. The generic solution is a countdown timing light that tells the people waiting exactly how long they have to wait until the lights change.

The *Generic* HTP question, "Who has faced this problem before and what did they do about it?" (Section 11.4):

- Is a key question which differentiates the systems approach to problem-solving from the non-systems approach.
- Helps to avoid repeating the mistakes of the past (Section 9.3).

11.7 TRIZ

This section contains a brief overview of the problem-solving aspects of TRIZ examined from the different HTPs as understood by the author. At this time, TRIZ has evolved and become more complex branching off into technology and providing databases of problems that have been solved in the past to be used as templates. However this discussion, to keep within the theme of this book, is limited to the problem-solving aspects. So consider TRIZ from the following HTPs:

1. The *Big Picture* perspective, discussed in Section 11.7.1.
2. The *Temporal* perspective, discussed in Section 11.7.2.
3. The *Scientific* perspective, discussed in Section 11.7.3.
4. The *Functional* perspective, discussed in Section 11.7.4.

11.7.1 The Big Picture *Perspective*

Perceived from the *Big Picture* perspective, TRIZ is:

- The Teoriya Resheniya Izobreatatelskikh Zadatch (TRIZ), developed by Genrich Altshuller in 1946, which has been rendered into English as, "the Theory of Solving Inventive Problems".
- An application of the *Generic* HTP perspective.
- A problem-solving process for finding an out-of-the-box solution whose underlying concept is, "Somebody someplace has already solved this problem (or one very similar to it.) Creativity is now finding that solution and adapting it to this particular problem" (Barry, Domb, and Slocum 2007), namely, incorporating Lessons Learned (Section 13.1.3.1) from other people in the problem-solving process by definition.
- A set of solutions looking for a problem, namely, working backwards from the solution (Section 11.8).
- A number of guidelines, rules or principles which indicate how to cope with a specific problem or situation (Valeri 1999).

11.7.2 The Temporal *Perspective*

Starting with the hypothesis that a patent described a solution to a problem, Altshuller examined more than 200,000 patents and classified the solutions in five levels, which he called "Levels of Inventions". The five levels are:

1. *Routine design problems*: (32%) adaptive solutions (Kirton 1994) identified by methods well known within the specialty.
2. *Minor improvements to an existing system*: (45%) adaptive solutions (Kirton 1994) identified by methods known within the industry, usually with some sort of compromise.
3. *Fundamental improvement to an existing system*: (18%) inventive or innovative solutions (Kirton 1994) identified by methods known outside the industry and resolving contradictions.

4. *A new generation*: (4%) inventive or innovative solutions (Kirton 1994) identified by using a new principle to perform the primary functions of the system.

5. *A rare scientific discovery or pioneering invention*: (1%) an innovative solution (Kirton 1994) essentially a new system.

Altshuller found 39 generic parameters each of which either improve or degrade a system. Accordingly every problem could be described as a conflict between a pair of the 39 parameters, wherein the requirement for one parameter contradicts the requirement for a second parameter. Typical parameters are weight, strength, size, ease of operation, ease of repair, and device complexity. So, for example, contradictions might exist when:

- Strength has to be increased, while weight and size have to be decreased.
- Ease of operation has to be decreased while device complexity is being increased.

After analysing the ways the contradictions were resolved in the patents, Altshuller concluded that there were only 40 generic inventive principles being used to resolve the contradictions in full.

11.7.3 *The* Scientific *Perspective*

Altshuller concluded that if a specific problem could be formulated in terms of a contradiction between any two of the 39 generic parameters, there was a high probability that the type of solution to the problem would be the same type of solution used in the patents to solve the problem posed by the contradiction between those two generic parameters. So all a problem solver had to do to use TRIZ would be to formulate the problem in terms of the contradiction, look up the generic solution that had been employed in the past, and use those generic solutions as a basis for developing a solution to the problem solver's specific problem.

11.7.4 The Functional *Perspective*

Perceived from the *Functional* perspective, TRIZ consists of the following process:

1. Identifying and gaining an understanding of the specific problem.
2. Classifying the problem to match a pair of contradictions.
3. Determine which generic problem-solving approach was used to solve the problem posed by the pair of contradictions.
4. Adapt those generic problem-solving approaches to solve the specific problem.

In addition, as Hillel is reported to have said in the Babylonian Talmud, "All the rest is commentary – now go and study it" (Rodkinson 1903).

11.8 Working Backwards from the Solution

The traditional approach to problem-solving is generally working forward, you start with a problem and you develop the solution. The systems approach on the other hand visualizes a solution (Section 7.11), and then works back to the problem (Ackoff 1978, Hitchins 1992: p. 120). In other words, "begin with the end in mind", Covey's Habit 2 (Covey 1989).

The systems approach:

1. Formulates the problem using the Problem Formulation Template (Section 14.3). The FCFDS is a visualization in general terms of the application of the solution in the problematic situation.
2. Identifies a template that suits the FCFDS. If we can't identify a template, we create one. However that should be the last resort because templates (Chapter 14) help to minimize errors of omission (Section 4.4). The solution is the creation and application of the solution in the undesirable situation.
3. Work back from the solution towards the problem. This can be thought of as climbing up the Waterfall (Section 14.9) instead of the traditional non-systems thinking approach of starting at the top and going down the Waterfall.

Examples in this book include:

- Creating the annotated outline (Section 14.1) before writing the document.
- Creating the student exercise presentation template (Section 14.7) before creating the presentation.

11.9 Summary

Chapter 11 provided seven process tools for systems engineers and project managers. In the systems approach, the generic problem-solving process is seen as a Causal Loop in which the solution is evolved and the traditional linear problem-solving process is but one iteration of that loop. This chapter then discussed the Cataract Methodology and its advantages and continued by discussing PDCA and pointing to some examples of PDCA in use. The process for creating technical and other project documents discussed next minimizes waste in document production, as well as saving time. This chapter filled two gaps in the current paradigm. The first gap is that while there is a focus on process in the current non-systems approach to project management and systems engineering, there is no guidance or process for tackling a problem or starting a project. This chapter discussed one. The second gap is that while there is a lot of encouragement to think out of the box, there's very little information on how to actually do it. This chapter provided a systemic and systematic approach to finding out-of-the-box solutions. This chapter concluded with a process from working backwards from the solution which saves time and minimizes errors in problem-solving.

References

Ackoff, R. L. 1978. *The Art of Problem-solving*. New York: John Wiley & Sons.

Arthur, L. J. 1992. *Rapid Evolutionary Development*. New York: John Wiley & Sons.

Athey, T. H. 1982. *Systematic Systems Approach. An Integrated Method for Solving Systems Problems*. Englewood Cliffs, NJ: Prentice-Hall.

Barry, K., E. Domb, and M. S. Slocum. 2007. *TRIZ - What Is TRIZ?* Accessed 31 October 2007. http://www.triz-journal.com/archives/what_is_triz/.

Bentley, C. 1997. *PRINCE2: A Practical Handbook*. Oxford: Butterworth Heinemann.

Boyd, J. 1995. "The Essence of Winning and Losing," 28 June 1995 Presentation. Accessed 13 November 2017. www.pogoarchives.com.

Covey, S. R. 1989. *The Seven Habits of Highly Effective People*. New York: Simon & Schuster.

Denzler, D. W. R., and J. E. Kasser. 1995. "Designing Budget Tolerant Systems." In the 5th Annual International Symposium of the NCOSE. St Louis, MO.

DERA. 1997. *DERA Systems Engineering Practices Reference Model*. Farnborough, Hampshire: Defence Evaluation and Research Agency (DERA).

Dictionary.com. 2013. "Problem." *Dictionary.com*. Accessed 15 May 2013. http://dictionary.reference.com/.

Fischer, A., S. Greiff, and J. Funke. 2012. "The Process of Solving Complex Problems." *The Journal of Problem-solving*, no. 4 (1):19–42.

Hitchins, D. K. 1992. *Putting Systems to Work*. Chichester, England: John Wiley & Sons.

Hitchins, D. K. 2007. *Systems Engineering: A 21st Century Systems Methodology*. Chichester, England: John Wiley & Sons.

Kasser, J. E. 1995a. *Applying Total Quality Management to Systems Engineering*. Boston: Artech House.

Kasser, J. E. 1995b. "Improving the Systems Engineering Documentation Production Process." In the 5th Annual International Symposium of the NCOSE.

Kasser, J. E. 2000. "A Web Based Asynchronous Virtual Conference: A Case Study." In The INCOSE - Mid-Atlantic Regional Conference. Reston, VA.

Kasser, J. E. 2005. "Introducing the Role of Process Architecting." In The 15th International Symposium of the International Council on Systems Engineering (INCOSE). Rochester, New York.

Kasser, J. E. 2016. "The Nuts and Bolts of Systems." In the 11th International Conference on System of Systems Engineering. Kongsberg, Norway.

Kasser, J. E., and D. K. Hitchins. 2013. "Clarifying the Relationships between Systems Engineering, Project Management, Engineering and Problem-solving." In Asia-Pacific Council on Systems Engineering Conference (APCOSEC). Yokohama, Japan.

Kasser, J. E., and R. Schermerhorn. 1994. "Determining Metrics for Systems Engineering." In The 4th Annual International Symposium of the NCOSE. San Jose, CA.

Kasser, J. E., and Y.-Y. Zhao. 2017. "The Myths and the Reality of Problem-solving." In the 27th International Symposium of the International Council on Systems Engineering. Adelaide, Australia.

Kirton, M. J. 1994. *Adaptors and Innovators: Styles of Creativity and Problem-solving*. London: Routledge.

MIL-STD-2167A. 1998. *Defense System Software*. Washington, DC: United States Department of Defense.

Rodkinson, M. L., ed. 1903. *Tractate Sabbath in The Babilonian Talmud*. Boston: New Talmud Publishing Company.

Schön, D. A. 1991. *The Reflective Practitioner*. Aldershot, England: Ashgate.

Shenhar, A. J., and Z. Bonen. 1997. "The New Taxonomy of Systems: Toward an Adaptive Systems Engineering Framework." *IEEE Transactions on Systems, Man, and Cybernetics - Part A: Systems and Humans*, no. 27 (2):137–145.

Simon, H. A. 1973. "The Structure of Ill Structured Problems" *Artificial Intelligence*, no. 4 (3–4):181–201. doi: 10.1016/0004-3702(73)90011-8.

Teague, L. C. J., and C. W. Pidgeon. 1985. *Structured Analysis Methods for Computer Information Systems*. Chicago: Science Research Associates, Inc.

Valeri, S. 1999. *TRIZ: A Systematic Approach to Innovative Design*. Accessed 2 October 2008. http://insytec.com\Knowledge Base\What is TRIZ.

12

RISKS AND RISK MANAGEMENT

Risk management is:

* Something that is performed to identify and mitigate the effect of risks.
* An activity (process) that requires competency in the problem, solution and implementation domains.

Risk management is an inherent part of project management and engineering in the systems approach. Therefore, while the risk management process is the same, more or less, it is interdependent with the rest of the project management and systems engineering activities not independent, and it is integrated into normal project management and systems engineering. Accordingly, it is included in the Three Streams of Activities (Section 8.14); it is not an additional stream. This chapter discusses the following aspects of risks and risk management:

1. The nature of risks, in Section 12.1.
2. Risk management, in Section 12.2.
3. Risks and uncertainty, in Section 12.3.
4. Ways of assessing/estimating/measuring uncertainty and risk, in Section 12.4.
5. Risks and opportunities, in Section 12.5.
6. The traditional approach to risk management, in Section 12.6.
7. Myths in the traditional approach to risk management, in Section 12.7.
8. Risk-based analysis, in Section 12.8.
9. Risk mitigation and prevention, in Section 12.9.

12.1 The Nature of Risks

One definition of a risk is the possibility of suffering loss. Risks in general are characterized by:

1. The probability of occurrence; namely, how likely they are to happen.
2. The severity of the effect of the occurrence; namely, how bad things will be should that risk come to pass.

The probability and severity of risks are plotted in a Risk Rectangle (Section 5.4).

12.2 Risk Management

Risk management is
1. Defined in different ways in different domains as discussed below.
2. A tool for:
   1. Figuring out what might go wrong.
   2. Ways of preventing it going wrong or mitigating the effect when it goes wrong.
   3. Monitoring the risk prone activity to make sure that, if the risk materializes and actually happens, the planned mitigation actually takes place.
3. Is also known as contingency management.
4. Is performed all the time to some extent. For example,
   - When you drive your car, you carry a spare tire. This is because there was a time when there was a high probability of a puncture in the tire, the consequences of which made the car un-drivable. Accordingly, to mitigate that risk, cars carried spare tires. These days the probability of getting a flat tire is very much lower, but we still carry spare tires in our cars.
   - When you're approaching a highway from a side street and you want to enter the highway, you do risk management. You make a subconscious decision when to enter the highway based on the distance and speed of the other cars approaching the intersection on the highway.

In the traditional non-systems paradigms of project management, risk management tends to be taught and performed as a separate activity that can be performed by project managers or engineers. Not only that, but it is defined differently in different areas of the HKMF (Section 5.2). For example, definitions of risk management include:

- "A software engineering practice with processes, methods, and tools for managing risks in a project. It provides a disciplined environment for proactive decision-making to assess continuously what can go wrong (risks), determine what risks are important to deal with and implement strategies to deal with those risks" (Van Scoy 1992).
- "The process of identifying, assessing, and controlling risks arising from operational factors and making decisions that balance risk costs with mission benefits" (FM-100 1998).

12.3 Risks and Uncertainty

The literature of risk management uses terminology that may have slightly different meanings in the different publications. Sometimes the term risk incorporates uncertainty and sometimes it does not. For example in the military domain, risk is subdivided into:

1. *Threats*: defined risks that may hinder the achievement of objectives.
2. *Opportunities*: risks that may help in the achievement of objectives.

In this definition risk is equated with uncertainty and is included in both the threat and the opportunity. However, Perceptions from the *Continuum* HTP indicate that there is a difference between risk and uncertainty. Where:

1. *Uncertainty*: the lack of complete certainty, that is, the existence of more than one possibility. The "true" outcome/state/result/value is not known and could have a positive or a negative effect.

2. *Threat*: a state of uncertainty where the possibilities are negative, namely involve a loss, catastrophe, or other undesirable outcome.

3. *Opportunity*: a state of uncertainty where the possibilities are positive.

The use of these three terms removes the ambiguity from the term "risk" by not using the term. This is an example of dissolving the problem. However, since the literature uses the term risk, the terms "risk" and "threat" will be used interchangeably for the remainder of this chapter but have the same meaning.

12.4 Ways of Assessing/Estimating/Measuring Uncertainty and Risk

Perceptions from the *Quantitative* HTP provide ways of assessing/estimating/measuring uncertainty and risk. For example:

- *Measurement of uncertainty*: a set of probabilities assigned to a set of possibilities.
  - Example: "There is a 60% chance this market will double in five years"
- *Measurement of risk*: a set of possibilities each with quantified probabilities and quantified losses.
  - Example: "There is a 40% chance the proposed oil well will be dry with a loss of $12 million in exploratory drilling costs" (Hubbard 2009) (emphasis added).

These definitions of measurement are subjective, because somebody has to estimate the probability and quantify them. The traditional approach is to use the Risk Rectangle (Section 5.4).

12.5 Risks and Opportunities

This section discusses:

1. Characteristics of risks and opportunities in Section 12.5.1.
2. Categories of risk and opportunities in Section 12.5.2.

12.5.1 Characteristics of Risks and Opportunities

Risks and opportunities can be characterized in the following way:

1. Risks and opportunities concern the future: anything that happened in the past or is happening in the present is a certainty not a possibility. So it's not a risk, it's an event that has already happened.
2. Risks and opportunities involve change: changes can be in places, actions, opinions, etc.
3. Risks and opportunities involve choices: because once a risk has been identified, a decision has to be made if something is or is not going to be done about. And if the decision is made to mitigate that risk, choices will have to be made as to what to do, what action to take, to mitigate the risk.
4. Risk is unavoidable; opportunities may or may not appear: there is uncertainty in the outcome of every action we take. For example, even the simple making a cup of coffee contains uncertainty. The power might fail, so the coffee maker will not be able to brew the cup of coffee. Now in most environments the probability of that happening is a low, so we ignore it. However, just because we ignore it doesn't mean it isn't there.

12.5.2 Categories of Risks and Opportunities

Categories of risk and opportunities can be general or specific to the situation. Typical generic categories include:

- *Financial*: the risk that the funding needed to meet budgets will not be available when required or the risk of financial losses should the event materialize. For example, the risk of financial loss should an oil well be dry.
- *Information*: The risk that information used in an analysis is incomplete, out-of-date, or inaccurate. Also the risk that information produced is wrong, irrelevant to the customer or inappropriately disclosed.
- *Legal*: The risk that an initiative, or action, will be in breach of a statute, regulation, contract, copyright, and that the entity

(individual or organization) will face litigation as the result of the risk materialising.

- *Non-performance*: the risk that a product will not perform the desired functionality.
- *People*: The risk that capable and motivated staff will not be available to complete a project. For example as a result of resignations, turnovers, inability to hire, strikes, injury, poor managers, etc.
- *Safety*: the risk that something may be unsafe and not protected. For example there is no cage near rotating parts so there is a risk of a person coming into contact with rotating parts and the resultant injury.
- *Security*: the risk that is associated with the protection of confidentiality and the probability of successful unauthorized access to secure facilities.
- *Technology*: the risk that the technology will not be available as and when needed which is why the TRL was developed (Section 8.12.2).

12.6 The Traditional Approach to Risk Management

The traditional approach to risk management is represented by the following process:

1. Identify all the process and product risks you can by reviewing the WBS (Section 8.18) elements identifying the risks.
2. Analyze each risk to determine probability of occurrence and consequences/ impacts, along with any interdependencies and risk event priorities.
3. Plan mitigation actions and contingency plans.
4. Translate risk information into decisions and actions (both present and future) and implement those actions.
5. Track the risks.
6. Monitor the risk indicators and actions taken against risks.
7. Control the risks by monitoring them and correcting deviations from planned risk actions.
8. Communicate the risks to the team and management.
9. Provide visibility and feedback data internal and external to your program on current and emerging risk activities.

12.7 Myths in the Traditional Approach to Risk Management

As perceived from the HTPs (Section 10.1), the traditional approach to risk management contains a number of myths including:

1. Risk management is a separate activity from design and project management.
2. Risk can be quantified as a single number. This number is the probability of occurrence of the risk multiplied by the severity of the potential outcome.
3. Published project risk assessment models provide consistent and rationale measures of project risks.
4. Projects with high cost-contingencies succeed and do not have cost overruns.
5. Maintain risk registers for all the risks.

From the systems approach:

1. Risk management is not a separate activity from design and project management; it must be integrated in a holistic manner.
2. Risk should not be quantified as a single number. A single number is too simplistic. By quantifying risks as a single number the risks with high probability and high severity are dealt with, but risks with high severity and low probability are not. Risks with high severity must be mitigated even if the probability is low, because the outcome is so severe.
3. Published project risk assessment models do not provide consistent and rationale measures of project risks. By not combining the ability and severity into a single number, but considering them separately in the form of a Histogram (Section 2.9), it's possible to create a Risk Attribute Profile such as the one shown in Figure 9.1. The Probability Attribute Profile would show how sensitive the system is to risk, and the Severity Attribute Profile would show the safety of the system. It would also be possible to compare different designs or proposals at the conceptual stage by comparing risk profiles as one of the selection criteria for selecting one of the designs. The assumption being the lower the risk profile, the higher the weighting to the selection criterion.

4. Projects with high cost-contingencies don't always succeed and often have cost overruns. Just because a project has a cost contingency doesn't mean it's not going to be poorly implemented.

5. Maintain risk registers for all the risks creates a lot of unnecessary work. Miller's Rule (Section 3.2.5) should generally be applied to maintain no more than the most important nine risks at each level.

12.8 Risk-Based Analysis

Risk-based analysis is a process for analysing risks. The traditional approach describes it as a separate process and not integrated into project management. In the systems approach, the process is part of the project management and systems engineering processes with all the non-risk-based analysis activities hidden. The risk-based analysis process is split into the traditional two parts; planning and doing. The planning section is basically as follows:

1. *Identification*: identify potential risks and their effects and store them in a List (Section 9.4). This list tends to be a database stored inside a project management tool. These risks may be process risks, or product risks. This activity is called contingency planning and mitigation failure analysis in the traditional paradigm. In the systems approach, it is integrated into all the states of the design process. Perceptions of the design from the *Continuum* HTP lead to questions such as,
   • What will happen if this... fails?
   • If... fails, how will the system behave?

2. *Analysis and classification*: the probability of occurrence and severity of the effect of each risk is analysed and the numbers assigned based on a scale that is agreed to by the interested or relevant project stakeholders. The scale may be project specific, or it may be adopted from some of the published Risk Rectangles (Section 5.4). Once the scale is agreed upon, it must not change for the duration of the project. When risks are reassessed and re-evaluated over time, and found to fall into a different area of the chart, they should be moved from one area of the chart to the other.

3. *Elaboration and study*: the risks are studied to discover their potential root causes. This provides an understanding of the nature of the risk. The Five Whys (Section 7.5) is one of the tools suitable for this purpose.
4. *Reduction assessment*: once the nature of the cause is understood, you can determine what needs to be done to either eliminate or reduce the probability of the risk occurring to an acceptable level.

The systems approach is to use perceptions from the *Continuum* HTP to seamlessly integrate the risk-based analysis process into the traditional workflow. In the product domain, risk-based analysis takes place during each state of the SDP. In the process domain, risk-based analysis takes place during the planning process (Section 8.11.2) each time the Project Plan (Section 8.11) is revised.

12.9 Risk Mitigation and Prevention

In the product domain, risk mitigation and prevention tends towards redundancy and higher reliability components to mitigate or prevent component failure. In the process domain, risk mitigation and prevention tends towards taking actions that prevent a risk from being experienced. For example, if a piece of equipment is needed for an activity and there is a risk of it not being available when needed, risk mitigation is to make sure that that equipment will be there when needed in working condition.

When planning a project using the working backwards from the solution methodology (Section 11.8), each activity and the products produced by that activity are analysed to identify the risks associated with the activity. Risk mitigation activities are inserted into the project timeline earlier as appropriate to either eliminate or mitigate the risks. For example, the whole concept of reorder levels in logistics and supply is risk mitigation. The workflow is analysed, and the consumption of material is noted. The time it will take from placing the order for additional material to the time that material is ready to be used in the production process is determined and sets the just-in-time order date. The amount of material consumed during that time is determined, and that sets the reorder level. Namely the material is reordered when the quantity drops to the reorder level. This concept can be used in the home as well. For example, if a household consumes five teabags a day, but only goes grocery shopping once a week, there is a risk of running out of teabags. In order to mitigate the risk, what is the minimum number of teabags that have to be stored in the kitchen to make sure that the household never runs out of teabags? The worst case situation would be running out of teabags the morning of shopping day. So the calculation is five teabags a day multiplied by the seven days of the week or 35 teabags. However the number 35 is only valid if the home runs out of teabags the evening before shopping day. So the amount of teabags used at breakfast on shopping day has to be added to the 35. That number then becomes the reorder level number. So when monitoring the level of teabags in the kitchen when the number of teabags drops to 38, teabags have to be added to the shopping list for the next week's grocery shopping. This is the whole concept of reorder levels used in the commercial world.

12.10 Summary

Chapter 12 pointed out that in the systems approach to project management, risk management is an inherent part of project management and systems engineering and is integrated into management and engineering instead of being a separate parallel activity. This chapter defined the nature of a risk and then discussed risk management, risks and uncertainty, ways of assessing, estimating, and measuring uncertainty, and risks and opportunities. This chapter discussed the traditional approach to risk management and some myths in the traditional approach to risk management and showed how the systems approach overcomes some of the defects and flaws in traditional risk management. After a discussion on risk-based analysis, this chapter concluded with a discussion on risk mitigation and prevention, showing how prevention can be included in the project planning process.

References

FM-100. 1998. *FM 100-14 Risk Management*, 23 April 1998. Houston, TX: U.S. Army AMEDD Center and School Fort Sam.

Hubbard, D. 2009. *The Failure of Risk Management: Why It's Broken and How to Fix It*. Hoboken, NJ: John Wiley & Sons.

Van Scoy, R. L. 1992. *Software Development Risk: Opportunity, Not Problem*. Pittsburgh, PA Software Engineering Institute.

13

SYSTEMS ENGINEERING TOOLS

This chapter discusses the following systems engineering tools:

1. Checkland's Soft Systems Methodology (SSM), discussed in Section 13.1.
2. The Concept of Operations Document (CONOPS), discussed in Section 13.2.
3. A Framework for Tackling Complexity, in Section 13.3.
4. Mathematical Tools, discussed in Section 13.4.
5. The Zone of Ambiguity, discussed in Section 13.5.

13.1 Checkland's Soft Systems Methodology

Checkland's Soft Systems Methodology (SSM) (Checkland and Scholes 1990):

- Is a tool for gaining an understanding of a problematic situation in social situations, situations in which people are involved, in a systemic and systematic manner.
- Was developed for the express purpose of dealing with soft problems in Layer 5 of the Hitchins-Kasser-Massie Framework (HKMF) (Section 5.2).
- Is used to convert an Ill-Structured Problem into a number of Well-Structured Problems (Section 5.3.2).
- Is a seven-stage customiszed version of part of the generic problem-solving process. "The function of stages 1 and 2 is to display the situation so that the range of possible, and, hopefully, relevant choices can be revealed, and that is the only function of those stages" (Checkland 1991: p. 166).

- Seems to be the most widely known version of SSM; there are others, such as Avison and Fitzgerald (Avison and Fitzgerald 2003).

This section describes this author's interpretation of Checkland's SSM. The interpretation is based on perceiving SSM from the HTPs (Section 10.1) and adapting SSM in the situation described in Section 13.1.2.

13.1.1 *The Seven Stages of SSM*

The seven stages of SSM are:

1. Recognizing the existence of a problematical or undesirable situation.
2. Expressing the real-world problematic situation.
3. Formulating root definitions of relevant systems of purposeful activity from different HTPs.
4. Building conceptual models of the systems named in the root definitions.
5. Comparing the conceptual models developed in Step 4 with the real-world situation documented in Step 2.
6. Identifying feasible and desirable changes.
7. Actions to improve the problem situation.

13.1.1.1 Stage 1: Recognizing the Existence of a Problematic or Undesirable Situation   This stage begins when a problem owner determines that an existing situation is undesirable and needs to be changed. The problem owner is someone who has or is given the authority and appropriate resources to initiate a project, to study the situation, to determine the cause or causes of undesirability, and recommend appropriate actions to make a transition from the existing undesirable or problematic situation to a FCFDS. The initial parts of the study are performed by the problem solver often an analyst.

13.1.1.2 Stage 2: Expressing the Real-World Problematic Situation   This is the stage that examines and documents the real-world problematic situation. The emphasis is on gaining an understanding of the real-world situation and documenting it. The original SSM documented the situation in hand-drawn Rich Pictures (Section 6.1.5) in accordance with the adage, "a picture is worth a thousand words".

SSM suggested three types of analysis be carried out on organizations in which people are involved.

1. *Analysis one*: the role analysis identifies the roles of three of the actors in the transformation. These three roles are:
   a. The "client" is the person or persons who caused the study to take place.
   b. The "would be problem solver" is whoever wishes to do something about the situation in question and "the intervention had better be defined in terms of their perceptions, knowledge and readiness to make resources available" in other words in the client's language.
   c. The "problem owner".
2. *Analysis two*: is based on a model that assumes a social system to be a continually changing interaction between three elements: roles, norms and values. Each continually defines, redefines, and is itself defined by the other two.
3. *Analysis three*: analyses the politics, "the processes by which differing interests reach accommodation". The analysis begins with the study of how power is expressed in the situation including authority (formal and informal), memberships of groups, committees, etc.

The analyst* perceives the problematic situation from a number of perspectives such as the HTPs (Section 10.1) collecting, sorting, and documenting the information. Examples of such observations include:

- Perceptions from the *Big Picture* perspective include:
  - The environment.
  - The boundary of the problematic situation.
  - Adjacent systems to the problematic situation.
  - The issues that the people involved in the situation think are problematical.

---

* Depending on the nature and scope of the problematic situation, the problem-solver may be a single analyst or a team with different disciplinary skills.

- Perceptions from the *Operational* perspective include:
  - The processes or transformations taking place in the situation. Each transformation process may be considered as a black box system, the input being an entity and the output being a transformed entity.
- Perceptions from the *Functional* perspective include:
  - The internal functions inside the processes or transformations (black box) perceived from the *Operational* HTP.
- Perceptions from the *Structural* perspective include elements slow to change including:
  - The organization chart.
  - Physical elements such as buildings, locations.
  - Information used in the functions.
  - How power is expressed in the situation including authority (formal and informal), memberships of groups, committees, etc.
- Perceptions from the *Quantitative* perspective include the following three minimal criteria for evaluating a process:
  1. ***Efficacy***: how well the process performs its intended task. This may not be the lowest cost process.
  2. ***Efficiency***: as measured by the amount of output divided by the amount of resources used.
  3. ***Effectiveness***: how well the process meets the longer-term aim.

Other criteria such as Ethical and Elegance may be added depending on the situation. A minimum value for each criterion should be set at the time the project begins.

13.1.1.3 Stage 3: Formulating Root Definitions of Relevant Systems   The perceptions from the *Operational* and *Functional* HTPs are summarized in root definitions.

A root definition expresses the core purpose of a purposeful activity system. That core purpose is always expressed as a transformation process in which some entity. The "input" is changed, or transformed, into some new form of that same entity, the "output". (Checkland and Scholes 1990: p. 33)

Any system generally can be conceived as being different things and performing different functions by the stakeholders many of which have no idea that a different perception exits. Different people have different ways of seeing things and belief systems, known as *Weltanschauung* (Checkland and Scholes 1990), worldviews or paradigms (Kuhn 1970). They may perceive problems or want different (and perhaps contradictory) remedies (solutions) to an undesirable situation or have different concepts of what the situation is all about.

In the development of SSM, the names of relevant systems had to be written in such a way that they made it possible to build a model of the system named. The names became known as "root definitions" since they express the core or essence of the perception to be modelled.

The root definition is a perception from the *Operational* HTP (Section 10.1). The simplest version of a root definition is "a system to do something" from the perspective of a stakeholder. However, perceptions from the *Continuum* HTP indicate that different stakeholders may have different root definitions. For example, a pub or bar could be (Kasser 2015: p. 134):

- *A profit making system* from the perspective of the owners.
- *An employment system* from the perspective of the (potential) employees.
- *A recreational system* from the perspective of the customers.
- *A social system* from the perspective of the local residents.
- *A revenue generating system* from the perspective of the taxation authority.

Each of these systems performs a different transformation process and can be considered as a subsystem of the whole.

13.1.1.3.1 CATWOE Checkland's root definitions are formulated as sentences that elaborate a transformation using six elements which are summed up in the template mnemonic CATWOE as follows:

- *Customers*: the victims or beneficiaries of a transformation process. These entities should be known as stakeholders since they have a stake in the process while the customers are the specific stakeholders who fund the transformation process.

- *Actors*: the stakeholders who perform the transformation process.
- *Transformation process*: the conversion of the input to an output, namely the purpose of a system.
- *Weltanschauung*: this world view, perspective, or paradigm (Kuhn 1970) which makes the transformation process meaningful in the context of the stakeholders. Perceptions from the *Continuum* HTP indicate that each stakeholder may have a different *Weltanschauung*.
- *Owner(s)*: the stakeholder(s) who has/have the power to start up and shut down the transformation process.
- *Environmental constraints*: elements that exist outside the system which it takes as given.

Checkland's version of a root definition is "a system to do something by means of something in order to achieve a goal or purpose". Checkland provides the following example of a root definition, "A householder-owned and manned system to paint a garden fence, by conventional-hand painting, in keeping with the overall decoration scheme of the properly, in order to enhance the visual appearance of the property" (Checkland and Scholes 1990: p. 36). The CATWOE template points to the following:

C: householder.
A: actor or person performing the transformation.
T: activity which transforms an unpainted garden fence into a painted fence.
W: amateur painting can enhance the appearance of the house.
O: householder.
E: hand painting.

The core of CATWOE is the pairing of transformation process T and the W, the Weltanschauung or worldview which makes it meaningful. For any relevant purposeful activity there will always be a number of different transformations by means of which it can be expressed, these deriving from different interpretations of its purpose. (Checkland and Scholes 1990: p. 35)

Table 13.1 Apparent Relationship between SSM's CATWOE and the HTPs

CATWOE	HOLISTIC THINKING PERSPECTIVE (HTP)
Client/customer	*Big picture*
Actor	*Operational*
Transformation	*Functional* and *Quantitative*
Weltanschauung	*Big Picture*
Owner	*Big Picture*
Environment	*Big Picture*

Perceptions from the *Generic* HTP indicate that this sentence is also an example of a Mission Statement (Section 8.9), a statement which is used as a way of communicating the purpose of an organization. Thus it seems that root definitions may be considered as Mission Statements and CATWOE can provide a template for Mission Statements. The CATWOE template seems to align with some of the HTPs (Section 10.1) as shown in Table 13.1.* The *Quantitative, Structural, Generic,* and *Continuum* HTPs are not implicitly invoked in SSM, and the *Scientific* HTP is implied by the findings of the study using SSM.

13.1.1.4 Stage 4: Building Conceptual Models of the Relevant Systems In this stage the analyst builds a set of models of each transformation process which is considered as a system. Once the set of models is complete, if there are more than nine models in accordance with Miller's Rule (Section 3.2.5), some of them should be combined into one or more complex models by appropriate grouping of functions. A useful tool for doing the grouping or aggregation task is the N^2 Chart (Section 2.10).

The model description should be in a format or language understood by all the stakeholders in the situation (Checkland and Scholes 1990, Chapter 2). Suitable tools to use include Rich Pictures (Section 6.1.5), Flowcharts (Section 2.7), PERT Charts (Section 8.10), Causal Loops (Section 6.1.1) or any process modelling language. Perceptions from the *Generic* HTP indicate that this model is also known as a "to-be" model in Business Process Reengineering (BPR).

---

* The boundaries do not align directly because the decomposition of systems thinking is different.

13.1.1.5 Stage 5: Comparing Conceptual Models with Reality The purpose of this stage is to generate debate about possible changes which might be made within the perceived problem situation. This is the stage in which the conceptual models built in Stage 4 are compared with real world expression at Stage 2. The work at this stage may lead to the reiteration of Stages 3 and 4. Perceptions from the *Generic* HTP indicate that this stage could also be known as a "gap analysis" which identifies the difference between the real world and the conceptual model. Checkland identifies the following four approaches for doing the comparison; ordered questioning, comparing history with model prediction, general overall comparison and model overlay.

1. **Ordered questioning**: an approach which can be used when the real world situation is very different from the conceptual model. The system models are used to open up debate about change. The model is used as a source of questions to ask of the existing situation. The questions are written down and answered systematically. The answers to the questions can provide illumination of the perceived problem. Perceptions from the *Generic* HTP indicate that Active Brainstorming (Section 7.1) which can be used irrespective of the relationship between the real-world and the conceptual model encompasses Ordered Questioning.

2. **Comparing history with model prediction**: a comparison method which reconstructs a sequence of events in the past and compares what had happened with what should have happened if the relevant conceptual model has actually been implemented. In this way, the meaning of the models can be exhibited and satisfactory of comparison can be reached. Checkland also warned that this method of comparison should be used carefully because it could reveal the inadequacies of the actual procedure and people might interpret the results as offensive recrimination concerning their past performance.

3. **General overall comparison**: identifies the features of the conceptual models that are especially different from the real-world and the reasons for the differences. This comparison is also generally discussed in terms of the "Whats"

(*Operational* HTP) and "Hows" (*Functional* HTP). Stages 3 and 4 produces systems models which themselves derive from the careful naming, in root definitions, of human activity systems which are relevant to the problem situation and to its improvement.

4. **Model Overlay**: overlays the conceptual model based on the chosen root definition with the second model of the real-world. The second model should have as near as possible the same form as the conceptual model; in other words, it is based on the same template. The direct overlay of one model on the other reveals the gap.

13.1.1.6 Stages 6 and 7: Action to Improve the Existing Situation   Stage 6 is the stage in which feasible and desirable changes are identified and discussed. Once consensus is reached, Stage 7 is the realization stage in which the changes are implemented. Checkland recognized three kinds of changes:

1. **Changes in structure**: changes made to those parts of reality which do not change during normal operations.
2. **Changes in procedure**: changes to the dynamic elements.
3. **Changes in attitude**: changes to the behaviour appropriate to various roles, as well as changes in the readiness to rate certain kinds of behaviour as "good" or "bad" relative to others.

Changes in structure and procedure are easy to specify and relatively easy to implement. At least, these can be done by the people who have authority or influence. Attitude on the other hand is relatively difficult to change because one must first understand why people have that attitude and what must be done to motivate them to change their attitude.

13.1.2 The Command, Control, Communications, and Intelligence (C3I) Group Morale Case Study

The discussion on SSM has been abstract, so this section provides an example of how SSM can be used (Kasser 2013b). This section tells the anecdote of how SSM was adapted and combined with the systems approach to problem-solving to investigate an organizational problem in a government organization. The case study has been set in the context of a fictional organization in a fictitious country. In early 2000, the Defence Systems and Technology Department (DSTD) within the government of Engaporia* performed a variety of research tasks that were aimed at upgrading the national Defence systems, and the acquisition and implementation of appropriate technology in the Engaporean Defence environment. DSTD worked in close cooperation with the Engaporean Defence Forces (EDF). At that time, the members of the Command, Control, Communications (C3), and Intelligence (C3I) group within the DSTD were concerned about the effect an impending reorganization would have on their jobs. They were concerned because they had the impression that they were underperforming because DSTD wanted them to do more research than they were doing and because the group's Research Leader was not spending any time with the group. The members of the group were so concerned about these issues that their morale had suffered and key members of the group were seriously considering leaving the DSTD for other employment. The group's Research Leader and the DSTD Big Chief were so concerned about the situation that they asked the Systems Engineering Centre at Hypothetical University to investigate the situation as a task under an existing task-ordered research contract. This section discusses the anecdote providing analysis and comments in the form of footnotes.

After receiving the task and analysing the situation, the plan† for the intervention investigation in the form of the systems engineering problem-solving approach to tackling a problem shown in Figure 11.3. This section just covers:

- *Task 2*: understand the situation and define the root cause (problem) discussed in Section 13.1.2.1.
- *Task 6*: perform trade-off to find the optimum solution discussed in Section 13.1.2.2.
- *Task 7*: formulate strategies and plans to implement the preferred option discussed in Section 13.1.2.3.

---

* A fictitious third-world country, ex-British colony used to provide a context for Case Studies in my classes in systems engineering.

† This section focuses on the activities and products elements of the task. Cost, schedule, and other resource information are omitted.

13.1.2.1 Task 2: Define the Problem   This task began with a review of the relevant documentation.* The documentation provided was sparse and mostly useless. However, what was gleaned was that:

- The situation had persisted for some time.
- The DSTD Big Chief was concerned about the situation.
- A consultant had been called in some months previously to analyse the situation and make recommendations with little apparent effect.
- This investigation would be the same type of activity that the C3I group performed on other groups with the EDF.

Once the information had been harvested from the documentation, preliminary discussions were held with the Research Leader to clarify points that were obscure in the documentation and receive an update on the situation. Then, after some consideration it was agreed that:

1. The systems engineering problem-solving process was an appropriate approach to resolving the situation since the task statement was a well-structured problem with a clear, singular objective.
2. The CONOPS for the solution system that would describe the activities performed by the C3I group would be part of the final report.

This was a people intensive situation; the solution system in the FCFDS would probably be a rearrangement of the work performed by the existing (and possibly) additional personnel. Consequently, the intervention approach to gain an understanding of the situation was based on SSM (Checkland 1993: pp. 224–225). The CATWOE elements in this instance were:

- *Customers*: The C3I group had two distinct groups of customers, namely:
  1. *External customers* in the form of the EDF where a client element within the EDF perceived a problem which was reported to DSTD who tasked the C3I group to

---

* This is not an unusual first step.

examine the situation and recommend improvements in a timely manner.*

2. *Internal customers* in the form of DSTD management and other groups within DSTD.

- *Actors*: the members of the C3I group, the Research Leader and the Big Chief.
- *Transformation process*: The then existing transformation process performed by the C3I group, which was based on scenarios describing the work performed by members of the C3I group gleaned from the documentation and the preliminary discussions, is shown in Figure 13.1. The group's goal was the improvement of the effectiveness of the EDF by performing organizational analysis tasks on elements of the EDF and then providing timely reports and recommendations to those elements (customers). The analysis sub-process was further broken out as shown in Figure 13.2. The transformation process was a "standard" process in which the C3I group collected relevant data about the specific situation they were investigating, performed a comparison with a conceptual reference model and acquired insight as a result of the analysis. The group then produced a timely report. At the same time the group reported the insight to DSTD and was expected to publish research papers in their field of expertise.†
- *Weltanschauung*: the first phase of the study quickly identified that the Big Chief, the Research Leader, and the members of the C3I group all seemed to have a different *Weltanschauung*.
- *Ownership*: resided in the DSTD.
- *Environmental constraints*: external and internal as follows:
  - *External*: military activities were changing; there was a so-called "revolution in military affairs" under way and military organizations were changing, and consequently, their external customers were changing. The reports of the

---

* Within two weeks or less.
† This study performed the same task on the C3I group as the C3I group performed on their customers.

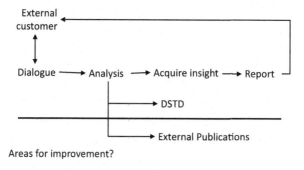

Figure 13.1   The transformation process.

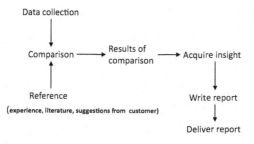

Figure 13.2   The analysis process.

group's investigations needed to be made in a timely manner in this changing environment.

* *Internal*: within DSTD, namely the Research Leader and indirectly the Big Chief.

13.1.2.1.1 The Apparent Undesirable Situation   The CATWOE information together with the domain knowledge pertinent to such situations provided sufficient information to formulate the preliminary hypothesis that the cause of the undesirable situation lay in the differences in *Weltanschauungs* exacerbated by a communications breakdown between the Big Chief, the Research Leader, and the members of the C3I group.

13.1.2.1.2 Supporting or Refuting the Preliminary Hypothesis   The investigator had to study the C3I group with minimal interference to their on-going activities. This translated to planning and carrying out short interviews with selected people and a sample of the remainder.

The algorithm for determining which members of the C3I group would be interviewed was as follows:

- Identify specific key persons who had to be interviewed. These turned out to be the Research Leader and the Big Chief.
- Sample the members of the C3I group. The sampling algorithm was simply to telephone each person for an appointment. If the phone was answered, an appointment for an interview was made; if the phone was not answered, the next person on the list was telephoned.

13.1.2.1.3 The C3I Group's Weltanschauung   After thanking the person for taking the time for the interview (Section 8.13) and explaining the sampling algorithm,* each interview began with the following five open-ended questions:

1. What do you like doing?[†]
2. What do you not like doing?
3. What does the group do?[‡]
4. What does the person feel the group should be doing but isn't?[§]
5. What does the person feel the Big Chief wants the group to be doing?[¶]

These questions and the subsequent short dialogue provided the maximum amount of information in the minimum time. The answers to the starter questions by the various members of the group were aggregated and are summarized below.

---

* The interview began with common courtesy and explained the sampling algorithm to avoid upsetting members of the C3I group.
† This was an interview about the nature of the person's work. Like and dislike of work has an effect on morale. The first two questions were posed to determine if the nature of the work could have been a cause of poor morale and were also an icebreaker to start the conversation moving.
‡ This question was posed to determine if (1) there was a common vision of the purpose of the group, and (2) to confirm the transformation process shown in Figures 13.1 and 13.2.
§ This question was posed to obtain ideas for improving the work and obtain buy-in to the results of the intervention.
¶ This question was posed to determine/confirm if there was a communications gap within the hierarchy of the DSTD.

13.1.2.1.4 What the Individual Likes

- The range of activities.
- Contributing to improvement of defence.
- Learning new things.
- Research.
- Interacting with co-workers.
- Making a difference.
- Being a change agent.

13.1.2.1.5 What the Individual Dislikes*

- Uncertainty of the future.
- Work overload.
- Changing directions.
- Political agendas.
- Nugatory work.
- Rushing through the process.
- Interfacing with customer.[†]
- Working in a new area without an adequate foundation in the subject matter.
- Not being sure of what the Research Leader wants them to do.
- Conflicting instructions.
- Each task is different.
- Unsure how group fits into DSTD structure.
- Complexity.
- The shifting of the task from tactical to strategic.
- Research without a purpose.

13.1.2.1.6 What the Group Does

- Responds to client's demands.
- Goes into organizations and evaluates them.
- Analyse structures and processes.

---

* Responses to these questions confirmed the presence of a communications gap between the members of the group and the Research Leader.
† This was from an individual whose job required meeting with customers!

- Analysis is not necessarily compared with a reference model.
- Research into group's own methodologies.
- Research into organizations.
- Assess impact of technology on capabilities.
- Gets additional work through satisfied customers.
- Considers aspects of:
  - Command, Control and Communications (C3).
  - Organizational analysis.
- Supposed to be in research context but is in evaluation context.
- Emphasis on current or short term.

13.1.2.1.7 What the Person Feels the Group Should Be Doing but Isn't

- Continue task to help implement recommendations (enterprise improvement).
- What if ... simulations.
- Research.
- Removing uncertainty.
- Being more proactive in developing customers.
- Transition planning into new tasks.

13.1.2.1.8 What the Person Feels the Big Chief Wants the Group to Be Doing

- More or less the same.
- Apply more academic rigor.
- Quote "sources used" as basis for recommendations.
- Implement own research program.
- Continue to satisfy external client's needs.
- Publish more.
- Promulgate credibility by referencing underlying principles for recommendations.
- More research.
- "No idea, I only hear things second- and third-hand".*

---

* A definite communication gap.

13.1.2.1.9 Research Leader's Weltanschauung   The open-ended starter questions and findings are listed below.

13.1.2.1.9.1 Questions to the Research Leader

- What should the C3I group be doing?
- How well are they doing it?

The answers to the starter questions are summarized below.

13.1.2.1.9.2 What Should the C3I Group Be Doing?

- Ultimate goal is to provide information to determine if the investment should be in C3 or in weapons systems.
- Need to work on these to show importance.
- Determine if C3 makes a difference.
- Operational and organizational analysis, synthesis, and evaluation.
- Determine if people understand doctrine and equipment.
- Form Measures of Effectiveness (MOE) for C3.

13.1.2.1.9.3 How Well Are They Doing It?

- Strengths:
  - Work together well as teams.
  - Glowing reports from satisfied external customers.
- Weaknesses:
  - The way in which the job is done.
- Is management satisfied?
  - Yes and no.

13.1.2.1.9.4 Research Leader's Additional Comments
The Research Leader made the following additional comments:

- Not unhappy with rate of change.
- Does not want to interfere with a good group.
- Group needs to evolve faster than customers and add new skills.

- Research Leader is not spending time with group because there are more urgent problems elsewhere.*
- Reduction of budget will have an effect.

13.1.2.1.10 Big Chief's Weltanschauung   The Big Chief was asked to:

- Comment on group.
- Define "research".
- Provide metrics for successful "research".

The answers to the questions are summarized below.

13.1.2.1.10.1 Comments on Group

- Group performed a useful role.
- She recognized the strengths of the group.
- Group had credibility with customers.
- Group was evolving too slowly.
- Good use of empirical techniques in the group coupled with a lack of "scientific" theoretical background.
- Analyses seemed shallow.
- Needed to use a stronger research based methodology on what they did.
- Needed to add researchers to the group.
- Failed to communicate items of importance.

13.1.2.1.10.2 Definition of "Research"

- Was not publish, publish, publish.
- Was:
  - Document in a manner consistent with Scientific Method (Section 11.1.10.5.1).
  - Use the Scientific Method in their work.

---

* The Research Leader seems to be applying Management by Exception (Section 8.7). However, the C3I group perceived it in a negative manner. There is a communication issue here.

13.1.2.1.10.3 Metrics for Successful "Research"

- Needed to be convinced on authority of conclusions.*
- Needed to quote from the literature to reinforce conclusions and justify methodology.†

13.1.2.1.11 Conclusions from the Interviews The interview responses were analysed with the following conclusions about the nature of the undesirable situation.

1. There was indeed a communications issue, namely a lack of communications between the Big Chief, the Research Leader, and the members of the C3I group. As a consequence, the group:
   a. Was uncertain about their future.
   b. Had an impression that the Research Leader perceived their work negatively.
   c. Perceived a conflict between performing their organizational analysis tasks for their customers and performing research.
2. There was an emphasis on short term or current problems.
3. The group needed to consider the enterprise architectural framework in which the customer organization operated both in the present and future (*Temporal* HTP).
4. The work straddled the boundary between soft systems and hard systems which meant they were pushing the envelope but had an excellent "name making" and publishing opportunity.

13.1.2.2 Task 6: Select the Preferred Option After considering several solutions,‡ the investigator felt that the perceived conflict felt by the group between performing their organizational analysis tasks and publishing in the research literature could best be overcome by modifying

---

* By citing references to the literature that support the conclusions.
† An application of Critical Thinking.
‡ Not described in this chapter since this chapter focuses on describing an application of SSM.

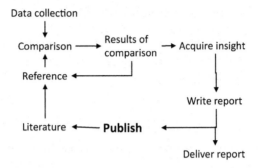

Figure 13.3   C3I group conceptual functional reference model.

the transformation model shown Figure 13.1 into the CONOPS (for what they should be doing) shown in Figure 13.3. The extra step in the modified process would be to take the same information in the report to the customer and reformat it for publication in a conference proceedings or journal.

13.1.2.3 Task 7: Formulate Strategies and Plans to Implement the Preferred Option   The strategies and plans to implement the preferred option took the form of a final report presentation containing an overview of the findings,* a description of the study methodology, the recommendations and an Action Plan.

13.1.2.3.1 The Recommendations to DSTD   The recommendations to DSTD were to open communications channels between the Big Chief, the Research Leader and the C3I group. Specifically the recommendations were for:

1. DSTD Management to remove the fear of "research" and uncertainty about future.
2. For the C3I group to:
   a. Take continuing education courses† on how to do "research", Command, Control, Communications, Computers, Intelligence, Surveillance and Reconnaissance (C4ISR)

---

* Presented first and then amplified later in the presentation.
† The intervention was performed by academics from Hypothetical University.

Architecture Frameworks, and SSM as applied to Information Systems.

b. Develop personal career plans.

c. Modify their methodology by adding architecture issues to customer dialogue and considering medium and long term impacts.

d. Develop conceptual models based on the literature for appropriate customer organizations which would speed task completion,* provide an objective basis for work and allow structured analysis of impact of technology to units and force structure.

e. Reorganize to match current and expanded functions to personal skills/likes dislikes.

f. Team within the group for publication in journals and at the annual Engaporean Systems Engineering Conference the following year.

g. Acquire mentors within DSTD on research methods, C4ISR Architecture Frameworks, and systems methodologies.

3. Carry out the Action Plan.

13.1.2.3.2 The Action Plan The Action Plan contained the following four elements:

1. DSTD Management to remove uncertainty about the performance and future of group within 30 days.†

2. Members of the C3I group to attend courses starting within two months.

3. Members of the C3I group to acquire mentors within DSTD within three months.

4. Create a target for acceptance for publication of at least three manuscripts within 12 months.‡

---

* By the use of pattern matching (*Generic* perspective).

† Each recommendation was quantified to be specific requirements.

‡ Acceptance is an output measurement. Specifying submissions for publications was useless because it did not require any academic standards and rigor to be applied to the manuscript. Publication was also useless because publications dates depended on the specific publication.

13.1.2.4 Preparation and Delivery of the Final Report   With the agreement of the DSTD customer, the report was delivered in the form of a PowerPoint presentation.* The presentation was discussed with the Big Chief and then made to the Research Leader and members of the C3I group. The format of the presentation also provided an example of how to implement some of the recommendations and included:

- An explanation of the sampling algorithm, stating that there was not a 100% sample, and that not being sampled did not equate to unimportance.
- References to the literature for the methodology and conceptual models providing some academic rigour.[†]

13.1.3 Comments

The *Big Picture*, *Operational* and *Functional* HTPs line up with CATWOE as shown in Table 13.1. In addition:

- The *Structural* HTP was used to develop the DSTD organization chart to match the people into the hierarchy and identify which people had to be interviewed and who could be sampled.
- The "to be" or reference model came from prior experience, namely going beyond systems thinking and using perceptions from the *Generic* and *Temporal* HTPs.
- The *Temporal* HTP provided the background information that an earlier intervention had not been successful which is why this intervention was invoked. This perception identified a need to also find out the reason for the failure of the previous intervention.
- The conclusion from the analysis of the initial observations produced the hypothesis (*Scientific* HTP) that the situation

---

* The intervention was performed within 40 man-hours. Creating a written report would have doubled the time and cost of the study. It was felt that a presentation would serve the purpose of distributing the findings of the intervention to the necessary personnel in the C3I group.
† As examples they could follow.

was the result of a failure in the hierarchical communications path between DSDT management and the C3I group. The interview questions were then phrased to test the hypothesis.

- Perceptions from the *Continuum* HTP points out that each of the different SSM actors may have a different Weltanschauung which may need to be considered. And indeed this was the cause of the undesirable situation in this instance.

13.1.3.1 Lessons Learned   The Lessons Learned (Section 9.3) from the experience included:

- Perceptions are more important than the reality when dealing with people. It was the perception that the Research Leader was unhappy with the C3I group that drove their morale down.
- Communications is the key to success. The failure in communications between the C3I group and DSDT upper management was a major contributor to the problematic situation.
- SSM needs to be tailored to the situation, like all methodologies.
- The HTPs were useful in scoping the intervention and determining the key interview questions.
- Hypotheses can be made based on a small data sample by experts who compare the situation at hand with similar situations that have been observed in the past (*Generic* HTP). However, the analyst performing the intervention has to make sure that if additional data does not fit the hypothesis, the extraneous data is not discarded but rather the data are verified and if found to be correct, the hypothesis is modified to fit the data.

13.2 Concept of Operations

A Concept of Operations Document (CONOPS) is:

- A tool for facilitating communication among the various stakeholders in a project.

- A descriptive document; its contents include descriptions of:
  - The problematic or undesirable current system or situation.
  - The justification and nature of the changes.
  - The FCFDS.
  - A summary of the impacts of the new system and its development.

There are several versions of the CONOPS in the literature including IEEE Standard 1320–1998.

13.2.1 IEEE Standard 1320–1998

The IEEE Guide for Information Technology – System Definition – Concept of Operations (CONOPS) Document is a document template containing an Annotated Outline (Section 14.1) for the contents of a CONOPS (IEEE Std 1362 1998). The relevant sections which cover the product and process are:

3.0 Current system or situation.

3.1 Background, objectives, and scope.

3.2 Operational policies and constraints.

3.3 Description of the current system or situation.

3.4 Modes of operation for the current system or situation.

3.5 User classes and other involved personnel.

3.6 Support environment.

4.0 Justification for and nature of changes.

4.1 Justification of changes.

4.2 Description of desired changes.

4.3 Priorities among changes.

4.4 Changes considered but not included.

5.0 Concepts for the proposed system.

5.1 Background, objectives, and scope.

5.2 Operational policies and constraints.

5.3 Description of the proposed system.

5.4 Modes of operation.

5.5 User classes and other involved personnel.

5.6 Support environment.

6.0 Operational scenarios.

7.0 Summary of impacts.

7.1 Operational impacts.

7.2 Organizational impacts.

7.3 Impacts during development.

8.0 Analysis of the proposed system.

8.1 Summary of improvements.

8.2 Disadvantages and limitations.

8.3 Alternatives and trade-offs considered.

13.2.2 *Creating a CONOPS*

The procedure to create a CONOPS is as follows:

1. Locate previously published CONOPS or a standard such as the IEEE template (Section 13.2.1) to use as a Template (Chapter 14).
2. Modify the template table of contents to fit your situation.
3. Create the Annotated Outline (Section 14.1) to show the contents of each section.
4. List the scenarios the CONOPS will cover in both the product and process domain as appropriate.
5. Fill in the Annotated Outline as appropriate to the situation.
6. For each scenario, visualize the scenario (Section 7.11) from:
   a. The *Operational, Functional,* and *Structural* HTPs, identifying inputs, outputs, and resources used or needed.
   b. The *Generic* and *Continuum* HTPs to identify similar scenarios in other situations, differences between the scenario and similar scenarios in other situations, and the effect of things failing or not being available when needed.
   c. The *Temporal* HTP to understand how the need arose and to identify any lessons that need to be learned (Section 9.3).
7. Follow the process for creating a document (Section 11.4) to complete the document.

13.3 A Framework for Tackling Complexity

Observations of the way people manage complexity have identified a dichotomy; managing complexity seems to be a major problem for some people and a way of life for others who just get on with managing it. The dichotomy can be explained by postulating that are two paradigms.

1. The non-systems paradigm in which managing complexity is a major problem.
2. The systems paradigm in which it is "a way of life" (Hitchins 1998).

Further observation of the systems paradigm for managing complexity is that it is mostly used without people realising they are using systems thinking to manage complexity. For example, complex systems that are being managed include fleets of cruise ships, financial and banking networks, oil rigs, airlines, transportation systems, and hospitals. Accordingly, before presenting the framework, the non-systems approach to tackling complexity needs to be discussed so that the different paradigm represented by this framework will be understood.

13.3.1 *The Non-Systems Approach*

The non-systems approach seems to have difficulty tackling complexity for several reasons including:

1. Not distinguishing between subjective and objective complexity discussed in Section 13.3.1.1.
2. Creating artificial complexity (Section 13.3.1.1) due to poor system decomposition and partitioning.
3. The systems optimization paradox discussed in Section 13.3.1.2.
4. The boundary of the system is not fixed for all purposes discussed in Section 13.3.2.3.

13.3.1.1 *Not Distinguishing between Subjective and Objective Complexity*
The non-systems approach does not distinguish between subjective and objective complexity. This is probably because the English language, rich as it is, does not have any words that uniquely define and distinguish the concepts of "subjective complexity" and "objective complexity" other than the word "difficult" which means subjective complexity. The commonly used words "complex" and "complicated" have been used for both concepts interchangeably

because dictionary definitions of their meanings contain both a subjective and objective meaning. However, once a distinction is made (*Continuum* HTP):

- Subjective complexity
  - Can be defined as, "people don't understand it and can't get their heads round it" (Sillitto 2009), namely difficulty.
  - Appears to have a different value for different observes, for example:

    > *A system is commonly thought of as 'complex' if it is made up of a large number of parts interacting in a nonsimple [sic] way. The linguistic usage, implying as it does that complexity is an attribute of the system itself, obscures the fact that complexity is a relation between an observer and the thing observed, i.e., that the same system can be seen as of greater or lesser complexity by different observers or even by a single observer before and according to comments, after he comes to 'understand' it.* (Conant 1972)

  - Can be measured using the levels of difficulty that range from "easy" to "hard" (Section 5.3.1).
- Objective complexity:
  - Can be defined as, "the problem situation or the solution has an intrinsic and measurable degree of complexity" (Sillitto 2009).
  - Has various definitions in the literature which makes measurement difficult; these definitions include:
    - "A complex system usually consists of a large number of members, elements or agents, which interact with one another and with the environment"* (El Maraghy et al. 2012).
    - "Colwell (Colwell 2005) defined thirty-two complexity types in twelve different disciplines and domains such as projects, structural, technical, computational, functional, and operational complexity" (El Maraghy et al. 2012).

---

* According to this definition the only difference between a system and a complex system is in the interpretation of the meaning of the word "large".

- "The measure of uncertainty in achieving the functional requirements (FRs) of a system within their specified design range" (Suh 2005).*
- Tomiyama D'Amelio, Urbanic, and El Maraghy introduced two different types of complexity: (i) complexity by design and (ii) the intrinsic complexity of multidisciplinary, from the viewpoint of knowledge structure (Tomiyama et al. 2007).
- Artificial complexity:
  - *An artefact of objective complexity defined as,* "a complex situation in which the non-pertinent aspects have not been abstracted out" (Kasser 2007).

The non-systems approach often does not differentiate between complexity and the structure of the problem because it includes the structure of the problem inside the definition of complexity, for example, "complex problems are equated to Wicked Problems" (Section 5.3.2.3) (APSC 2012). By including the structure of the problem inside the definition, the problem often becomes insurmountable (Section 5.3.2). This is because they are no solutions to Ill-Structured Problems. Ill-Structured Problems have to be converted to Well-Structured Problems before the undesirable situation can be transformed into a desirable situation (Simon 1973). The Problem Classification Framework (Section 5.3) abstracts objective complexity out of the issue and considers subjective complexity and the structure of the problem.

13.3.1.2 The Systems Optimization Paradox   The systems optimization paradox has been stated over the years in various ways including the following examples:

- "The principle of suboptimization [sic] states that optimization of each subsystem independently will not lead in general to a system optimum, and that improvement of a particular subsystem actually may worsen the overall system. Since every system is merely a subsystem of some

---

* Sun also stated the need to abstract out things that were not pertinent to the issues at hand.

larger system, this principle presents a difficult if not insoluble problem, - one that is always present in any major systems design" (Machol and Miles Jnr 1973 page 39).

- "Conventional systems engineering wisdom has it that if subsystems are optimized, then the system cannot be optimum" (Wymore 1997).

Accordingly, according to the principle of suboptimization a system can never be optimized, hence the paradox. The paradox in the principle of suboptimization is dissolve in the systems approach to system optimization because although Wymore articulated the paradox, he then used a mathematical approach to show that conventional wisdom was mistaken and how it was possible for systems engineering to ensure that optimum design of the subsystems can result in optimum design of the system. System optimization at one level is always a subsystem optimization of the meta-system. If any system is a subsystem of the containing or meta-system, then where does the optimization take place? The answer in the systems thinking paradigm is that system optimization at any level optimizes the interactions between the subsystems of that system level within the constraints imposed by the systems engineer of the meta-system. For example:

- Consider an allied naval convoy crossing the North Atlantic Ocean in 1942. The convoy is a system.* Each ship in the convoy can be considered as both a subsystem of the convoy, or as a system.† There was a CONOPS (Section 13.2) for the convoy.‡ There were separate CONOPS for the naval escort ships and the merchant ships describing the actions and interactions

---

* Some people might call it a System of Systems or a complex system.

† Alternatively, the naval ships could be one subsystem and the merchant marine ships a second subsystem of the convoy. Each ship is then a subsystem within the naval or civilian subsystem of the convoy. If there are ships from the navies of more than one allied country in the convoy, then the ships of each country could constitute a subsystem within the naval subsystem. The choice of subsystem partitioning depends on the issues being considered.

‡ The documents may not have been called CONOPS but would have contained much of the information in today's CONOPS.

of these subsystems of the convoy in various scenarios. The system was optimized to minimize the interactions between the individual ships.

- Consider the complex problem of docking two spacecraft (Kasser and Palmer 2005). Once the spacecraft are close, the problem is simplified by minimizing artificial complexity (Section 13.3.1.1) and creating a closed system view to only consider the:
  - Relative positions of the spacecraft.
  - Relative velocity of the spacecraft.
  - Relative alignment in X, Y, and Z orientation of the spacecraft.

The optimization problem is then set up in the context of a closed system view to produce a relative docking velocity close to zero with the docking collars on both spacecraft properly aligned.

13.3.2 The Systems Approach

The systems approach used by those who can deal with complexity seems to be based on a different paradigm and disssolves the problems faced by the non-system approach in the manner of a new paradigm (Kuhn 1970). The framework includes a number of interdisciplinary methodologies as summarized in the following sections:

1. Distinguishing between subjective and objective complexity as discussed in Section 13.3.1.1.
2. Reducing artificial complexity by abstracting out the non-pertinent aspects of objective complexity as discussed in Section 13.3.2.1.
3. Partitioning the system as discussed in Section 13.3.2.2.
4. Redrawing the boundary of the system to suit the purpose discussed in Section 13.3.2.3.
5. Attempting to dissolve the problem as discussed in Section 13.3.2.4.
6. Using the Problem Formulation Template (Section 14.3) to think through the problem and solution before taking any action.

13.3.2.1 Abstracting Out the Non-Pertinent Aspects of Objective Complexity The systems thinker abstracts out the non-pertinent aspects of the complexity by applying the following:

1. Minimizing artificial objective complexity by abstracting out non-pertinent aspects of the situation complexity (Section 5.3.2).
2. Applying the "Don't Care" situation (Section 3.2.2) to abstract out other non-pertinent aspects of the situation.

13.3.2.2 Partitioning the System "The choice of partitioning is a major factor in the efficacy of any system description" (Aslaksen and Belcher 1992). Thus optimal subsystem boundaries must be designed for simplicity, namely:

- To abstract (hide) non-relevant information.
- To bound subsystems into self-regulating or self-sufficient entities with maximal internal cohesion of subsystems and minimal coupling between them.
- That the maximum number of subsystems at any level of decomposition should generally be no more than 7 (±2) to comply with Miller's Rule (Section 3.2.5).

Maier and Rechtin recommend that the way to deal with high levels of complexity is to abstract the system at as high a level as possible and then progressively reduce the level of abstraction (Maier and Rechtin 2000: p. 6). However, as they point out:

- Poor aggregation and partitioning during development can increase complexity (i.e. artificial complexity) (Section 13.3.1.1).
- The concept that a complex system can be decomposed into a single set of smaller and simpler units omits an inherent characteristic of complexity, the interrelationships among the components (i.e. real-world complexity).

However, Simon set forth strong arguments for believing that hierarchic structure is the rule rather than the exception in physical, biological, social, symbolic, and many other types of systems. Accordingly, when trying to understand or create a complex system, start by assuming that that it has a hierarchic structure and is decomposable into subsystems within which the interaction of variables is relatively intense (maximize cohesion) and between which the interaction is relatively weak (minimize coupling), for if that is the case attention can be turned to the detailed workings of each subsystem (Simon 1962).

13.3.2.3 Redrawing the Boundary of the System to Suit the Purpose   A system is an abstraction from the real world of a set of objects, each at some level of decomposition, at some period of time, in an arbitrary boundary, crafted for a purpose (Kasser 2013a). The purpose is not in the system, it is in the mind of the person drawing the boundary that creates the system because people draw boundaries (Churchman 1979: p. 91). Accordingly, the boundary of the system need not be fixed for all purposes or from all perspectives. Thus, observe the situation from a number of viewpoints or perspectives on the Perspectives Perimeter (Chapter 10) instead of the complex and complicated single views discussed in Section 13.3.1.1. For example, consider:

- *A camera*: when we consider:
  - The device that takes the photograph or captures an image, we draw the system boundary around the camera.
  - The act of taking the photograph we redraw the system boundary to include the photographer.
  - Transporting the camera, we redraw the system boundary to include the transportation elements.
    Developing one system representation that includes all the elements for photographing and transportation and then requiring the elements under consideration for a specific situation to be abstracted out of the representation, creates artificial complexity (Section 13.3.1.1). The three separate simpler views, abstracted out of the real world. are simpler for understanding the various aspects of the use of a camera in photography.
- *A human being*: some areas of the real world can only be fully understood by examining the internal components of the system and observing it in action in its environment. Mechanical systems may be disassembled and reassembled, but some systems such as biological systems cannot

be disassembled without destroying the sample. Consider a human being, a biological system. To learn about:

- The interaction between internal subsystems we may have to observe the sample in action in specific situations and either observe or infer the interaction.
- The internal subsystems we have to dissect a sample of the system. Once dissected, an individual example cannot usually be restored to full functionality. However, we have learned something about the class of systems it represents which can be applied to other instances of the class of systems.
- *Two theories of electromagnetic wave propagation in physics.* Scientists use the:
  - Wave theory (Huygens 1690) to explain some aspects of electro-magnetic radiation.
  - Particle theory (Newton 1675) to explain other aspects.[*]

13.3.2.4 Attempting to Dissolve the Problem   Recognize that when faced with extremely complex problems, the best way to deal with them is to understand that the complexity may indicate that there is a defect in the current paradigm[†] and there is a need to look for an alternative paradigm (Kasser 1995) while trying to develop the solution in the current paradigm.

13.4 Mathematical Tools

Mathematical tools:

- Are used in the front-end of systems engineering in column A of the HKMF (Section 5.2) to analyse systems and situations.
- Used by systems engineers include: (Alexander and Bailey 1962, Wilson 1965, Chestnut 1965, Goode and Machol 1959)
  - Probability.
  - Single thread – system logic.

---

[*] Mind you this could also form the basis of an argument that there is no underlying theory of electronic-magnetic radiation.

[†] But not necessary the nature of the defect.

- Queuing theory.
- Game theory.
- Linear programming.
- Group dynamics.
- Simulation and modelling.
- Information theory.

13.5 The Zone of Ambiguity

The Zone of Ambiguity (Kasser 1997) is a tool for getting useful information from small sample sizes, a situation when conventional statistics are not valid.

13.5.1 Use of the Tool

The tool is best explained by an example describing how and why it was developed. This was a situation in which 13 reasons for something not happening were identified and a survey was performed to determine the degree of agreement or disagreement with each reason (Kasser 1997). The three key questions which led to the development of the tool came from the *Quantitative* HTP were:

1. "Do the 13 reasons need to be ranked?" discussed in Section 13.5.1.1.
2. "What is the required level of confidence in the data?" discussed in Section 13.5.1.2.
3. "What is the relationship between sample size and level of confidence?" discussed in Section 13.5.1.3.

13.5.1.1 "Do the 13 Hypotheses Need to Be Ranked?" The answer was negative because of the way the research was framed (bounding the problem). Framing the research problem to avoid ranking the hypothesis simplified the survey by eliminating the need for the respondent to do PWC (Section 4.6.4).

13.5.1.2 "What Is the Required Level of Confidence in the Data?" Research into statistics indicated that the answer was 0.95 for standard statistics (Downie and Heath 1959).

13.5.1.3 "What Is the Relationship between Sample Size and Level of Confidence?" This question provided the key to the innovation. Research into statistics indicated that the relationship is expressed in the following equation (Downie and Heath 1959):

$$n = (z^2 * \sigma^2)/H^2 \qquad (13.1)$$

where:

    n = sample size.

    z = level of confidence factor (for a 95% level of confidence, z = 1.96).

    σ = estimated Standard Deviation of the data.

    H = accuracy of the estimate (±).

Changing perspective, the equation was rearranged to provide a Zone of Ambiguity (± accuracy) on the median (the innovation) namely:

$$H = \sqrt{(z^2 * \sigma^2)/n} \qquad (13.2)$$

Since the sample size is the number of responses to the questionnaire, the equation could provide three results for each reason.

1. **Supported**: if value of the Median is positive and the Zone of Ambiguity does not overlap the zero line, i.e., (Median>0) and (Median-H)>0.

2. **Refuted**: if value of the Median is negative and the Zone of Ambiguity does not overlap the zero line, i.e., (Median<0) and (Median+H) <0.

3. **Ambiguous (no clear result)**: if the value of the Median is zero or the Zone of Ambiguity overlaps the zero line when overlaid on the median, i.e., (Median = 0) or (Abs (Median) <H).

For example, for a given sample size H = 2:

1. If the Median of the responses is more positive than +2 the hypothesis is supported.

2. If the Median of the responses is more negative than −2 the hypothesis is refuted as shown in Figure 13.4.

3. If the Median of the responses is somewhere between −2 and +2, namely inside the Zone of Ambiguity, then there is no clear result; it is ambiguous.

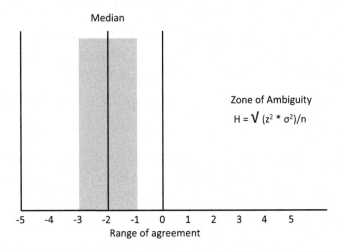

Figure 13.4   The Zone of Ambiguity.

In the figure the Zone of Ambiguity around the median does not overlap the zero, so the result is unambiguous on the negative side of the X-axis; namely the hypothesis is refuted.

13.5.2 Using the Zone of Ambiguity

Using the Zone of Ambiguity is an extension of the way data is processed in a spreadsheet as follows:

1. Collect the survey results.
2. Store the data in a spreadsheet.
3. For each item calculate:
   a. The median using the built in formula in the spreadsheet.
   b. The Zone of Ambiguity using equation (2) above.

As stated above, there could be one of three results for each issue, namely the issue is:

1. **Supported**: if value of the Median is positive and the Zone of Ambiguity does not overlap the zero line.
2. **Refuted**: if value of the Median is negative and the Zone of Ambiguity does not overlap the zero line.
3. **Ambiguous (no clear result)**: if the value of the Median is zero or the Zone of Ambiguity overlaps the zero line when overlaid on the Median.

Table 13.2   Results by Number of Employees

EMPLOYEE SIZE	Q1	Q2	Q3	Q4	Q5	Q6	Q7	Q8	Q9	Q10	Q11	Q12	Q13
1–10	S	S	S	S	S	S	S	S	S		R		R
11–25	S	S	S	S	R	R	S	S	S	S	R	R	R
26–50	E	S			S	S	S		S	S		E	R
51–100		S					S		E	R			R
101+	R	S	R	R	R	R	R				E	E	R

Table 13.3   Results by Company Age

COMPANY AGE	Q1	Q2	Q3	Q4	Q5	Q6	Q7	Q8	Q9	Q10	Q11	Q12	Q13
1991–1996	S	S	S		S	E	S	S	S	S	S		S
1986–1990			S	S	S	S	S	S	S				R
1981–1985		S	R	R	E	R	S		S	S		R	R
Pre-1981	R	S	E	S	R		S	R	R	S	R		R

Support (S) and refute (R) can be clearly seen for some of the hypotheses (questions) in Table 13.3 and Table 13.2 where:

- **S = Support**: more than 50% of the survey results agreed with the question.
- **R = Refute**: more than 50% of the survey results disagreed with the question.
- **E = Even**: where the degree of support and refute is about the same (Support =Refute ±2%).
- **C = Complacent**: where more than 50% of the survey results did not care or were neutral.
- **Ambiguous**: no letter, just a gray area means the median was inside the Zone of Ambiguity, so no clear result could be inferred.

Changes in the responses as a function of the subsets can be clearly seen in some instances. For example, the response to Q1* in Table 13.3 changes from support for new companies to refute for companies that have been in business for more than 15 years. Accordingly, we

---

* Q1 to 13 are the survey questions.

can infer that the findings for Q1 reflect that a learning curve may be in operation. Other results such as the responses to Q4 in Table 13.2 and Q8 in Table 13.3 need further data.

13.6 Summary

Chapter 13 discussed five systems engineering tools. Checkland's SSM is a tool used in the front-end of the SDP to gain an understanding of the undesirable or problematic situation and determine the type of intervention needed to remove the undesirability in the situation. This chapter also contained a case study in which Checkland's SSM was successfully applied. The CONOPS is one of the fundamental project documents containing both a vision of the solution system in operation, and the transition process that will upgrade the undesirable or problematic situation to turn it into a desirable situation sometime in the future. This chapter continued with a framework for tackling complexity based on the systems approach to solving problems using a different approach to the current non-systems paradigm. This chapter then included a list of mathematical tools that are used in the front-end of systems engineering, and this chapter concluded with the Zone of Ambiguity, an original tool that allows the analyst to obtain information in situations in which the sample size is too small to use conventional statistics.

References

Alexander, J. E., and J. M. Bailey. 1962. *Systems Engineering Mathematics.* Englewood Cliff, NJ: Prentice-Hall, Inc.

APSC. 2012. *Tackling Wicked Problems: A Public Policy Perspective.* The Australian Public Service Comission, 31 May 2012, accessed 25 February 2018. http://www.apsc.gov.au/publications-and-media/archive /publications-archive/tackling-wicked-problems.

Aslaksen, E. W., and R. Belcher. 1992. *Systems Engineering.* New York: Prentice Hall.

Avison, D., and G. Fitzgerald. 2003. *Information Systems Development: Methodologies, Techniques and Tools.* Maidenhead, UK: McGraw-Hill Education.

Checkland, P. 1991. *Systems Thinking, Systems Practice.* Chichester: John Wiley & Sons.

Checkland, P. 1993. *Systems Thinking, Systems Practice.* Chichester: John Wiley & Sons.

Checkland, P., and J. Scholes. 1990. *Soft Systems Methodology in Action*. New York: John Wiley & Sons.

Chestnut, H. 1965. *Systems Engineering Tools*. Edited by Harold Chestnut, *Wiley Series on Systems Engineering and Analysis*. New York: John Wiley & Sons, Inc.

Churchman, C. W. 1979. *The Systems Approach and its Enemies*. New York: Basic Books, Inc.

Colwell, B. 2005. "Complexity in Design." *IEEE Computer*, no. 38 (10):10–12.

Conant, R. C. 1972. "Detecting Subsystems of a Complex System." *IEEE Transactions on Systems, Man, And Cybernetics* (September 1972):550–553.

Downie, N. M., and R. W. Heath. 1959. *Basic Statistical Methods*. New York: Harper & Row.

El Maraghy, W., H. El Maraghy, T. Tomiyama, and L. Monostori. 2012. "Complexity in engineering design and manufacturing." *CIRP Annals - Manufacturing Technology*, no. 61 (2):793–814.

Goode, H. H., and R. E. Machol. 1959. *Systems Engineering*. New York: McGraw-Hill.

Hitchins, D. K. 1998. "Systems Engineering... In Search of the Elusive Optimum." In the 4th Annual Symposium of the INCOSE-UK.

Huygens, C. 1690. *Treatise on Light*.

IEEE Std 1362. 1998. *IEEE Guide for Information Technology – System Definition – Concept of Operations (ConOps) Document*. New York: The Institute of Electrical and Electronics Engineers, Inc.

Kasser, J. E. 1995. *Applying Total Quality Management to Systems Engineering*. Boston: Artech House.

Kasser, J. E. 1997. *The Determination and Mitigation of Factors Inhibiting the Creation of Strategic Alliances of Small Businesses in the Government Contracting Arena.*, Washington, DC: The Department of Engineering Management, The George Washington University.

Kasser, J. E. 2007. *A Framework for Understanding Systems Engineering*: Booksurge Ltd.

Kasser, J. E. 2013a. *A Framework for Understanding Systems Engineering*. 2nd Ed. CreateSpace Ltd.

Kasser, J. E. 2013b. "The Engaporean Air-Defence Upgrade: A Framework for a Case Study Development Project." In the 23rd Annual International Symposium of the International Council on Systems Engineering. Philadelphia, PA.

Kasser, J. E. 2015. *Perceptions of Systems Engineering. Vol. 2, Solution Engineering*. Createspace.

Kasser, J. E., and K. Palmer. 2005. "Reducing and Managing Complexity by Changing the Boundaries of the System." In the Conference on Systems Engineering Research. Hoboken NJ.

Kuhn, T. S. 1970. *The Structure of Scientific Revolutions*. Chicago: 2nd Ed., Enlarged. The University of Chicago Press.

Machol, R. E., and R. F. Miles, Jr. 1973. "The Engineering of Large Scale Systems." In *Systems Concepts*. New York: edited by R.F. Miles Jr., pp. 33–50. John Wiley & Son, Inc.

Maier, M. K., and E. Rechtin. 2000. *The Art of Systems Architecting*. 2nd Ed. CRC Press.

Newton, I. 1675. *Hypothesis of Light*.

Sillitto, H. 2009. "On Systems Architects and Systems Architecting: Some Thoughts on Explaining and Improving the Art and Science of Systems Architecting." In the 19th International Symposium of the International Council on Systems Engineering. Singapore.

Simon, H. A. 1962. "The Architecture of Complexity." *Proceedings of the American Philosophical Society*, no. 106 (Dec. 1962):467–482.

Simon, H. A. 1973. "The Structure of Ill Structured Problems." *Artificial Intelligence*, no. 4 (3–4):181–201. doi: 10.1016/0004-3702(73)90011-8.

Suh, N. P. 2005. "Complexity in Engineering." *Annals of CIRP* no. 54 (2):46–63.

Tomiyama, T., V. D'Amelio, J. Urbanic, and W. El Maraghy. 2007. "Complexity of Multi-Disciplinary Design." *Annals of the CIRP*, no. 56 (1):185–188.

Wilson, W. E. 1965. *Concepts of Engineering System Design*. New York: McGraw-Hill Book Company.

Wymore, A. W. 1997. *Subsystem Optimization Implies System Suboptimization: Not!* Accessed 30 September 2013. http://www.sie.arizona.edu/sysengr /wymore/optimal.html.

14
TEMPLATES

Templates are:

- Tools that maximize completeness and minimize errors of commission and errors of omission (Section 4.4).
- The first thing to look for when starting a project, try the:
  - *Structural* perspective for format, e.g., systems engineering document templates available in Military Standards (MIL-STD) and on the Internet and the presentation outlines discussed in this chapter.
  - *Generic* perspective for content (e.g., similar products).
- Checklists that provide reminders for what needs to be in something.

This chapter discusses the following templates:

1. Annotated outlines, discussed in Section 14.1.
2. Four different Idea Storage Templates (IST), discussed in Section 14.2.
3. The Problem Formulation Template, discussed in Section 14.3.
4. A generic functional template for a system, discussed in Section 14.4.
5. A template for a document, discussed in Section 14.5.
6. A generic template for a presentation, discussed in Section 14.6.
7. A template for a student exercise presentation, discussed in Section 14.7.
8. A template for a management review presentation, discussed in Section 14.8.
9. The Waterfall Chart, discussed in Section 14.9.

14.1 Annotated Outlines

An annotated outline:

- Is a thinking tool template for expediting the document production process. It is a smart template for a document.
- Elaborates a table of contents by adding a paragraph or two on each section describing the contents of the section (Kasser and Schermerhorn 1994). The paragraph might begin with the words, "This section will contain …". This approach:
  - Organizes the author's brain dump in a somewhat more structured manner.
  - Provides a clue as to what to expect in the document.

Before starting to prepare the annotated outline, think of the document as a presentation in which each PowerPoint slide is a chapter. The bulleted (dot pointed) lines on the slides are the section headings, and the written text is the verbal expansion of the points made by the presenter. These guidelines can be modified according to the length of the document. Plan the contents so the document flows in an orderly manner. Develop the contents as a list of headings using the inverted pyramid or newspaper writing style wherein the information begins with a general overview and then branches out to specific details. This way the audience can read as far as they need to. The outlining capability of modern word processors facilitate this implementation approach because you can see the appropriate levels of detail and readily expand sections of the document as appropriate. Annotate each heading with a description of the future contents. If the material exists, inserting the material at this time will clutter the document with too much detail. Instead, so do not insert it into the initial version of the annotated outline, insert the material after the review and approval of the annotated outline.* For example, consider the following extracts from two of the sections of an annotated outline for a postgraduate class study guide.

---

* Alternatively, insert it as hidden text.

Section 2 The classroom sections

This section will contain the schedule and 14 paragraphs, one paragraph for each session, each providing details of:

Objectives - a list.

Knowledge - the topics to be covered in the session.

Skills - to be learned/developed or exercised

Exercise - a description of the functions performed by the students.

Readings - a list of required readings containing the knowledge to be learnt during the session.

Student presentation - the nature of the topic the students will present

Section 3.2 requirements of assignments

This section will contain the complete set of requirements for the individual assignment.

The normal table of content elements are in bold, and the annotations are in the regular text. Perceptions from the *Generic* HTP show the similarity between the extracts and a PowerPoint presentation. These annotations to the section headings communicate the future contents of the section to the reader. Annotated Outlines can be thought of as document templates when applied to specific types of document such as study guides, requirements documents, proposals, contracts, etc.

While the abstract introduces the document, the last part of the document summarizes the document and draws the attention of the reader to the main points in the document. Sometimes the summary may be a copy of the abstract or the introduction but written in the past tense explaining what the document did. For examples, see the summaries at the end of each chapter of this book. The summary should be finalized at the same time as the abstract is updated, namely at the end of the preparation part of the process.

If the document is going to be summarized in a presentation, for example in the way a System Requirements Document is summarized at the SRR, the annotated outline should also be used as part of the Presentation Template (Section 14.6) as the annotated outline has identified the sections the presentation.

14.2 Idea Storage Templates

Idea Storage Templates (IST) are templates for storing ideas. One of the most widely known ISTs is the Strengths, Weaknesses, Opportunities, and Threats (SWOT) Template (Learned et al. 1969) in the business domain (Section 14.2.1).

This section introduces three original blackboard-style, multiple person access, parallel working memory, problem and remedy ISTs for organizing and storing ideas. When used with the ideas generated by Brainstorming (Section 7.1) and Active Brainstorming (Section 7.1) the flow of ideas is as shown in Figure 14.1. The initial set of ideas generated in the Brainstorming session (Section 7.3) is stored in the temporary memory. When the flow of ideas dries out, the Active Brainstorming session (Section 7.1) begins and generates more ideas. When the Active Brainstorming set of ideas ends, these ideas are then sorted into the appropriate IST. The act of sorting often generates more ideas which then need to be stored as well. The sorting process generates ideas because often when an idea is sorted into one of the

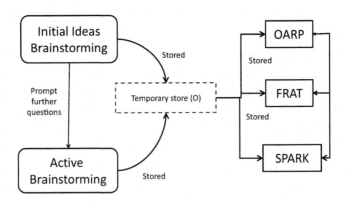

Figure 14.1   Flow of ideas.

ISTs, it generates a related idea that belongs in one of the other ISTs. The ISTs are:

1. *OARP*: discussed in Section 14.2.2 for ideas or concepts pertaining to the problem.
2. *FRAT*: discussed in Section 14.2.3 for ideas or concepts pertaining to the solution (product).
3. *SPARK*: discussed in Section 14.2.4 for ideas or concepts pertaining to implementing the solution (process).

The three ISTs are temporary or working memories used to store and share information between people working on an issue. The ideas are to be used in the later activities that realize the solution. At the time the issue is being examined, the focus will be on filling in OARP. However, during this process, ideas pertaining to the solution and its implementation will be generated and discussed and stored in FRAT and SPARK. Some of these ideas will reflect on the feasibility of answers or on the understanding of the underlying real problem.

During each state of the SDP various tools are used to generate ideas and information depending on the domain and the problem being faced. OARP, FRAT, and SPARK can provide temporary storage of those ideas which are later used to realize the solution system.

14.2.1 The SWOT Idea Storage Template

SWOT is a:

- Planning tool used to help think about a project or product (Learned et al. 1969).
- A methodology using a template to generate ideas and facilitate making decisions about opportunities a risks.
- Piece of paper or whiteboard template divided into a 2x2 Framework (Section 5.1); four areas corresponding to the letters in the acronym SWOT (Strengths Weaknesses Opportunities and Threats) used as a blackboard-style multiple-access working memory (Nii 1986).
- Four-viewpoint Perspectives Perimeter (Chapter 10) for discussing a specific type of problem.

An example of the use of the SWOT approach in the making decision to market a product, a SWOT analysis of a product would be used to consider:

1. **Strengths**: characteristics of the product that gives it an advantage over similar products.
2. **Weaknesses (or limitations)**: characteristics of the product that places it at a disadvantage relative to other products.
3. **Opportunities**: things to take advantage of, to improve performance or sales of the product.
4. **Threats**: things that could cause trouble or problems for the product.

From the *Generic-Continuum* HTPs,* SWOT is Brainstorming (Section 7.3) using a Perspectives Perimeter (Chapter 10) with just four viewpoints corresponding to each area of the SWOT Template in turn. The facilitator asks questions pertinent to each area of the template in turn. Typical questions asked in a SWOT analysis might start with the questions:

- What are …?
- Why are …?
- Where …?

However, unlike Active Brainstorming (Section 7.1), where the ideas are sorted after the session, in a SWOT session, the ideas are generally stored in the appropriate area as they are generated because the answers to the questions usually lie in the same areas as the questions. The SWOT process may be enhanced using Active Brainstorming as shown in Figure 14.2. The normal SWOT session produces ideas which are stored in the SWOT Template. Then the Active Brainstorming session generates even more ideas which are also stored in the template either during or after the session is complete.

---

* Perceptions from the *Generic* perspective perceive the process as being similar to Active Brainstorming; perceptions from *Continuum* perspective recognize the four different viewpoints are different to those in the HTPs. SWOT are characteristics of the perspective; for example, at the strategic level, SWOT is used within the *Big Picture* perspective.

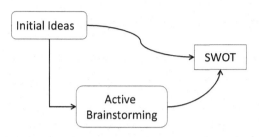

Figure 14.2   Better 'SWOTting'.

14.2.2 The Observations, Assumptions Risks and Problems Template

The Observations, Assumptions Risks, and Problems (OARP) Template for storing ideas related to the underlying cause or real problem is a four-part IST (Section 14.2.2) consisting of:

1. ***Observations***: ideas concerning perceptions relating to the need, problem, and symptoms. This part of the template:
   a. Helps to develop understanding of a situation by containing questions, answers, analyses, and other relevant information.
   b. May also contain analyses of ideas.
   c. Begins as the initial repository of ideas from the Brainstorming and Active Brainstorming sessions.
   d. Ends up as the repository for the leftover ideas that remain after moving the other ideas into the other areas of the three ISTs.
2. ***Assumptions***: the assumptions implicit in the thinking. A critical area, since undocumented assumptions may be incorrect and may cause the wrong solution to be realized.
3. ***Risks***: ideas about reasons the activity to remedy the problem could fail. During the discussion of the problem, there are bound to be ideas or concepts generated that incorporate solutions since we often use solution language instead of problem language, namely we say, "we need a car" when we should be saying, "we need transportation". By identifying risks associated with realizing the car solution we can more readily identify solution related concepts and transform them to problem related concepts and focus on the underlying cause or real problem.

4. *Real Problem*: ideas concerning the cause or problem. The ideas from this part of the template often eventually produce a clear and concise statement of what has to be done to change the situation. The problem statement is generally developed after considerable discussion.

OARP is a template which is used after the ideas have been generated by any of the idea generation methods (Chapter 7) such as Brainstorming (Section 7.3), Active Barnstorming (Section 7.1), NGT (Section 7.9), and Slip Writing (Section 7.10). Once the ideas have been generated, they are examined and stored in the template.

14.2.3 *The Functions Requirements Answers and Test* Template*

The Functions Requirements Answers and Test (FRAT) Template is:

- A tool for thinking about functions and requirements in systems and software engineering. For example, the relationship between problem and solution in Figure 14.3 shows that a problem can be described in terms of the need for functions which perform the solution and that requirements quantify functions.
- A tool for thinking about processes in project management.
- A four-area template based on the FRAT views of a system (Mar 1994, Mar and Morais 2002). However, in this instance FRAT has been adapted for use as an IST (Section 14.2) to store:
  1. *Functions*: ideas concerning the normal and contingency mode mission and support functions or activities the solution system performs or needs to perform (mainly ideas from the *Functional* HTP).
  2. *Requirements*: ideas concerning how well each function must be performed (Mar 1994) (mainly ideas from the *Quantitative* HTP).[†]

---

* The late Brian Mar seems to have had a sense of humour. Perceive the acronym from the *Continuum* perspective and transpose the letters R and A.

[†] Some systems and software engineers equate requirements with needs. These persons are working in the 'B' paradigm. The systems engineers who use requirements to quantify functions are working in the 'A' paradigm.

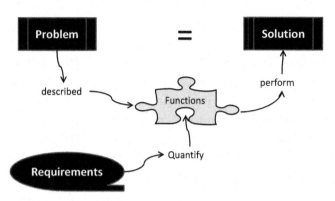

Figure 14.3 The relationship between functions and requirements.

3. *Answers:** ideas concerning (feasible and non-feasible†) candidate ways of performing the functions so that they meet the requirements.
4. *Tests*: ideas:
   - Concerning the selection criteria for evaluating or selecting the answers or solutions.
   - Pertaining to how and what will be done to determine how well the answers or solutions perform the needed functions.

14.2.3.1 Example of FRAT Applied to Systems Consider how FRAT could be used to store ideas with reference to the Luz system. The first Luz Solar Electricity Generating System (SEGS-1) (Kasser 2008) generated electricity using the sun as fuel. The system was conceptualized as an array of parabolic trough reflectors mounted north–south rotating from east to west during the day. There was a pipe placed the focal points of each of the parabolic trough reflected mirrors so that as the mirrors rotated the sun's rays were focused on the pipe. As oil was pumped through the pipe, the sun heated the oil. The oil was pumped

---

* The word "answer" is used instead of "solution" in the template because (1) it keeps the original Mar acronym and (2) it prevents confusion because the "S" character is used in the SPARK template for schedules rather than solutions.

† Non-feasible ideas may also be generated during Brainstorming and Active Brainstorming. These ideas need to be stored until they can be processed. None-feasible ideas may be useful as goals or triggers for alternatives.

through a converter which used the high temperature of the oil to boil water to produce steam, and the steam drove a turbine to generate electricity for Southern California Edison. The initial system and the follow-ons were built in the Mojave Desert in California in the 1980s. Had there been an Active Brainstorming session (Section 7.1) to discuss the control and electronics system, the ideas generated could have been sorted into the FRAT (Section 14.2.3), OARP (Section 14.2.2) and SPARK (Section 14.2.4) ISTs. The ideas stored in the FRAT Template might have included the following.

14.2.3.1.1 Functions   A list of ideas about the functions performed by the system might have included the following:[*]

- Deploying the entire array of mirrors (>600) when $Power_{(generated)} > Power_{(used)}$
- Tracking when and while the sun shines
- Idling for periods of cloud cover
- Stowing the array when $Power_{(generated)} < Power_{(used)}$
- Gathering, displaying, and storing status information about the operation of SEGS-1
- Interfacing with the operator

14.2.3.1.2 Requirements   The requirements would pertain to the system level and to the subsystem level and quantify the functions. The requirements might have included the following:

- In operation, SEGS-1 shall generate more power than it uses.
- SEGS-1 shall generate the maximum possible amount of power each day.
- The mirror pointing accuracy shall be ±0.2 degrees.

14.2.3.1.3 Answers   A list of ideas from the *Structural* HTP might have included the following:

- AC or DC motors.
- Power distribution at 110, 220 and 440 V.

---

[*] Note the use of the ending 'ing' for the functions.

- Local control units for each mirror.
- Power distribution units in the field.
- Command and control using Ethernet.
- Position sensors to sense the angle of the mirror with respect to ground.
- Electromagnetic interference from adjacent systems.

14.2.3.1.4 Tests A list of ideas pertaining to testing might have included the following:

- The need to simplify troubleshooting in the field.
- Ethernet is brand-new expensive and risky.
- Position sensors can be absolute or relative.
- Local controllers could be smart and do some computations, or could be simple and just pass on instructions from a central minicomputer.

14.2.4 The Schedules, Products, Activities, Resources and risKs Template

The Schedules, Products, Activities, Resources and risKs (SPARK) Template is a five-area template for containing ideas pertaining to the implementation of the answer or solution namely information used in project management, where:

1. *Schedules*: ideas concerning the time to be taken by the activities.
2. *Products*: ideas concerning the products to be produced.
3. *Activities*: ideas concerning the activities which produce the products.
4. *Resources*: ideas concerning resources used in or by the activities to produce the products
5. *risKs*: ideas concerning anything that could prevent, delay, or increase the costs of, the production of the products. These ideas may be product or process related.

The ideas stored in the SPARK Template feed directly into a plan.

14.3 The Problem Formulation Template

The Problem Formulation Template is:

- A tool to overcome the generic problem of "poor problem formulation".
- Based on the generic problem-solving process (Section 11.1).
- A way to assist the problem-solving process by encouraging the planner to think through the problem and ways to realize a solution when formulating the problem.
- Made up of following five parts:
  1. *The undesirable situation* as perceived from the each of the pertinent descriptive HTPs.
  2. *Assumptions*: about the situation, problem, solution, constraints, etc. that will have an impact on developing the solution. One general assumption is there is enough expertise in the group formulating the problem to understand the undesirable situation and specify the correct problem. If this assumption is not true, then that expertise needs to be obtained for the duration of the activity. Providers of the expertise include other people within the organization, consultants, and members of the group looking it up on the Internet.
  3. *The Feasible Conceptual Future Desirable Situation (FCFDS)* (the *Scientific* HTP) as inferred from the descriptive HTPs. Something that remedies the undesirable situation and is to be interoperable with evolving adjacent systems over the operational life of the solution and adjacent systems.
  4. *The problem*, which is how to convert the FCFDS into reality.
  5. *The solution* the creation of a set of activities, and the performance of those activities that produce the FCFDS. In non-complex systems the solution is often the FCFDS. The solution is made of two interdependent parts:
     a. The SDP or transition process that converts the undesirable situation to a desirable situation.
     b. The solution system operating in the context of the FCFDS.

Placing the FCFDS before the problem is based on the dictum of working backwards from the solution (Section 11.8) and allows risk management to be incorporated into task planning instead being an add-on in the current systems engineering and project management paradigms. The risk management is achieved by ensuring that risks identified in a task are mitigated or prevented in earlier tasks in the project schedule.

The first version of the Template generally does not include a solution. The problem is to create the solution that implements the transition to the FCFDS.

14.3.1 Framing Classroom Exercises Using the Problem Formulation Template

This section provides an example of a generic Problem Formulation Template for framing classroom exercises as follows:

1. *The undesirable situation* is the need to successfully* complete the exercise in a timely manner.
2. *The assumption*: the exercise can be completed successfully within the allotted time.
3. *The FCFDS* is having successfully completed the exercise in a timely manner
4. *The problem* is to figure out how to create and deliver a product that meets the requirements of the exercise.
5. *The solution* is creating and delivering a product that meets the requirements of the exercise.

Students should be provided with the opportunity to practice using the template by framing the problem posed by the specific exercise or assignment by adapting the generic Problem Formulation Template to their situation.

14.4 A Generic Functional Template for a System

Ensuring that a design for the solution system is complete constitutes a significant problem. The standard functional template for a system is a tool that provides a remedy to the problem. From the *Generic* HTP, the use of a standard or reference set of functions in the form of a template

---

* Success is defined by achieving the desired grade.

that can be tailored to describe a specific system can ensure a greater probability of design completeness as described in this section.

A generic functional template for a system is pictured in Figure 14.4 as a jigsaw piece because systems can be represented by a number of functions (components or subsystems) fitted together to perform the function of the system. Generically a function converts inputs to outputs using resources. Hitchins grouped the complete set of functions performed by any system into the following two classes (Hitchins 2007: pp. 28–129):

1. *Mission*: the functions which the system is designed to perform to remedy the undesirable situation in its operational context under normal and contingency conditions, as, and when required.
2. *Support*: the functions the system needs to perform in order to be able to perform the mission under normal and contingency conditions, as and when required. Support functions can further be grouped into:
    a. *Resource management*: the functions that acquire, store, distribute, convert, and discard excess resources that are utilized in performing the mission.
    b. *Viability management*: the functions that maintain and contribute to the survival of the system in storage, standby and in operation performing the mission.

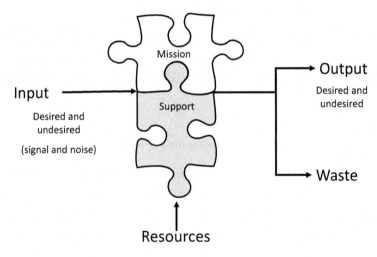

Figure 14.4   Functional template for system.

14.4.1 Some Advantages of the Use of Functions

The use of functions has a number of advantages including the following:

1. Supports abstract thinking by encouraging problem solvers to think in abstract terms in the early stages of identifying a problem and providing a solution discussed in Section 14.4.1.1.
2. Maximizes completeness of a system by allowing for the inheritance of generic functions for the class of system discussed in Section 14.4.1.2.
3. Provides for the use of standard functional templates for various types of systems which can help maximize completeness of the resulting system discussed in Section 14.4.1.3.
4. Improves probability of completeness by making it easier to identify missing functions in system functional descriptions than in implementation (physical) descriptions discussed in Section 14.4.1.4.
5. Allows the system to be modelled in its functional form at design time to determine how well the solution functionality appears to remedy the problem.

14.4.1.1 Supports Abstract Thinking People tend to use solution language to describe functions. For example, we often use the phrase, "need a car" when we should be using problem language and saying, "need transportation". Using solution language in the early stages of problem-solving tends to produce results that may not be the best solution to the problem even if it is a complete solution, as well as generally not being an innovative solution. This is because solution language tends to turn examples into solutions with little exploration of alternative solutions. For example, if the need is stated as "we need a car", the problem-solving process tends to focus on selecting the car to meet the need. A need should be stated from the *Operational* and *Functional* HTPs as, "need a transportation function to move people from A to B". The non-atomic requirement will then be stated from the *Operational*, *Functional*, and *Quantitative* HTPs as, "provide a transportation function to move N people with B (Kilograms/cubic meters) of baggage M Kilometres in H hours over terrain of type T with an operational availability of O".

Creating the solution concept in the form of capability or functionality is in accordance with Arthur D. Hall who stated that if a problem can be stated as a function, then the total solution is the needed functionality as well as the process to produce that functionality (Hall 1989). In holistic thinking terms, state the need using functional or problem language not structural or solution language. Using the language of functions in the early stages of problem-solving will nudge the stakeholders into abstract thinking rather than fixating on an implementation. For example, they might stop saying, "I need a car" and start saying, "I need transportation".

14.4.1.2 Maximizes Completeness of a System   From the *Generic* HTP, any system is an instance of a class of systems and once the first one has been built, subsequent systems can inherit properties and functions. Consequently, any system can have two types of mission and support functions:

1. *Generic*: to that class of system.
2. *Specific*: to that instance of the system.

For example, when building a spacecraft the necessary thermal-vacuum properties and functions needed to survive the launch and operate in space can be inherited from previous spacecraft of that type. Once inherited the properties need to be examined to determine if they are applicable with or without modification. Other specific properties and functions for that spacecraft must then be examined to determine if they conflict with the generic ones.

14.4.1.3 The Use of a Standard Functional Template for a System   Figure 14.4 shows a template for a system in which the functionality has been grouped into mission and support functions. Note how Figure 14.4 does not show details of the mission and support functions because these details have been abstracted out since they belong in lower level drawings. An immediate advantage of the Figure 14.4 *Functional* template is that one can see that there are two system outputs, the desired output labelled "output" and another output labelled "waste". If applied to the incandescent light bulb, the desired output is light; the undesired or waste output is heat.

Process improvement and cost reductions efforts tend to focus on the effectiveness of producing the desired output, namely the mission functions. The template shows that there is also a need to focus on reducing the amount of waste or exploring ways in which "waste" can be used or treated as a desired output and sold to someone who wants the waste. For example, waste heat might be sold or used; waste food in a restaurant might be used for fertilizer or animal food, and so on.

By using the inheritance concept, it should be possible to inherit functions from the set of reference functions for the class of system being developed. This seems to be the concept behind Hitchins' Generic Reference Model of any system (Hitchins 2007: pp. 124–142). Problem solvers and application domain experts working together[*] would assemble the detailed functions to be performed by the solution system from the set of reference functions for the class of system being developed, tailoring the functions appropriately. For example, if the solution is a:

- *Spacecraft*: the support functions for surviving launch and the out-of-atmosphere environment would be among those inherited.
- *Information system*: the functions displaying information to ensure that data is not hidden due to colour blindness in the operators would be among those functions inherited. In addition, a typical template for data processing system might look like that shown in Figure 14.5. This method for developing a system design should decrease the number of missing functions.

14.4.1.4 Improves Probability of Completeness at Design Time This method for developing a solution system design should decrease the number of missing functions and allow innovative designs as shown in the following example. A bank's Automatic Teller Machine (ATM) is a system to which most people can relate, having had some interaction

---

[*] In an integrated team.

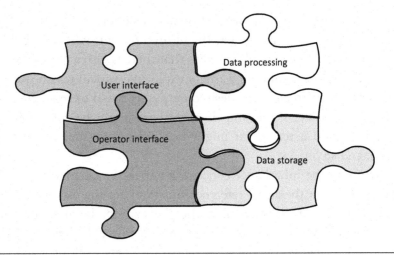

Figure 14.5   Functional template of a data processing system.

with such machines. The mission functions for which the ATM was designed include:

- Withdrawing funds.
- Depositing funds.
- Checking the balance in the user's accounts.

The support functions for the ATM include:

- Removing and replenishing bank notes.
- Deterring theft.
- Countering attempted theft.
- Servicing the electromechanical components to keep them operational.

By considering the CONOPS for each of the scenarios of the ATM and how the functions in each scenario can be implemented, alternative innovative design approaches may be identified for implementation sometime in the future. For example, the physical realization of the ATM is based on the use of a plastic card containing a magnetic memory and a Personal Identification Number (PIN). Thirty years since the initial implementation alternative implementations have become possible based on thumb prints, laser retina scans, cell phones and other techniques to ensure security without the need for the plastic card. The functional approach allows the holistic thinker to pose the following question, "Is the financial industry trading off the costs of developing and deploying newer more secure ATMs against the cost of the losses incurred from the current generation of ATMs?"

14.5 Generic Template for a Document

The purpose of a document is to communicate something to someone. While documents come in all shapes and sizes, they all comply or rather they should all comply with the following three-part generic template:

1. An introductory section which:
   a. Introduces the document.
   b. States the purpose of the document.
   c. Provides a list of the contents/sections of the document.
2. The information being presented section.
3. A closing section which:
   a. Summarizes the document.
   b. Invites questions and comments.

The information section of the document will depend on the situation. Search the Internet for at least one document that performs the same function as the one you are planning to write to use as a model. Examine these documents for good and bad points using the process for critical analysis of an argument (Section 3.2.8). Create the annotated outline while examining the model documents.

14.6 Generic Template for a Presentation

The generic template for a presentation is the same as the generic temperate for a document (Section 14.5 and accordingly contains the following three parts:

1. An introductory section which:
   a. Introduces the presentation.
   b. States the purpose of the presentation.
   c. Provides a list of the contents/sections of the presentation
2. The information being presented section.

3. A closing section which:

   a. Summarizes the presentation.

   b. Invites questions and comments.

A typical introductory slide which states the objectives of a workshop is shown in Figure 14.6. The eight objectives are listed in a table; each objective is numbered. It makes the presentation simpler because it is easier to talk about objective "Number 3" than to talk about objective "learning about systems thinking". The slide shown in Figure 14.6 is one of a pair; the second slide shown in Figure 14.7 is shown as part of the closing section of the presentation. It is a Compliance Matrix (Section 9.5.2) pointing out that the first seven objectives have

#	Objective
1	To provide you with >25 useful conceptual systems thinking tools for problem-solving
2	To explain that systems engineering is the application of systems thinking tools to remedy complex problems
3	To learn about systems thinking
4	To boldly go beyond systems thinking
5	To learn about the holistic problem-solving process
6	To understand the benefits of holistic thinking and the holistic thinking problem-solving process
7	To practise holistic thinking
8	To encourage you to explore holistic thinking on your own

Figure 14.6   Workshop objectives.

#	Objective	
1	Provided you with >25 useful conceptual systems thinking tools for problem-solving	✓
2	Explained that systems engineering is the application of systems thinking tools to remedy complex problems	✓
3	Learnt about systems thinking	✓
4	Boldly went beyond systems thinking	✓
5	Learnt about the holistic problem-solving process	✓
6	Explained the benefits of holistic thinking and the holistic thinking problem-solving process	✓
7	Practised holistic thinking	✓
8	Encouraged you to explore holistic thinking on your own	?

Figure 14.7   Workshop - meeting the objectives.

been met, but there is no way of verifying that the last objective has been met during the workshop session. The slide usually comes right after the summary so that the parts of the presentation in which the objectives were met are stated verbally instead of being written down on the slide.

14.7 Template for a Student Exercise Presentation

Students seem to have a lot of difficulty when they first have to prepare presentations in class. This generic template for a student exercise presentation is:

- A tool to overcome the difficulty.
- A modified version of the generic template for a presentation (Section 14.6).
- Made up of three sections as follows:
  1. An introductory section
  2. One section for each of the requirements for the contents of the presentation
  3. A closing section

For example, if the students are required to present five items, there are seven sections in the template. They are:

1. The introductory section.
2. The first item.
3. The second item.
4. The third item.
5. The fourth item.
6. The fifth item.
7. The closing section.

14.7.1 Example of Creating a Presentation Using the Template

Students often have difficulty in figuring out what needs to be in the presentation. This is a reflection of the real-world when given a problematic situation we need to figure out what needs to be done. That's the first problem. Once we figured out what needs to be done we can formulate the problem of filling in the presentation outline using the Problem Formulation Template (Section 14.3) and then proceed to implement the transition from the problematic situation to the FCFDS. For example, consider the exercise I often give students in a workshop as follows. The slide in which the exercises presented is as follows:

- This Workshop is a system
- There is something undesirable about this Workshop
- Think up ideas about this Workshop
- Focus on Operational and Functional HTPs
- Use Brainstorming and Active Brainstorming
- Group ideas into functional mission and support systems and subsystems
- Use *ing words (present tense of verbs), e.g. drinking, eating, speaking, etc.
- Use Concept Maps and N² Charts to show how the systems and subsystems seem to be arranged
- Formulate the exercise problem using the Problem Formulation Template
- Create the Compliance Matrix for the exercise
- Prepare a <5 minute presentation containing:
  - Formulated problem
  - Representative sample (not all) of functions
  - Lessons Learned from this exercise
  - [a list of] Which thinking tools you used and why

What generally happens is that the students start working on what they think is the first thing that needs to be done, complete that, and then move onto the next thing, and so on. The result is that they generally run out of time and do not complete the exercise. The undesirable outcome of the failure to complete the exercise is a lower grade because what wasn't presented cannot be graded. However, once the students practised developing and began using the Problem Formulation Template (Section 14.3), their time management skills improved tremendously and they generally completed the exercise usually with time to spare.

I teach my students to read the whole slide and only then determine the requirements for what needs to be presented. In this instance there are four items that need to be presented. That means the six-part template is as follows:

1. An introductory section.
2. The formulated problem in five parts according to the Problem Formulation Template (Section 14.3).
3. A representative sample (not all) of functions.
4. The Lessons Learned (Section 9.3) from this exercise.
5. A list of the thinking tools used and why they were used.
6. A closing summary.

I then tell them that to complete the exercise they have to determine the requirements for each section. By the way, by the time this exercise is given to them, they have learned about Compliance Matrices (Section 9.5.2) and how to use them. They should do this using the planning process (Section 8.11.2) and working backwards from the solution (Section 11.8).

The most complex section of the exercise is item 3.

14.8 Template for a Management Review Presentation

This generic template for a management review presentation contains the following parts:

1. Cover slides stating title, date, and agenda (list of topics to be covered) as an ETL Chart (Section 8.16.2); see Figure 8.21 for an example.
2. The overall health and status of the project or projects. An effective way of presenting this is to use the ETL Chart (Section 8.16.2). If the presentation is for a single project the chart will only contain a single row and may be combined with the following chart.
3. The financial state of the project, presented in the form of an EVA Chart of the type shown in Figure 2.10.
4. The current schedule of the project, presented in the form of a Gantt Chart (Section 8.4) of the type shown in Figure 8.4. The chart should be at a high level and contain no more than nine bars in accordance with Miller's Rule (Section 3.2.5).

5. CRIP Charts showing the summary of the workflow (Section 8.1).
6. Details of the activities performed since the last review presentation starting with the cost and schedule information showing the planned and actual values. The information should be presented using EVA Charts (Section 6.2) and Gantt Charts (Section 8.4).
7. Risk report showing the status of the outstanding risks and the mitigation activities.
8. Supporting information presenting details about any cost and schedule variations.
9. Any other pertinent information.
10. Lessons Learned (Section 9.3) during the reporting period.
11. Plans for the activities to be performed during the next reporting period.
12. Closing part with any additional information that is relevant the presentation.

14.9 The Waterfall Chart

The Waterfall Chart (Royce 1970) is:

- Simple to explain, so teaching of systems engineering* has focused on using the Waterfall model (Biemer and Sage 2009: pp. 152–153).
- A planning tool for visualizing a sequence of activities.
- A template of the SLC incorporating the SDP version of the problem-solving process which provides a planning view of a notional project containing a predefined set of objectives, activities, milestones and products, performed in a time-ordered sequence, ideal for use in MBO (Section 8.8).
- A Concept Map (Section 6.1.2) that showing the relationship between the activities in a project in the different states of the SDP assuming that nothing goes wrong.

---

* And project management.

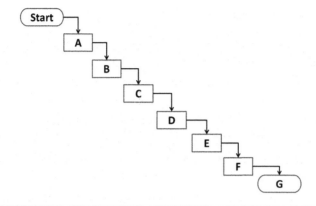

Figure 14.8 The Waterfall Chart template.

- A *Temporal* perspective of a notional project that does not take into account the effect of changes as a result of changes in the customer's needs or problems arising during the SDP.
- Not representative of the real world since most projects do experience changes in the customer's needs or problems arising during the SDP.
- A Gantt Chart (Section 8.4) with connections between the activities and the row and column lines abstracted out.
- Shown in Figure 14.8.

14.9.1 States in the Waterfall Chart

Perceptions from the *Continuum* and *Quantitative* HTPs identified the following nine different states in the Waterfall view of the SLC defined in generic terms as:

A The Needs Identification State.
B The Requirements State.
C The System Design State.
D The Subsystem Construction State.
E The Subsystem Test State.
F The System Integration and System Test States.
G The Operations, Maintenance (O&M) and Upgrade State.
H The Disposal State which may be a project of its own.

States A to F constitute the SDP subset of the SLC. Each state:

- Has a set of pre-defined objectives in the form of products to be produced before the milestone at the end of the state. For example, the documents produced during the Requirements State generally include a requirements document, a requirements presentation, and the handouts distributed at the presentation.
- Normally commences and terminates at a major formal milestone. Different projects use different names for the formal and informal milestones, but a milestone by any name is still a milestone.
- Has two exit conditions:
    1. The normal planned exit at the end of state milestone review which documents consensus that the system is ready to transition to the subsequent state as shown in Figure 14.9.
    2. An anticipated abnormal exit anywhere in the state that can happen at any time in any state and necessitates a return to an earlier state in the SDP due to:
        a. Any flaw other than replacing a defective item.
        b. An approved change that necessities rework.

The second type of exit is recognized and the Waterfall view is often modified to show iteration in the SDP as in Figure 14.9. This really represents the effect of change as a chaotic view of the SDP

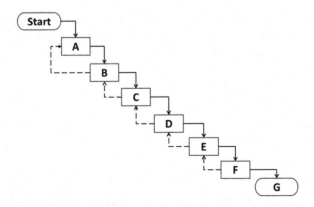

Figure 14.9   Iteration in the Waterfall.

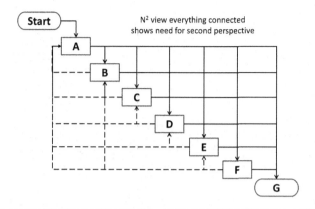

Figure 14.10   Chaotic Waterfall view of SDP.

which shows every state connected to every other state in drawings similar to Figure 14.10.

14.9.2 Milestones in the Waterfall View

There are no uniformly agreed-to names for milestones. Milestones can be major and minor, formal and informal. The purpose of a major milestone is:

1. To provide the customer with a sense that the project will deliver the promised product within estimated cost and schedule and that the product will perform as specified in the requirements.
2. To document consensus that the project may proceed to the subsequent phase (Kasser 1995).
3. Not to dispute any aspect of the project causing delays.

Minor milestones may be monthly management meetings or informal reviews such as software walkthroughs. The notional major milestones used in this book are:

1. Start of project which formally starts the SDP.
2. Operations Concept Review (OCR).
3. Systems Requirements Review (SRR).
4. Preliminary Design Review (PDR).
5. Critical Design Review (CDR).
6. Test Readiness Review (TRR).
7. Integration Readiness Review (IRR).

Table 14.1   The Notional States in the SDP

STATE	START	END	PRODUCES
Needs Identification	Start	OCR	Common vision of the system in operation, System architecture
System Requirements	OCR	SRR	System requirements System Management Plan
System Design	SRR	CDR	System design
Subsystem Construction	CDR	TRR	Subsystems
Subsystem Test	TRR	IRR	Tested subsystems
System Integration and System Test	IRR	DRR	The tested system
O&M and Upgrade	DRR	End	The products or services for which the system was created
Disposal	Start	End	The absence of the system in use

8. Delivery Readiness Review (DRR).

9. End of project which formally terminates the SDP.

The relationship between the states, milestones, and major products produced during each state for delivery at the milestones is shown in Table 14.1.

14.9.3 Misuse of the Waterfall Chart

Misuse of the Waterfall Chart includes:

- Being used as a lifecycle model for projects in systems and software development when it was intended to be a view of a notional sequential view of an iterative process (Royce 1987).
- Being used to show the effect of change such as in Figure 14.9 and Figure 14.10. These figures are views from the *Functional* HTP, and consequently do not relate to changes in schedules. Schedule changes must be viewed from the *Temporal* HTP using Gantt Charts (Section 8.4) as shown in the example in Section 8.4.2 and PERT Charts (Section 8.10) to see changes in the critical path.

14.9.4 The V Model

In the non-systems thinking paradigm, the V model or diagram is often described as a depiction of the systems engineering process.

When examining the V model or diagram from the HTPs, the perceptions include:

- Perceptions from the *Temporal* HTP found the first mention of the V diagram in 1986 (Rook 1986) where it was introduced as a software project management tool illustrating the concept of verification the process-products at established milestones. The original figure was captioned, "The stages in software development confidence". It was drawn to show that the intermediate process products produced at each state of the software development process were to be verified against previous baselines before starting work on the subsequent state. The V diagram also seems to have been introduced to the systems engineering community (Forsberg and Mooz 1991) as a project management tool.
- Perceptions from the *Structural* HTP show that the V Chart is actually a view of the Waterfall Chart in the shape of the V so that the product produced in the early stages can easily be related to the states later in the Waterfall in which those products get their final tests as shown in Figure 14.11. The V is a redrawn Waterfall and suffers from the same defect if used as a process model, namely lack of consideration of changes in customer needs. Some attempt however is sometimes made to include the effect of these changes by drawing two Vs in series.
- Perceptions from the *Continuum* HTP indicate that when the V diagram is used in a simplistic manner to depict the relationship between development and T&E there seems to be no place in the diagram for the "prevention of defects".

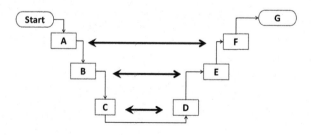

Figure 14.11   The V view of the Waterfall.

14.10 Summary

Chapter 14 discussed nine templates used in project management and systems engineering. The Annotated Outline is a template for maximising completeness and correctness of a document by providing prospective readers with the contents before the document is written. The original ISTs provide a location to store ideas after an ideation session. The Problem Formulation Template is the basic tool in the systems approach to problem-solving. It helps formulate the problem and conceptualise solutions and the solution development process, which makes the problem solver think through the problem and solution before beginning the process of tackling the problem. The generic functional template of a system helps ensure completeness of the system by incorporating the concept of inheritance. The template for a document helps maximize the completeness of a document by providing guidelines for what should be in the document. The generic template for a presentation and the example templates for a student exercise presentation and a management's review presentation provide for better presentations by providing places for the types of information that need to be presented. The Waterfall Chart is a template for the states in the SDP that provides a template for MBO.

References

Biemer, S. M., and A. P. Sage. 2009. "Systems Engineering: Basic Concepts and Life Cycle." In *Agent-Directed Simulation and Systems Engineering*, edited by Levent Yilmaz and Tuncer Oren. Weinheim: Wiley-VCH.

Forsberg, K., and H. Mooz. 1991. "The Relationship of System Engineering to the Project Cycle." Chattanooga, TN: In the Annual Symposium of the National Council on Systems Engineering.

Hall, A. D. 1989. *Metasystems Methodology: A New Synthesis and Unification*. Oxford: Pergamon Press.

Hitchins, D. K. 2007. *Systems Engineering: A 21st Century Systems Methodology*. Chichester, England: John Wiley & Sons Ltd.

Kasser, J. E. 1995. *Applying Total Quality Management to Systems Engineering*. Boston: Artech House.

Kasser, J. E. 2008. "Luz: From Light to Darkness: Lessons Learned from the Solar System." In 18th INCOSE International Symposium. Utrecht, Holland.

Kasser, J. E., and R. Schermerhorn. 1994. "Determining Metrics for Systems Engineering." In the 4th Annual International Symposium of the NCOSE. San Jose, CA.

Learned, E. P., C. R. Christiansen, K. R. Andrews, and W. D. Guth. 1969. *Business Policy: Text and Cases.* Homewood, IL: Richard. D. Irwin, Inc.

Mar, B., and B. Morais. 2002. "FRAT: A Basic Framework for Systems Engineering." In the 12th annual International Symposium of the International Council on Systems Engineering. Las Vegas, NV.

Mar, B. W. 1994. "Systems Engineering Basics." *Systems Engineering: The Journal of INCOSE*, no. 1 (1):7–15.

Nii, H. P. 1986. *Blackboard Systems, Knowledge Systems Laboratory Report No. KSL 86-18.* Knowledge Systems Laboratory, Department of Medical and Computer Science, Stanford University.

Rook, P. 1986. "Controlling Software Projects." *Software Engineering Journal*, no. 1 (1):7–16.

Royce, W. W. 1970. "Managing the Development of Large Software Systems." In the IEEE WESCON. Los Angeles, CA.

Royce, W. W. 1987. "Managing the Development of Large Software Systems: Concepts and Techniques." In ICSE '87: the 9th International Conference on Software Engineering. Computer Society Press. Monterey, California.

Author Index

Subject Index

Printed in the United States
by Baker & Taylor Publisher Services